D0052674

AN AMERICAN QUILT

AN AMERICAN QUILT

Unfolding a Story of Family and Slavery

RACHEL MAY

PEGASUS BOOKS
NEW YORK LONDON

AN AMERICAN QUILT

Pegasus Books Ltd.
148 W 37th Street, 13th Floor
New York, NY 10018

First Pegasus Books cloth edition May 2018

Interior design by Maria Fernandez

Library of Congress Cataloging-in-Publication Data is available.

ISBN: 978-1-68177-417-6

10 9 8 7 6 5 4 3 2 1

Printed in the United States of America
Distributed by W. W. Norton & Company
www.pegasusbooks.us

For Ezra & Lily

&

For Minerva, Eliza, Juba Simons, Jane—and the dozens of people, names recorded & not, whose lives are connected to this story

Contents

A Note from the Author

This is a work of creative nonfiction. I'm a creative writer and scholar, and have researched the stories of the Crouch-Williams-Cushman family and the people they enslaved: Minerva and her children Cecilia and Samon, Eliza, Juba Simons and her son Sorenzo, Boston, Bishroom, Jimmy, William, George, Jenny, and Jane. These were not the only people the Crouch-Williamses enslaved in Charleston over the years, but these are the people whose lives I came to know, as much as I could, and whose traces I followed, as much as was possible, from the 1830s to the 1860s.

The records that remain tell us more than usual about Eliza, Minerva, Juba Simons, and Jane, on whom I primarily focus. Nonetheless, because the records of enslaved people in the antebellum era are so scant, I have imagined their lives based on historical and contextual information. I make clear within the text what is known fact and where I'm imagining. I hope that you, the reader, will follow me in these moments, and that you come to fill in the story as you imagine the lives of all these people who lived almost two hundred years ago but seem to stand alongside us today.

All errors in the quoted letters are as they were originally written. In places, I have added punctuation and/or capitalization within these family letters for purposes of readability and clarity.

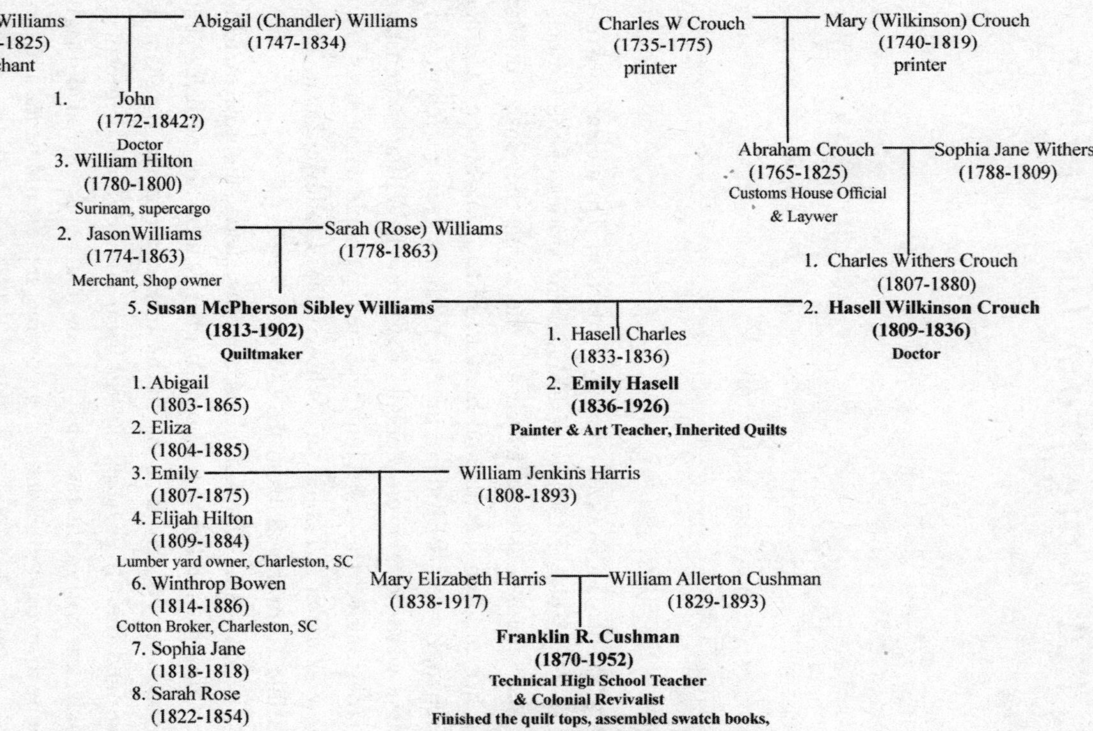
Williams-Crouch Family
Elijah Williams
(1744-1825)
merchant
Abigail (Chandler) Williams
(1747-1834)
Charles W Crouch
(1735-1775)
printer
Mary (Wilkinson) Crouch
(1740-1819)
printer
1. John
(1772-1842?)
Doctor
3. William Hilton
(1780-1800)
Surinam, supercargo
2. JasonWilliams
(1774-1863)
Merchant, Shop owner
Sarah (Rose) Williams
(1778-1863)
Abraham Crouch
(1765-1825)
Customs House Official
& Laywer
Sophia Jane Withers
(1788-1809)
1. Charles Withers Crouch
(1807-1880)
5. Susan McPherson Sibley Williams
(1813-1902)
Quiltmaker
2. Hasell Wilkinson Crouch
(1809-1836)
Doctor
1. Hasell Charles
(1833-1836)
2. Emily Hasell
(1836-1926)
Painter & Art Teacher, Inherited Quilts
1. Abigail
(1803-1865)
2. Eliza
(1804-1885)
3. Emily
(1807-1875)
William Jenkins Harris
(1808-1893)
4. Elijah Hilton
(1809-1884)
Lumber yard owner, Charleston, SC
6. Winthrop Bowen
(1814-1886)
Cotton Broker, Charleston, SC
7. Sophia Jane
(1818-1818)
8. Sarah Rose
(1822-1854)
Mary Elizabeth Harris
(1838-1917)
William Allerton Cushman
(1829-1893)
Franklin R. Cushman
(1870-1952)
Technical High School Teacher
& Colonial Revivalist
Finished the quilt tops, assembled swatch books,
donated to URI & other archives

"Cloth as a metaphor for society, thread for social relations, express more than connectedness. . . . The softness and ultimate fragility of these materials capture the vulnerability of humans, whose every relationship is transient, subject to the degenerative processes of illness, death, and decay . . . Precisely because it wears thin and disintegrates, cloth becomes an apt medium for communicating a central problem of power; social and political relationships are necessarily fragile in an impermanent, ever-changing world."

—Annette B. Weiner and Jane Schneider, *Cloth and Human Experience*

"These seemingly isolated episodes reaching back to the nineteenth century and carrying forward to the twenty-first, once fitted together like pieces in a mosaic, reveal a portrait of a nation: one that is the unspoken truth of our racial divide."

—Carol Anderson, *White Rage*

1
Piecing the Quilt

There is the sound of a baby in the house, a delight. He is a fat baby, a happy baby, full of laughter and mischief, Susan writes. The light falls through the window of their house on Cumberland Street each morning, when the baby wakes her early, and she gazes at him and makes him smile. Touches his sweet, soft skin. Leans toward him to kiss him and linger at his cotton-soft tendrils of hair. He is always getting into things; she can't turn away from him for a moment. He kicks his father in bed at night, and in the morning, they laugh about it together—*his kicks are no joke!* But he is so easy at bedtime, going off to sleep contented. Susan is a mother for the first time at twenty-three. *Come for a visit*, she tells her sisters in letter after letter. *Come and see my baby. He's such a* good *baby*, she tells them, he's so easy.

She is proud. She has gone to housekeeping with her new young husband—now a doctor, no less. Their life is a delight.

She is an expert sewer, and when the baby goes to bed each night, she bends over her hexagons, basting them one after the other with swift, quiet stitches—and her husband sits and thinks to the sound of thread running through cloth and paper. He thinks about the patients he saw that day, some of their cases simple—rheumatism, a cold—while others were intricate puzzles—chronic stomach pain, headaches, an inexplicable bulge in one's side. Susan hands him a hexagon, and he sews. He's designed the pattern, and together, they make the quilt that I'd come to know almost two hundred years later.

In 1833, when Susan was twenty, there were pelerine collars on dresses—what we'd call "boat neck collar" today, straight across the breastline with the collarbones exposed. There were leg o' mutton sleeves, poofed at the top, slender at the wrist. There were bonnets with bows and feathers. When the head was bare, a woman's 'do was two puffs at each side of her face, and a single high twisted bun at the top. It reminds me of a primped samurai. Susan must have worn this look in her early twenties.

But first. Imagine: In 1820, Susan is seven. Her mother will cut the vegetables brought in by Susan's brothers from the kitchen garden, stoke the fire in the iron stove, dice the beef. Unlike her wealthier neighbors, she doesn't have a girl to help. She has boarders to feed—a family staying the night between Boston and Newport and two Brown University students. Sometimes, she has more than twenty boarders. She'll come to Susan to look at the sampler, examine her stitches to see if they're fine enough. How is the arch of the lowercase *a*? How straight is the line of the *y*? Susan has made three alphabets this week, and then she'll start the phrase her mother dictated to her this morning: "Behold the child of innocence how beautiful is the mildness of its countenance and the diffidence of its looks." Maybe Sarah Rose, her mother, stitched the same when she was a child. It's Sarah Rose's job—as it will be Susan's—to make the coverlets, the quilts, the dresses, the petticoats, the corsets, the pantaloons, the trousers, and the jackets. Sarah Rose's family depends upon her skill to keep them clothed, warm, respectable, and in fashion. Their clothes, the stitched objects in their home, signify their class and status in this world, and influence every element of their lives, from love to business. Susan has been sewing since she was three.

Next, she cross-stitches the phrase "Be good and be happy." She makes the red stitches in *x*'s across the linen, carefully pressing the needle in and out, piercing the white cloth at the top and bottom of each *x* until she's built a *B* out of what feels like a hundred small *x*'s. And then the *e*, and so on. Her mother is satisfied with her stitches. She does not ask Susan to tear them out. They remain.

One hundred years later, Susan's grandnephew Franklin would find this sampler, along with three quilt tops, in a trunk that traveled from Charleston back to Providence and remained sealed shut after Susan's heartbreak. Franklin would be the first to examine its contents in almost a hundred years, and I would be the first to fall in love with the quilt and its story after he passed away, another near-century later.

On the first day, before I even saw the quilt tops, I was captured by their mystery, my sense of the secrets they must hold and the knowledge that I'd get to touch the cloth and study hundreds of paper templates made from ephemera. As a quilter and writer seduced by the tactile and drawn to a good story, I approached them with wonder and delight. I was finishing a book on modern quilting and lived in a Rhode Island house built in 1738; it was rumored that George Washington stayed at this house in Little Rest on his way down to Delaware in the 1781. I'd walk across the original wide pine floorboards in my apartment, the sound of squirrels chuckling in the walls throughout the winter, trying to imagine who else had walked these floors, if I might be walking in Washington's ghostly trace.

When Prof W. mentioned these quilt tops I might study as part of a material culture theory course, I was intrigued. We knew only that they were made by a newlywed couple in Charleston, South Carolina—he was a doctor who worked on the quilts with his wife when he had a "difficult case"—and donated in 1952 by a colonial revivalist from Providence. It was a snowy winter day when Prof W. led me down the overheated hall of the Textiles, Fashion Merchandising and Design department at the University of Rhode Island. With a jingling set of keys, she unlocked the old wooden door of the flat-storage room, and once inside, slid open the metal drawer of what looked like a map case. As it opened, I saw the first quilt top, its sky-blue, red plaid, white floral, green zigzag hexagons slowly revealed. My intrigue became entrancement. I couldn't wait to touch it.

Prof W. slid both arms underneath it, gently, as if it were a sickly lamb. The only sound was the crinkle of the tissue paper that had been set between its layers to keep it from pressing against itself in storage. She set it down on top of the case and slid her arms out from underneath.

"The papers are fragile in the back," she said. "Every time you move them, a few crumbs fall away."

We looked over the front of the quilt, unfolded it once and found a central star of colorful calico hexagons with a white center. And around the star, "'flowers' of hexagons . . . separated by rows of white hexagons," some of which were yellow and brown with age. The "checks, stripes, indigos, chintzes, calicos, drabs, and rainbow prints" dazzled me. There were white parrots' heads framed in repeating hexagons around a central patch of red, sweet red ginghams and plaids, a pink floral print on a white background.

I imagined the makers' hands on the quilt, sewing what today we quippily call "hexies," in just the same way I've been taught: make the paper template, baste the scrap of fabric over each edge, then whip-stitch them together and, finally, remove the paper template. Since these tops had never been finished, the paper templates remained. Prof W. could tell that the fabrics were cottons from the 1830s or '40s, machine-woven and printed with blocks, plates, and cylinders, "all three of the main printing techniques of the period."

As I held the quilt tops, in my mind's eye I saw Susan and Hasell (pronounced "Hazel"), a young couple hunched near the light of an oil lamp and a fire, carefully cutting out each paper hexagon template, then the fabric scraps left over from dresses and men's shirts and children's clothes. I could hear the metallic slice of their shears' edges meeting. Could see the fire beside them burning hot on a rainy southern night. Could hear its crackle and the pull of the thread through paper and fabric—one long *shhhhhh.* A pause. And then another. That soothing rhythm of hand-stitching that every sewer knows. Today, it's a privilege to have time to sew and we romanticize the hand-stitched, making precious gifts for one another with stitches that illustrate for the recipient our care and love: *I made this for you. With my own two hands.* But in the days of this quilt, these hands (at least, the woman's) would have known a lifetime of sewing, a skill that was necessary for survival. Sitting by the fire, or in a quiet few minutes while the baby slept, she would have stitched dress seams and hems, buttonholes, hat trimmings, cloth diapers, and undergarments. She'd have decorated her home with embroidered tablecloths and napkins, lace doilies. Together, the couple made hexagon after hexagon with long basting stitches—one stitch across each side—that they'd tear out later, once they'd whip-stitched the hexagons together.

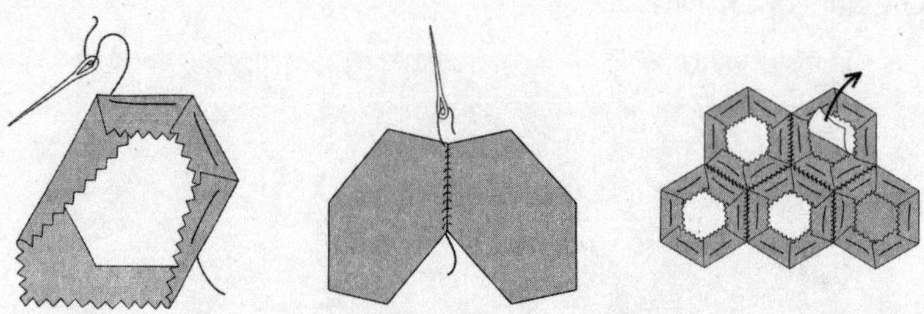

Why was a man sewing with his wife in the 1830s? What did they talk about? What were their lives like? How had the quilt tops come from Charleston to Providence? Why did they remain unfinished?

As we stared down at the quilt top, Prof W. said, "It's the back you'll want to see."

We moved the quilt top to an empty classroom and pressed several tables together, threw a clean white sheet over them, and then unfolded the quilt facedown so that the papers in its backing showed. It was slow, the unfolding. I was cautious. We'd both washed our hands. I tried to remember not to touch my face, because the oils from our skin would damage the fabric and papers.

Finally, the quilt was flat—a gasp—and there they were: a collage of hexagon papers that ranged in color from brown to cream to white, some in glossy full color with typed print, and some in loopy old-fashioned handwriting that no one without special training could replicate today. It was obvious before we even examined them that these browning, handwritten pieces were the oldest, crinkling and dry, corners disintegrating. A few paper flecks fell to the floor.

Carefully, I leaned over the quilt top and saw the words on oldest paper (matte, beige): *friendship, sloop, schooner*, and on the newer papers (glossy, whiter): *invest, see, fame*. There were lists of numbers, handwritten and typed, snippets of glossy articles on investment opportunities, yellow mimeographed announcements about high-school faculty meetings in the 1930s. None of this made sense yet. It was a great, swirling collage of times and places and language and numbers, of the nineteenth century enjambed with the twentieth, of sweetnesses like *dear sister* next to business contracts: *signed in the presence of.* There were four languages, sheet music, repeating words lined up beneath one another as if a child had been assigned the task of perfecting each letter's shape: *Knowledge, knowledge; friendship, friendship; maintained, maintained, maintained; communicate, communicate, communicate.*

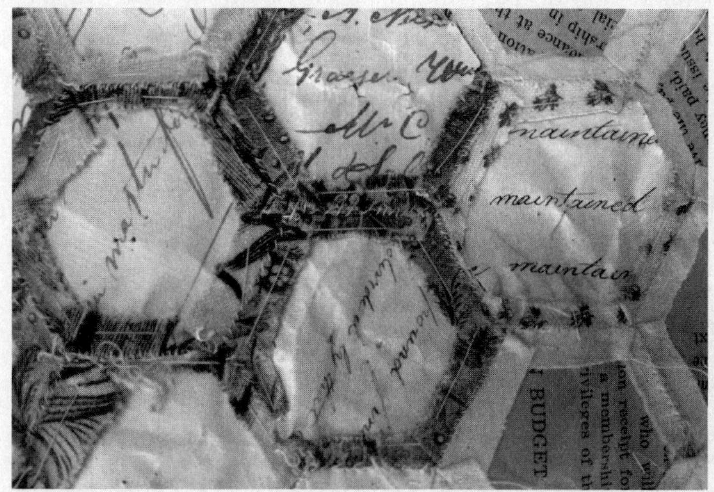

Older snippets, "maintained," and "master for" (probably referring to master for a ship, an oft-repeated phrase in the quilt top papers), enjambed with typed text on yellow paper probably from the 1930s.

Prof W. receded to the background, her voice faded out, and it was like that night in college down South when I was drunk, staring at the boy I loved; all the world was gone but him and me, and we spoke in a vacuum. It was like that once more. Just me and this quilt. I recognized the strangeness: I was falling in love with an object and the stories it promised. But here I was, touching a two-hundred-year-old object that would normally be kept behind the safety of museum glass, and its collage of papers looked like a puzzle to solve. I was allowed to trace the fabrics with my fingers, lift up one of the half-loose paper templates ever so slightly to read its reverse side, take pictures, read and reread the words in the hexagonal snippets of text.

When sound reached me again, I heard Prof W.'s voice. "There are two notebooks that go with the quilt tops. You'll want to look at those next."

Before I got to the notebooks, I spent weeks with the quilt tops, studying the fabrics and reading and recording the papers in the back. It became obvious that there was one—or more—expert sewing hands in the quilt; I could read in each tiny stitch a lifetime of training as a sewer. Other stitches were sloppier—crooked, longer, uneven. The variation in stitch quality meant that multiple people had worked on them. *Who?* I wondered. The young couple, or were there more people involved?

As I recorded words from the papers, I noticed repetitions: *shuger, casks, West Indies, West Indies, West Indies*, over and over, along with *Havana, Barbados*, lists of numbers and calculations in a small nineteenth-century hand, juxtaposed with the bigger, loopy words *friendship, kindness, government, incident.* A child's handwriting practice. The sweetness of that repetition and the concentration it must have taken to make each perfectly arched *a* and *h* and *l.* Cursive. Shapes our children don't make anymore. And juxtaposed against that sweetness, the smaller, experienced hand of someone connected to the mercantile industry of the nineteenth century;

the people who worked on this quilt had money at their disposal. They were calculating shipments on *schooners* and *sloops*, making manifests of the ship's holdings—*casks, shuger, barrels*—and those who would sail it—*seaman, master*—to and from locations like *Havana, Barbados, Carolyna, Newport.*

Returning to the department's accession records, made when the quilt tops were donated, I learned that the quilt tops had been stowed away, first in a trunk that was closed in 1838 and left unopened until 1917, when Franklin, who donated them, was given them by his aunt; they were made by her mother, Susan, and her new husband, the doctor Hasell. The accession note read: "Planned and sewn by Dr. and Mrs. Hasell Crouch. It is said that when he had a difficult case to prescribe for, he would work on his patchwork while trying to decide what to do for his patient . . ." After the tops were donated in 1952, just before Franklin died, they were left more or less undisturbed—studied here and there by a student whose research faded into now-defunct floppy disks and lost notes—until Prof W. and I removed them that winter afternoon in 2012.

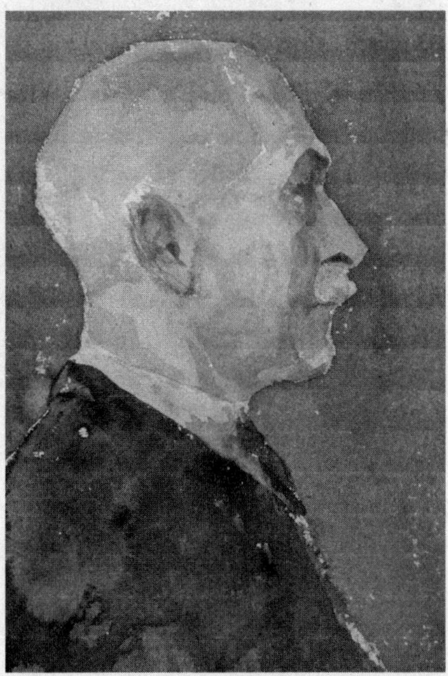

A watercolor portrait of Franklin.

Alone each day on the third floor of that overheated old stone building, accompanied only by the disarrayed crowd of cloth-covered mannequins used by fashion design students, I'd open each paper-lined box and remove one of the quilt tops. The floor-to-ceiling windows in that corner room cast in honey-thick, three o'clock light in blocks along the floor, hitting one corner of the quilt. Each day, it was like finding a present that someone had left for me almost two hundred years ago, with dropped clues about their lives: There were the 1830s-era fabrics with small prints of red, blue, plaid green, and floral whites, the teakettle print in brown and red; the fragile papers in the back with the dates 1798, 1808, 1813, 1824. This was a treasure trove, an unfolding, ever-expanding story with hints buried like a crooked trail to follow: artifacts housed at the historical societies in Providence and Charleston, the family gravestones at St. Philip's Church in Charleston and Swan Point in Providence, stacks of letters in file folders and notebooks that Franklin had transcribed.

It's 1833 in Charleston, South Carolina, and Susan and Hasell Crouch are young and in love. They were married in October 1832, in Providence, and then she moved to his hometown, Charleston, to "go to housekeeping," as she said, with him. For years, Hasell had been friends with her brothers, since they met, most likely, when Hasell boarded at their family home while a student at Brown University. It's possible their families had a long-standing connection. Just before Hasell graduated in 1830, he went to visit Susan's brothers, Hilton and Winthrop, who worked as clerks in nearby Worcester, Massachusetts. Their weekend entertainments included bird-hunting, and, perhaps, planning their futures; within two years, Hasell, Winthrop, and then Hilton moved south to Hasell's hometown, Charleston, South Carolina, to make their fortunes. Somewhere along the way, amid family dinners and stays at Susan's Providence home, Susan and Hasell began to court.

The house on George Street in Providence in which Susan grew up.

In 1830, while she was finishing the education her brothers encouraged her to complete—since she never knew, they said, when she may need it—Hasell sent her a letter from Charleston; he'd gone home in December, just after graduating a month earlier. He'd have sailed to Charleston on one of the schooners or brigs that ran up and down the coast, trading goods in each of the port cities. Susan was eager to know if her father would rent a piano so she could learn the instrument from an instructor in Cambridgeport, Massachusetts, where she was staying. Back in Charleston, Hasell must have been setting his affairs in order, preparing to marry. In 1832, Susan and Hasell had a small Providence wedding, witnessed by her younger brother Winthrop. From Charleston, in 1833, Susan writes home that she'd like Winthrop to have something made for her to commemorate the occasion.

> *Winthrop ought to give me something seeing as how he stood up with me [at my wedding]. It is customary here for the bridesmaids each to give a suit that is a cap and frock. Now I should think Winthrop must buy the materials and let Sarah Hamlin make it. Such things here are talked more about than they are with you. They are made such secrets of*

While Susan strives to learn the ways of Charleston women and waits to deliver her first baby in August, she hopes her brother and friend Sarah will help her make her way in this new town.

She feels like an outsider with the women in town, but she and Hasell are young and seem blissfully in love; they make cordial and preserves that they drink with friends and send to Susan's family in Providence via the brigs that run the coast. They dye a bonnet together. Soon, they'll start this quilt.

Susan misses home and wishes she lived as close as her older married sister, Abby, does, but she's happy making a new home with Hasell, and likes having her brothers and brother-in-law nearby.

> *The weather is delightful now, just warm enough. Blackberries have been ripe about three weeks. All kinds of vegetables are in market. Peaches are quite large. I suppose they will be ripe in about a month. I think we shall have a great deal of fruit. Blackberries are very plenty indeed. Charles* [Hasell's brother] *and Hasell bought near a bushel for 37 ½ cents. I made some jelly and Hasell's making some cordial. I intend to send you some jelly as soon as I get an opportunity. I made it rather too sweet. I think I boiled it away too much. I never made any or saw any made before so I did not know. I put the same quantity as you do for currant jelly.*

Susan's letters are full of stories of their young, domestic bliss. She thanks her mother for sending "sheets and spreads," a quilted coat, and table spoons. The family constantly sends goods and food back and forth on the brigs. Apples from the North, peaches and figs from the South, pickled vegetables and wine. Susan sends north "barberries, gingerbread, jelly and dried apples" by the brig *Mary* and particular types of pots and pans, "Ma knows the size," that she needs for her "housekeeping." Susan's brother Hilton, also in Charleston, asks for "a ½ barrel pig pork and a small keg of good butter, both scarce articles here." Hasell and Susan send home the rose brandy they made together: "We have a great quantity of roses in the garden." At one point, Susan requests a stove to be sent down. But most often, she asks for fabric.

> *I wrote in the letter that was sent by The Eagle for some flannel 3 yards of nice and three yards for some coats for little Hasell. I have not bought any coats since those first ones and they are worn thin.*

At other times, she asks for calico, merino, "linnen," "cambricks," and white muslin. Some of these fabrics make up the quilt tops that Susan and Hasell made together.

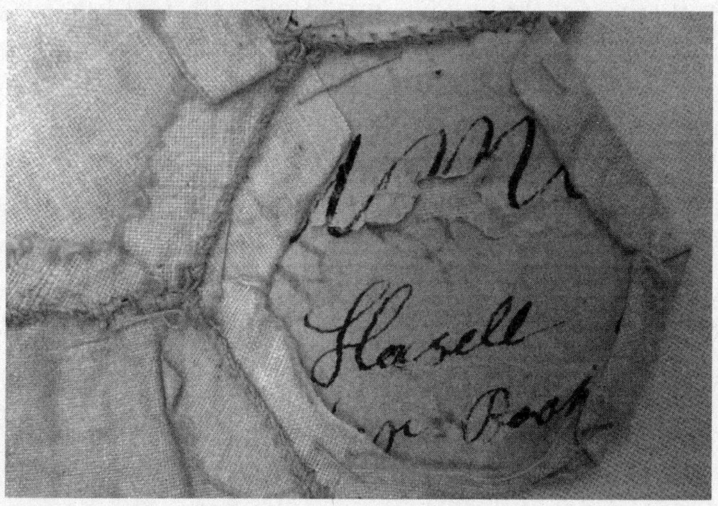

One November day in 1834, maybe the weather is cooling, and Susan is soothing the baby, Little Hasell, as a rainstorm passes over the city. Maybe her husband, Hasell, is off at the medical college, learning his trade. On November 8, her brother Winthrop, working as a clerk in Columbia, writes home to send news to his father. In the course of the letter, he asks for cotton batting and calicos to be sent south for his sister, sister-in-law, and aunt.

> *Susan wants you to send her six pounds of cotton batting to make a comforter. Mrs. Thorne and Eliza would like to have enough to make them each one—you may as well send 20 pounds in all and Father can charge it to Hilton so they will settle with him for it here. You can buy it much cheaper with you than here. Susan likes the quilt you sent her very much. She has made it up and wears it. She is very thankful for it. I don't think it would be a bad plan to send some cheap calicos to make the comforter for it will cost her a great deal more here than at the North, perhaps you have some old stuff in the house that will answer.*

And so this was the start of the quilt. Susan's sisters and parents up in Providence would send down twenty pounds of batting and "some cheap calicos" to make the quilt, maybe "old stuff" they have left over from their sewing projects, or new materials they could buy cheaply near the textile mills and with their father's connections as a dry-goods store owner and former shipper. (The "quilt" that Winthrop says Susan has made up and wears was quilted fabric she'd probably made into a petticoat to wear under her dresses, for warmth and to help billow out the skirts.)

Susan and Hasell began work on the quilt together, that much we know, but the details are unclear. There is the problem of memory: While one note indicates that Hasell stitched the quilt, another states that Hasell designed the quilt top and Susan stitched it. While men sometimes quilted—injured Civil War soldiers, for example, took it up when they were bedridden and needed to occupy their hands—it's unique that Hasell and Susan worked on this quilt top together. There's something so hopeful in this. The quilt was intended to be for their great four-poster bed; they must have imagined they'd spend winter nights under this quilt for many years to come.

Susan and Hasell could have had no idea that their quilt would remain unfinished, that tragedy would befall them, that the hexagons would be taken up by their descendants in Rhode Island a century after they'd started it in South Carolina, that because they'd made so many hexagons and modern beds were smaller, it would be transformed into three quilt tops of slightly different designs—that I, a stranger to their family, would come upon the quilt and this story almost two hundred years after they started it.

Weeks passed before I came back to the notebooks Prof W. mentioned. They were donated with the quilt tops by Franklin in 1952, along with hundreds of other objects, including clothes and paintings. These two small binders included fabric connected to the quilt tops. I removed them from an acid-free cardboard box and carried them carefully, as ever. I imagined they were one of the empty, paper-thin robin's eggs I used to find in the grass under ocean-side hedges; I'd tote them home in cupped palms to show my sister, steadying my steps, eager but careful not to crush the blue shells. This was the first notebook: a delicate surprise.

I walked through the high-ceilinged halls, to the classroom, set the notebooks down, and opened them page by page. In the center of each page, there were squares of fabric, sometimes two or three layered on top of one another, and underneath, in neat cursive, a note that I realized was made by Franklin: *from the pocket of Sarah Rose Williams*. And, in the lower right-hand corner, the year, *1917*.

I didn't yet know what this meant—a pocket? I didn't know who Sarah Rose Williams was or how she was connected to this story. The classroom was quiet. I sat on faded green metal chairs that reminded me of my elementary-school days, and took notes in pencil—everything around the archives must be done in pencil, because it does less harm than pen if its marks should go astray on precious objects. I turned the pages, noting fabrics that were in the quilt. Most were listed as being "ante 1840."

And then I saw, in Franklin's neat penciled cursive, the note that added still more questions, which superseded all those that came before: *Probably for slave gowns.*

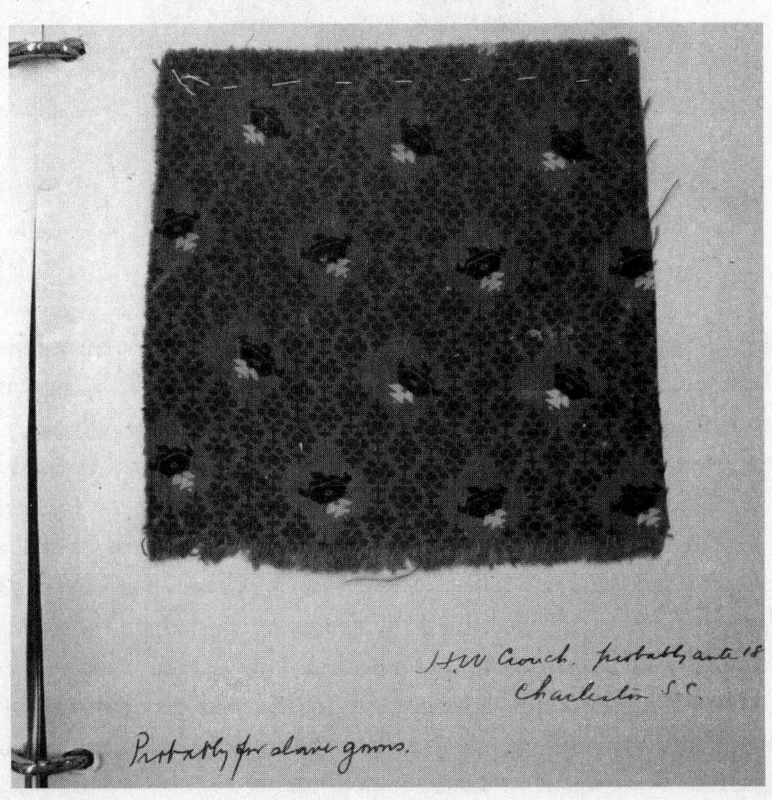

At first, I sympathized with Susan as a northern transplant in the South, as I grew up outside Boston and went to school in North Carolina. It was the mid-nineties. When I visited the college campus my junior year of high school, I remember having arrived tired from all the previous tours, on which students told me the merits of the college union or the cafeteria or the dorms. When I arrived here, I found myself enamored of its quiet beauty—the empty, wide green lawns and pillared brick buildings, the ringing bells that marked the hours, the water dripping from the greenery around the dorms. There were few students on campus that weekend; they were on spring break. I remember sidewalks crisscrossing an empty green, and I filled that green with my imagination of my life to come—long days talking literature with the other students, sprawled on the lawn with our books open, or playing Frisbee in the afternoons—the movie version of college. No one I knew from my high-school class was planning to go afar; they were all staying in New England. Families in Concord seemed to have been there forever, and they seemed to stay forever. My family had moved to town when I was older, and I never felt I fit in there; I imagined that if I went to a new land, I'd find my people. I wanted something different, an adventure, casting myself as far away as possible. The short of it: I didn't know what I was getting into.

A year and a half later, I found myself struggling with the differences between Concord, Massachusetts, the suburb where I grew up, and the small, conservative liberal arts college I'd chosen to attend. I didn't know, when I applied, that the school's student body was 98 percent white, 2 percent people of color, nor that the majority of the students were from old southern families, nor even that the school had such close ties with the Presbyterian church. At Easter, great wooden crosses were placed on the lawn at the entrance to one of the academic buildings, slurs were made against the few Jews enrolled, and when an African American speaker was scheduled to come to campus, swastikas were scrawled across his face on the posters advertising the visit. Two of my good friends, one who was from Turkey and the other who was Indian American, transferred out by the end of that first year. The town was divided between black and white by the railroad tracks—the African American side poor, the white side prosperous. I remember finding it strange that I never saw people of color from town on the main street we often visited to get shakes at the old soda shop, where the college's sports paraphernalia from the '20s, '30s, and '40s—old football sneakers, a helmet, black-and-white photos of men—white men—smiling in their uniforms after a game—hung on the walls.

But what was most alarming to me was the way that my classmates spoke. In the early weeks of my freshman fall, I sat outside with my hallmates and their friends. We were in the midst of the O. J. Simpson trial, waiting for the decision, and one of the students said, "I hope O.J. loses so that we can snipe black people from the tops of buildings." I remember his face in this moment. The snarl and delight. And the woman who laughed loudly and said, "Cal! That was so southern of you," and slapped him five. I was stunned, sickened. There were many other moments like that one to follow. Later that year, I'd hear someone call her puckering lips while smoking a cigarette "nigger lips." I had never heard a white person use that word before. She was drinking, when she said it, and after, she and a friend giggled. Sometime that year, I visited a friend's Charleston home, and when I said about the cottage out back, "What a cute little house," she replied that it was the slave quarters. I didn't know how to understand this at the time. She had a black nanny, whom she called "nanny" or "mammy," I don't remember which, but I remember the moment when I heard this, stunned, when she and I were introduced in the kitchen. At an event I attended in the city, all of the guests were white and all of the servers were black. It was simply regarded as the way things were. We could not talk about this history, nor even the fact of racism in the South. When I tried to talk about it, my classmates would laugh at me: "Go home, Yankee!" they'd say, laughing, or, "Carpetbagger!" or, "The South will rise again!" I was told that, as a northerner, I had no history, no roots that ran deep like theirs did. Many students hung Confederate flags in their dorm rooms. I'd ask why? Why would they hang that flag? They'd say it was about their heritage, not about racism or slavery. I kept talking, pushing, questioning, believing that these conversations might change things, even ever so slightly. I was too overwhelmed to transfer as my friends had; the thought of tackling applications again was daunting. So, I decided, brimming with hubris, I'd stay and try to change things.

I was naïve. I wasn't good at negotiating those conversations; I was too strident, pushed too hard. Meanwhile, I learned how slow the world is to change.

It wasn't just this school. I'd come to see that the problem was that I believed in the myths I'd been taught. During those four years in North Carolina, I had to confront my own experiences in Concord, Massachusetts, which I'd told people was a liberal bastion compared to the college. I grew up believing the stories about the houses with the black-striped chimneys, which were said to be part of the Underground Railroad, and the legends of Thoreau and Emerson and the transcendentalists. I'd never heard that people in town owned enslaved people—that would have been unfathomable to me, and to many New Englanders it still is, though the story is now being told more publicly: A house once inhabited by enslaved and then free African Americans in Concord has been moved next to the Old North Bridge and converted into a small museum, the Robbins House, named for the family who lived there. I'd never heard of the Royall House and Slave Quarters in Medford, half an hour from Concord, where the only known extant northern slave quarters still stand today and that history, of colonial northern enslavement, is told fully by its historians and docents.

These quilt tops led me to a history of the North to which I had been blind. Now, when I tell people that Newport and Bristol, Rhode Island, were the largest slave-trading ports in the country in the late eighteenth and early nineteenth centuries, they're most often shocked. New Englanders continue to believe that the North was abolitionist, was *always* abolitionist, free from the damning history of slavery that plagues the South. People in the North don't talk about that history, would not acknowledge it in their backyards the way my classmate had noted her home's former slave quarters. That history and its markers and legacies, though, are just as fully present in and around Boston.

If you walk through the acres of woods in South County, Rhode Island, where I lived when I began researching the quilt tops, you'll see miles of moss-grown stone walls that cross and zigzag over the hills—many of them built by enslaved people in the seventeenth and eighteenth centuries. The walls were built in grids so that overseers could mark the progress of those who planted and picked in each section while also keeping each enslaved person contained. Stop and look at those stone walls when you see them in a colonial town, or out in the woods, almost forgotten: The way the walls are built is masterful—stones that fit together as if cut like puzzle pieces, they've stood for three hundred years, a testament to the skill and artistry of the people whose hands touched them, lifted them, and set them here.

Havana, Barbados, shuger, casks, Carolyna, West Indies.

I knew when I read these snippets in the quilt's backing that someone in the family was likely implicated in the triangle trade. But exactly who was connected, and how closely, was a mystery. *Probably for slave gowns* was more definitive. It meant that a woman who had grown up in what I once believed to be the abolitionist nineteenth-century North had moved south and owned enslaved people. How did a woman from the 1830s North come to terms with owning people? And, the question I wanted to answer most of all—who were these enslaved people?

I went back a generation to learn more about Susan, sinking into the reams of letters and account books held in Rhode Island archives. I found myself in the mercantile Atlantic world, a world I'd known about in vague terms, growing up around Boston and my mother's hometown, Salem, and living now near Newport and Bristol. This is a world where it was faster to travel by boat than by land; there was as yet no railroad, no car. Horse and wagon were slow, and the rides were rough over potholed and rocky dirt roads. Wooden sailboats traveled smoothly across the sea, skimming up and down the east coast of what we now call the United States, and down to what we now call the Caribbean, buying and trading goods.

Out on a schooner for an afternoon, I heard the creak of a thick rope as the wind pressed at the sail, felt the ship heeling as it gained speed. I'd been seasick all morning in the muggy, still air, the sail luffing, and now I delighted in the wind, bracing my feet against the rail of the boat. This was a wooden schooner with two masts, the sails attached by metal hoops and raised by hand. *Heave, ho! Heave, ho!* You know those words. Hauling down on the line, and then shifting the hands up to grab higher, and hauling down again.

We sailed across Gloucester Harbor, and I saw in the distance another wooden schooner, and beyond, the rise of the land. An old warehouse painted red, a brick building, and the patchwork blur of colonial houses that scaled the hill in the center of town. The wind carried us out toward the sea, that great, open, windy expanse that awaited us, with all its ancient myths of mariners and monsters and pirates and wrecks. But just before we reached the open water, the crew called to jibe, and we ducked our heads to avoid the swinging boom; the ship turned back toward the safety, the quiet—the disappointment—of the docks.

Susan's father, Jason, and his father, Elijah, were Rhode Island merchants whose ships traveled these Atlantic waters, captained by men they hired. Between 1799 and 1808, they invested in sloops, schooners, and brigs that traveled the Eastern Seaboard, from Rhode Island down to South Carolina and the West Indies. The repeated words in the quilt's papers—s*loop, schooner, seaman, West Indies, Barbados, Havana, casks, shuger*—were likely remnants of his shipping manifests and contracts. Their ships carried New England rum south and molasses and sugar back north, along with muslin, silk, tea, coffee, and other goods traded from the West Indies. So it was Susan's father and grandfather who were part of the mercantile system of the eighteenth and nineteenth centuries—a cyclical system that fueled, and was fueled by, the slave trade.

The Seaman's Friend. *Types of ships, schooner sloop brig.*

After one of the ships in which they'd invested was captured by the British during the embargo of 1808, Jason and Elijah cut their losses.

Jason would continue to pay off these debts for years. To sustain himself and his family, he and his wife continued to take in boarders. Because their house was right next to Brown University, they always had plenty of students in their home; Sarah Rose, his wife, was responsible for their care.

Jason focused on the dry-goods store he owned in Providence, which was likely the source of his access to cheaper fabric and goods than Susan would have had down South. He bought and sold from Atlantic merchants every day. He could get yards of fabric—and anything else she and Hasell needed—at lower prices than she could if she were to shop in Charleston.

In addition, the Providence textile mills—Sprague Print Works, Allen Print Works, among others—were making yards of cloth just a few miles from Jason's doorstep. He had easy access to the cottons Susan used in the quilt, along with the fabric she requested for clothes for herself and her family. Thus, the quilt tops and the notebooks (the latter of which include handwoven as well as machine-made cloth) marked the start of the United States' booming Industrial Revolution, which would drastically change the lives of Susan's family and enslaved people in the South.

Those letters that are full of requests for goods from Susan and Hasell are evidence of the way the family profited from their connections between North and South. Letters went back and forth between the two branches of the family as they asked each other for hominy, potatoes, figs, cotton, dried apples, stoves, "tin kitchens," pots and pans, shoes, hats, and feather beds—among so many other goods that were shipped on the brigs that ran up and down the coast. Eventually, Hilton and Winthrop would use their father's merchant connections to build their southern businesses; they sent raw goods from the South to factories and consumers in the North with whom Jason had connections. As an "old New England family," store owners, and former shippers, they had a solid network of buyers. Jason had easy access to buyers of Hilton's lumber and Winthrop's cotton, and he sent south all the goods his children needed as they built their businesses and furnished their homes.

"Ask Father," Hilton tells his sister Eliza in Providence, "what clear northern pine boards are worth at Providence and what the prospect is of there being a supply in market in the spring." After requesting his business tips, he goes on to request "a box of Flagg Tooth Powder it can be purchased at Dr. Johnson's Apothecary Shop in Weyboset Street," and "Susan wishes you to send a piece of cotton about the quality of my shirt. She would like it bleached and about a yard wide as she wishes it for pillowcases &c. Father can charge it to me and I will settle with him one of these days." He also wonders if his father paid "Brown" for his coat and says one of the sleeves smells so bad he doesn't wear it. He wishes he could send the family potatoes from the barrel he bought, "but nearly all of them have spoiled and I cannot find any that will keep; all that I can see have been touched by frost, which makes them rot. If the vessel does not sail tomorrow, I will send you a barrel of flint corn but you need not send me any more grayham flour . . . Susan does not make any bread. We do not use any except bakers. I would like very much to have some of your nice Grayham bread." And so their letters went back and forth with requests for the food they missed, barrels of hominy and dried meats, flour, fabric, and later, other supplies.

While Hilton worked to found a lumber mill in Charleston, young Winthrop, struggling in his early days in South Carolina (he was working for a clerk in Columbia when Hilton wrote about the lumber), would become a rich man from the cotton industry and his northern connections. After working for Mr. Ewart in Columbia for several years, he and Ewart cofounded a cotton-trading business. Ewart secured northern buyers from his New York hometown, and Winthrop organized the buying of cotton from plantations around Columbia and the selling of it at the ports in Charleston. Both Hilton and Winthrop would come to own enslaved people, as would Susan, and Winthrop, the more extreme and daring of the two brothers, came to be known as a "fire-breathing southerner," in favor of secession, by the time of the Civil War. Winthrop shifted up in class, from a working professional back in Providence to a respected "factor" and bank president in Charleston. He'd amassed what amounts to millions in today's dollars, lost it all in the war, and built it again. His sisters Emily and Eliza

Williams remained in the North and were opposed to slavery and his way of life.

It was strange to watch their lives unfold in the letters before me, from youth to old age—Hilton's verve and ebullience, even sometimes a hint of sarcasm (he asked Winthrop to write him a few lines and "lo and behold!" he had), to striving, longing to be successful in business and family, to his old age. I sank into their lives in the 1830s, as I sank myself into the Atlantic trading world. Here were Providence and Charleston a few decades after the start of the Industrial Revolution, with their bustle of commerce at the wharves, their markets for meat and vegetables, their residents in long, swishing skirts and corsets and snug-fitting suits and ties and black hats. I zigzagged between archives, from my days with the quilt, to Charleston's various collections—emerging between each visit to what Winthrop once described as "intolerable hot" summer days, sweat slipping down my skin, which pinked in the sun—back to Providence. There were piles of letters, hundreds of letters, neatly stacked in manila folders that were filed tidily inside acid-free boxes, like the wooden nesting dolls I loved as a child, eagerly uncapping each one to find the tiniest solid doll in the center, the answers that filled the gaps. Several times every day at the historical society, a hushed room with researchers settled at wooden tables around me, I awaited each box that held another piece of the story; it was rolled down on a cart for me by patient and peculiar archivists—people with the same penchant for unspooling a trail as I've found in myself. I grabbed my cotton-covered page weights to hold the pages open, and I read and read and took picture after picture. I went back to Charleston, to St. Helena, to Columbia, South Carolina, to talk to more people, to look for more contracts. The days became weeks, months, years. I followed the lives of the family and dug to find more on the enslaved people. I found the weight that rested on Little Hasell's life—a tiny child whose fate would come to determine Susan's, Hasell's, and Eliza's, Minerva's, Juba's, and their children's lives, too.

Mosaic quilt top.

In Susan's first days in Charleston, fresh from Providence, she and Hasell live with his brother and sister-in-law, Charles and Eliza Crouch.* Susan is eager to "go to housekeeping" with her husband, but they have to wait to set up their own home when he's done with medical school. While Hasell and Charles are accustomed to—and defend—the slave system, Susan comes from Providence, where slavery had been declared illegal at the end of the previous century and, by the 1830s, had been completely eradicated. Susan dislikes owning enslaved people, not for moral reasons but because she found them lazy and destructive.

> *You mentioned in one of your letters that you would like to send me something but did not know what to send. I will tell you what I would like to have, some old linen and an old tablecloth. For I shall want some such things very much. Eliza has nothing of the kind. Everything is destroyed or stolen by the negroes. I never saw so much destruction in*

* I'll refer to Charles's wife as Eliza Crouch from here on, as there are three Elizas in this story. Eliza Williams is Susan's sister. Eliza with no known surname is the enslaved woman owned by Susan.

one house as there is in this. I do not know what Ma would do if she had these negroes to deal with. They are so careless. I think it is partly owing to their not being managed right. Eliza is easy with them. There is not one of them that has one quarter of the work to do that either of you have. There is no regularity or order about everything and for that reason it takes a great deal longer to do the work and nothing is done properly. I do wish we would keep house. It would be so much pleasanter. It would seem more like a home for I could have one of you with me then. But it will be an impossible thing until Hasell gets his profession.

. . . I wish Emily could come here and live. This climate would be of great benefit to her health. If you could only look at Hilton and see how much better his health is. I wish we could go to housekeeping but it would be much more expensive.

Back home, Susan's sisters either do the work themselves or have domestic workers who help in the home. Abby has a housekeeper and a "young girl" to watch the children. She mentions an Irish girl Susan hired after her return to Providence in the late 1830s, who is "as good as any other." Before Susan moved to Charleston, she lived with her parents and two sisters in their house on George Street, in Providence. The family was wealthy enough to send their children to school—Susan and her sisters finished their education through early high school in Massachusetts boarding schools—but still needed to hire boarders to supplement the income that Susan's father brought in from his general store. Susan and Abby bemoaned this burden in their letters home, wishing that their parents didn't have to work so hard and that they could eschew the trouble of taking in boarders.

Despite Susan's initial misgivings about having enslaved women do the housework, she adjusts quickly, as do her brothers. Over the years, she mentions in her letters home the names of enslaved people they owned at different times: Minerva, who would have a daughter, Celia or Cecilia, and a son, Samon or Lamon. A woman named Juba and her children. They rent a man named Jimmy who is "let with [the Sullivan Island House]" each summer; sometimes he comes to the city house with them. Susan's brothers Hilton and Winthrop, and her brother-in-law, Charles, and his wife, Eliza Crouch, own enslaved people as well, and they all live within a few blocks of one another.

Susan seems to adjust to the system quickly. Two years after her initial assessment of Eliza Crouch's enslaved women, she writes:

> *I want to come on very much this summer but it will not be possible for me to leave.*
>
> *I think of you all very often and wish I could go home as easily as Abby can. I am sorry to hear she has no help. It is so bad to have all the work to do in the warm weather. Has not she a little girl to mind the children. I should think she might take one to bring up. I hope you have help. I do not think Father ought to do the white washing himself. I have thought of you a good deal this spring. I know what a job it is to clean house. I do wish you could all live here you would not have to work so hard.*
>
> *I have Juba to cook for me, the one that Eliza had to cook for her when I first came. She behaves as well as I could wish. If I send her anything to bake or cook she will do it as nice as possible. She washes and irons very well. She does all our washing but Hasell's shirts and those I put out. I iron my frocks and muslins. Last summer I ironed Hasell's shirts but this summer I thought I would not. I get them done for 37 ½ cents a dozen. I do not wish for a better servant. She likes Hasell and tries to please him. She is very fond of little Hasell. He calls her mammy. He hears her children call her so.*
>
> *Hilton is in very good health. He comes to see us every Saturday and stays until Monday. He is loading two vessels for Providence. He has done a good deal of business this summer. He is doing very well indeed. He is doing more business than any other lumber merchant in the city.*

Here, Susan writes about the enslaved woman who was part of the group of "negroes" she'd so harshly criticized two years ago, now judging her performance with glowing remarks. She wishes her mother and older sister didn't have to work so hard back home, that they could some south, where enslaved women could ease their burden. She envies her sister,

Abby, who lives in New York and can visit Providence more easily than Susan can; Susan's journey home takes about ten days by ship.

By this time, the baby, Little Hasell, is a bubbly toddler, tearing apart the house with his enthusiastic curiosity. Susan can't turn her back on him for the trouble he'll get into. He doesn't speak yet, she says, but that's fine. She's two months pregnant with her daughter, Emily. She may know as much, since she says she can't travel to the North in the summertime. These sections of the letters also reveal, again, the connections between North and South of which Susan and her brothers are always taking advantage; Hilton is "loading two vessels for Providence," where he ships lumber from his mills. Winthrop has started a cotton business through which he sometimes sends cotton bales north for his father to sell, and consistently sends goods north through his business partner's northern routes. Both boys, as well as Hasell and Susan, profit from these connections. As their letters are exchanged consistently from the '30s through the Civil War, their ties become more complicated over time, especially as Winthrop becomes more entrenched in southern politics and Susan has moved back to Providence.

What was most important to me about these letters, though, was the information about the enslaved people, especially Juba and her children, Minerva and her children Cecilia and Samon, and, mentioned elsewhere, Eliza, as well as Hilton's enslaved men Boston and Bishroom, who worked at the lumber mill. Now I knew their names and their roles within the household. I'd soon follow trails around Charleston and Rhode Island, and later, Cuba, to piece together the rest of their stories.

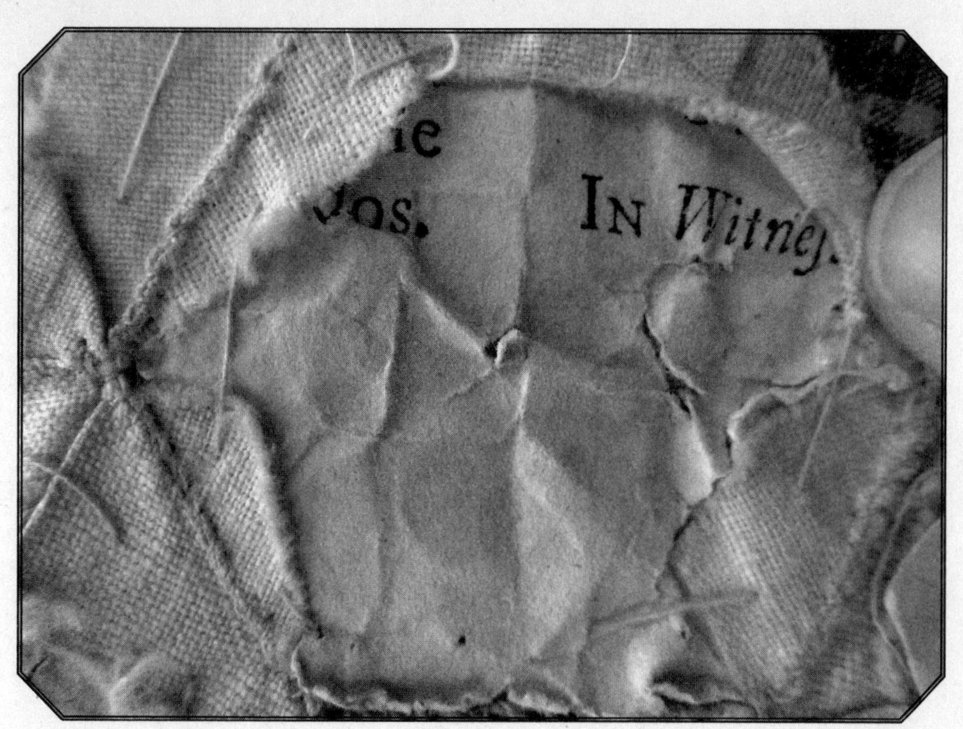

2

Eliza, Minerva, & Juba

Suppose she is “small of her age.” That she “had . . . two short gowns, one of white linen,” the other, as we know from the quilt, of brown or red with a black print that looks like a teakettle; perhaps she has a dress in each colorway, or versions of the print in red and brown, both those prints that we see in the quilt, now just tidy hexagons, scraps left over from these “slave gowns” now repurposed.

The dresses would have been worn to rags. Unlike Susan’s fine silk and muslin dresses with piped seams and ruffles, they would have been simply made with plain seams; and, because they were worn until they were threadbare, they're not preserved. Laurel Thatcher Ulrich—the material culture historian who coined the phrase "well-behaved women rarely make history"—writes about this disparity between the preservation of the objects of the wealthy and the disappearance of objects of the poor.

> Surviving needlework often has the very same biases as letters and diaries and was probably produced by the same relatively small group of women. For every cross-stitched picture of Harvard College thousands of plain shirts and aprons were produced in New England. Although a few survive, most were worn till full of holes, then recycled into dishcloths, pocket, rag coverlets, scrap bags, and lint.

Ulrich adds that some of the worn pieces of cloth were even recycled into paper. This disparity between saving the elite's objects but not those of the working class and enslaved is certainly evident in the case of the Crouch family and their enslaved people's stitched objects. From the Crouches, we have a man's jacket, several dresses, including the white muslin gown Susan wrote about letting out during her second pregnancy, and three quilt tops, as well as a photograph, hundreds of letters, documents, weather journals, a medical notebook, and other ephemera. There are five boxes full of their documents in the historical society, and scattered documents in Charleston on microfiche rolls and in tidy manila folders. I can trace the ownership of their home for almost seventy years through sales records and deeds. Their names are even immortalized in online records of South Carolina slaveholders. But to find the stories of the enslaved people, that takes far more work—and imagination. I'm told, over and over, at archives and research centers around Charleston, and when I meet activists and historians, that I won't be able to find the trail for the enslaved people, that I'll have to make it a composite story out of historical records and slave narratives. That's part of the frustration of this archive—reading what's on the surface and digging for what's been disregarded, suppressed, quieted. The enslaved people were simply considered property, so there aren't records to be found as there are for the white family—contracts for their marriage, court cases to reclaim or buy property, birth and death certificates—all the bureaucratic minutiae that mark our lives today, missing for people who weren't considered citizens nor even humans. Even the records of their purchase and sale weren't always recorded. Some sales were private. Some sales contracts were destroyed over time, or never made at all.

The cloth Susan requested for "servants" used in the quilt, probably from scraps leftover after making dresses.

The calico bought for the teakettle prints, for the "servants' gowns," as Hilton called them when he wrote home requesting cloth, was not of as fine quality as the calico that Susan requested for herself. In February of 1835, Hasell writes home to his father-in-law, in Providence, with a list of requested items enclosed.

½ Bushell white beans
½ Barrel of dried apples and peaches, separate, about equal quantities
1 piece brown sheeting, yard wide or over, 12 or 13 cts. a yard
8 yards fig. calico for Susan a summer dress 12 to 16 cts.
16 yards calico for 2 servants from 9 to 12 ½ cts.

He asks that they be returned by the brig *Commerce*, a ship that often takes their letters and goods back and forth. Susan wants finer quality cotton for her own dress, at the higher price of twelve to sixteen cents a yard, while the calico for two "servants"—the deceptively more genteel name for enslaved people—should cost only nine to twelve and a half cents. It wouldn't be of as fine a weave, perhaps coarser and of fewer, less desirable colors. This is the print that looks like a black teakettle on either red or brown (which was then called "drab") fabric, preserved in the fabric notebook with the note *probably for slave gowns*, and in tidy hexagons within the quilt. Those would have been made from the scraps left over after the dresses were made, either by Susan or by Minerva, Eliza, and Juba themselves.

Suppose we imagine Minerva and Juba, one wearing red and one wearing brown. These are plain dresses with cinched waists and cartridge pleated skirts, bodices that hug their chests and long straight sleeves with a slight poof at the top—nothing so dramatic as Susan's gowns, it would have been a less elaborate pattern. Perhaps Minerva, who's about twenty-seven, is holding her child in her arms, swaddled in a blanket she stitched herself. That's Celia or Cecilia, an infant in the spring of 1835. Maybe Minerva used a few scraps from their dresses, combined with other scraps Susan gave her or that she traded for with women at the market, to piece a small quilt. She sways side to side to soothe Cecilia, then gently shifts her into a sling on her back so she can haul in a pot of water for Susan to bathe herself. And do you see Juba, with her son pressed against her, her arms on his shoulders? She's wondering how long she'll get to keep him by her side. She's thinking she needs to cut his hair tonight.

We know Juba had more than one child; Susan wrote that little Hasell called her "Mammy" because he heard her children call her by that name. We know the name of only one of her children, Sorenzo (perhaps Lorenzo, but he was likely named for the white owner William Sorenzo). We might imagine that in 1835, Sorenzo was ten, and stands beside his mother momentarily before running to play with the other children in the yard. See him reach for the child who runs from him, his hand outstretched, laughing when his fingers catch the cloth of the child's billowing shirt? *Got you!* he hollers. Imagine that he returns, breathless, to stand beside his mother again, and that her hand reaches for him almost unconsciously, finding the side of his head, then his cheek, in a caress. The glow of sunlight falls across his cheek, down his neck, across his lanky body where it catches the bottom of his mother's brown skirt, illuminating them together in the stillness. He is laughing at something he sees in the distance.

Now imagine a third woman. "She had two petticoats, one of which is drugget, the back parts striped with red, green, and yellow, the fore parts is striped with blue and brown," and "new shoes, with wooden heels, tied with strings, and half-worn stockings." She stands a little apart from the other two women. She's about the same age as Minerva, thirty, and doesn't have with her any children. This is Eliza.

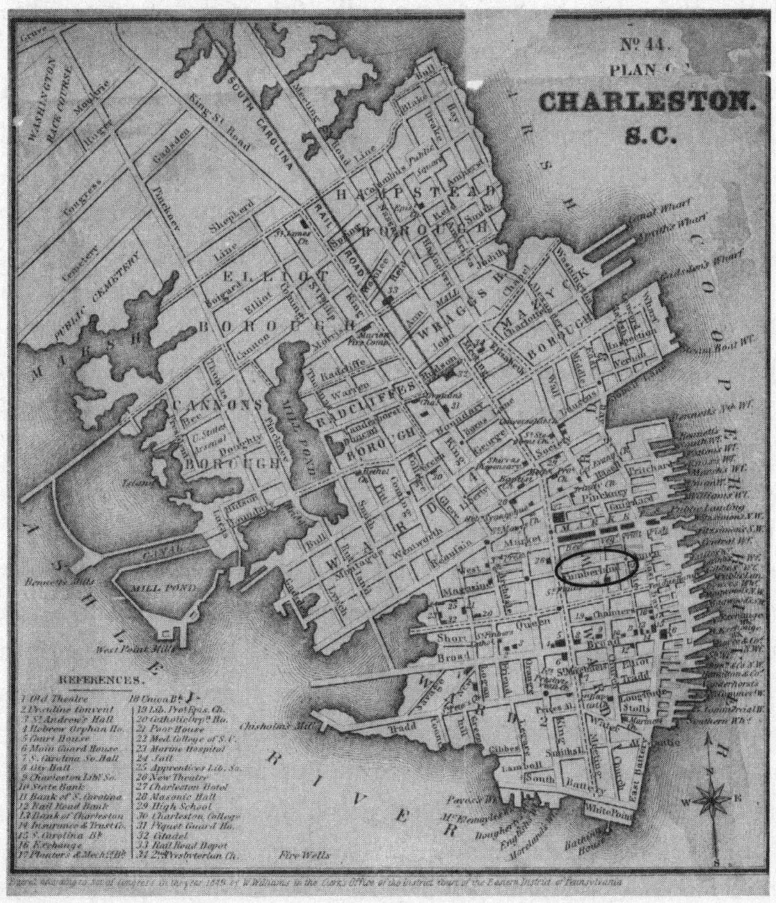

1849 map of Charleston. Crouchers lived on Cumberland Street, circled on lower right of map.

Imagine that it's morning, just after dawn, pink lighting the sky over the horizon on Charleston's peninsula. The Crouches and Eliza, Minerva, and Juba live at 6 Cumberland Street, just half a block from the bay. When Eliza catches sight of the sun coming up, she remembers, for a moment, holding her mother's hand as a child; it's her only memory of her mother. She smells the salt in the air, hears the distant call of a shipmaster approaching a wharf. Eliza moves back inside quickly, hauling water to the washbasins upstairs, spilling none; she's become adept at this, no matter how tired she feels. She was up late the night before with the baby Hasell, soothing him while Susan slept. She heard the doctor snore in the middle of the night. She is unwilling witness to their every intimacy. When she brings Susan and Hasell their breakfast in bed, she avoids their eyes, pretends they each live in private and distant worlds. She appeases them with a smile—another expertise—and then walks out of the room and down the stairs and out the door to the yard, where she watches the sun come up over the bay. This moment is hers.

Back in the kitchen, she talks to Minerva about the garden, asking who will take the vegetables to market. Minerva misses the market, where she sees her friends and steals moments of autonomy in the one place that gives her authority. Here, she can determine her own prices for her produce. She can decide to whom she will or won't sell. She can meet and talk with friends without fear of retribution. There will be no trip to the work house on market day.

The enslaved people at the market could "collectively defy white authority in ways that would have been impossible individually." They were predominantly women who grew vegetables in small gardens, made sweetgrass baskets, or knitted or stitched goods to sell. They could name their own prices, keeping a portion of the proceeds in agreement with their masters. One of the traps of enslavement was that owners realized they had to concede some freedoms to the people they owned in order to keep them within that patriarchal system—*See, I'm a good owner, allowing you to keep the proceeds you get for your vegetables*. Because owners, outnumbered by enslaved people in Charleston, realized they could be overtaken at any time, they made concessions to keep the people they owned "content," and then held this over their enslaved people's heads as if they had done them a favor. These favors, they might have reminded the women and men they owned, could be revoked.

Perhaps while Eliza hauled water for the washbasins and cleaned the house, Juba was tending to the children and cooking breakfast. We know that Juba was the cook, based on that letter Susan wrote in July 1835: "I have Juba to cook for me, the one that Eliza [Crouch] had to cook for her when I first came." Juba and Eliza and Minerva did the heaviest work of the household, cooking, tending fires, washing the clothes, and Susan took care of the lighter loads—ironing her "frocks and muslins," making decorative pieces for the home like the hexagon quilt—an object that would take dozens of hours to make—that set her status as a lady, a member of the master class. Only white women could be ladies.

The work that Eliza, Minerva, and Juba did allowed Susan to escape the most laborious and time-consuming aspects of "housekeeping." Even washing clothes was hard work in the 1830s. I think of this every time I toss a load of laundry into my washing machine, pour in the detergent, close the top, and walk away to watch TV or walk my dog—these machines give me an easy life. In 1830, washing was done with lye soap that was tough on the skin. First, if it wasn't store-bought, the soap had to be made, as it always was in the colonial days before the factories produced it. To make soap, women needed first to make lye from ashes, which were easy enough to find under the cooking hearth. The ashes were compressed in a container with an opening in the bottom, and then water was poured over them to produce lye water; it dripped out of the bottom of the container into another. Lye water was combined with animal fat, like beef tallow, which was saved when women cooked, and more water. Lye burned the skin, so women would have been careful not to spill it on themselves. Through a process of boiling, stirring, and then pouring the concoction into molds, soap was made. It had to sit for one and a half to two months outside of the mold before it could be used.

All this just for soap. You can imagine what a thrill it would have been to buy a ready-made bar from the dry-goods store, saving hours of work. We don't know whether Susan bought soap ready-made for the enslaved women to use for laundry, or if she had them make it themselves.

Minerva would have had to shave the soap into flakes, then boil some of the shavings in water, in an immense copper or cast-iron pot that could hold ten gallons. She'd have hauled in the water from the nearby well, one or two heavy buckets at a time. She'd submerge the clothes and linens (separately, of course), mix them with a great wooden spoon or stick, move them to clear water to rinse, then wring them hard and hang them on the line in the yard. Dirtier clothes could have been scrubbed on the washboard, but those that were too delicate for washing (suits and fine dresses) were spot cleaned and brushed. Only underthings were washed in their entirety. Quilts were washed or beaten clean once a year.

In 1835, Minerva would have done the laundry at least once a week, with a baby, Little Hasell, in the house, along with the doctor and Susan. Juba, the cook, would have gone for the day's groceries at the market, come home with eggs and a cut of beef from the meat market, or fish from the wharf, okra and tomatoes from the vegetable market, bread from the baker. She'd have made all of the day's meals on the family's cast-iron stove, in pots and pans that Susan and Hasell requested from Jason

(Susan's father) to be delivered from Providence in 1834. Susan, performing her lighter duties to illustrate her role as lady, made gingerbread and preserves that she sent north (her first batch, she said, was a disaster—far too watery), and probably toyed with the new recipes in ladies' domestic guides and cookbooks that had been emerging more and more frequently since Amelia Simmons' *First American Cookbook* of 1796.

In thanks for all this labor, Minerva, Eliza, and Juba would have either slept on pallets in the kitchen, rolled out on top of the hardwood floors, or else in beds built against the wall with hay for mattresses. Each would have had a blanket to share with her children, or, if she was lucky and had sewing skills as well as time and fabric of her own, a quilt—if a quilt, she made it in her "own" small hours, after putting the children to bed and cleaning up the evening meal and before the morning work began at dawn—and a pillow that had been flattened over the months to a hard cotton slab. On Sullivan's Island, where the family retreated in the summertime, they probably slept in a separate cabin in the yard—what my classmate had referred to as "slave quarters"—and had pallets. Maybe it felt like a small luxury to have their own private space and a window that faced the shore. Susan was proud to have one of the best spots on Sullivan's Island, but Minerva might have cared only that she could hear the ocean waves at night and could sleep apart from Susan and Hasell.

One night in Somerville, Massachusetts, I stood in a kitchen with six other women, stirring great vats of boiling dye. These were all-natural dyes made from avocado pits, small bugs called cochineal from Mexico and the southern United States, walnut husks, and fustic, wood bark. I was stunned to find that the old brown tree bark made a vibrant yellow, the walnut husks made a soft brown, the avocado pit was meant to be pink but instead turned gray, and the cochineal, crunched up with its red shell, turned pink (meant to be a stronger red). It took six hours to dye these fabrics, first cutting or crunching the cochineal pieces to be dyed, then boiling the water with the dye elements in the pot, including alum to fix the color, and stirring, slowly stirring, like weary witches. Until, finally, it was time to submerge the fabric.

Afterward, we gently squeezed out the liquid and hung it to dry. It was dappled, imperfect, and some of my favorite fabric. Now when I see fabric from the 1800s, I imagine the hours that went into its making—from picking the cotton, to spinning it into thread, and then weaving it into cloth, then dyeing it by hand. Our efforts that night, even led by an experienced dyer, were unpredictable and imperfect, but women in the nineteenth century who relied on dyed cloth for their clothes and bedcovers would have had the process down pat, and their finished products would have been even and smooth. Enslaved women often spun, wove, and dyed their own cloth: "Slave narratives frequently refer to the fact that slaves learned how to use plant dyes expertly. Some dyes could be purchased in dry goods stores, while others grew naturally. Beech bark was used to achieve a slate color. Hickory bark and walnut bark colored fabric brown; cherry, elm, and red oak imparted red (a favorite color) . . . wild indigo gave blue. . . ." Even poison ivy could be used for dye, and "vinegar and water, or 'chamber lye' (urine)," could be used to set the dyes. Nearly two hundred years later, there I was in a quilting shop frequented by hipsters, learning a more "sustainable" form of hand-dyeing fabric with natural materials, setting them with alum (one of several mordants used then and now) just as enslaved women did in the 1800s and the colonial women who preceded them had done, and the women who preceded them through ancient history twenty thousand years ago had done, too. While the job of weaving shifted over time between the genders, it was women who sewed, dyed, and spun yarn over time, sustaining their families through cold weather, blistering sun, and harsh winds. In the nineteenth century, enslaved women often spent evening hours, after a long day's work, spinning cotton and weaving cloth for their own use.

Princess Feather, Jackson Hill, Nine Patch, Drunkard's Path, Lily in the Valley, Feathered Star, Swan's Nest. All the hope and whimsy in these quilt names, patterns made by enslaved women as well as free African American and white women. The skill of sewing as a seamstress was passed down from mother to daughter, and talented seamstresses were more valuable than enslaved women without a skill or trade. I sank myself into *Stitched from the Soul*, by Gladys-Marie Fry, to learn about quilts made by enslaved and formerly enslaved women.

A spinning wheel at the Slater Mill Museum in Rhode Island.

It was enslaved women who made the clothes for other enslaved people on large plantations, who cut the patterns and stitched the seams from "negro cloth," or osnaburgs, cheap, rough cloth that was far less expensive than even that lower-quality cotton Susan ordered for her "slave gowns." Negro cloth scratched the skin, like burlap; one man recalled that as a boy, he'd ask his older brother to wear his new clothes until they'd been worn in.

Rhode Island's South County, where I lived in that old tavern house when I began studying the Crouch quilt, was at one time a center for the production of "negro cloth"; this was in the early 1800s, with the proliferation of new textile mills in the North, which spun cotton picked by enslaved people down South. The cotton was picked in the South, then shipped north to be spun into cloth, then shipped south again to be sewn—by enslaved people—into their own horridly uncomfortable clothes. A vicious circle of industry.

In spite of the suffering, the determination of the planter society to make a profit at any cost, the lives divided and truncated, there were these incredible triumphs of beauty born of skill and talent. "A former Georgia slave describes another slave's pride in her quilt-making skills. 'When Vanna brought the gay pieces up in a "double-burst" (sunburst) [quilt] pattern, Nancy fingered the squares with loving fingers. "Hits poetry, ain't it?" she asked wistfully.'" Poetry made of scraps salvaged or woven and dyed.

I flipped through Fry's book again and again. See the turning pink and white swirls on this quilt from the 1830s? The red *x*'s and coffin shapes around flowers on this one from the '40s, made to memorialize a baby or to help one heal? The fine appliquéd flowers on this one from the '20s? This is broderie perse, in which a central fabric is cut from one fabric and sewn onto another with fine stitches that turn under the rough edges of the cloth, leaving a central flower bouquet on a printed cloth, or a circle of flowers like a wreath.

People think that all African American quilting is Gee's Bend–style quilting. Because of the way the Gee's Bend quilts were made, the circumstances under which they were made, the artistry and aesthetic with which they were made, the Gee's Bend quilts *are* distinctively African American quilts—but African American quilts are *also* those made with the precision of sharp points, the patterns that one of the Gee's Bend quilters described as feeling constrained or too fussy.

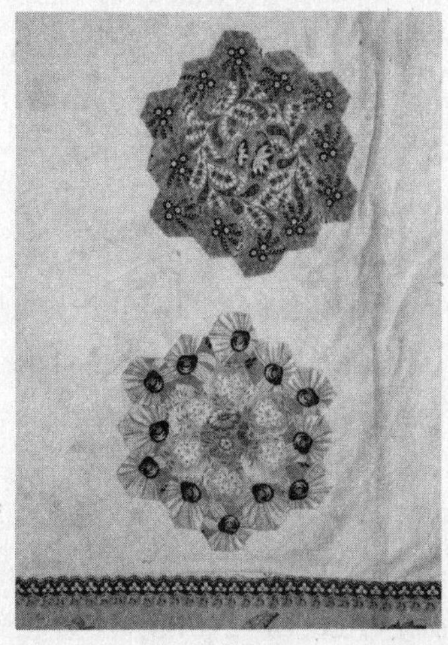

LEFT AND RIGHT: *Hexagon flower from quilt made by "a negro seamstress in 1780" on the Drayton Hall Plantation, Charleston, SC. (See color insert for other images of this quilt.)*

If you haven't seen them yet, the Gee's Bend quilts are those gorgeous pieces that were displayed at the Whitney in 2003, which changed everyone's perceptions of quilts and modern art. Gee's Bend quilts were made with gloriously bright, bold colors in simple, sometimes asymmetrical designs that have been compared to jazz music. They were improvised but carefully created, made with bright, bold colors. My favorite of the Gee's Bend quilts aren't square, as if they're resisting that convention that a quilt must be so. The patterns and sense of aesthetics were passed down within family lines and evolved generation after generation.

Many of the quilts selected for the Whitney exhibit were made contemporaneously with modernist paintings, even though local white people prohibited the Gee's Bend women from gaining access to the twentieth century art world. The quilters are descended from enslaved people in rural Alabama. In the Jim Crow era, their peninsula became especially isolated when the local white community suspended the ferry to the mainland. Impoverished but surviving, the women's quilting patterns, which were unique to each family and passed down from mother to daughter, remained strong for generations, evolving over time as women experimented with new twists on the patterns. What's most remarkable about the quilts is that they were masterfully designed with scraps of old work clothes and dresses; you can still see the marks of shoulders and elbows and knees in the denim quilt, shades of faded blue that bleed to dark. When thread ran out for one quilter, she turned to fishing twine. No one was buying yards of fabric for these designs. They used what little they had, and the results are art. As Nancy said, it's poetry.

Anna Williams, born outside Baton Rouge in 1927, became famous for her hand-pieced quilts that some say "embody a polyrhythmic African-American aesthetic." She'd cut pieces of fabric by hand with scissors rather than a rotary cutter—a pizza cutter tool that quilters use to expedite clean cutting—and sew together each tiny piece to create a splash of color across the quilt in triangles, rectangles, and squares, no shape perfect or regular. She improvised her designs, though she had an overall scheme in mind. Nancy Crow, a prominent art quilter (who is white) was inspired by Williams's work and went on to found the Quilt

National show that's attended by thousands each year. Crow also uses this hand-cutting improvisational technique. She found that rotary cutters are too precise; scissors make imperfect lines, their crooked arch part of the character and beauty of the piecing.

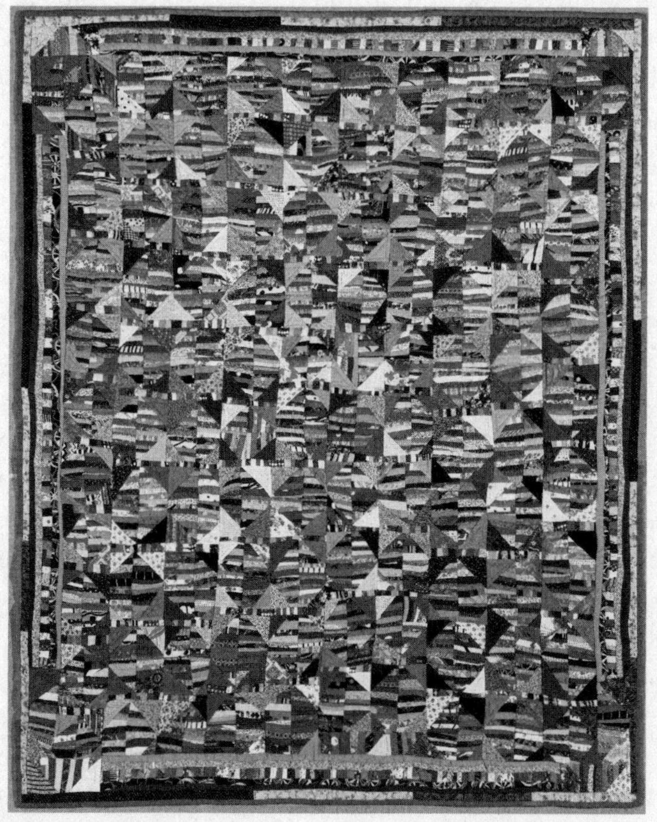

Anna Williams Quilt, 1995. Cotton, synthetics, 76 ¼ × 61 ½ in. (193.7 × 156.2 cm). Brooklyn Museum, (See also her quilt in color insert.)

Countless white women have been inspired by the work of the African American Gee's Bend quilters and Anna Williams's work, myself included. Modern quilters—predominantly white and middle-class—call themselves "improv quilters," with whole books recently dedicated to the topic (a chapter of my own book was about "improv"). I've worried that we're co-opting a form that was innovated by African American women and works like jazz, with riffs and jagged lines and poetic loops and arcs. The Gee's Bend quilters seemed to "break the rules" of quilting by which others had told me I must abide: no need for precise corners, tidy seams, sharp points, or following the pattern. This imperfect form was liberating, and I found myself making improvised quilts, too. Like most "modern" quilters, I was cutting up yards of expensive fabric to make a form that had been innovated by the Gee's Bend women, out of necessity, using what was available in a limited market, with scant resources, all thanks to racist oppression and discrimination.

Before the Industrial Revolution—and in all but wealthy circles after, too—no one would have cut up yards of whole cloth to make a quilt. Even today, a woman I know who grew up poor in New England scoffed when I told her I was buying fabric for a quilt. *Buy it and cut it up? What an absurdity!* She laughed. Quilting was an art of scraps, creating something new and useful of whatever was left over from the dresses and suits and shirts a woman spent her days sewing. Seamstresses, who made the clothes, were also, of course, some of the expert quilters, but all women were trained in the skill; quilts were a necessity for cold nights. Gladys Marie-Fry notes that enslaved boys also picked up the skill that they saw their mothers teaching their sisters: "According to oral testimonies, obtained from descendants of former slaves, the male slaves simply watched and listened as mothers transmitted sewing skills and needle crafts to their daughters." A white northern woman noted upon visiting a Georgia plantation in the 1800s that, ". . . among the Southern field hands, the women can hoe as well as the men, and the men can sew as well as the women, and they engage in all departments of labor according to the necessity of the case without regard to sex." This blending of men's and women's labor, scholar Stephanie M.H. Camp notes, added another layer of oppression to women's lives: "Another badge of slavery was the androgynous appearance imposed on some bondwomen by work and dress . . . With a mixture of pride and bitterness, Anne Clark recalled that during her life in bondage she had 'ploughed, hoed, split rails. I done the hardest work a man ever did' . . . Fleming claimed that the women he knew even resembled men in the field." While free white women were cultivating their cult of domesticity in fine dresses and corsets, enslaved women "wore pantelets or breeches" to work in the fields. Eliza, Minerva, and Juba, as house slaves, were given dresses (or cloth to make their own dresses), of finer cloth than the rough "negro cloth" that field slaves had to wear, but still of lesser quality than that used for Susan's dresses.

Though they lived several decades earlier, Eliza, Minerva, and Juba may have dressed similarly to these women who were photographed in 1879 in Charleston, SC.

Enslaved women wouldn't have been preoccupied with conforming to the performance of domesticity that so concerned Susan. As Cynthia M. Kennedy explains, "Enslaved girls were taught household skills from the time they were toddlers, and youthful slaves learned early that their lot in life comprised hard work and an endless quest for self-preservation rather than balls and parties followed by marriage." This is the contrast between Susan and the three women she enslaved—Minerva, Eliza, and Juba. While it was Susan's job to marry well—her access to upward mobility was a good husband—and maintain a lady's home (the "cult of domesticity"), it was an enslaved woman's job to sustain herself and her family while keeping her owners satisfied enough with her performance of the labor they demanded. Alice Walker points out that in the midst of the hard work of survival, which included enduring sexual abuse, black women made art in the everyday: "What did it mean for a black woman to be an artist in our grandmother's time?" she asked in the 1970s. "In our great-grandmother's day? It is a question with an answer cruel enough to chill the blood."

> Did you have a genius of a great-great-grandmother who died under some ignorant and depraved white overseer's lash? Or was she required to bake biscuits for a lazy backwater tramp, when she cried out in her soul to paint watercolors of sunsets, or the rain falling on the green and peaceful pasturelands? Or was her body broken and forced to bear children (who were more often than not sold away from her)—eight, ten, fifteen, twenty children—when her one joy was the thought of modeling heroic figures of rebellion, in stone or clay?
>
> How was the creativity of the black woman kept alive, year after year and century after century, when for most of the years black people have been in America, it was a punishable crime for a black person to read or write? And the freedom to paint, to sculpt, to expand the mind with action did not exist.

The answer to this question lies in the garden Walker's mother tended every day, bringing to the world a burst of beauty that was her art, just as Walker's art—permitted and possible for her generation—is her writing. She writes about Phillis Wheatley, beloved American poet of the eighteenth century who was enslaved by a Boston family. Walker says it's no wonder Wheatley's health failed, when she was surrounded by the "contradictions" of her world: being taught that her homeland was a savage place from which she'd been "saved," working all her life under enslavement to serve an elite white family, yet with the talent that would have earned her the title of genius had she been a white man. She wonders how many women who were enslaved had ancestors who made art on their walls back in Africa, sang with voices like Bessie Smith, and had daughters who became writers like herself, women who were finally permitted to make the work they were born to make. She wonders how enslaved women survived without being able to make their art, and the answer is in how they treated their everyday objects—their talent was channeled into their gardens, their cooking, sewing their clothes, or making their quilts. Stephanie M.H. Camp writes, "Women, whose bodies were subject to sexual exploitation, dangerous and potentially heartbreaking reproductive labor, and physically demanding agricultural labor, worked hard to bring personal expression and delight into their lives. Women wove and dyed color, patterns, and designs into their clothing." Minerva, Eliza, and Juba wouldn't have been preoccupied with the cult of domesticity as Susan was; instead, they'd have defined their individuality and found joy in the works they created and perhaps wore, in the slim hours of their own time.

From the Smithsonian's National Museum of American History: "The embroidered inscription 'Frances M Jolly 1839' graces the center medallion of this quilt top. This signed and dated silk-and-wool-embroidered quilt top came from an African American family, and the maker, Frances M. Jolly, was said to be an ancestor of one of the donor's grandparents. The family, of whom little else is known, is said to have lived in Massachusetts and moved to Pinehurst, North Carolina."

Log cabin, Streak o'Lightning, Whole Cloth, Appliquéd, Courthouse Steps, Tulip pattern, Grandmother's Flower Garden. I scanned each of these quilt patterns made by women of color before the Civil War, pictured in Fry's book. Grandmother's flower garden, this last one, catches my eye because, like Susan and Hasell's quilt, it's made of hexagons that became popular as a result of the publication of the 1835 *Godey's Lady's Book* pattern. These quilts represent only some of designs that that enslaved women made. People think of African American–style quilts as being only those with improvised patterns made as a result of a lack of access to enough fabric to make a consistent, symmetrical pattern, just as clothes were patched as needed, becoming, as Fry notes, quilts themselves. Enslaved people were given clothes once a year, sometimes twice, sometimes only once every few years, or worse. Camp explains, "Old, torn, shredded, and dirty clothing resulted in more than saved costs for slave owners; it had social effects. Poor quality attire reflected and reified slaves' status and played a role in their subjugation. Former bondwoman Harriet Jacobs wrote bitterly in her narrative of life as a bondwoman that the 'linsey-woolsey dress given me every winter' by her mistress was 'one of the badges of slavery.'" Consequently, "when bondpeople, especially women, outfitted themselves for their own occasions, they went to a great deal of trouble to procure or make clothes of quality and, importantly, style." Women traded "homespun goods, produce from their gardens, and pelts with itinerant traders for good-quality or decorative cloth, beads, and buttons . . . Enslaved South Carolinians had an especially independent economy." Maybe Eliza, Juba, and Minerva made sweetgrass baskets, or sold vegetables grown in their own kitchen gardens, in exchange for cloth of their own.

Now when I see a quilt made by a woman who was enslaved, I see a piece that must have been the product of much negotiating for fabric and dye, and hours spent working to dye the cloth over boiling vats on an open fire, drying it in the yard, cutting it into sweeping symmetrical shapes, and then gathering or making other goods in exchange for enough cotton to fill the quilt, and spending hours over a loom for any homespun cloth that was also used. Some surviving "everyday" quilts that enslaved people used for themselves are made of varied, irregular shapes of cloth pieced together as in the style of crazy quilts that would become popular with white Victorian ladies in the late 1800s—whatever shape scrap one had, one used. Enslaved women couldn't typically spend a lot of time making decorative quilts for their families when they needed them for warmth and comfort during cold nights, and spent all their daytime hours making quilts and doing other heavy labor for their masters. The quilting style that began out of necessity flourished and proliferated as a distinctive style, imitated by quilters who say they're making "improv" quilts today. They are artistic masterpieces. But so were the "fancy" quilts they made for the master's house, sometimes in partnership with the mistress. Most of what enslaved women made did not survive because it was used every day, until it was positively worn out. But we can recognize that their hands were in the work of countless dresses and quilts and coverlets used by wealthy white women on plantations and in city houses. When Eliza's and Minerva's brown and red dresses wore out, maybe they turned them into quilts for their own use; maybe, somewhere in the past, there was a quilt made entirely with their hands, with these same snippets of cloth that Susan and Hasell used in their bed quilt. When I touch the quilt, run my hands across its seams and hundreds of white stitches, I wonder if some of this is the work of Eliza, Minerva, and Juba. I feel the ridges of the seams between hexagons, where the whip-stitch bound them. There's no signature, no record to indicate that this is the work of enslaved women. And even if they didn't work on this quilt (Camp argues that urban enslaved women didn't share stitching labor as plantation enslaved women did), it was Eliza, Minerva, and Juba's labor that gave Susan the time to make this piece. The enslaved women are not overtly recognized in the archives of documents and in the quilt tops that mark Susan and Hasell's lives, but they're decidedly here. We can recognize their labor and the legacies they created—the gardens, food, clothes, and quilts that were their art.

Sullivan's Island panorama by Hugo Bosse, 1860.

Imagine that it's ten o'clock at night on Sullivan's Island, and Susan and Hasell have gone to bed. Maybe Minerva, Juba, and Eliza talk about their lives together at night, about their own children, about, perhaps, the latest marriage between neighbors on Sullivan's Island. Eliza's hands might be sore from hauling pots and weeding the gardens and washing and stirring and wringing the clothes, and sewing Susan's hexagons. But she'd return to the cabin in the yard, and pick up a quilt she's making with Minerva and Juba for their children to use at night. Before they know it, winter will be here with its chilly, rainy nights, and Juba and Minerva want to keep the children warm when they're back in the city kitchen with its doorways and windows whose drafts can't be defeated by the stove's fire. Maybe they have fabric from the trade they made with friends at the market in Charleston, and black sailors at the docks—handwoven hats in exchange for pieces of fabric. They have scraps, too, from Susan's sewing; she's been ordering yards of fabric from the North, so the women have her remnants, whatever she doesn't use after her dresses are cut and the quilt hexagons are made. Imagine that they pick up needles with hands sore and stiff from the day's work, and sit by the fire in their cabin, and sew for an hour before falling asleep side by side, Minerva with Cecilia nestled on her chest, her soft breath lulling Minerva into sleep; maybe Sorenzo sleeps already under coverlets Juba made back on the plantation in North Carolina, with patterns and stitches taught her by her mother Judith, and by her mother and grandmother and great-grandmother before her. These skills, talents, and knowledge are inherited legacies of wealth, too.

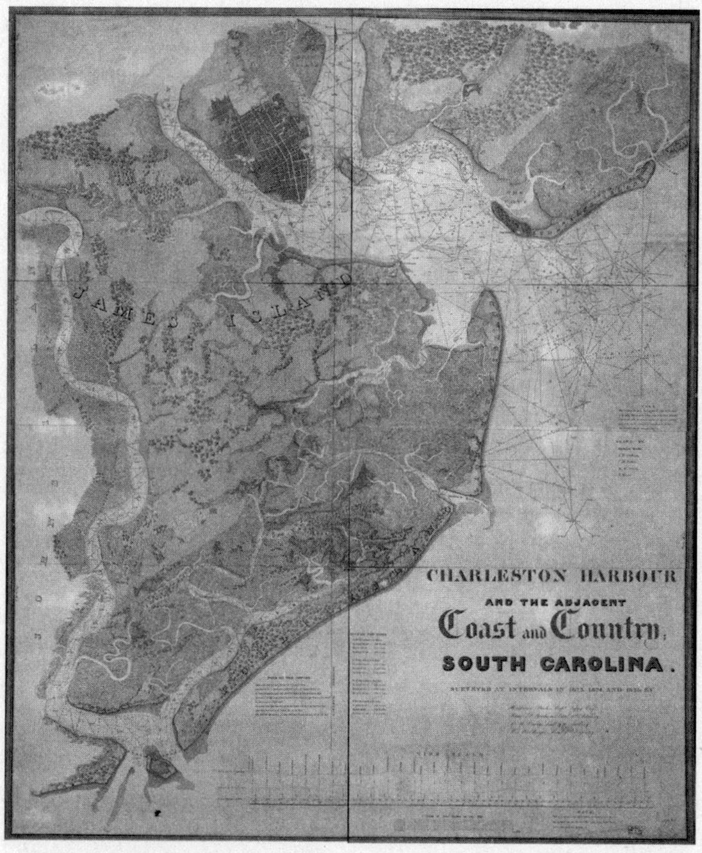

Sullivan's Island as depicted in 1860, and a map of the city of Charleston (central peninsula) and Sullivan's Island (top right corner).

3

Warp & Weft: Agriculture & Industry

The long stitches across the hexagon are the basting stitches; the short stitches between hexagons are the whip stitch. Typically, when a quilt is finished, the papers are torn out so the quilt can be layered with batting and backing. That may not have been the intention with these quilt tops.

When the machines start up in the textile factory, they roar; it's as if the whole building is shaking to life, a clatter of metal on metal, the belts charging over the wheels. There are rows of great looms in this cavernous building with its floor-to-ceiling windows. The windows have latches on the bottom, but in 1835, they couldn't be opened because the breeze would cause the cotton threads to blow in the wind, tangle the machines, make the particles fly through the air in a flurry. Just down the road from Susan's Providence home, where her parents still lived in 1835 and where she'd grown up laboring over samplers, Slater Mill had been functioning since the late 1790s. Slater Mill was the first textile mill in the United States, founded by Samuel Slater.

Slater Mill's opening set off the American Industrial Revolution and the burgeoning textile mills that would come a few years later in Lowell, Massachusetts, where I stand now, in the midst of the roar. How did Susan and her brothers so easily adapt to owning enslaved people in the South? These mills are part of the answer.

The looms at the American Textile History Museum, in Lowell, MA, which closed in 2016.

Once Susan and Hasell move south in 1833, their new lives together begin, though not as prosperously as Susan would like. First, they live with Hasell's and Susan's relatives, including her brothers, Hilton and Winthrop. Like Susan, Hilton and Winthrop moved south in hopes of upward mobility. While her chance came through marriage, the boys' came through business ventures—lumber and cotton trading, both of which thrive thanks to their father's connections back in Providence.

It takes only two short years for the siblings' lives to begin to flourish in Charleston. But in 1833, Hilton's nascent lumber business is tenuous and Hasell is still waiting for his "profession" to get under way. Hilton writes from Charleston to his father asking for advice about whether to pack up and head home to Providence, or to stick it out in Charleston. If he stays, he says, he'll need money from his father—or another relative—to get his business running.

> *The question now is if I had better go on with the business or close out and return to the north. Of one thing I am certain: situated as I am now I cannot make money. As it is I have not capital enough to carry*

it on to advantage. Find[ing] eight hundred dollars soon would enable me to do a very handsome business, but with my present capital I can do scarcely anything. You must have money on hand to take advantage of the market, for if you buy on a credit, you have to buy of the second person and consequently pay a profit on it, but by having cash you buy of the country people that bring it down, and often get great bargains. My present lease of the yard expires on the last day of July, and I can by that time sell out all my stock and collect all the accounts due now, but if I could get five hundred or eight hundred dollars more I should much rather continue in the business as I am confident with that addition to my present capital I could do well.

Hilton is both asking for advice as well as money from his father here, believing that if he only has "more capital," he'll be able to get a better start in the business. He's writing to his brother Winthrop, who's still living at home. Hilton goes on to emphasize his point:

I wish you to let Father read this letter and both of you write me fully on the subject what I had best do how the lumber business is at Providence and if Father and myself could do anything at it. Or how the grocery business, the same kind you are in, would succeed? Suppose you and myself should go in company in the fall and open a store of that kind? Do you think you understand the business well enough, and why could not we succeed as well as Mr. Paddiford? I think were you and myself in company and had a snug store managed it well and economically that with Father's judgment purchasing goods we might do well, but as you can judge of the state of the market better than I can, you can of course tell better the thing would succeed but as soon as you receive this for I cannot conclude about buying more lumber till I hear from you. If Father can get the money for me and thinks it would be better for me to go on with the business, I would in that case like him to engage a cargo of White Pine lumber, should I conclude to give up business I cannot leave until July, and if I had sold out I should not have been able to have left for some time as I should have had to [stay] and [settle] my accounts. That was one reason why I was not anxious to sell out, as by retailing it out I get much better prices for my stock and have something to do in the same time.

Hilton entreats his brother to consider opening a grocery with him, as their father has done back in Providence; with their connections in the North, they could run a "snug store" with their "Father's judgment purchasing goods." He'll take advantage of his family's experience and connections between north and south to help make his living. As he thinks about his future, he worries that he's getting too old to be on the brink of indecision for too long.

There is one thing to be considered and that is that I am getting old, and that it is quite time I was settled in some permanent business, for changes you know are bad, and I am now of an age to be permanently settled, but I am not as well situated now as when I was 20 years old then I was doing a large business, now I am doing but little.

Franklin, the grandnephew making notes on this collection in the 1950s, writes that at this point, poor harried Hilton is twenty-four. He hardly seems old through my twenty-first-century eyes—after all, millennials often live at home into their late twenties and thirties and can remain on their parents' health insurance until they're twenty-six. But, of course, in the 1830s, Hilton's peers have been in established careers for several years, embarking on new marriages, and bearing children. He's four years older than his now-married sister Susan. Maybe he is experiencing what we'd call today a "quarter-life crisis."

Hilton is the more conservative, and, says Franklin, gentler, of the brothers. Winthrop is wilder, a ladies' man, always on the lookout for "female acquaintances." He breaks the heart of a girl named Phrania, one of Susan's friends in Providence. Susan writes that he had treated her poorly. Phrania seemed to expect a proposal from Winthrop, and he didn't offer one. This wasn't just a matter of the heart. If Phrania spent a great deal of time with Winthrop, if she took risks in spending time with him, her reputation might have suffered, affecting her future marriage prospects. For a woman of her time and class, marriage was her only potential livelihood; a middle-class woman like Susan and her sisters and friends could not have gone to work in the factories.

This division between the classes in the factories persists even into my own lifetime; when I asked a family member if my grandmother's lung disease might have been from working in one of the textile factories in Salem, Massachusetts, she said our grandmother wasn't of that class. My father and aunt, who grew up in nearby Lawrence, another industrial town, tell me stories of their summers spent working in factories—one that made lockers and another that made sneakers. My aunt spent a summer lacing shoes, and my father worked with the sheet metal that became those sorts of lockers we'd slam open and closed in our high-school hallways.

Winthrop and Hilton emphasize over and over the value of education when writing to Susan. The girls were to become educated in case they needed to support themselves, but the education—piano, sewing, languages—would also help them become ladies, find a good husband, and keep house once they were settled.

While Hilton seems to agonize over each of his decisions, Winthrop is a bit reckless, and not just with his female acquaintances. Once, while out shooting pheasants, he shoots himself in the hand, and his brother teases that it was because he was upset about a lady. Winthrop's sense of daring, however, comes to "pay off" in business, as he's more willing to take risks and made large profits by taking advantage of enslaved people's labor.

Meanwhile, young Hasell is also trying to find his way back in his hometown as he finishes his medical degree. He and Susan are newly married and living with Hilton and his brother, Charles, and Charles's family, until they can "go to housekeeping" on their own, after medical school. Hilton writes:

> *You wish to know of Hasell's going in the country and ask what will become of his school and his profession. Charles* [Hasell's brother] *has taken the school on his own account and for the present gives Hasell a certain sum to assist him. He took it before Hasell thought*

of going to the country that H. might have an opportunity of getting his profession. He will take his medical degree one year from this time. One reason for his going in the country is that he may have a place to practice for you know he can be a Planter and practice his profession at the same time. He is now waiting to hear from the person who owns it, and he will probably know in a week if he can get it or not. I think it will be a very good move as the place is said to be very healthy one, and should he not have practice, he will have his plantation to support him. But if he settles in this city he would stand a chance to starve the first five years, for the place is now literally crowded with young doctors and it would take him at least five years to get any practice.

Hasell *is* worried about "getting practice" in the city, but he doesn't end up buying the plantation. Instead, he and Susan settle on Sullivan's Island for the summer months, when diseases ran rampant in the city. This is a good solution to the problem of competition from other doctors in Charleston, as well. Since the professionalization of medical practice after the Revolutionary War, and the founding of the medical college in Charleston, many men had decided that this was the career for them. On the island, Hasell has less competition and, as the island was only for the wealthy, more clients who are able to pay; in addition, the family is safe from mosquito-borne illnesses like malaria, yellow fever, and what they called "bilious fever," which was any fever they didn't know how to categorize otherwise. They knew that the breezier, cooler island wasn't susceptible to diseases, but they didn't know why—that it was mosquitoes that carried yellow fever and malaria. They only knew that the "close" city quarters in the summer months spread disease, and that they were safe to return after the first frost. Of course, we know now that the frost is what killed the mosquitoes.

Susan and Hasell spend the summers of 1834, '35, and '36 on "the Island," as they call it. Winthrop, who has decided that Columbia is too quiet a city socially, joins his family in Charleston in 1834. He writes:

We have been upon the Island ever since we landed until the day before yesterday when we moved up here to a house in the center of [Charleston]. *Hasell has been very much plagued to get* [rent] *a house* [in the city]. *He came up to the city 5 or 6 times before he found the one we now occupy. I will give you an idea what sort of a house it is—a wodden* [sic] *3 story house—2 rooms in front, making 6 good upright ones and 2 garretts, besides a kitchen and several rooms attached to it for sleeping rooms for the slaves, a stable and a small yard. The rent is $250 per annum.*

Charles and his wife, Mrs. Thorne and her children, Hilton and myself board with Hasell. Hasell nor Charles were able to find a small house to suit them so they concluded to come under the present arrangement [of sharing]. There were several small houses that they looked at but not of them were less than $300 per annum, therefore they think themselves fortunate in obtaining the house we occupy. To be sure it would have been much pleasanter if we had been able to live separate, but as it is for economy's sake we must try to put up with it.

Susan and Hasell were very much disappointed in not seeing one of you here with us. The baby has grown very much since he left Providence, he is now a great boy. He begins to walk. I do wish you could see him, he is one of the best boys I ever saw.

Hasell has 2 girls, an old woman who cooks, a boy about 6 years old, and a girl about 3 years old to do the work. We breakfast about 8 o'clock, dine at 2, and have tea about 6 ½ o'clock. Things go on more regularly than they used to when Charles kept house.

The baby is little Hasell. "He is now a great boy. He begins to walk. . . . he is one of the best boys I ever saw."

The family continues to delight in their first nearby nephew; Abby, Susan's sister, has children already but lives far away in New York. Meanwhile, Winthrop agrees with Susan that Charles and his wife are inferior housekeepers, noting that with Susan and Hasell in charge, things "go on more smoothly." Of course, this is thanks to Eliza, Minerva, Juba, and their children, who keep the place running for the family. "2 girls, an old woman who cooks, a boy about 6 years old, and a girl about 3 years old to do the work." What sort of work could a six-year-old and a three-year-old do? I try to imagine my friend's three-year-old daughter, her wild energy, her inability to sit still. What kind of work could she do?

Enslaved children followed their mothers throughout the day, so were taught to do the work their mothers knew—if cooking, the children learned to cook, if sewing, the child learned to sew, if basket-weaving, the child would have begun to weave as a toddler. They'd have carried dishes, stirred pots on a hot fire, swept the floors, cut vegetables, and stuffed quilts with cotton batting. On the plantations, children were taught to shoo flies from their napping owners, help with chores like sweeping, and pick cotton alongside their parents. Surely you've seen those photographs of toddlers trailing cotton bags behind them in the fields, their tiny hands grasping a boll that they'd plucked from that prickly plant. "The slave narratives indicate that few slaves escaped work in childhood: 48 percent of those who discussed the subject began working before age seven, 84 percent before age eleven, and only seven percent reported that no work occurred before age fourteen." Scholar Cynthia M. Kennedy argues that enslaved mothers really had three jobs: the work of taking care of the masters, the work of taking care of her children, and the work of teaching her children the work of being a slave.

Juba would have been cutting the vegetables and hauling water for the soups and stews and buying meat from the butcher. Minerva would have made the beds, stripping them on wash days, scrubbed the stairs of the dust that constantly blew in from the dirt road, dressed and undressed Susan. Minerva's daughter Cecilia would have followed her around the house, learning what her mother did, becoming indoctrinated in the world of enslaved labor, much to the pleasure of the Crouches, certainly, who knew that teaching the little girl would only increase her value. But she was also learning the ways that her mother resisted and declared her autonomy, in the subtlest motions of her head, the way she feigned illness when she no longer wanted to mop up Hasell's mess or clean his medical equipment, the scraps of fabric she slipped into her pockets to save for her own quilts, working on them in those rooms off the kitchen at night.

The machines clack louder and louder and the New England mill girls—in the beginning, they were local women, white women, from the farms—move their hands quickly to slip the spindles onto the machines, thread the shuttles, clear a tangle. All the while, they're dreaming of dinnertime at the boardinghouse with their friends, of their now-faraway home on the farm—a mother, a father, brothers and sisters who worked all day in the fields while now she works in the factory. This is her chance at a good living, a job of her own with wages paid in her name alone. She sends most of it home, of course, but it is hers to reap.

She learns to let the sound of the machines wash over her, to let it become a drone like the swarms of flies that bother the cows in the milking shed in the summertime. She remembers kneeling beside their udders, pulling at each teat, as she now reloads a spindle, checks to see the warp threads haven't broken on her machine. She knows all of the machine's parts and functions. She takes pride in this new knowledge. The drive belts run from the ceiling to the machine, powering it with the river's water rushing beside the mill, a miracle of diversion.

A loom in the American Textile History Museum and a 500 lb. bale of cotton as seen at Slater Mill in Rhode Island.

This is the mill where the cloth in the quilt is spun, from those great bales of cotton—about three hundred and seventy pounds—that are bound down South. They're picked by enslaved people on plantations around Charleston, then loaded onto wagons that bring them to that port, where Winthrop buys them and loads them—forces the enslaved people to load them—onto the ships that will take them north, to Slater Mill, in his and Susan's hometown, or to the Lowell Mills in Massachusetts.

The cotton is carded—brushed, essentially, with tough-toothed combs so that all the fibers run in the same direction, to be more smoothly spun into thread. The thread is wound onto spools or bobbins. The loom is warped with yarns that will go up and down while the shuttles are loaded with weft yarns, back and forth. The warp threads are pulled apart by harnesses, creating a sort of tunnel, or shed, through which the shuttle passes, making the weft.

You probably made weavings like this as a child, on a very small loom. You might have used fat, colorful yarn, or stretchy cords, or even elastic loops. It was fun then, remember, to make a pot holder? I was given one of these by a friend's child. It hangs on my stove in orange and yellow, too small to really use, though I tried. She was proud of her weaving. She was nine when she made it. In 1835, in the years to come, girls her age would take over at these looms; she'd be useful for her small fingers, which could get into the machine's innards more easily, and her small body, which could duck under the looms to free a thread too far away for an adult woman to reach.

For all the dangers and risks inherent in the new textile factory jobs, they were still a privilege granted only to whites. Christy Clark-Pujara notes that this was a freedom to which people of color weren't granted access because "white [textile factory] employers preferred to hire whites and white workers often refused to work alongside black people." While osnaburg, or "negro-cloth" factories in South County, Rhode Island, and elsewhere in New England, "help[ed] perpetuate slavery in the south," free people of color were being discriminated against as they sought work in the Industrial Revolution that allowed all whites, even the lower classes, to profit. "In the North, industrial work was the purview of whites; it was associated with free labor, and even though most blacks in the antebellum North were free their race marked them as slavelike." People of color were supposedly "free," Clark-Pujara writes, but they weren't granted rights and citizenship, and were thus conscripted to a life of poverty and "disenfranchisement."

In 1835, the Crouches go to the island in May and don't return to the city until November 7, having waited for the first frost. Susan writes that by the time they departed, the island was deserted, with the houses boarded up for winter. She leaves Juba and her children behind there, perhaps to finish packing up the house and preparing it for the off-season. Susan writes:

Young girls and boys worked at the mills alongside the women.

> *We are staying at Charles' as the house we intend to occupy is not vacant yet and we were obliged to come up as lectures commence next Monday. We left all our furniture on the Island, only brought our bedding and clothes. We have not had a frost yet and the planters are afraid to move into the country. But the house will be ready for us frost or not in about 10 days or less. We left Juba and her two children on the island and brought Jimmy up with us. I should rather have staid* [sic] *on the island until the house was ready if I had had any one to stay with me.*

Jimmy was the old man who was "let," or rented, "with the house" on Sullivan's Island. Like many enslaved people in Charleston, he was rented out by his owners so they could continue to profit from their "investments." In explaining this to me, someone likens it to buying blue-chip stocks today; they're a reliable investment that will keep yielding dividends. It's an apt and sickening comparison.

By this time, 1835, Hasell is a busy practicing physician whose plan to summer on the island has worked—he now has so much business that Susan is often left alone, to her displeasure. She becomes lonely and constantly tries to persuade her sister Eliza to come down to Charleston to stay with her, promising that the island is very "pleasant" and that it will improve her health; she should see how well Hilton looks now, she writes. "Eliza [sister-in-law] spent last week with me. It is so much cooler [on the Island] than the city that they enjoy a week on the Island very much. I think it is pleasanter here of anything at the North. Every day we have a delightful sea breeze . . . I think of you all very often and wish I could go home as easily as Abby can." Three months later, further along in her pregnancy with her second baby and anticipating even more isolation with her last trimester confinement back in the city, she writes: "I shall feel the want of someone this winter very much, as I expect to be confined about the first of February and I shall be quite lonely. Hasell cannot be at home much as he is Demonstrator at the Medical College and therefore if one of you can come I shall feel much better satisfied." Hasell will now teach at the college where he earned his degree. Susan hopes that either Emily or Eliza Williams will come stay with her when she's alone.

Their sister Abby, married and living in rural upstate New York, was lonely as well. Susan's friend wrote: "Abby complained feeling very lonesome, and well she may for R. boarded very near to her and they were almost inseparable. In her last letter she says, 'I may imagine her in a land of mostly strangers to her, and with only one female friend with whom to be intimate and have that one taken away.' I may then know how lonesome she is." Abby was ten years older than Susan, and married Elita Stickland Elles, a printer, in 1828, when she was twenty-five (incidentally, Elita would go into business making "cambric" cases, cotton-covered books, among other things, tying him into the family cotton connection). Together, they had six children who survived and several more who did not. She suffered with the loss of her children and often wrote to Susan about it, often but not always reflecting the stoicism that women of her day were trained to portray in the face of sorrow: "Women of the master class did not merely discuss and correspond about their ongoing tragedies, they also cultivated a stoic, religious resignation to suffering. . . . They shared their sufferings, confessed the depths of their disquiet and grief, looked to each other for strength . . . and lauded one another for properly resigning themselves to a loved one's death."

Eliza, Minerva, and Juba, would have been well aware that enslaved women more often died in childbirth than white women, and that enslaved babies died at higher rates than free brown and white babies. They would have known ample suffering, too, and, if they were friends with one another in those years in which they were together in the Crouch house (they might have been more likely to be friends, even perhaps family, if they'd been together for years in North Carolina), they would have shared their grief and held each other up through sorrow.

Susan's sister Eliza Williams, to whom Susan and Hilton and Winthrop wrote, back in Providence, was nine years older than Susan but had the "freedom" of mobility—traveling to keep house with Susan, if she so chose or if her parents decided they couldn't support her—because she was single, a widow living back home with her parents. It wasn't entirely *freedom*, since she was reliant on her parents or a married sibling to take her in and support her; a woman's fate was almost always reliant upon a man's, but of course, she wasn't under anything like the constraints that Eliza, Minerva, and Juba faced. After watching her older sister Abby and younger sister Susan marry and move away, Eliza Williams must have been resigned to living with her parents and helping tend to their boarders. She'd have worked hard in the house, alongside her mother, washing sheets and preparing meals for the people who came through their house. But then, in 1834, at the quite elderly age of thirty, she, too was married, and set off on what might have been a hopeful new life with her husband. It isn't clear whether she was happy with the match or not, as there aren't any letters between her and her sisters from this time, and none of her letters to her siblings down South have been preserved (or at least, I haven't found them yet). However, she was considered lucky to be married at that age, as everyone seemed to have given up hope of her prospects by that time.

After all that waiting, and all that hope for her new life, Eliza Williams' marriage ended within weeks, with the tragedy of sickness.

> *Eliza has been married and with short space of two months from the day she left here, she returned a widow. Her prospects have suddenly been blighted, it is a dreadful shock to her. I have not seen her since she returned. She does not feel like seeing any but the family. Her husband had the smallpox, was in a most shocking situation before he died. I should leave for Winthrop to tell you about them.*

Smallpox was a painful, ugly disease that caused a high fever and covered its victims in erupting pustules. The "most shocking situation" her husband was in "before he died" was the result of the fast course the disease took. Eliza Williams must have cared for him, watched him become disfigured and riling in pain and the delusions of a high fever—alternately shivering and sweating—until he passed away. She was lucky not to have caught it herself, since it was highly contagious. She returned home with her "prospects blighted," meaning that at this old age, the rare luck of marriage would surely not come again.

Now, a year later, Susan hopes Eliza Williams will come visit her in Charleston but understands that she has to stay home to help Emily prepare for her wedding. How bittersweet that must have been for Eliza Williams, who had, just a year earlier, prepared for her own wedding. Her younger sister Emily probably helped dress her and do her hair that day. She'd part her hair in the middle and braid it into two long plaits that she wound up at the sides of her head: "The hind hair is dressed very low, the front platted on each side, and the ends brought under a gold enamelled comb at the back of the head," an article in a lady's monthly described the 'do of the day that accompanied a model evening gown of 1834. Eliza and Emily Williams weren't wealthy, but their middle-class status allowed them access to the cloth, shoes, and hats that their father bought for them, as well as monthly magazines like *Godey's*, on which all white middle- and upper-class women then relied for the latest in fashion advice, food preparation, and housekeeping (both of which were gaining more respect with the Victorian era), quilt patterns, marriage, and the day's fiction. Eliza Williams, Susan, and Emily kept up with the day's fashions. In the same letter in which she wishes her sisters Eliza or Emily could visit Charleston, Susan writes:

> *I am much obliged to you for having my silk dress cut for me as it will help me a good deal but I do not like to have you pay for the whole of it. I shall not need it this winter as I have a good black silk which I shall wear whenever I go out. I think they will dress here very much as with you this winter. Calicos will be worn very much and plaid silks.*

Susan wants to be part of the circle of society women in Charleston. She said, in 1833, when she wrote for her friend Sarah to make something from one of Winthrop's shirts from her wedding, that this is what women in Charleston do to commemorate the occasion, and that "these things are made such secrets of," more so than in Rhode Island. She's making a hexagon quilt that was commonly made by Charleston ladies in 1835, and she slips into the ownership of enslaved people. Already a part of the master class, she longs to be accepted by Charleston women. She was probably ostracized by them, a Charleston woman tells me when I talk about this project. The community is closed, and hard to understand unless you grow up in it; it was nothing like Providence. When I tell this woman about my attempts to contact the living white family members in Charleston, to try to find those missing letters, she says, "Of course they didn't want to talk to you! You're an outsider. And you sound like—" I interrupted her, knowing what she was about to say, "—like a Yankee," I say, laughing. "I know."

The divisions remain.

To help Susan in her mission to acclimate, to find acceptance, she requests things that are fashionable, using her connections in the industrial North to get those things that would be more expensive in agrarian Charleston, where finished products were shipped in from England or New England. This was a source of tension that led to conflicts between the North and South, and prompted the secessionism that was avoided until the 1860s. Winthrop would write home about his frustration with the North as the political conflict unfolded.

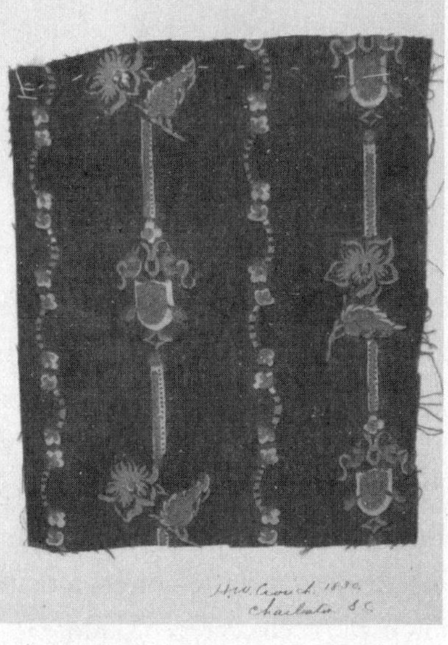

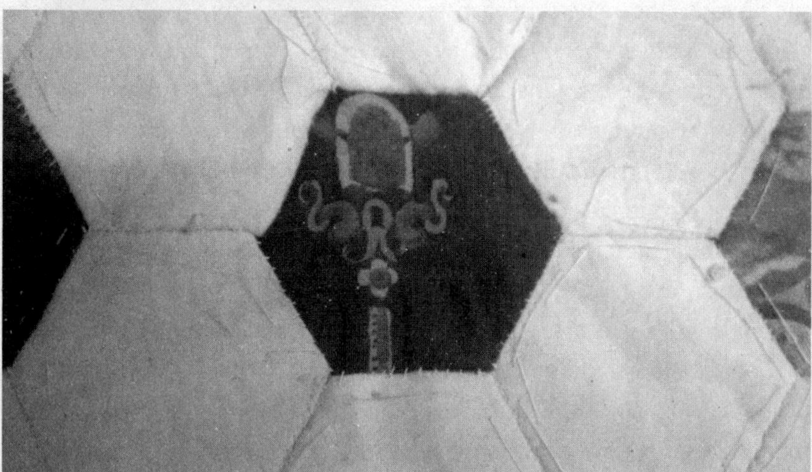

This is one of the dresses Susan likely wore in the 1830s. She was a talented sewer and a small woman; another of her dresses is approximately 26 inches at the bust and 22 inches at the waist. This dress was donated without its sleeves and has since been restored; we surmise that Franklin cut off the sleeves to include the fabric in one of the notebooks. The same fabric is also included in the quilt tops.

Susan makes sure to get her cloak fitted just right, measured just a bit shorter than what her sister would require, as she must be a bit shorter than her. A woman she knows near their home in Providence will cut the pattern for her, but Susan is careful to note that she'd like her to come to the house to cut and sew the cloak, rather than taking it to her own house to work on it—presumably because her sisters can better oversee the production of it in their house.

> *I am sorry to trouble you to get as many things for me as you have so much to do. We have written for a carpet and several other things. Eliza, if you come do not leave your woolen stockings at home as you will find them comfortable. The winters here are much colder than they formerly were. I should like a couple pairs of merino or worsted stockings but I am almost afraid to write for them as we have written for so many things. But woolen stockings are much dearer here than with you. I do not want you to trouble yourselves to make any preserves for me as we can do with out them and you have so much to do. I do wish you could give up keeping boarders. It is such a laborious way of getting a living. You do not take any comfort of your lives. I shall feel very glad to hear that you can live otherwise.*

Susan's very concerned about that cloak, as it comes up again in another letter, with more instructions to her sisters on how to have it made, and then at last in December 1835, she writes to say it's arrived.

> *My cloak came safe without the least injury. I think it very handsome, very cheap, It fits me very well indeed. I could not have got it here under thirty dollars. I am very well satisfied with it. I think it a beautiful color.*

She also thanks her family for the preserves and apples they sent down; they often sent apples to Winthrop and Hilton, too, since there weren't any to be found that they thought were as good as those in New England. These were the benefits of their family connections in the North.

The marmalade and jelly were in good order but the quince had fermented a little. We are much obliged for all the preserves. I was sorry you had sent so much as I know you all have so much to do. I think the juice makes as good a preserve as there is. I think the marmalade is as good as any I have ever eaten. I shall be very choice of it as it keeps so well. The apples are very good . . . I picked them over and did not get a half a peck that were specked. We have enjoyed eating them very much. I found a few sweet apples among them which I cooked for tea. They reminded us of home. For the old clothes I am much indebted to you. They will be of service to me. I am astonished to perceive that Sarah has grown so much. I made a nice frock for Hasell out of the plaid dress and have got enough to make another which I shall do as soon as I have time.

Susan often requests things of her family and says she'll send money home, or that she'll send figs, cordial, and other goods to them in exchange. Here, she's gotten her sister's outgrown clothes to make clothes for Little Hasell; she used Sarah's dress to make a "frock" for Little Hasell, and the clothes give her a sense of her sister's growth—another connection to home across the thousand miles that are bridged only with the newspapers and these letters and other goods that take days or weeks to arrive.

Susan is thrifty—middle class, not elite—but she says when they move into the city house that it was the dirtiest she's ever seen and "had it cleaned from top to bottom," meaning, this was the work she assigned to Minerva, Eliza, and Juba and their children. At the same time, she's trying to save money by getting this used cloth from her family; maybe the scraps from her sister's clothes that remained after she finished Little Hasell's clothes became part of the quilt. She mentions in this letter that they're burning coal instead of wood, which is "very high" this winter, and she fears they'll have a "sorry" Christmas because food (butter and eggs) are so expensive (for Thanksgiving, they ate some of the goods her parents sent down). She didn't have to make butter like her mother and grandmother did in the colonial era, as now they have the means to buy it. She asks her family to send a firkin of sweet butter if they can get some for less than twenty-two cents; it's thirty-seven and a half in Charleston. And always, she emphasizes how much she misses the family, and longs to hear from them more frequently—and, even more, for them to visit her. One letter arrived in December, though it was dated September; Susan writes that she doesn't know where it was in the interim. She misses home.

> *I wish you could see how comfortably we are situated Eliza if you went to Andover you must have had a cold journey as I see by the papers that it is very cold at the north. It has not been very cold here. A fortnight ago Sunday I went to Church and wore a muslin dress and thin cape on my neck and I found a fan very comfortable. Mrs. Carpenter mentioned that the same day they had a snow-storm in New York. Mrs. Carpenter called to see me last week. She left town the next morning for Columbia. I was very glad to see her indeed. I was glad to hear from her that Emily is growing so fleshy and how I wish I could see you all. I tried to persuade Mrs. Carpenter to stay and spend the day with me but she said she could not. I intended to call and see her in the evening but it rained.*

The Carpenters are from Providence, and always bring news of the North with them. Mrs. Carpenter must have been good company for Susan, because she wishes she'd stay longer. In these letters, there's news of the family, and, of course, always a bit of gossip, too—who's married to whom back in Providence, who's had a child, what's wrong with so-and-so's child rearing or ugly husband. In this December letter, she writes that Mrs. Thorne, who has been living with the Crouches, has just lost her husband. Apparently, it was no great loss, because they'd already been separated and as Susan says, "I do not think there was a person that was sorry he was dead. It was a great relief to Mrs. Thorne. I am glad on her account and the children for he was a great mortification to them." He didn't drink but was doing something that embarrassed his family, and died of a sudden "fit" in the street. In May of the following year, Hilton writes that Mrs. Thorne will be traveling to New England and will meet his family: "Mrs. Thorne intends visiting the North. She will leave for the North the first of June and will visit Providence in the course of the summer. You will be much pleased with her and I hope you will make her visit pleasant and agreeable to her." Hilton and Mrs. Thorne would soon marry, and he'd take charge of her two children, one of whom, it would become apparent, had epilepsy.

At other times, Susan is critical of her brother-in-law, Charles, and his wife, Eliza Crouch. Here, she talks about their daughter Harriet and the new baby.

> *[Little Hasell] has had very few clothes in comparison with Harriet Crouch. I do think she is the crossest child I ever saw in my life. The baby does not cry half as much it is a very quiet child but they are spoiling it with indulgence. They walk about with it all the time. I never saw people humor children more than they do.*
>
> *Hasell is no trouble at all. He takes care of himself. He goes to bed by sunset. He lays down and goes to sleep without any trouble. He does not drink tea, just takes a piece of bread. Do write soon as I am anxious to hear from you.*

Eliza Crouch carries the baby, Harriet, around too much, "indulging her," and thinks she's a very cross baby. She and Winthrop don't like Hasell's brother; Winthrop once called Charles and Eliza Crouch "the most disagreeable couple I ever saw." They don't get along, and Winthrop would later call them lazy. Susan notes that Eliza and Charles call the baby by different names for several months because they can't agree on one.

> *I wish you could see little Hasell. He is as full of mischief as he can live. Eliza's baby is a much more quiet child than Harriet ever was. It appears to me that Harriet [their firstborn] is more troublesome than the baby. She cries more than the baby does. It appears that they have changed the baby's name again. They call it Julia but I do not know that that is the child's name. What pleases Eliza does not please Charles.*

In spite of her misgivings, Susan sounds grateful for Eliza Crouch's company when she visits her on the island.

Susan repeatedly wishes that her parents and sisters didn't have to work so hard, saying in another letter that she feels badly that they have to work so hard while she has it so easy. She wishes her sisters could come live with her so that they, too, could benefit from the ease that enslaved people's labor creates for her in the household. She asks her mother and sister Eliza to come during the winter of 1835, when she's anticipating her pregnancy confinement as well as Hasell's long hours as a "demonstrator" at the college. But when Winthrop chimes in on this issue, he agrees that their parents should quit taking in boarders and that Eliza Williams could relieve herself of the worry of being a burden on her parents by coming to live with Susan. However, he doesn't agree with Susan that their mother should come south. He argues that she'd be dissatisfied with Juba's cooking.

> *You speak of breaking up the house and living by yourselves. I think it a very good plan, for I should think Father could get along with what he can earn and the house rent. You need not be any expense to him for Susan would be glad to have you with her.*
>
> *As to mother's plan of coming out South, I know it would hardly be the thing for her. She never could eat after the negroes' cooking and it would not answer to do otherwise. I despise such cooking as I see every day. I am astonished sometimes to see the boarders put up with it. Even the most simple things, for instance the potatoes are not half cooked; all the negroes care for is a good mess of cabbage and bacon the biggest and fattest they can get it is the height of their ambition. As for bread, there is nothing but corn bread that is fit to eat and that only at dinnertime, for when they make it for breakfast they always shorten it too much with hogs' lard, sometimes strong enough to cut your throat. I have told them several times to save some from dinner to last me at the rest of my meals but this is always forgotten.*

At this time, Winthrop is living in Columbia while working as a clerk in Mr. Ewart's store and boarding with a woman in town. He's being served by enslaved people who probably make his food, wash his clothes, and clean and stock the store. Mr. Ewart has shipped from the plantations bales of cotton that are bought from the plantation owners and then sold to traders in Charleston who ship them north, or to Liverpool, and sell them to the textile mills.

This system was the result of what Sven Beckert describes as the "feverish rate of growth" of the "world's mechanized cotton industry," noting that "in 1810, there were 269 cotton establishments in the United States with a total of 87,000 spindles," and just fifty years later, "in 1860, there would be 5 million spindles, making cotton textiles the United States' most important manufacturing industry in terms of capital invested, workers employed, and net value of its product." The founders of the mills in Lowell and Waltham, Massachusetts, had, "by 1823, . . . creat[ed] the largest integrated mills anywhere in the world." Part of the work of those mills was to produce "negro cloth." The owners were implicated in US enslavement not only in what they produced at the mills, but also in their trade; they "all had ties to the slave trade, the West Indian provision trade, and the trade in agricultural commodities grown by slaves. The 'lords of the lash' and the 'lords of the loom' were, yet again, tightly linked." The "cotton industrialists" were connected to the trade in which Jason Williams, Susan's father, as well as Winthrop and Hilton, were so intricately entangled, though, of course, the Crouch-Williams families' investments and profits were much more modest than the cotton mill owners who had invested more than 400,000 dollars in the Waltham mills. Still, Jason Williams' mercantile trade up and down the coast brought goods from the West Indies north and vice versa, and his last ship, destined for the West Indies, was seized in the US embargo of 1807 that propelled the US cotton industry forward as it blocked entry of British textiles to the States. Winthrop, like Hilton, had moved south to proft from the growing cotton trade and the chance to export raw goods north and abroad for production.

His letter home in 1835 marks the start of his career, and he's learned quickly—not only how to make profits off of enslaved people's labor but also how to behave as part of the master class. "It would not answer to do otherwise," he writes, meaning that their mother could not cook for herself as she did at home; she'd have to let the "negroes" cook for her—and she would hate their cooking. Winthrop couldn't have been accustomed to southern cuisine yet, and here, he perpetuates the myth of the slovenly, bestial "negro" who doesn't care about the quality of her food and simply adds bacon lard to everything, "sometimes strong enough to cut your throat."

I still wince when I read how Winthrop, Susan, and Hilton write about the enslaved people who take care of them, who meet their every need and do the tasks that Susan's sisters and mother find so difficult at home. When I first read the phrase, in that fabric notebook that their descendant Franklin compiled, *probably for slave gowns*, I was surprised and suddenly disgusted by the quilt that I'd fallen in love with. Looking back, I'm embarrassed at my naïve reaction. This is an object from 1830s South Carolina made by a white merchant family; *of course* they owned enslaved people. But they had come from the North, I thought, and wasn't the North abolitionist by then? Shouldn't they have been abolitionists, not slave owners? Most enslaved people had been freed by 1830 in New England. How did the Williams siblings slip so easily into this life? And what was Hasell's background, which allowed him swift entrée into Charleston's master class and the wealthy Sullivan's Island community as a new doctor?

It's a rhythmic sound that comes from each machine as the heddles rise and fall, the belts hum, the shuttles run through the weft threads. The roar comes when each machine's rhythm overlaps the others; it all becomes one great clatter.

This is the clacking roar—*chacka*-clack, *chacka*-clack, *chacka*-clack—constant, a rhythm that echoes in the fan I hear above me later in the day while stretching my legs. Once I've been with the sound, I can't forget it. It's a roar that deafened women or left them with forever-ringing ears. A mill girl was lucky if she didn't die of white lung—inhaling tiny cotton fibers all day long—lucky if she left factory life without losing fingers let alone her life; sometimes, the warp threads caught a woman's loosened hair and pulled her in, scalping her. Her screams couldn't be heard above that roar.

Hilton's lumber business is now thriving. He owns a mill in Charleston that he says is doing the most business of any in the city, and he frequently ships lumber back and forth between Providence and Charleston, occasionally bringing down rare lumber that Charleston builders want from the North, but most often sending up what is needed from the South. He uses his father's merchant and Providence connections to find northern buyers and supplies some of Providence's most prominent builders, Tallman and Bucklin, with South Carolina lumber for their projects.

John Lewis Krimmel, Black Sawyers Working in front of the Bank of Pennsylvania, *Philadelphia, c. 1811–1813.*

Susan gave me this to write a few lines but as I am much engaged in business it will be but a few. We were all very much pleased to hear of

> *Emily's engagement in fact I suspected such would be the case when I was on and it gives me pleasure to congratulate her. I would like very much to be on at the wedding but it will be impossible. My business occupies all my time. Tell Father that Mr. Fall has brought out a very large Cargo of dear Northern Boards which we have purchased.*

At other times, he ships as many as forty thousand boards to his father, to be sold to Tallman and Bucklin, who built Rhode Island Hall on the Brown campus where Hilton's uncle had studied, and many other buildings around Providence (sometimes in partnership with Russell Warren). Rhode Island Hall was funded by "wealthy" Brown donors, much of whose money was connected to the slave industry, and perhaps made with boards cut and planed by enslaved people in the South. Tallman and Bucklin designed Rhode Island Hall, now Brown's "fourth oldest building on the main green," which once housed the department of taxidermy: "Rhode Island Hall, the fourth oldest building on the main green, has seen a variety of occupants since its construction in 1840. It was originally built as 'another College edifice for the accommodation of the Departments of Natural Philosophy, Chemistry, Mineralogy, Geology, and Natural History' (letter from Nicholas Brown to the Corporation, March 18, 1839), and was largely funded by donations from wealthy Rhode Islanders—explaining the building's name."

The slave trade was booming in Bristol into the start of the 1800s. Jay Coughtry writes that "Throughout the eighteenth century, Rhode Island merchants controlled between 60 and 90 percent of the American trade in African slaves. . . . [T]hey soon surpassed Massachusetts as the chief colonial carrier, and by 1770, controlled 70 percent of the trade." The entire Rhode Island economy was tied into the slave trade in ways no other state was. Coughtry writes, "From 1725 to 1807, what has been called the 'American Slave Trade' might be better termed the 'Rhode Island slave trade.'" The end of the international trade was coming, by 1800, but then, with the pulse of industrialization and the need for cotton, it would shift to domestic trade.

I would never have guessed, walking the Brown campus, that their buildings on campus or elsewhere in the city might have been made with lumber made by enslaved people. I'd have assumed that the materials were sourced locally, or shipped down from Maine's forests. But this was the Atlantic mercantile economy, sending goods up and down the coast as the nation developed its own products for export. Just as raw cotton was shipped north in the 1820s to '50s, to be spun and woven at the northern textile mills, so raw materials from the South were sent north for construction. Hilton's enslaved men—Boston, Bishroom, Adam, and George, among many others whose names I don't know—worked at his mill, hauling and cutting the lumber, shaving rough logs into fine boards that could be used in construction for those northern buildings amidst which Hilton had grown up. Coughtry writes the "majority of workers employed by the Gibbes and Williams Steam Saw Mill," Hilton's mill, were enslaved people.

Hilton's family connections in the North help him build his lumber business. He often asks his father what lumber is going for in the North, and whether it's advisable to send deliveries or not. Sometimes, his father sends certain "dear" northern lumber not available in the South, down to South Carolina for Hilton to sell. In May 1836, he writes home that Susan is very busy with the children, they wish they could be there for Emily's wedding, and then he shifts into the business of his lumber:

> *The business has increased wonderfully. I am in expectation of sending Tallman and Bucklin a quantity yet, for the last 6 weeks there has been but a very small quantity that came to market. In about a week or ten days there will be an immense quantity. I would like Father to see* [Tallman and Bucklin] *and say that Lumber has risen. I would like them to write us.*

His father's proximity to the architects allows Hilton to negotiate prices and keep them apprised of his business and plans for shipments. A month later, he writes regarding another client, William Brown, who had written to Hilton's father the fall before to ask about getting lumber from Hilton. Now Hilton writes that he needs to return to him a "belt," perhaps something for the mill.

> *Sometime since I sent by the Grand Fork a Bundle containing the belt that Captain William Brown sent me. You mentioned that it was not received. If it has not yet come to hand, I would like Father to call upon him and pay for them. I intended to mention it in my last letter but forgot it. . . . We are now loading a vessel for Tallman and Bucklin. Lumber is coming in now plenty but very high, almost double what it was last year.*

A month and a half later, that shipment is sent off to Tallman and Bucklin—Hilton notes they've sent about 150,000 feet of lumber to the partners—and Hilton says he's too busy to visit Providence that summer or fall, as he'd hoped to do.

> *. . . for our business to go on profitably, at the same time it requires the attention of one of us to be constantly in the yard to deliver lumber and one to overlook the Negroes and keep them at work, and it is as much as one can attend to in doing our collecting. Now if I am away, one of [my partners] must suffer, for I cannot hire any one that will pay the same attention to it that I do.*
>
> *We have done a very good business this season for Charleston has improved very much within five years. There are many buildings going up at this time and very many more will be put up next season. We shipped a cargo of lumber to Tallman and Bucklin yesterday.*

Archived contracts reveal that he bought two men, Bishroom and Boston, on February 17, 1835. They'd have worked at the steam mill when it was over one hundred degrees, pushed logs through the planer, and shaped boards into tapered shingles that would come to grace houses and roofs in Charleston and Providence. They must have been skilled laborers to have been bought for the steam mill. Hilton bought Bishroom from Edward McCrady, another resident of the city who held strong beliefs about secession and how enslaved people should be "managed."

Hilton wrote that Boston and Bishroom and the other men working beside them were being supervised by himself or his partner, Mr. Gibbes. Hilton likely kept the men at work in inhumane conditions, including high heat and humidity, with mosquitoes biting, without good food and with little water to keep them hydrated. Hilton said he's best at it. I wonder what this means. That he delivers the best beatings? That he's the most severe and exacting, or reminds the men most often of his power over them? Franklin describes him as the "gentler" brother, but it's hard to see him as anything near gentle in this light.

In 1799, Hilton's uncle William Hilton Williams was a student at Brown, and his notes are in the archive. I read his loopy handwriting, looking for answers to how this family became who they were, why they engaged in the trade to the West Indies, why they moved south and bought enslaved people, if they understood the implications. William wrote in his notebooks:

1. *Happiness consists in health and the free exercise of our mental and corporal faculties.*
2. *Virtue and patriotism are the brightest ornaments of the citizen.*
3. *Riches and idleness are the enemies of virtue.*

He then translated each line into Latin, phrases that were meant to improve his language skills but also espoused the morals of the day. Hilton was taught these same values—that his worth was in his honor. He was born almost a decade after his uncle passed away at sea while working as a supercargo, a manager of a mercantile ship, in Suriname. Thirty years later, here is Hilton, carrying forth these values as a young businessman new to South Carolina, managing his own enslaved people.

> *One of my negroes ran away during my absence and I caught him the day after my return. I have since sold him for $600. I gave $500 for him about seventeen months since, he was a great rogue, would steal from me every opportunity he had. I bought another fellow last week for $462 that I think will answer my purpose much better. Negroes are now selling very high. The other negroes behaved very well during my absence.*

We don't get the names of the enslaved men in this letter, but in the 1840s, Winthrop would recount the loss of Hilton's enslaved man,

Boston, saying that the man's death wasn't such a great loss to Hilton because he'd been drinking and acting unreliably for weeks. He meant, of course, Hilton's *financial* loss when he spoke about Boston's death. Whether or not Boston had really been drinking for weeks, we don't know. If he had been, maybe he was trying to ease some of the pain he felt—whippings, degradation, the loss of his wife or children, the loss of his home. Maybe the bottle he could buy from the local grocery owned by a free black woman helped him slip away from the hardest edges of his sorrow.

Virtue and patriotism.

How did kinder, gentler Hilton move from Providence, Rhode Island, during the early days of abolitionism and not even question slavery? If he was taught to value virtue and patriotism, weren't these the qualities that would make him question the institution?

It takes time to learn all this—and to unlearn what I've been taught. I've made the mistake of thinking that because he's the more sensitive brother, he'll be more honorable and resist engaging in slave ownership. I stumbled on my twenty-first-century logic, reading him as a hypocrite. I didn't yet understand the connections between honor—the basis of a timocratic society—and slave ownership. One didn't negate the other; living in a society that valued honor above all else meant that Hilton was even *more* likely to own enslaved people. Hilton believed he needed enslaved people to make his living. He moved to Charleston to benefit from that system, and he bought enslaved people as soon as he could, proving himself a competent businessman and a member of the master class. His definition of self—a white man in antebellum Charleston—and his upward mobility depended upon his ownership of enslaved people. He defined himself in contrast to Boston. This is what W.E.B. Du Bois and Ida B. Wells and James Baldwin teach. Baldwin famously said, *What white people have to do, is try and find out in their own hearts why it was necessary to have a nigger in the first place, because I'm not a nigger, I'm a man, but if you think I'm a nigger, it means you need it.* Hilton could not be a master without a man to enslave.

It takes years to find, but there is a glimmer in this story—one of several—and it is Bishroom's autonomy, in spite of his enslavement. In

1822, Bishroom is mentioned in a class list at the Trinity Methodist Church as a married man. He's listed with his "class," people with whom he'd have studied Bible stories and verses, talked about his life, shared his story. They met on Thursday nights, so Elizabeth Vale, the woman who owned him in 1822, must have given him permission—or he must have claimed it for himself—to attend.

Maybe on Thursday nights, he learns to read, or teaches someone else to read, claiming and sharing literacy, too. Maybe he and his friends talk about the news they read that week, covertly, in the *Charleston Courier*, or about Denmark Vesey's plans for a revolt that they might debate whether to join or not. Maybe they mourn his death and the deaths of his co-resisters, when they're later executed. Maybe they laugh and joke together about the ridiculously extravagant hat they saw a white woman wearing that week, or how their friend had gambled too much in the grog shops the week before and lost all the money he'd earned hiring himself out the month before. I imagine one of Bishroom's friends sitting across from him, shaking his head as he chuckles, his face transforming into a more serious expression as he worries about his now-broke friend, knowing that man had planned to buy his wife's freedom with the money.

He had a wife, presumably a woman he loved, and he was able to marry her at a time when, in most of the country, marriage was illegal for enslaved people and often barred by owners. In Charleston, enslaved people found more liberties than they could have elsewhere. They had access to church communities and could be married in the church even when they were prohibited from doing so by the government. Bishroom "refused to simply be property," as Clark-Pujara says all enslaved people resisted in various ways around the country. Now, I begin to wonder whom he loved, when they married, and whether they had children. There was a woman in the same class at Trinity Methodist, also listed as married—the only other married person listed—and her name was Mary. She, too, was owned by Elizabeth Vale, who said upon her death in 1834 that she wanted her enslaved people to remain together if possible, and she wanted them to be given mourning clothes—a substantial "gift" for people who would have typically been given one set of clothes a year.

Was Mary Vale Bishroom's wife?

When Mary died in 1831, before Elizabeth Vale, before Bishroom was sold to Hilton, she was listed as being sixty years old. I don't know how old Bishroom was when Hilton bought him, nor how old he was when he was sold again years later, if he ever was sold. Maybe he and Mary were a couple in their sixties who had been together for years, and lived together in Elizabeth Vale's possession. Maybe they had children somewhere, even in Charleston. Maybe they'd met as older people and fallen in love.

If Mary was indeed his wife, Bishroom would have been heartbroken in 1831 when he lost her. He'd have mourned her loss in the midst of his daily work—because, for all of Elizabeth Vale's so-called kindnesses, she still owned enslaved people, and they still had to work. It was illegal to manumit enslaved people in Charleston as of 1820, except by going to court for a special ruling; since she couldn't free her enslaved people, maybe Elizabeth was doing her best as a woman living in this time. Maybe. The genealogist tells me that, even with his pro-slavery commencement speech in mind, Hasell may have been a reluctant slaveowner because he, too, inherited the enslaved people he owned and wouldn't have been easily able to free them. Minerva, Eliza, and John were able to rent themselves out and would have kept some of that money for themselves, perhaps saving for their own or their families' freedom. But, Hasell also surely kept most of their earnings, and we know that he also used them to serve himself and Susan. One of the women was likely the nurse Susan said was so good to baby Emily, and Susan notes that Juba worked for her family since leaving her sister-in-law Eliza Crouch's house. Hasell's uncle Charles was a lawyer who could have gone to court to manumit the enslaved people for Hasell, if he'd so chosen.

I think of Bishroom and Mary, their love, and those meetings where they spent time each Thursday with other people of color at Trinity Methodist, where they could talk freely, and laugh, and be at ease together. I imagine they were the married couple, and I see their hands clasped together throughout the whole meeting, and the way Mary leans slightly toward Bishroom as the minutes tick on and she gets tired. They're both getting older and feel the pain of the day's labor more deeply—an ache in her hip joints and fingers, the stiffness of his knee broken by a master years ago. Now, I see her head resting on his shoulder in the final moments of the night, and how he puts on the straw hat she wove for him just as they rise together and walk to the door, her hand on his arm, showing their love for one another in a space where it's safe. As the door opens, she lets go of his arm, and there's the creak of wooden planks behind them, the sound of their friends approaching, the laughter of two women sharing a story; outside, dark is falling while the hum of cicadas rises, an incessant whir on this hot summer night. Mary loves the hydrangea and rose blooms they pass on their way back, and pauses to smell a red rose on a bush that spills over a wall, before any of the patrolmen can spot her. She sinks her face into the bloom, and inhales deep, blissfully lost for a second, while Bishroom protects her by scanning the road ahead.

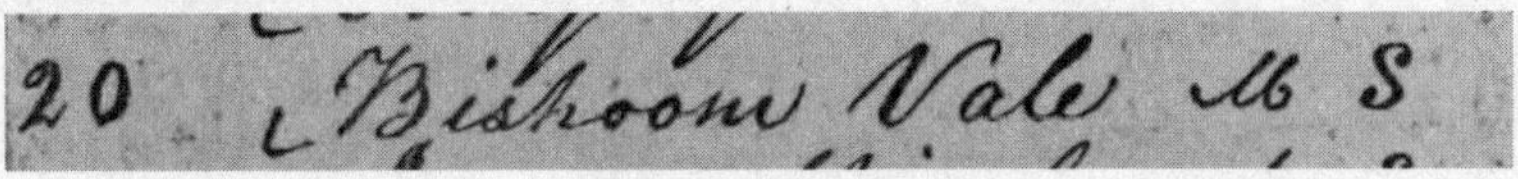

The page from the Trinity Methodist Church's membership rolls that record Bishroom Vale, listed with the surname of his owner Elizabeth Vale, between 1822 and 1826. He's noted as "married" and "slave." Bishroom was sold to Hilton in 1834, but here he is, a member of the church group, a married man, living his own life.

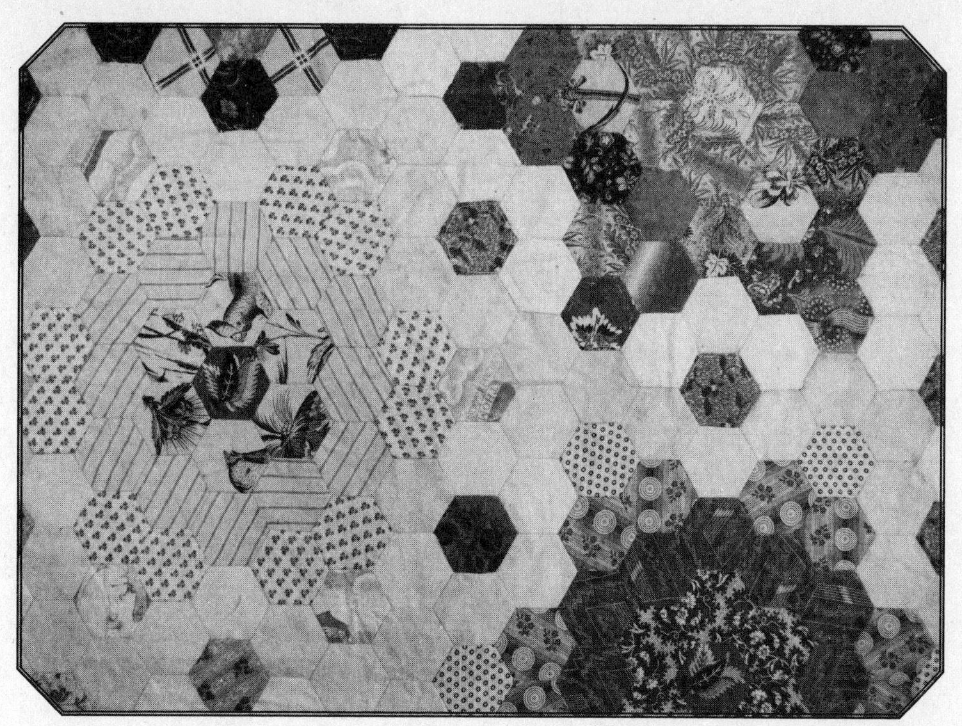

4

Mosaic

In 1835 Charleston, a white man is arrested for murdering a "negro." The white man was looking for his runaway slave when he "entered a negro house . . . where he thought he might find him." It's early spring. The tulip trees bloom pink outside the window at the house that Susan's brother Winthrop Williams lets. He writes to his younger sister Eliza Williams, back home in Rhode Island.

> *A negro was lying sick on the floor near the door; in passing him,* [the white man] *tread on his foot or hand. The negro asked him not to do*

it again, or something to that effect; the man turned and said he had a good mind to shoot him and pulled a pistol from his pocket and shot him dead indeed.

Winthrop notes that it's unlikely the white man would be found guilty.

It is doubtful whether he will be convicted as there was but one white person present and he the murderer's friend. There were several negroes, but their testimony is not taken in any case whatever.

At this point, Winthrop and Hilton are still new in Charleston. Hilton, five years older than Winthrop and four years older than Susan, has founded his now-thriving lumber business, and Winthrop has just taken a job in Columbia working for a factor, "a merchant who would sell a planter's cotton, supply him with goods, and provide credit;" part of his job with the factor entails working in the store that is, in part, similar to his father's in Rhode Island, with one significant difference: Cotton is traded here.

I have at last a stopping place. I arrived here last Thursday and through the kindness of our friend Penuel Carpenter have obtained a situation in the store of Mess'rs. D&J Ewart & Co., who do a large business in Dry Goods, Hardware, Groceries, etc., and buying cotton from the Planters as it comes in. They have about $50,000 worth of cotton on hand at present.

Today, that would be more than 1.3 million dollars. This is the beginning of Winthrop's career as a cotton factor, inspired no doubt by the vast amounts of money he saw he could make from the trade. In a few years, he'll go into a business partnership with his boss, Mr. Ewart, who comes from New York. Ewart uses his New York connections while Winthrop uses his Providence and Charleston connections to move cotton from the plantations around Columbia and Charleston, to the ports and then north or overseas to Liverpool, where it will be spun into cloth used for a quilt, and made into dresses for ladies and house slaves. In another letter home, written about the same time of his new employment, he writes about the man, Adger, who's from Providence.

> *I became acquainted with my present employer. . . . The store is close by; only a few doors below the Ewarts are engaged in two stores, the lower store, which in fact is 3 or 4 stores together. They do business in Dry Goods, Hardware & Iron of all kinds, Groceries, Crockery, and everything almost that is used by the Planters. They employ here 6 or 7 clerks, at the upper store where I am they keep a general assortment of all kinds of goods but on a smaller scale, the principal business is buying cotton as it comes in. They have now on hand about $50,000 worth most of it in the hands of James Adger of your city* [Providence, RI] *who does their business. All of our trade is in cash; we pay cash for cotton if we cannot sell goods in exchange for it but try to sell them as much as possible.*

Winthrop's family was like many merchant and planter families who lived between Boston or Providence and Charleston, South Carolina, and profited from their North-South and mercantile connections. I'd come to learn, in the course of this project, how closely tied Rhode Island and South Carolina were. All of these planters and merchants were involved or implicated, in some capacity, in the slave trade. There was the Middleton family, for example, who owned Middleton Place, a plantation outside Charleston, along with eighteen other plantations in which their hundreds of enslaved people worked to build their wealth. They produced some of the rice—thousands of pounds of rice—for which Charleston is still famous, Carolina Gold; their enslaved people made those symmetrical pools at which I stared when I visited Middleton plantation. Jamaica Kincaid stared at these pools, too, and said of them: "At the foot of the terrace are two small lakes that have been fashioned to look like a butterfly stilled by chloroform." She describes an encounter she has with a wealthy man whose last name is Cabot, and I wonder if he's related to the Cabots of Massachusetts whom, Beckert says, made their wealth from cotton production and the slave trade. Kincaid says that what she didn't mention to this wealthy man (who resented her discussing enslavement in the context of gardens), was that Arthur Middleton was one of the signers of the Declaration of Independence; he, like DeWolf, was sustained by his properties at home and abroad: in South Carolina, Barbados, and England. Middleton was part of the planter aristocracy, descended from parents who were also powerful citizens. He likely saw no irony in his signing of the Declaration in spite of his ownership of enslaved people, because to his mind, enslaved people were not, in fact, human. Furthermore, he was not an anomaly; the majority of the signers of the Declaration of Independence owned enslaved people. The Middleton generations to come summered in Newport, Rhode Island, and intermarried with the DeWolfs, the powerful slave-trading family of Bristol, Rhode Island.

The Nathaniel Russell Middleton House in Charleston is one of the city's most opulent, with a "self-suspended" spiral staircase (it has no supports from the floor). When I took the tour, the guide was eager to tell us about that staircase and about how tenderly the home had been restored. "Look," she told the group, "at that design along the woodwork." We looked up to see a pattern along the molding in the circular room; I scanned down again, to take in the portraits of the family—a little blonde girl, smiling—and the dining table set with fine china, roped off from tourists who might get too close. She did not like it when I asked who would have served the family at that fine dining table, who would have polished all that silver and cleaned all those dishes. "Well, the servants," she said.

The servants.

The Middletons and DeWolfs had married; Nathaniel's wife, Anna, was from Bristol, Rhode Island. It was her family who was largely responsible for Bristol's notoriety as a large slave-trading port. And while the Crouch-Cushmans were in a different class than the Middleton-DeWolfs, both would stay intimately connected and suffer through the same familial tensions during the division of North and South in the Civil War. Everything that Winthrop, Susan, and Hilton did in the South in the 1830s set them more deeply apart from their northern siblings as the war approached. In the 1830s, war wasn't so far off, as the country seemed to periodically veer closer, then swerve away, avoiding it once more.

The DeWolf house in Bristol, Rhode Island.

After telling his sister Eliza Williams about the murdered man, Winthrop goes on to tell Eliza the family news, how Hilton and his wife have moved out of Susan's house in Charleston to their own home, about the differences between a Charleston boardinghouse and "a New England house," and how they eat "wharfles for breakfast and supper, Johnny cake, rice, Turnips for dinner."

When he recounts the story of the murdered "negro" to his sister, he doesn't comment on whether or not this is just, but he does call the white man "the murderer" and notes that the authorities arrested the white man. How did Susan, Winthrop, and Hilton so easily come to terms with these sorts of events that discounted enslaved peoples' lives, and with owning enslaved people themselves? My initial mistake was in the question itself—in not understanding their New England roots, which mirror my own.

I first look to South Carolina to understand the slave-holding culture. Unlike Susan and her siblings, Hasell and Charles were indoctrinated in a culture that sustained enslavement, and grew up in a grand three-story house by Charleston's battery, where, as of 1820, they were waited on by twelve enslaved people. Their childhood brought them into contact with planters, the largest slaveholders in the country, as well as countless elites and more common people who owned a few house slaves, like Susan and Hasell did.

8 Meeting Street, now known as the Tucker Ladson house, where Hasell grew up with his father Abraham and brother Charles.

Susan and Hasell's quilt is called a "mosaic quilt," common for this era in the South Carolina Lowcountry, land of rice plantations and indigo—the plant that can make sky blue, midnight blue, almost-baby-blue when faded light, and best of all, a deep sky blue that bleeds almost to violet. Dip it in the dye and pull it out to oxygenate and then dip it again to deepen its hue. The more often it's oxygenated and submerged, the darker it gets. Hands come out stained. Bind the fabric and you have *shibori*. Tie-dye. Paint on wax before dyeing and you're left with pretty starburst and zigzag and flower-like patterns of white amid the blue. This is called "resist dyeing," because the waxed parts, now scraped clean, have resisted taking on the blue. My favorite color is Prussian blue, an almost electric, popping color that was popular in the 1830s. While the cochineal I used to make red comes from insects' shells, and fustic comes from bark,

Prussian blue comes from minerals, the earth. That particular vibrant sky blue was discovered in the early 1700s, by a color-maker in Berlin, and, like the aniline purple dye mauveine in the mid-1800s, its discovery was an accident of oxidization. Prussian blue comes from the oxidization of iron, while mauve or mauveine comes from the oxidization of aniline and helped propel the production of synthetic dyes that would follow. Every color has its own long history, the story of its discovery, use, or invention. Madder makes red, too, from a root that was used thousands of years ago, in ancient Egypt, Rome, and Greece. Scholars tell us that the Egyptian Pharaoh Tutankhamun was buried with cloth that holds madder in its fibers. I imagine Egyptian women weaving, together, linen from flax on large looms, and then using madder root to dye it that beautiful vibrant red. The root, like indigo, originated in Asia.

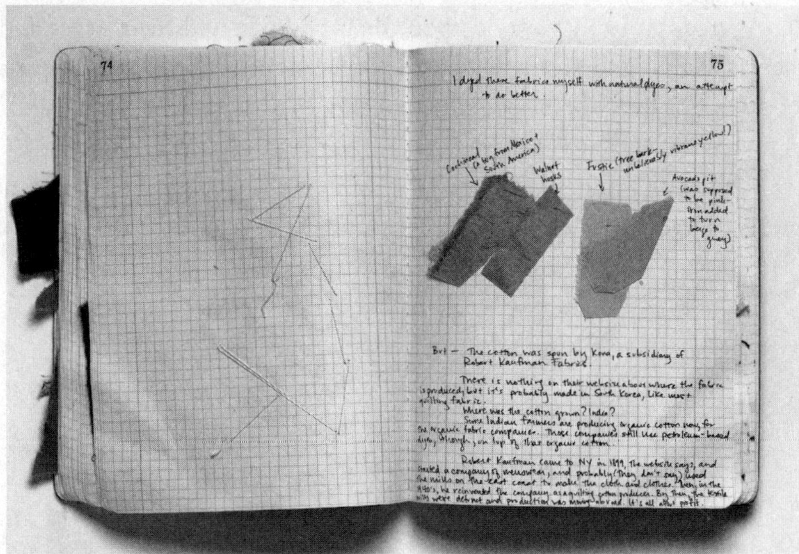

The notebook I made after dyeing fabric.

Behind all the pretty colors there's the story of indigo as a crop, a product, like rice and wheat and corn and denim and cotton, *the fabric of our lives*, and every other thing we wear and eat and use. Scholar Catherine E. McKinley tells us that indigo cloth was traded for human lives in Africa. Like New England rum. On the other side of the Middle Passage, indigo and rice were cultivated by enslaved people in the seventeenth, eighteenth, and nineteenth centuries in South Carolina Lowcountry swamps and marshes, in what one white visitor described as "putrid water." Imagine the mosquitoes swarming, biting, and filled with disease.

I saw those half-moon pools at Middleton Place, the chloroformed butterfly that was part of rice irrigation, on a cloudy day in January when the wind riffled their surfaces. I wondered how anyone could have made such perfectly arched, perfectly symmetrical pools before they had access to mechanized tools and under the conditions in which they were forced to live. These builders would have waded into muddy waters hoping the water moccasins wouldn't find them, hoping the rats and vermin would leave them be, swatting off the malarial mosquitoes their masters escaped when they rode off to their summer cottages each year. They were probably hungry, probably ill-clothed, probably hot and dehydrated, probably worried about their children and their wives and their husbands and all the people they'd been torn from along the way. The straight line where the halves meet didn't waver. Kincaid reminds us that West Africans brought this skill of rice cultivation and irrigation across the sea, and here was one piece of its evidence, hundreds of years later, reflecting twenty-first-century clouds in its surface.

Beyond there's the Ashley River, which was diverted to make these pools and others that have been lost to the tides; the river rushes toward Charleston's port at the mouth of the Atlantic, where Minerva, Eliza, and Juba lived at 6 Cumberland Street, a few blocks from the harbor. Imagine Minerva and Juba in those cotton dresses with the teakettle print, one in red and one in brown. Imagine Minerva prefers the red. Imagine she wears it out sooner than the brown because she wears it so often, especially on market days when she sells her vegetables to her neighbors. Imagine she hides this vegetable money away in the pocket she wears under her dress, a cotton pouch, muslin she claimed from Susan's scraps; it holds her children's futures, the freedom she will buy for them.

How does this happen? How does a plantation become what it is? How does a city come to host populations of both enslaved and free people of color, poor whites and those who call themselves the masters?

This is the South Carolina Lowcountry, hot and humid. From the air, its waterways reach like tendrils for miles between drips of green land, then blend into the blue bay and sea. This is flat land, swampy, where you can still buy Carolina Gold rice, marketed for tourists in small cotton sacks in gift shops, where you can take horse-and-wagon tours through the old city, which people still see as charming southern genteel. Restaurants have *sugar* and *cotton* in their names. One of the hotels is named after a hotel from Susan's day—the Planter Hotel. There is something about this myth that still seduces people. I think of the restaurants where I ate in college, the ones I visit in Charleston, where chefs serve shrimp and cheese grits, hush puppies, collard greens cooked with pork, fried okra. I look for okra soup, which Winthrop notes he ate one evening, food that Michael Twitty writes that enslaved people cooked for their masters, popularizing dishes we now think of as southern cuisine. I think of Juba, standing in the kitchen or the yard, chopping collards while her son brings in water for the pots, humming to herself. Jimmy brings in the horse and carriage as Hasell enters in the front door; she hears his call to Susan. Sorenzo shows her younger child how to pour the water into the pot without spilling. Let's say the younger child was a boy, too.

Imagine how she loves his patience with his little brother when she hears him say he'll race him back to the chickens.

How did Juba and Sorenzo come to inhabit a place whose economy is driven by enslavement? The lowcountry became plantation country over time, its crops changing with demand:

> *Beginning in the last decade of the seventeenth century, the discovery of exportable staples, first naval stores and then rice and indigo, permanently altered the character of lowcountry South Carolina. . . . African slaves began pouring into the region; and sometime during the first decade of the eighteenth century, white numerical superiority gave way to the lowcountry's distinguishing demographic characteristic: the black majority. No longer societies with slaves, lowcountry South Carolina, then Georgia, and finally East Florida became slave societies.*

What's the difference between a society with slaves and a slave society? This was a distinction applicable only in the pre-Revolutionary period. Christy Clark-Pujara writes that the difference "is not static; however the North was only ever a society with slaves," though small parts of the North (including South County, Rhode Island, where I lived when I started studying the quilt tops) were slave societies. The South, on the other hand, would have been a slave society because "slavery stood at the center of economic production, and the master-slave relationship provided the model for all social relations: husband and wife, parent and child, employer and employee, teacher and student. From the most intimate connections between men and women to the most public ones between ruler and ruled, all relationships mimicked those of slavery." In slave societies, the master class "rule[d]" and "nearly everyone—free and slave—aspired to enter the slaveholding class." Ira Berlin explains that people of color could become slaveholders themselves, and describes the codes that slave societies enacted to keep people in bondage. What prompted a society to shift from a society with slaves to a slave society was the discovery of crops that required a large labor force to harvest, produce, and export them. Rice, indigo, cotton.

It's 1820 in Charleston, twelve years before Susan and Hasell marry, and Hasell Crouch is still a child. He lives with his brother, Charles, and father, Abraham, in a fine house by the port. It's three stories high with a square façade. Imagine two boys who stand at the third floor window to look out at the sea. From the top floor, they can watch the brigs and schooners sailing into port with the goods their father will document at the Customs House, known today as the Exchange Building, down the street, a few blocks away. The port is always busy, and between here and there, there are neighborhoods their father won't let them traverse, where sailors and merchants, freemen and enslaved people commingle, everyone shouting, selling their wares or pushing their way through the streets.

Abraham owns twelve enslaved people who run their home. His wife, Sophia, the boys' mother, died a month after Hasell was born, when she was just twenty-one. She was descended from the elite planter class through her mother. Her mother, Hasell's grandmother, was Mary Ancrum Walker, and she owned a large plantation, at least two thousand acres, in Wilmington, North Carolina, and then in 1808, she became a respected part-time resident of Charleston. As a widow with her own protected property, she was able to operate as a *feme sole*, passing down her enslaved people to her grandchildren. Married women were counted as one person with their husbands, and their husbands maintained all control, while single women could have slightly more autonomy. Hasell and Charles inherited from their grandmother several enslaved people, and were "gifted" Jenny by her. The record is incomplete, but also listed as Mary Ancrum Walker's property or that of her daughters' (to whom she passed down her property) are Flora, Chloe, and Minerva. In her second marriage settlement, when Mary Ancrum Walker married a second time, she listed as her property to be passed to her daughter Sophia and then to Sophia's children 24 enslaved people including Roxana and her children Tom and William, Cynthia, Damon, Diana, and Juba and her son Sorenzo.

Hasell and Charles inherited some of these people. Minerva. Juba and Sorenzo. Hasell and Charles grew up being cared for by enslaved women who worked as their nurses, housekeepers, and cooks. These women soothed them to sleep each night and dressed them each morning, probably longing to soothe their own children to sleep, to wipe their own babies' faces clean, to feed their own children such great feasts of fine food. These boys would come to own these women. In 1830, when he graduated from Brown, Hasell gave a commencement speech on the "necessary evils" of slavery. The papers reported his speech to have "enlisted the favor of the audience from the candid and unassuming manner in which the subject was discussed." So, his delivery was appreciated, even though the topic wasn't "exactly fitted for a Rhode Island atmosphere." In 1830, Rhode Islanders, at Brown at least (which was founded by slave traders and funded at least in part with money made from enslavement), had more abolitionist leanings, after all.

specimen of neatness and elegance in elocution, highly acceptable to a very respectable audience.'

In a notice of the celebration of the late commencement at Brown University, we find in a Providence paper,the following paragraph:

The modest defence of slavery, as an unavoidable existing evil in the Southern States, by H W Crouch of Charleston S. C. though not exactly fitted for a Rhode Island atmosphere, enlisted the favor of the audience from the candid and unassuming manner in which the subject was discussed.

American Tobacco, has been cultivated with success in several parts of Russia.

In 1819, when Hasell was just ten years old, he might have looked upon the miniature their father had done of his wife the year they were married; perhaps Hasell gazed at her big eyes, oval face and narrow chin, ran his fingers over the locks of hair in a fleur-de-lis on the back of the frame, surrounded by pearls. Their mother died on September 10, 1809, a month to the day after Hasell was born. Maybe she died of complications from childbirth, or from a disease, an accident of some sort, or of infection. Perhaps he felt guilt alongside the pain of his loss, perhaps blaming his own birth for her death.

While the people enslaved in Abraham's house aren't named in the census records, they likely included the people passed down to Sophia from her mother; their presence is indicated by twelve tick marks on the 1820 census. There could have been six women and their children to care for the boys, cook the meals, and clean that tremendous house, and six men who acted as butlers or waiters, hauled the coal and wood for the fires, chopped the wood, fed and groomed the horses, tended the stable, drove the carriage. These people were possibly born in the United States (the international import of slaves having been outlawed in 1808), and may have been sold away from their own parents as children. Since Mary Ancrum Walker had owned several generations in one family, though—Judith, her daughter Juba, and her son Sorenzo—maybe there were other people who were able to stay with their relatives as well. Juba probably did everything she could to keep her children with her, making them indispensable to Abraham so that he wouldn't sell one away without the other—staying up later than anyone else to prepare the morning meal, churn the butter thick and creamy, dice carrots into the smaller pieces as he preferred. Maybe Roxana spent hours mending Hasell's suits with the tiny, even stitches that she knew made her more valuable as an object, and, she knew more deeply, more talented as a woman. Imagine she was given this skill that allowed her some bargaining power, becoming her last mistress's favorite, recommended to Abraham's late wife by her last mistress and sold, therefore, along with her children Tom and William.

Probably, at some point in these women's lives, they were raped by their masters or the white men around them. Charleston socialite Mary Boykin

Chestnut writes in her Civil War diary about how common "mulatto" children were: "The mulattoes one sees in every family exactly resemble the white children—and every lady tells you who is the father of all the mulatto children [in everybody else's household], but those in her own she seems to think drop from the clouds, or pretends to think so." I wonder if Sophia or Susan made similar observations in their days. White men's rape of enslaved women, their use of enslaved women as "mistresses," was an open secret. Stephanie M.H. Camp writes that "By the antebellum period, planters has so thoroughly assimilated ideas that reduced enslaved people to their bodies that they often referred to them by their parts: 'hands' was a common term and 'heads' was not unfamiliar . . . Women slaves . . . were as one with their farming tools and called, simply, hoes." How many times have I heard this word, and never known its origin? Camp goes on to say that "Planters, and white southern men generally, had also learned of black women's tough, sexual nature, and preyed on them shamelessly." Of course, here Camp is also emphasizing the problem of white men and women stereotyping black women as "tough" and "sexual."

I don't know if Abraham visited local high-class brothels after Sophia died, nor if he ever raped Minerva or Juba or Jenny, or any of the other women his wife Sophia owned. But if he was like most of the other white masters in Charleston at the time, it's more likely than not. William and Ellen Craft, who ran to freedom and wrote their story, say that, "It is common practice for gentlemen, (if I may call them such), moving in the highest circles of society, to be the fathers of children by their slaves, whom they can and do sell with the greatest impunity; and the more pious, beautiful, and virtuous the girls are the greater the price they bring, and that too for the most infamous purposes." Bernard E. Powers writes that "the largest single group of emancipated slaves gained freedom by the last will and testament of their masters." Sometimes, he says, "masters emancipated their mistresses along with their illicit offspring." Thus, "In 1860, 75 percent of the free black residents of Charleston County were mulattoes," while only "8 percent" of the "county's slave population . . . was mulatto." In 1820, manumission was limited by law, but some enslaved people, Powers says, found ways around this by saving money to buy their relatives.

Imagine that, several decades into the future, one of Minerva's children is sold away from her. Her child wouldn't have a portrait to hold to trace his or her mother's face. Maybe somewhere there was an eleven-year-old boy working in a field in Georgia, on a hot day when his thirst was heavy, dreaming of the mother who, by an accident of birth, was forced to care for a white woman's child instead of her own son.

Susan cut the hexagons from fabric her parents sent her from Providence via the brigs that ran the coast. From her house, she'd have been able to hear echoes of the harbor's daytime hustle—the shouting of merchants and captains and food sellers hawking their wares. She'd have sent Juba to buy for the cooking, and walked along the harbor past the Exchange building where Hasell's father once worked as a customs inspector. Her sister-in-law, Eliza Crouch, lives nearby. Now, in the night, it's quiet. She's sent the women to bed, all but Minerva, who stays up to undress Susan before retiring for the night.

The mosaic quilt that Susan and Hasell began together was popular with elite Charleston women since the pattern was published in women's magazines similar to *Godey's Lady's Book* in 1835. Paper piecing had been practiced in Charleston since the early 1800s, perhaps introduced from England by a visiting lady. In 1835, Susan wanted to be accepted by these women. She longed to know their ways. She said as much when she asked for Winthrop to give her something in commemoration of her wedding. "Such things here are talked more about that they are with you. They are made such secrets of." She was trying to break into a new society. She was learning quickly, like her brothers, Hilton and Winthrop, that if she were to thrive in Charleston, she had to prove herself a lady who followed the codes of the master class. It probably wasn't easy for Susan to fit in with Charleston women; she didn't seem to have many friends around except for Mrs. Carpenter (the wife of Penuel, who helped Winthrop get his job in Columbia), from the North, and her sister-in-law, Eliza Crouch. When Susan prepared for her confinement in the winter of 1835–36, she feared she'd be alone the whole the time.

Susan was a middle-class merchant's daughter, not an elite woman of leisure like the daughters of planters with whom Hasell grew up. Her parents had to run a boardinghouse to make ends meet, hardly a luxurious lifestyle. They hired a "domestic" to assist with housekeeping (in 1820, their domestic was a woman of color), but much of the work was done by Susan's mother and single sisters. Susan and her sisters were educated at a boarding school in Andover, Massachusetts, and then came home before they were married. Thus, they fulfilled the middle-class ethos of education as a means of "self-improvement," in addition to "encourage[ing] children to stay at home, sometimes into their twenties, a practice that maintained the parents' moral influence and gave young people material support." Winthrop and Hilton left home after high school, in their late teens, in pursuit of their careers: "As well as extending children's time at home, middle-class parents in the first decades of the 19th century advocated and sustained educational institutions that prepared their sons for business and their daughters to marry upward." This was precisely the path that Susan, Winthrop, and Hilton followed—Susan and most of her sisters married "upward" while Hilton and Winthrop founded their own businesses in Charleston. Hasell's family valued education, too, and while they were from the upper classes, education was a means to further ones' class and social connections; his father Abraham graduated from Brown and went on to become a lawyer before he became a customs house official. Hasell's grandmother had stipulated that Hasell and Charles must be educated, and left money for that purpose. All Susan's siblings, including Susan's other sisters, were educated so that they could move up in the world, "acquir[ing] cultural capital and learn[ing] how to spend it wisely while maintaining a genteel status." Susan wrote home in 1830 about her piano lessons and hoped her father would rent a piano so she could practice; because Hasell was indebted to Susan's father for his father Abraham's burial in 1826, Hasell gave her money—ten dollars—for the lessons. She planned to learn French, and to write to Winthrop sometimes in French to practice. And, for Susan and her sisters, this education included needlework.

Writers in the early 1800s were espousing the benefits of a woman's proper education: "Mrs. Friendly explained that a woman who lacked a well-furnished mind, well-governed temper, love of domestic pleasures, and the inclination and capacity for domestic employments would be unhappy in herself and a torment to her friends." Women were better mothers when they were educated, writers argued, and a substantial part of that education, of the "self-construction of the middle-class person," included "drawing and needlework." Those mills that thronged on in Susan's Providence and just north in Massachusetts were part of this construction of the middle class and Susan's new role as a housewife (as opposed to her mother's and grandmother's more labor-intensive roles as colonial housewives). "In industrialized urban areas, servants were hired in order to relieve their employers from having to do many of the more arduous tasks themselves. As Christine Stansell writes in *City of Women*, 'Being a lady . . . meant not doing certain kinds of housework.'" Since enslaved women and men did the household work for Susan, she was expected to develop her sewing and cooking skills. "Labor-saving technology slowly began to be introduced into the more affluent households in the 1830s and 1840s, but cooking largely continued over open hearths, for instance, and the work of supplying the most basic needs, such as heat, continued to be heavy labor. Along with the new technology, however, the standards of cleanliness increased and the aesthetics of the Victorian home became so ornate that leisure time did not increase." Stansell explains that women of this new middle class had to assert their superiority over servants by proclaiming problems with them. She's referring to life in northern cities, where immigrants served as "domestics" whom Susan's mother and sister Abby hired (they complain about their "help" to one another in their letters, as Susan would do when she returned north later in life). Women who "were not entirely confident of their own class identity, assert[ed] judgment over the immigrant poor" to "[affirm] their position and status."

The same definition of self in contrast to other applied to define oneself as middle class—and master class—in the Charleston slave society. This—defining herself as *not* enslaved, as not just a woman but a *lady* displeased with the work of the enslaved people Eliza Crouch owns—this is what Susan did when she arrived in Charleston and complained about the enslaved women who were supposedly poorly managed by her sister-in-law, Eliza Crouch. In those early days, conflicted and trying to adjust to this new society, Susan also claimed she'd prefer to do the housework herself, as her mother and sisters did back home, because she thought she'd do a better job. And, she wished her sister could help her with the housework so she could keep her company in Charleston. "I do wish we could keep house it would be so much pleasanter it would seem more like home for I could have one of you with me then. But it will be an impossible thing until Hasell gets his profession." But then, a year later, she sang Juba's praises as her cook and nurse—the same woman she'd criticized while living in Eliza Crouch's house—saying that Little Hasell called her "Mammy."

In 1835, Winthrop was becoming a cotton factor, in charge of getting the cotton from the plantations around Charleston to the city's docks and selling it north and abroad. Beckert writes that factors were "American middlemen" who "accepted planters' cotton on commission, transported it to ports, and then sold it to merchants. . . . This service was of enormous benefit to planters, as it enabled them to sell their products in large coastal markets or even in Europe, giving in effect even the remotest of them access to distant markets." He explains that factors also did the work Winthrop described in his letters, "provid[ing] planters with manufactured goods and food supplies." Factors played a significant role in the cotton industry, and Winthrop seized this window of opportunity. He and Mr. Ewart would found their business in 1836. He wrote about the wagons that brought the cotton in. He wrote about how when the weather was bad, the wagons couldn't come. He wrote about how, by the Civil War, he'd stored enough cotton bales for himself to support his family for years to come. He lost more than $50,000 worth of cotton and goods in the Civil War's destruction. Whenever I tell African American historians in Charleston that he was a cotton factor or trader, they chuckle and say, "Oh sure!" meaning: Cotton trader is a nice way of saying he was trading slaves, that this was his guise in the 1830s. He may have been a trader, but I haven't found evidence of this in the contract files. There are no extant records of his purchase or sale of enslaved people, except for what he writes in the letters. His brother, Hilton, on the other hand, is listed as a "trustee" for the property of several people on contracts for enslaved people in the 1840s and '50s, benefiting from his wife's inheritance of enslaved people from Mary Ancrum Walker, Sophia Jane Withers' mother. How Harriet was related or connected to Mary Ancrum Walker isn't clear. But, as her sister was Eliza Crouch, married to her husband's Uncle Charles, Hasell's brother, it's possible that the enslaved people owned by Hilton, Charles, and Hasell were related, as they all came from the same North Carolina plantation and at least some of them had managed to stay together as multi-generational families—Juba, Judith, and Sorenzo, as well as Minerva, her children, and her mother Dianna.

Winthrop's business was tied up with industrialization and the northern mills, and thus with enslavement. Factors "were the most significant deliverers of capital into the cotton-growing regions of the U.S. South, channeling credit to planters who used the money to acquire the supplies they needed to tide themselves over until the next cotton harvest and to purchase more land and more slaves to expand the production of cotton." Factors weren't necessarily "the wealthiest traders in the empire of cotton," Beckert writes, but they were "the most numerous." And, because they were extending credit to planters, which might have been "advanced by European merchants" and others in the northern states, too, when the planters couldn't pay, their enslaved people were used as collateral for the debt. This was in the 1840s and 50s, decades after England had banished slavery. And yet, here they were, still bound up in the system.

Winthrop sent his cotton to Providence and Lowell, as well as Liverpool. As plantations shifted from the production of rice and indigo to cotton, the northern landscapes changed, too. "Between 1826 and 1836," when Lowell's textile mills were booming after their founding in 1821, "Lowell's population jumped from twenty-five hundred to eighteen thousand. . . . The population continued to grow steadily into mid-century, when it declined briefly because of the discovery of gold in California."

As the industrial north's landscapes and routines changed with technological advances, so did the personal lives of every person living through the time. The production and distribution of readymade cloth and other household goods changed Susan's life as a housewife, Hasell's work as a doctor, Susan's brothers' careers in the lumber mill and cotton trade, and the lives of the enslaved people they owned. While Susan strived toward status as a lady, Minerva, Juba, and Eliza probably loathed that concept. Thavolia Glymph writes that some of enslaved women's first acts upon emancipation were to buy themselves new dresses and household goods, not in an attempt to mimic white women's engagement with domesticity but to claim their own identities in the clothes and items they chose, to declare their liberty to buy what they selected rather than what someone else demanded they wear and use. Minerva, Eliza, Juba, and Boston's lives were determined by "the long night of American enslavement," as Ira Berlin calls it, their enslavement seemingly even more certain now that vast quantities of cotton needed to be planted, cultivated, and picked each season.

The workhouse in Charleston, where enslaved people were sent by their owners for punishments.

Eliza, Juba, and Minerva lived in a two-story house at 6 Cumberland Street, a block from the harbor, several blocks from the work house, and about six blocks from Denmark Vesey's old house, though he had long passed by the time Minerva and Eliza inhabited the Crouch house. Vesey led the 1822 rebellion that prompted slave owners in the city to install heavier wrought-iron gates with spiked tops like thorny rosebushes, and sharp traps on the house-side of the fence to injure anyone who made it over the thorns. Gates were topped with six-inch spikes. Walls were made higher. You can still see these gates in the city today. Walk around the battery neighborhood, and there they are, before the two-hundred-year-old houses, guarding the yards and the old carriage houses that serve as garages or guesthouses now but were once stables for the horses that drew the carriages, or shacks for the people owned by the big house's inhabitants. The gates and walls still serve to keep the public out; tourists wander the neighborhoods now, walking or in horse-drawn carts, listening to the tour guides' tales. The well-to-do locals who live here now—still predominantly white—give the tourists disapproving looks as they pull into their drives and carry groceries inside; the locals gripe about the tourists and the ever-clopping hooves of those big workhorses running through their neighborhoods. They still wish for privacy; they still wish for distance from what's distasteful—and that includes the past. Most people in this neighborhood do not want to talk about slavery.

I'm told by someone in the North that I can't make this assumption. This is the neighborhood in which Susan and Hasell lived. It's where Nathaniel Russell Middleton's house stands, and the infamous Calhoun's mansion. North, at the peninsula's center, John C. Calhoun's statue stands in Marion Square. Jamaica Kincaid wrote about the statue in her essay on Middleton Place, saying she couldn't imagine how black citizens of Charleston walked past his statue each day. He's the "inventor of the rhetoric of states rights and the evil encoded in it, who was elected Vice-President of the United States twice," she says. States needed to create their own laws, Calhoun argued, so that slavery could be sustained. He wanted to secede from the Union. And there he stands in the middle of Marion Square, standing over the city.

"Do you think I can say this?" I ask Joseph McGill, a Charleston historian and activist. "Someone told me I can't know that people in this neighborhood don't want to talk about slavery."

"Oh," he says wryly, "I know. Trust me."

A treadmill wheel used in Jamaica in 1834, similar to the one used at the Charleston work house. We don't know if Hasell and Susan sent Eliza, Minerva, Juba, or the other people they enslaved for punishments at the work house. Certainly, the enslaved women would have known of friends or family who had been sent there.

In 1822, Vesey organized an uprising in Charleston uniting hundreds of enslaved people in the city to rise up against the minority population of whites. I've heard people ask why, if the enslaved were the majority, they didn't *just revolt and take over*, as if to imply that they weren't smart or savvy enough to do so. Wasn't it that easy—to change the rules by force? The people asking this question don't think of the system of slavery as a nationwide institution reinforced with organized armies, police forces, laws, and weapons—guns. Enslaved people were not allowed to own a gun, of course, and they were rarely allowed to ride a horse (which would give anyone more speed, and more power), so when they organized any kind of revolt it was on foot and with weapons like clubs and farm tools—pitchforks, hoes, scythes, and if they were lucky—as in the case of Vesey's revolt—the occasional stolen gun. What defense was a hoe in the face of a man on horseback with a gun? Or a few guns in the face of twenty or thirty? And, if enslaved people made it out of one region alive, how would they get through the next, where any black man on the street could be stopped by any white man on the street, and questioned, and beaten, and arrested, and killed, simply out of a sense of suspicion, or anger, or resentment, or because the white man was in a bad mood that day?

Escape meant weeks running through woods and fields without access to food, being chased by vicious hunting dogs and men on horseback who had nothing more to do with their time—who were motivated by the reward of money and another man's respect—than to find an escaped man or woman who was hungry, on foot, perhaps without shoes, and often insufficiently clothed. What chance did a black man have in the face of a system built to keep him in check, under the power of not just his owner but any white man, anywhere? "The lowest villain in the country, should he be a white man," write William and Ellen Craft, who escaped enslavement, "has the legal power to arrest, and question, in the most inquisitorial and insulting manner, any colored person. . . . If the colored person refuses to answer questions put to him, he may be beaten, and his defending himself against attack make him an outlaw, and if he be killed on the spot, the murderer will be exempted from all blame."

And yet, in spite of the odds, people did escape, and they did make it to the free northern states, which offered refuge until the Fugitive Slave Act of 1850 was passed. Until then, free black communities in Boston and Philadelphia could safely welcome those who had escaped slavery in the South. The ingenious Henry "Box" Brown had his friend, Samuel A. Smith, box him up, nail the box shut, bind it with hickory hoops, and mail him from Richmond, Virginia, to Philadelphia, Pennsylvania. The box was "two feet eight inches deep, two feet wide, and three feet long," and he had with him, "one bladder of water and a few small biscuits." The box was marked "This side up, &c.," but was not respected by the mailmen, who "hesitated not to handle the box in the usual rough manner common to this class of men. For a while they actually had the box upside down, and had him on his head for miles." Henry made it safely to Philadelphia, but when Samuel tried to send two more enslaved men north in boxes, he was caught, arrested, and imprisoned.

William and Ellen Craft, "married slaves from Georgia," escaped together by disguise: Ellen, so fair-skinned she could pass for white, dressed as an elderly male plantation owner, and her husband posed as his slave. In order to keep her from having to speak much to other wealthy train passengers, they wrapped a bandage around her jaw to make it look like she suffered from a toothache, and they put her arm into a sling so she wouldn't have to write or sign for her husband's passage as "her slave" (she did not know how to write). Together, they rode the train from Georgia to Philadelphia and then settled in Boston, where they lived until they were hunted by slave catchers from Georgia, seeking to reclaim them under the Fugitive Slave Act of 1850. The Crafts decided to seek safety in England, where they were "highly respected." They had several children, whom they "spared no pains in educating for usefulness in the world."

Eliza, Juba, and Minerva would have had access to the free black community in Charleston, which included a temperance society, churches, a dry-goods store, and a network of friends who supported one another. People could buy their own freedom with the money they earned from goods sold at market or by getting a portion of the money they made from being rented out, themselves, to others. Before 1820 in Charleston, they could have been emancipated upon their owner's death, through the will.

Making a quilt out of hundreds of hexagons was time-consuming and an inefficient way to make a warm bedcover. But when Susan and Hasell worked on the quilt together in 1834 and '35, they weren't making something utilitarian; this was to be something beautiful, a shared pursuit—and she was practicing her status as a lady who could make things that proved her position; this was the more elaborate housework that came in the Victorian era. "Mosaic patchwork is not a particularly practical technique, and it does not seem to have been used in utilitarian bedcovers. Instead, it provided opportunities to show off the maker's skills, personal artistry, awareness of fashion, patience, or determination." Susan and Hasell were becoming part of Charleston's society—not the high society of the balls and parties that kept them up at night when they wanted to sleep, but they were moving upward through the middle class, gaining wealth, buying property; in 1836, just before Little Hasell died, the doctor Hasell bought a house on Sullivan's Island. And, of course, there were the enslaved people they owned—more signifiers of the white family's wealth and place in society.

I traveled to Virginia to work on an extant slave cabin that was being restored. I'd learned about it from Joseph McGill, the man who runs The Slave Dwelling Project, which offers a series of overnight stays in slave dwellings to raise awareness and to preserve the buildings in which enslaved people lived alongside the mansions and the fine houses where the white people lived. We need to tell both sides of the story. We need to remember the people who brought their skills to this world—cultivating rice in complex irrigation systems, weaving baskets, inventing looms and corn grinders and ways to separate the rice from the husk, to make the food edible. The Gullah language survives around Charleston on the sea islands. The songs. The instruments and rhythms.

This cabin was on the grounds of an old plantation in the blue hills of Virginia, a ninety-minute drive west from D.C. I stayed in a hotel and drove out at dusk, when the crew leader said they'd be breaking for dinner and would have time to talk. The sun was going down on the hills, green and yellow in the light, the sound of crickets and cicadas and the heat of July pressing in. I turned down a dirt road, wound around and over another hill, and there it was: a three-room cabin reinforced with leaning two-by-fours, and a crew of hard-hatted people walking and crouched around it.

At dinnertime, one of the men showed me his Darwin-era replica microscope, through which he studies samples of dirt and water. This microscope was made of wood that had been sanded into circles, a lens mounted on the top; it was an important—and technologically advanced—tool in his day but looked rudimentary to my eyes. Darwin took this microscope on his voyage on the *Beagle*, which began in 1831, just before Susan left Providence for Charleston. While Susan settled into her new home in humid Charleston, Darwin set sail for South America, Australia, and—the part of the trip I remember learning about most vividly—the Galápagos Islands. He saw those tremendous tortoises, some of whom have lived long enough to have met both him and you (the oldest recorded Galápagos tortoise lived from about 1830 to 2006).

The man with the microscope told me about water bears, tardigrade, which he'd seen with this microscope. He tried to find one for me to see. "They look like little hippos," he said. The project director said, when I asked how it feels to work on a cabin once inhabited by enslaved people, "Well, it's actually a lot of fun most of the time." He chuckled, wondering—I think—why I was so *serious*. The others nodded and agreed. The microscope man's partner was the only one of the volunteers who would talk about race, telling me about her sons from her first marriage, her sons who are biracial, and how she worries for them when they go out at night. She always wonders if they'll come home safe.

Clermont Farm is a learning site for architectural preservationists, and that's why they were here: to learn about restoring old buildings. They were not here to talk about race. Still, when the preservation board leader, an older white man, took us on a tour, he told the stories of the slave cabin, of the enslaved people who were here—what little he knew—as much as he told the story of the white people and the big house. "That's our concern here," he said, "to tell the whole story."

I was captivated by a chopping block stored in the back room, from what era they were not sure. It might have been as old as the eighteenth century. It was a worn stump of wood, smooth-edged, where countless chickens must have been slaughtered, where pork was cut into portions for meals, where, probably, the white family got their meat and the black families took as much as they could without anything being missed. The block was on three legs now and painted blue, a newer addition, said the preservation board leader. It was tucked in among dressers, paintings, and chairs used by the whites. It sat beside a great stone fireplace, in what was once the kitchen. This was where the enslaved women would have worked.

The kitchen on the left side of the house, with a large chimney, where enslaved women would have cooked for the household.

It was nearing midnight, and we could hear the cicadas hum, the crickets chirp. It was mid-summer, and when we stepped into the darkness to walk back to the crew's tents, I imagined how this darkness would have felt to the women who worked in the kitchen. Would they have talked on their way to their cabin, a few hundred feet away? Would they have stopped to look up at the stars? Would they have been spooked by the sound of a coyote howl from the woods beyond the scope of the lantern's light? Would they have dreaded the sound of a man from the big house walking up behind them?

❧

At Magnolia Plantation and Gardens in July, it was over one hundred degrees and humid. I thought of Clermont, the rolling fields outside the cabin window on a farm that had turned back to woods and open fields, as I hustled toward the slave cabins at Magnolia to catch Joseph McGill's tour. This was a different scene, with great oak trees that arched over the road, and tidy manicured lawns and gardens that had been maintained for decades. Joseph McGill, the Slave Dwelling Project Founder, and I were both sweating, me more than him, while we chatted in the back of the tram that carries guests around the plantation. He told a dozen visitors about the four slave cabins that sit on Magnolia Plantation under great arching oaks dripping with Spanish moss, and a Chinese Fringe tree, not in bloom now, but beautiful with its fat green leaves.

As we drove under the shade of the trees—quick relief—I thought about how far these plantations would have felt from the city by horse and carriage, boats up the river, or the railroad. It would have taken an hour or two to get here. I wondered if Minerva ever saw these places, if she came from a Wilmington plantation and had become accustomed to the sounds of the fields or woods at night. In Charleston, she and Juba and Eliza wouldn't have lived like people enslaved on plantations did. She lived in rooms attached to the kitchen in the city house, and on the island, probably in a small cabin behind the house, the sort that people in Charleston today have transformed into pool houses, or adorable guesthouses that you can rent on Airbnb for a few hundred a night—nice "extra income," Joseph noted, reminding me that descendants of slave-owning families continue to profit from but often silence and erase this history.

His mission is to help preserve and bring awareness to such extant slave dwellings. The story he told at Magnolia Plantation was of people who brought their skills in rice cultivation to the States, digging rice beds and waterways around the timing of tides and water levels, harvesting and husking the rice with baskets that would help to separate the rice from its shell, making it edible, sellable. It was hot work, amid deadly water moccasins, snapping turtles, alligators, and vermin, and resting at night on blankets atop hardwood floors in the cabins, too many to a room, swarmed by mosquitoes come summer. In one of the four two-room cabins at Magnolia, a man who is descended from the enslaved people who worked on the plantation raised his thirteen children and lived there until the 1990s, when he was moved for the plantation's restoration of the dwellings. He works and lives in another part of the plantation now.

When Joseph raised the question of whether the plantation owner was "humane," or a "good" slave owner, something guests often ask, Joseph said, "Of course he wasn't. He was a slave owner, therefore, he was inhumane."

The truth of Minerva's life was that she worked from before sunrise to after sunset, and that her labor and her children and their labor were Susan's and Hasell's from which to profit, to sell if they so chose. Was Susan "kind" to the people she enslaved? This question misses the point.

Every nineteenth-century family had to endure heavy losses. Sophia Jane Withers, who was eighteen when she married Hasell's father, Abraham, would die three years later. Hasell's own marriage, twenty years later, would be similarly short-lived, another three-year marriage.

You can see Sophia and Abraham in their married years, painted in miniatures now held in the Gibbes Museum's collection. She looks out with large, doleful eyes, a long fine nose, full pink lips that might be smiling, or resigned in acceptance of a moderately satisfied life. We don't know. For a nineteen-year-old, she looks tired—there's that shadow against the underside of her right eye. Maybe this is just the way her eyes are set, or the lighting of the portrait. Her hair is parted in the center and hangs loose against her neck. She's wearing an empire-waist dress with a low-cut neck, typical for her time. Maybe this was her wedding dress. The frame of the portrait is set with pearls, and on the back side, there's a brown lock of Sophia's hair that might have been added after her death (it's possible the portrait was made posthumously, in memoriam). If we had the desire and the permission from the museum, we could test her hair to see what it told us about her genetic history, a scientific advancement she and Abraham couldn't have imagined. The portrait was painted "circa 1805," and she and Abraham were married July 15, 1806. In another year, she'd have a son, Charles. Two years later, her youngest, Hasell, our doctor, would be born and she would die a month later.

Sophia and Abraham lived in that grand three-story house by the battery, where ships came in with goods for sale, near the markets that ran chaotic and quick-paced all day long. That was where Abraham worked, in the counting house that noted the ships coming and going, the goods they bought and sold, the sailors and captains aboard. He worked at the building that's today called the Exchange building, which you can visit and tour.

In the basement, the prison cells used for delinquent taxpayers or captured criminals, including pirates, remain, now filled with statues of pirates dressed in classical pirate garb (minus the stereotypical eye patches): tapered pants that come to the calf, high white socks, ankle boots, and poofy white shirts with openings that tie at the top. Billowy sleeves. Famously, several women pirates made their names in these waters, too. When I took the tour, a mother who was homeschooling her children made sure to tell her daughter the story of these female pirates.

We mythologize pirates today, but they were always—as they still are—simply sailors who terrorized and stole from other sailors. They could take possession of a ship at sea, and then sell its wares for their own profits in port. Those wares could include enslaved people; in fact, it was far more profitable to pirate a slave ship than to organize and fund one from the start. Slavery was a dangerous and risky business, one that didn't always return a profit. So many things could go wrong on that triangular route—the ships could run into bad weather and sink, sickness could strike the whole crew and cargo, enslaved people could riot and take over, murdering the crew, or—most likely—most of the enslaved people could get sick and die along the way. A ship that had made it almost all the way home with its "cargo" intact was a profitable rarity, and pirates would wait until such ships were close enough to the selling ports along the East Coast or the West Indies that they could safely make it to the auction blocks, securing a high profit with little risk. All they had to do was overtake the crew; they didn't have to invest thousands of dollars in the voyage, nor wait the weeks or months the journey would take, nor hire the crew, negotiate with slave dealers in Africa, navigate the wide and wild seas, control and feed the hundreds of people in the cargo hold. All they had to do was battle a crew, take command, and sail into port to make their sales—hundreds of people sold off, and there was a tidy profit. This was the work of our mythologized villains, like Captain Kidd.

Abraham would have been familiar with these stories, and would have seen the captured men and maybe even have stopped in to ogle them in their cells below his office. He was a Custom House official, so he signed off on all that came through the port as well as the sale of those goods once they left the port. The market was there on the docks, so it was easy to transport the dry goods, textiles, meats, fruits and vegetables, and people from the docks to the blocks. The front steps of the Custom House were used as an auction block, and the neighborhood around the building was full of traders and agents who sold enslaved people; Abraham would have passed those sales every day as he walked into and out of work, must have heard the auctioneer shouting out prices and the attributes of those people on the block through his open windows in the summertime.

Eyre Crow—"Slaves Waiting for Sale—Richmond, Virginia" 1861.

This engraving reveals the scene—several people scantily clad, standing for sale as the crowd below bids on them. This was what Minerva, Eliza, and Juba witnessed every time they walked to the market to buy and sell their goods; their heart rates must have quickened, their skin raised with goosebumps, as they walked past the block and heard the auctioneer describe women and babies for sale. We don't know if they were ever sold on an auction block before, or when, Mary Ancrum Walker bought them. Those we're able to track were sold by Susan in private sales after Hasell's death.

The enslaved people for whom Abraham was trustee in 1825, when he sold the house, would have been passed to his sons, Hasell and Charles, as soon as they came of age. Since Charles returned to Charleston before Hasell, Charles took ownership of their enslaved people when Abraham died in Providence in 1826. It was Susan's father who paid for his burial. Apparently, the families were likely long connected, before Susan's brother Winthrop befriended Hasell, before Hasell courted and then married Susan. Their families might have become acquainted when Mary Wilkinson, Abraham's mother (Hasell's paternal grandmother) went north to Newport each summer with her young sons, or through the link between Mary Wilkinson, a Rhode Island native and journeyman printer, and her husband Charles, a Charleston native; they were newspaper printers who distributed Charleston's news. Mary took over the paper when her husband passed away, and later moved north to Salem, to start a paper of her own—a remarkable feat for an eighteenth-century woman.

Rhode Island and South Carolina had strong ties. They were trading the goods that propelled the slave trade—rum, sugar, molasses, cheese, and cod. And it was common practice for southern planters and those wealthy enough to afford escape from Charleston's hot, humid summers, to head for Newport, where their arrival was published in the local paper. In Charleston's swampland, the risks of sickness in the city were high. Just a few decades later, conditions had not much improved, and Susan and Hasell were glad to have the island house to escape the sicknesses; when it was hot and "close" in the summertime, they encouraged Hilton to leave the mill and stay with them on the island, where they said it was as safe as in the North.

Mary, Hasell's grandmother, went to Newport at least three summers. Her arrival was announced in the Newport newspapers, which recorded all the town's comings and goings. This was the news of the day: who was in town, who had left, what was happening on the docks and in the city. As Mary disembarked, she'd have seen the brick market building with its high first-floor arches that led to an open-air room. Here, vendors sold their goods—baskets of fruit and vegetables, paper-wrapped meats, live chickens, eggs, and the dry goods just unloaded from a recently docked ship. She'd have passed all this with her young sons in tow, the threesome well attired. She'd have taken the best lodging on board with her sons on the ten-day journey north, and been accompanied by a male escort—a family friend, another couple or family.

Newport didn't look so different from Charleston. Its coast was less intricately niched than Charleston's, with fewer nooks and crannies, but the harbor would have had the same air—that nearly identical market building, the two-story houses made of pine less grand than Charleston's in the main square, but more lavish along the outskirts of town, by the shore. Along the harbor, there was the familiar hustle of the docks and market as sellers and buyers rushed in the midst of sailors, merchants, and yes, even in Newport, enslaved people for sale. Though there was no public auction block, many of the houses that still stand along the harbor served as sites of private sales of enslaved people. It's hard for New Englanders to imagine this, sometimes—at least, in the informal surveys I've been taking for the last few years, though I find it's changing more and more of late—but Newport and Bristol, Rhode Island, were slave ports, just like Charleston, South Carolina. Bristol even surpassed Charleston as the largest slave-trading port in the country in the late seventeen and early eighteen hundreds, thanks in part to the DeWolf family, who kept the international trade running until it was outlawed in 1808. As Joseph McGill and Keith Stokes told me, Newport's market and city center were designed by the same man in exactly the same layout as Charleston's and Barbados's Bridgetown, one more thread that united North and South and the cities of the triangle trade. They were all part of the same circuit in the nation's early years; they were all interdependent.

Abraham has an oval face, slender arched eyebrows, a fine concave nose, and a narrow mouth. He smiles just slightly, so that the edges of his lips press into his cheeks and make his mouth look prim. He has thin lips. He has a thick double chin almost hidden underneath his high collar. His ears are set low, and his hair is brushed forward against his cheeks, dark curls dressing his forehead. He wears a fine buttoned coat, has narrow shoulders around that wide neck—in fact, his neck is impossibly long. The portraitist is off. No one's neck can be this long. The object description of Sophia's portrait states it might have been made by an artist "who was beginning his career." Abraham's miniature, which is said to have "an especially rich and elaborate case of gold, enamel, and seed pearls," is attributed to the artist Vallée, a well-known French portraitist.

When Winthrop sent a letter home in the 1850s, he wrote that Charles was as slovenly as his father. Maybe Abraham lost his money, or his mind, after his wife died. Maybe he was heartsick, depressed, sad. Maybe he stopped doing all that he should have, or he drank too much. We don't know who he really was, nor what happened. In 1825, he lost his employ and sold his grand house on Meeting Street and moved to a smaller home, indicating he was in some kind of trouble. A year later, in 1826, he'd travel to Providence and die there, leaving his estate in the hands of Susan's father to settle. Perhaps he'd traveled north to bring Hasell to school that fall.

Abraham's parents were educated enough to read and write and run their printing business. Like Hasell's wife, Susan, Abraham's mother, Mary Wilkinson (Hasell's grandmother), was from Rhode Island. Perhaps they met when the family had traveled north. Mary was bold to move back home to Rhode Island as a widow, work as editor of a newspaper there, and then to move to Salem, Massachusetts, another port town (and, of course, another slave port), to found her own paper. She died on October 24, 1818, at seventy years of age; she outlived her husband Charles by forty-five years. Abraham was only eight when Charles died in 1775. I look for echoes of the loss in Abraham's eyes, in that portrait, but all I see is the slender mouth, the long neck.

In 1814, an enslaved woman named Jenny was given to Charles and Hasell by their grandmother, Mary Ancrum Walker. Jenny, in other words, was a gift. She is described as "a young sound negroe woman named Jenny" in the contract that notes her sale. Charles and Hasell were only seven and five, respectively, in 1814, and lived in that fine house near the battery with their father. Maybe Jenny was intended to help nurture the boys and ease the loss of their mother five years earlier. Maybe she was meant to help when their father was grieving. Did Jenny stay in Charleston after Abraham left in 1825? Did she get to escape? Did she live fifty more years to see emancipation? How many children did she have, if any? Whom did she love? I think of her life, try to imagine her in that three story house, carrying food upstairs to the boys or cleaning the floors or answering the door. I imagine her telling her story to the girl who worked beside her, talking about where she came from. Maybe she lived somewhere else in the city before she was sold to Mary Ancrum Walker; maybe she had a sister or brother nearby, whom she slipped out to see when she was given a pass to run errands for the Crouches. There she is at the entrance of the grand Crouch home, walking a block west to find her brother at the Russell house, or up to the Aiken-Rhett house, the "urban plantation" that's still maintained in the city today as a museum. I see her at the back gate, speaking to the man who leads a horse back to the stables. She asks the man to bring her brother a message and a piece of fruit—a peach she bought at the market just for him.

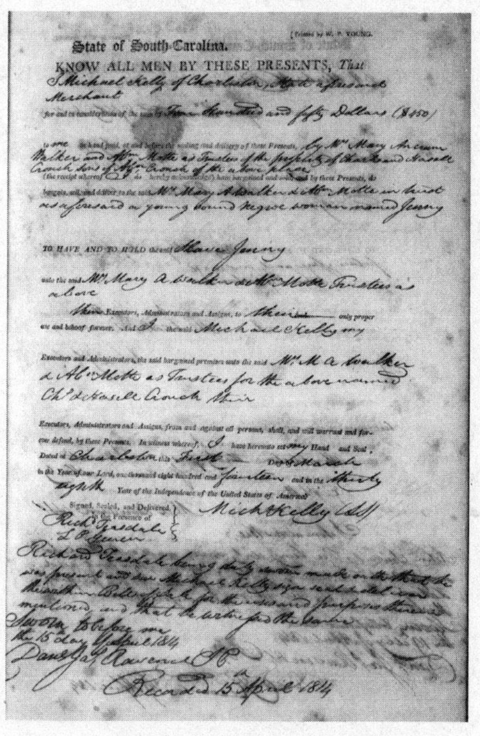

[Printed by W. P. YOUNG.

State of South-Carolina.

KNOW ALL MEN BY THESE PRESENTS, That I Michael Kelly of Charleston, [illegible] aforesaid Merchant

for and in consideration of the sum of Four hundred and fifty Dollars ($450)

to me in hand paid, at and before the sealing and delivery of these Presents, by Mrs Mary Ann Walker and Mrs Motte as Trustees of the property of Charles and Russell Crouch sons of Mrs Crouch of the above place

(the receipt whereof I do hereby acknowledge) have bargained and sold, and by these Presents, do bargain, sell, and deliver to the said Mrs Mary A Walker & Mrs Motte in trust as aforesaid a young [illegible] Negro woman named Jenny

TO HAVE AND TO HOLD the said Slave Jenny

unto the said Mrs Mary A Walker & Mrs Motte Trustees as above

their Executors, Administrators and Assigns, to their only proper use and behoof forever. And I the said Michael Kelly my

Executors and Administrators, the said bargained premises unto the said Mrs M A Walker & Mrs Motte as Trustees for the above named Chs & Russell Crouch their

Executors, Administrators and Assigns, from and against all persons, shall, and will warrant and forever defend, by these Presents. In witness whereof, I have hereunto set my Hand and Seal, Dated at Charleston the First Day of March in the Year of our Lord, one thousand eight hundred and fourteen and in the thirty eighth Year of the Independence of the United States of America.

Signed, Sealed, and Delivered, in the Presence of
Richd Teasdale
[illegible]

Mich Kelly (LS)

Richard Teasdale being duly sworn made oath that he was present and saw Michael Kelly sign seal & deliver [illegible] Bill of Sale for the uses and purposes therein mentioned and that he [illegible] the same

Sworn to before me the 15 day of April 1814
[illegible] Q.U.

Recorded 15 April 1814

Mosaic quilts were made by "upper-class women in Charleston" who "came from and married into wealth, education, and influence." Other quilts in the Charleston Museum collection were made by the planters, merchants, lawyers, and ministers. These were the ranks Susan hoped to join, yet she was conscious of being thrifty, asking for fabric her parents could get for less in the North, and for batting to use in the quilts (this was a difference as well, since most of these mosaic quilts were actually made to be coverlets, without cotton batting, unlike a typical quilt—Susan obviously planned to use batting and backing in her quilt). Still, she was able to buy yards of fabric new and cut them into pieces, in addition to reusing fabric the family had on hand from dress and clothes making. Susan, like those other women, "fussy cut" some of her fabric, selecting particular prints to highlight, like the bird's head that repeats. "Selective cutting makes extravagant use of fabric, converting yardage into 'Swiss Cheese.' . . . This apparent lack of concern about economizing on fabric is yet another indicator of the economic standing of the makers." Susan had been prepared for a life of homemaking as a middle-class woman since she was a child, making samplers and learning the needle arts. A description of one of her samplers is preserved in the Massachusetts chapter of the National Society of the Colonial Dames of America's *American Samplers.* Susan was seven when she made it, in 1820 Providence. She stitched three alphabets and two phrases:

> "Behold the child of innocence how beautiful is the mildness of its countenance and the diffidence of its looks."
>
> "Be good and be happy."

Ethel Stanwood Bolton writes in the 1920 introduction to the re-published collection of samplers, "The conclusion I draw from these incomplete premises I believe tenable: namely, that throughout the whole range of sampler poetry the only trace of originality to be found is in the signature and the dates." She goes on to explain that most of the quotes included in the samplers come from Bible verses or common sayings, sometimes even local sayings like the New England phrase, "When this you see, remember me." Indeed, Susan's phrases are an excerpt from William Kenrick's "The Whole Duty of Woman, Comprised in the Following Sections," outlining expectations of a woman in the late eighteenth century. The whole of the excerpt Susan quotes is Section XI, "Modesty":

> Behold the daughter of innocence! how beautiful is the mildness of her countenance!
>
> How lovely is the diffidence of her looks!
>
> Her cheek is dyed with the deep crimson of the rose; her eye is placid and serene, and the gentleness of her speech is as the melting softness of the flute.
>
> Her smiles are as the enlivening rays of the sun; the beauty of her presence as the silver light of the moon.
>
> Her attire is simple; her feet tread with caution, and she feareth to give offence.
>
> The young and the old are enamoured with her sweetness; she carrieth her own commendation.
>
> She speaketh not the first in the conversation of women, neither is her tongue heard above her companions.
>
> She turneth not her head to gaze after the steps of men; she enquireth not of them whither they are going.
>
> She giveth not her opinion unasked, nor stoppeth her ears to that of another.
>
> She frequenteth not the public haunts of men, she enquireth not after the knowledge improper for her condition.
>
> So becoming is the behaviour of modesty, so lovely among the daughters of women!
>
> Is there who hath forgotten to blush, who playeth with the wanton glances of her eyes, who replenisheth the cup when the toast goes round, and despiseth the meekness of her sister.
>
> Shame shall overtake her in the prime of her days, and the years of her widowhood shall be infamous as they are many.

Of course, Kenrick is defining—and reflecting upon—gender roles, a woman's proper place in society. A woman's job is to remain quiet, to be gentle, not to speak over others or to gaze after men but to keep her head on her stitching. She who breaks these rules will suffer a life of widowhood.

Though Susan, of course, didn't have the opportunity to attend Brown like her husband did, she attended high school and was educated for her time and class. In 1830, when Susan was seventeen, Hilton, her older brother, encouraged her to complete her schooling "in case she should have to support herself in the future." Three years later, at twenty, she'd marry Hasell. Her sampler, "chain and cross-stitched," as Bolton notes, was just a training ground for the sewing she'd do all her life, making dresses for herself, clothing for her husband and children, quilts and bedcovers and other goods for the home. The stitches around her hexagons are perfectly even, tiny stitches. It's hard for anyone who wasn't raised like Susan, sewing by hand every day, to make such perfect stitches.

While Ethel Bolton argues that samplers such as Susan's childhood piece are unoriginal, material-culture studies theorist Roszika Parker would have taken issue with Bolton's argument, noting that many women modified samplers and staid sayings to speak their own voices and undermine social strictures placed on women. Parker's analysis focuses on the Middle Ages through the twentieth century, explaining how embroidery has both "constrained" women and offered them "a weapon of resistance." She traces examples of samplers with images of power, along with other forms of subversion, like Polly Cook's sampler, embroidered with, "Polly Cook did it and she hated every stitch she did in it." Parker cites women who spoke out against the inculcation of femininity through embroidery. For example, "Sixteenth-century feminist poet Louise Labé of Lyon had no doubt that the demand for women to practice domestic arts prevented them from doing anything else . . . Domestic arts were equated with virtue because they ensured that women remain at home and refrain from book learning. Ignorance was equated with innocence; domesticity was a defence against promiscuity." In the nineteenth-century middle class, femininity was bound up in the relationship between mothers and daughters: "The key to the hold embroidery and femininity established over middle-class women was that it became implicated in an intense relationship, shot through with as much guilt, hatred, and ambivalence as love." The "cult of domesticity" relied upon the association of femininity, domesticity, and chastity. As David Jaffee notes, the development of the parlor as an important space in the mid- to late 1800s was part of this "cult of domesticity." "The Bixbys, like many other provincial families throughout the northeast, fashioned a parlor for performing the rituals of social life."

And yet, also connected to cloth production, even as these parlors were developed, lower class "mill girls" occupied the textile mills in Lowell, in the midst of these middle-class women.

> In encouraging women to stay at home, the cult was resisting the new industrial world, or positioning women as a bulwark against it. Meanwhile, that world was beckoning women to enter it, including some of the very ones the cult addressed. As their traditional work of spinning and weaving was transferred to the factories, young women who were being deprived of that work in the home yet who remained skilled in it followed it into the new mills, where they became the first industrial workers.

While the first mill girls were the (often educated) daughters of New England farmers, they soon ceded their role to immigrants—"French-Canadian and Irish immigrant women, men and children . . . Factory work had become exploited work, and native-born white women avoided it." Even as the demographics in the mills changed, the cult of domesticity went on, until the early twentieth century.

This is the just-burgeoning New England that Susan left to join Hasell in Charleston, entering a world of strangers who seemed reluctant to accept her. She'd embroider and quilt her way into the "cult of domesticity" as a young wife and mother. However, she'd leave Charleston sooner than she expected and would have to support herself after all, as her brother had cautioned her to prepare herself to do by finishing high school. She'd come to know the fate of women who rejected modesty, though she had done everything to conform to a patriarchal society's rules. The tragedy that befell her family would come to change the lives of Eliza, Minerva, and Juba and their children, too.

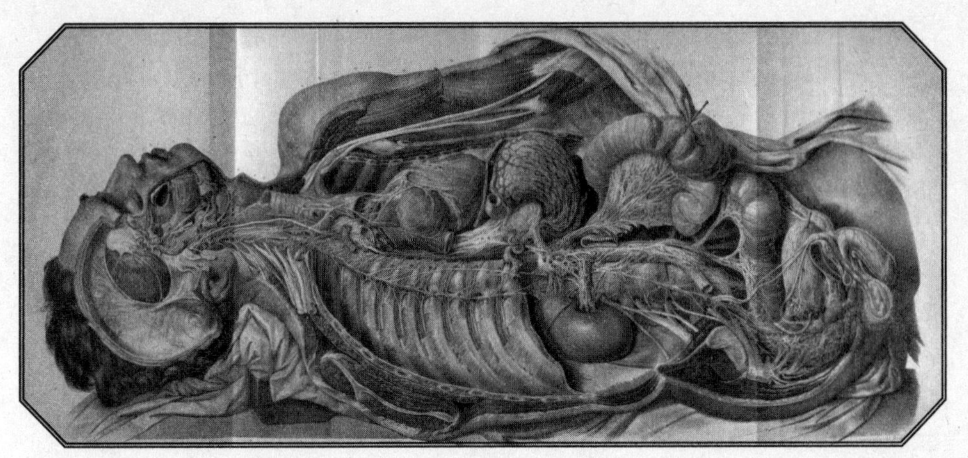

5
Medicine & Its Failures

Charleston, Dec 10, 1835

. . . I wish you could see little Hasell. He is as full of mischief as he can live. It is almost impossible to do anything where [he] is. He is quite fat, eats apples all day. . . . [Little] *Hasell was very much pleased with the mug and plate. He is so full of mischief I can hardly write. I wish you could have him for a short time to pull about the things. He is more mischievous than Harriet ever was. I cannot keep anything in its place two minutes for him.*

Did Sarah Cady go with the Capt.? Have you ever heard anything of Mrs. Cook? Capt Cook left her in Liverpool last winter. I must stop as it is time to send this. . . .

Susan

Imagine life before insulation, before plumbing, before indoor toilets, before vacuum cleaners and pesticides that instantly kill ants, fleas, termites, ticks, and spiders. Before sealants to keep out snakes and mice and rats. It's the hot South, on a one-hundred-degree day. There are thermometers, but no washers and dryers. Nor deodorant nor toothpaste. No tampons, no showers, no easy bath for a child. Water is hauled from the well. In the winter cold, it is heated on the fire before a washtub-bath that leaves the shoulders exposed. One can only hope that the fire is close and hot. When it is hot, there are no screens on windows to keep out the moths and flies and mosquitoes that carry malaria. This is before layers of weather-proof glass in winter. Eliza must have heard the wail and creak of wind coming through the cracks, whipping around the corner of the house. On a plantation or in a cabin in the yard or in the basement quarters, there is dirt on the floor, and in the dirt live worms that invade the skin. In the dirt in the garden that the white and black children run in, there are more worms. Was Minerva subjected to the constant itch of ringworm? Did her babies suffer from intestinal worms, the way Little Hasell did? Did anyone treat her baby, as they treated Little Hasell with pink root and coffee?

There are dishes washed in twice-used water, clothes washed in washbasins or the rivers. There are outhouses and, in the "lower" parts of the city, areas for defecation too close to the houses. This is where the sailors and free blacks live, along with enslaved blacks who live on their own and are rented out to employers, by their masters or of their own accord. Down near the water is where the yellow fever runs thick come those hot summer days. Sailors from other cities stay in Charleston and are frequently taken by the "Stranger's fever" in the summertime. Susan writes, in 1836, during yellow fever's rampant spread in the decade of the '30s, that it was "confined almost entirely to the negroes and low white people." The poor. The "bad" neighborhood. Those of higher rank were also, they thought, of higher moral standing. One couldn't get the lowly diseases if one's morals were right. Except there is that "almost entirely," acknowledging, passively, that the diseases couldn't be contained to the lower classes and to people of color; wealthy whites were susceptible, too.

Susan and her family were safe out on Sullivan's Island, where the wealthy escaped in the summertime. Did Hasell and Charles go to the North in the summertime, to Newport, Rhode Island, as their father Abraham had with his mother and brother? One couldn't leave Charleston for too long a spell or immunity to yellow fever would be lost, locals warned. Had Hasell been away from Charleston too long when he went north to study at Brown?

Charleston, May 7, 1836

Dear Sister,

Your letter of Apr 16 came duly to hand and the perusal of it afforded us much pleasure. I have kept your letter in my hat, ever since expecting to answer it by every mail but I have had so much business to attend to that I scarcely have a leisure moment and now . . . I am counting there is a person waiting for me to get out some lumber.

Hasell and Susan went down to the Island this 22 April. They have taken the same house that they had last season. It is one of the pleasantest on the Island. They were up to the City yesterday and spent the day with [sister-in-law] *Eliza* [Crouch]. *They are all in very good health. Little Hasell and* [his infant sister] *"Emily Harris" are in fine health and very good children.* [Little] *Hasell does not begin to talk yet. He is very backward.*

Hasell purchased a house on the Island a short time since. He paid $1000 for it and will rent it out this season at $175. I am not boarding at Mrs. Fells in Broad St. The same place that I staid at last summer.

By your letter you mention that Emily is to be married the first or second week of this month which is about this time now. I would not be surprised if this letter came to hand on the day she is married. We have had much speculation and "guessing" to find out the House you have moved to, but we cannot make it out. You say it is near the Arcade but do not mention the street it is on. There are many houses near the Arcade. We have some curiosity to know the street it is on. We were under the impression that you were to give up taking Boarders, but your saying that you have 8 in the family and also that Mr. Foster is with you that you take some still. Do mention who is in the family. Your house must look very well if we take the parlour as a sample. I should like very much to be at Emily's wedding. I would help to plague [tease] *her a little. We shall expect a big cake sent on to us. . . . Susan has so much sewing to do and her children take up all her time. . . . Lumber is very good . . .*

—Hilton

In December, he was full of mischief. By May, he was "very backward" and didn't yet talk, at two years and ten months. Why didn't he speak yet? The shift from mischievous and lively to "backward" and quiet perplexed and plagued Susan and her husband.

Two weeks after Hilton sent this letter home, Little Hasell died, on the same day that Susan's sister Emily was married to William Jenkins Harris, stepson of Moses Brown, the brother of the famous John Brown, trader of enslaved people. Moses was the slaver-turned-abolitionist, after his Quaker conversion in 1774.

Hasell C Crouch

In 1833, Hasell graduated from the medical college. He was thinking of buying a plantation outside the city and becoming a planter so that he could make a living with his crops if the practice was at first slow. There was a glut of doctors in Charleston in 1833, Hilton wrote, so Hasell needed something else to help him along in the beginning. The plantation he was thinking of buying was profitable, he said.

He didn't buy it. Would he regret this forever after, in the days he mourned Little Hasell's death? Would he wonder, as we often do in the wake of tragedy, *what if—what if—what if—?* Would he gaze at his own signature on the death certificate, and see his son seizing in his arms over and over and over again in his mind? Maybe, in the days after Little Hasell died, the doctor began to forget what was real and what was not—that his son was not still seizing, that he was not still in the midst of making choices for his son that would lead to his death.

Instead of buying that plantation, Hasell decided they'd go to Sullivan's Island in the summer. It was just outside the city and reachable by small packet boats. It would be expensive to get a house there, but Hasell believed it would be worth it to get some practice. And, he thought, it would be good for the family, keeping them safe from the summer diseases. So often, they urged their siblings and parents in the North to come visit, for Sullivan's Island was *as safe as in the North.* Sullivan's Island it was. And so Little Hasell's fate was sealed in the hindsight of his father. And so, also, were the fates of Susan, and Minerva and Eliza and Jimmy and Jane and a boy named George. I likely wouldn't have learned that Jane and George lived in this household, owned by Susan and Hasell, unless this change had come to pass—unless Little Hasell had died.

Charleston 1st June 1836

. . . We have been anxiously expecting a letter from you for the last two weeks but have not received one as yet. I should not write at this time but that Susan requested me to let you know of the death of little Hasell. He died on Thursday last the 26th of dropsy on the brain produced by injury in his head. Last summer he fell off from the bed on the back of his head, and this last winter he fell from a new crib that Susan had made, and struck the back of his head again, and since which time he has not been well although we did not anticipate any serious results from it, yet it affected him very much. He was not as lively as formerly, slept a great deal, and was not inclined to play as he did previous to the fall. Hasell had other Physicians to see him but the disease was so masked that they could not say with certainty what was the matter with him.

I was at the Island on Sunday. He was unwell and Susan gave him some medicine but they did not think he was dangerous [that anything serious was wrong] *until the morning he died. He was brought up to the City and buried on Friday. Susan and Hasell are very much affected by his death. They miss him very much. I think he was the best child I ever saw. He was always pleasant and good natured. He was 2 yrs 9 months and 16 days old. The baby is in good health. Susan wishes very much that you could come on and make her a visit. She is alone so much that I think if you can come it would be a good plan as it would be perfectly healthy on the Island and it is very lonesome for Susan. Hasell and Susan went back to the Island on Saturday. I spent Sunday with them. Hasell cannot get reconciled to the loss as he has taken all the care of him ever since this child has been born.*

. . .

If you can come on now I think it would be a good plan to do so as Susan will be alone so very much. Mrs. Thorne will leave for New York on the 11th of this month. She is not certain that she will visit Providence as she goes in company with Mr. and Mrs. Green. I do not know that Eliza will accompany her.

Do let us hear from you soon. I had a letter from Winthrop a short time since. He was very well. In haste yours EHW [Hilton]

Give my love to all the family.

He seemed all right. He fell from the crib and bumped his head six months ago. Susan had a new crib made, to safeguard Little Hasell. Probably, she asked a local carpenter, maybe Jimmy who was enslaved by them. The crib was high, Prof W. said, higher than our cribs today, so he would have sustained quite an injury from a fall off the top of the crib. I imagine Jimmy sawing wood in the yard, body shifting with the motion of his arm. He hammers in nails, a whapping sound that startles Little Hasell when he's outside with Minerva and Cecilia. When Little Hasell cries, Minerva lifts him into her arms, and takes Cecilia by the hand to go inside.

Then Little Hasell fell again, and Hasell sawed off the legs this time—probably in frustration, in anger, in a sense of disbelief that their child should have fallen twice and bumped his head twice; the doctor would have known this wasn't good, did not bode well for their beloved child.

Prof W. consulted her doctor-brother, who confirmed that Little Hasell's symptoms were consistent with those of a head injury—he stopped speaking, was not as active, slept all the time. These days, you'd be asked to wake a child every few hours and check his pupils. He'd be given a CAT scan and then, perhaps, an MRI, to find the splotches of blood that could threaten his life. He wouldn't be permitted to sleep that much. He would be given medicine to help clear the clots. If it was necessary, he'd have surgery to reduce the swelling or release the pooling blood so it couldn't kill the brain tissue.

I can see Susan and Hasell in their home, Little Hasell asleep upstairs, finally giving them a little peace—they don't think much of it—they're making a pot of tea, the task Susan commands as lady of the house, and she pours it for her tired husband into a simple white teacup sent by her parents. Hasell touches her back with a gentle hand, and she turns up to look him in the eye, half grateful half resentful. *Where have you been?* she wants to ask him. She doesn't want to hear the answer. She's heard from all the women in her company and knows too well what men do here in the South, with all the enslaved women at their mercy. Is that what he's been doing? Does she doubt his faithfulness to her, though she knows he's busy with his practice? She asks him about his practice. Who did he treat tonight? Will he look over the letter she's written home? *Hasell is learning me to write.* These letters were her opportunity to practice, supplementing the education she received in those high school years she completed. The doctor traces his hands over her letters, correcting her grammar, advising an introductory clause here, a more formal phrase there. And all the while, baby Hasell sleeps upstairs in the crib whose legs Hasell sawed off after the last fall. Little Hasell sleeps, unaware of the blood seeping across his brain, the slow death coming to his body. Downstairs, Susan and the doctor talk while she finishes working on her hexagons. Eliza and Minerva settle into bed in the rooms beyond the kitchen, talking about the money they've tucked away from the market day the weekend before, talking about what a fuss Little Hasell was today. Minerva tells Cecilia a story, sings her a hymn while she falls asleep. *There is a balm in Gilead.* Maybe she sang those words to her daughter, or in church on Sundays or Thursdays, if she, like Bishroom, was allowed to attend the meetings. I see Eliza roll onto her side to face the wall, so that Minerva has a few moments alone with Cecilia—as alone as they can be in this shared space. I imagine Juba lying beside her children, her arm on Sorenzo's arm as she falls asleep. And upstairs, in the crib, Baby Hasell sleeps, dying.

Wake him up! I want to scream as I read the letters. *Wake the baby! Wake the baby! Little Hasell is dying! This is going to change all of your lives!*

I holler back into time, or forward—which way does time go, if it's always circling, overlapping, palimpsesting? It furls off the spool and piles on the floor, or maybe it falls in folds like silk ribbon. See how the silk shines under the light? See how the fibers are woven so tightly that their sheen is almost like gold?

From Susan and Hasell,
Moultrieville June 6, 1836

Dear Sister,

We are quite anxious about you all as it is so long since we have heard from you even if you have a great deal to attend to. I should think either you or Abby might find time to write us a few lines. I am fearful that some of you are sick. Emily I suppose is married before this. It is near two months since we have heard a word from you.

I suppose you will receive Hilton's letter today announcing little Hasell's death. It was very sudden indeed. Two hours before his death we did not think him dangerous. He had not been well for near three months but we thought it was worms that troubled him but since his death I have thought about it and recollect that he has not been well since he fell out of the crib the first night he slept in it. After the nurse left me, the crib was standing by our bed. There was a window at the head of the crib. The curtain projected out from the window so that it touched the crib. He was sitting on the banister of the crib and as he leaned back against the window lost his balance and fell over the top of the crib. It was very high indeed. After that Hasell sawed a foot from the bottom so that it is now the same height of our bedstead. He had been very sleepy for a week before his death but he did not have the least fever until the morning before he died and that did not last long. For several hours before his death he was in a profuse perspiration. He did not appear to lose his senses to the last, for whenever we called him he would open his eyes. Every one that saw him said the child was not much sick as he had no fever. He would not eat anything at all for several days before he died. All he wanted was to lay and sleep all the time.

Dr. Deas saw him the day before he died twice and told Hasell that he was not much sick, only a slight irritation of the stomach.
—from Susan

from Hasell: *He had no alarming symptoms but his sleeping so constantly and headache. We gave him considerable medicine, which seemed to relieve him but slightly. The morning of his death he was sitting in his crib* [word missing]. *And afterwards played with the baby* [his sister Emily]*—laughing and smiling upon her and us. He soon laid down to sleep again and never rose again. He was taken with convulsions in about an hour after and died about one o'clock. His convulsions were not severe, nor long continued. He did not appear to suffer except from the Blisters &c which we applied at that time. He seemed conscious until a short time before his death.*

We buried him in St. Philips by the side of my mother, [Sophia]. *It rained so incessantly that we had to remain till near evening before the funeral could take place and I think I never witnessed such a rain as till that night. He is now at rest and we hope enjoying that happiness which his infancy and virtues entitle him to. His countenance after death was sweet and serene and he seemed to be happy.*

Now Susan: *Eliza, I have wished you were here now very much. It seemed so lonely when we came down after the funeral. Eliza* [Crouch] *had been staying with me a day or two at the time of Hasell's death. It was very fortunate for me that she happened to be* *down here at that time. I wish you could see the baby,* [Emily]. *She is the most quiet child I ever saw. She never cries. You would not know there was a baby in the house until you saw her. She is much more lively than Hasell ever was. Every one says she looks like her father and I think she does, too. I do not have any trouble with her. She sleeps all night, always goes to sleep about sunset and sleeps till after sunrise. I think it is on account of my having so good a nurse when I was confined. My health never was better than it is now and it has been so for the year past.*

Hassell once more: *The sudden and unlooked for loss of our dear little boy has been a great shock to us, but when we reflect upon his probable condition had he lived, we are reconciled his mind has been impaired for some time, and I think it probable he never would have recovered fully. The baby is in good health, very lively. My love to all, your affectionate son, HWC*

"Sleepy for a week before he died." Hasell sawed off the crib's legs, and it was "the same height as our bedstead." Little Hasell seemed fine, just troubled by his stomach. Worms, they thought. Maybe he needed a concoction that might help him pass a worm again, as he'd done the summer before—pink root and coffee, that was the medicine—and blisters, they applied blisters. This would be the cure. The doctor had a plaster that would produce a blister—something made from mustard seeds, perhaps—it produced heat, made the skin pucker up, and then the skin would be lanced and the fluid oozed out, and with it, the sickness and the pain. Mustard plaster, sinapism. Cantharides, ground blister beetles—the Spanish fly, for example, its shiny green shell a hint of the sting it could emit. Crunch up the shell, make a paste, apply the paste and wait for the blisters to appear. Feel the skin heat as the plaster sits. See the skin rise. These were Hasell's tools. For a time, leeching had been in vogue. One the same as the other, who could say. The doctor said that the blisters hurt Little Hasell, but that it was the only pain he felt before he died. Were the blisters applied to his head? His stomach? Where did the doctor apply the blisters to ease the baby's pain? How must it have felt to have been blistered, at two years, nine months, and sixteen days old? How must it have felt to apply blisters to one's own child's skin, inflicting pain in the desperate hope of healing? The baby must have looked at his father and wondered why he was hurting him so much, and if he'd lived, he might have come to associate love and pain as necessarily intertwined for the rest of his life, might have sought out all the things that hurt and then ruptured into relief, believing this was love.

The white muslin gown Susan likely stitched for her pregnancy with Emily.

This was the state of medicine before vaccinations or even variolations (the prelude to vaccines), before the flu shot and the shot for mumps, measles, and rubella, before the whooping cough shot or even over-the-counter Tylenol to bring down a fever. Before heating pads to soothe and cold packs and ice cubes easily stored in the electric freezer to bring down swelling, before Ace bandages and quick-set casts, before x-rays and—worst of all, if the break was bad—before anesthesia, before the pins and plates we've developed to stabilize fragments of bone, before open-heart surgery, blood transfusions, the ability to check blood for disease. There was no nurse marching down a hospital corridor with the promise of pain relief in her hands—codeine, morphine, muscle relaxers. There were ambulances, but they were drawn by horses. Imagine racing down the road at ten miles an hour, pulled by a pair of draft horses as you rocked in the back, your appendix bursting in your side, seeping into sepsis. If a leg was infected or too badly broken to save, it needed amputating;

it was sawed off with a handsaw, and a piece of wood was stuffed between the patient's teeth so he wouldn't bite off his own tongue from the excruciating pain of bone and muscle and skin being torn from flesh, the shaking of the body as the doctor moved the saw back and forth, the blood spurting up against the walls with sufficient or insufficient tourniquets, as the case may be. The patient was luckiest if he passed out.

Before there were laws determining on whom medicine could be practiced—not practiced, as in served, but practiced as in *working on skills*—there were other ways of finding bodies that could be forced to submit. Today, there are dummies for the insertion of needles and compression of chests. There are cadavers donated for dissection. But then? In 1835 and 1836? There were enslaved people of color. That is one of the most disturbing truths—that white doctors and medical students learned and practiced their craft on the enslaved men and women from the city. They chose to experiment on people of color, to learn which incision was most effective, which knife most precise, which stitch the best for stitching wounds—which the doctors would first have had to make—which procedure—no matter how invasive—the swiftest for healing ailments. Hortense Spillers cites William Goodell's 1853 anti-slavery text that includes an advertisement in the *Charleston Mercury* in 1838; Dr. S advertises for sick enslaved people, to be used for medical experiments. Goodell notes that enslaved people were commonly "*bought up* . . . by medical institutions, to be experimented and operated upon, for purposes of 'medical education.' . . ." The ad reads:

> To planters and others—Wanted, fifty Negroes, any person, having sick Negroes, considered incurable by their respective physicians, and wishing to dispose of them, Dr. S. will pay cash for Negroes affected with scrofula, or king's evil, confirmed hypochondriasm, apoplexy, diseases of the liver, kidneys, spleen, stomach and intestines, bladder and its appendages, diarrhea, dysentery, etc. The highest cash price will be paid, on application as above, at No. 110 Church St., Charleston.

Just five years earlier, there was Hasell at the medical college in Charleston, attending lectures and observing procedures before trying them himself—this was how you pulled a tooth (*take out this man's molar*), this was how you conduct a vaginal exam (*put your fingers inside this woman*), this was how you make an incision to cut only the top layer of skin, now deeper, now into muscle, and alongside bone (*ignore the young boy's screams, keep on cutting*). *Let us try this treatment for diarrhea and dysentery, let us try to remove the kidney to find the cure.* There was no anesthesia, no pristinely cleaned room that today is labeled "sterile." There was a house or an operating theater. There was *Coster's Phisician's Practice, Coster's Surgical, Reports on Cholera, Engravings of Arteries*—Hasell's semi-useful books, the best of his time.

They did not help Anarcha, Betsy, and Lucy, who were brought from a plantation in Montgomery in 1845, to be the patients—subjects—of Dr. Sims, who wrote about them in his work on resolving vesicovaginal fistulas. This is a hole between the bladder and the vagina, so that urine runs into the vagina and drips out constantly, onto, Sims said, the linens and clothes and produces, he said, a "burning similar to . . . smallpox, with constant pain and burning." Except, says Deborah McGregor, writing in our time, Anarcha was not *dying* of the fistula, as one would have died from smallpox. She was not the "disgusting" creature Sims described, but a seventeen-year-old who had probably been raped, whose uterus had retracted because of rickets (a disease caused by a lack of vitamin D, a disease of malnutrition); she was a woman in pain—a teenager, we would call her today, and she would be in high school—she was probably always hungry, sore from rickets and from overwork, but she was not dying, and she was not foul. She was strong, to have survived her childhood, the rape, the birth, and then the experiments that followed.

Bettina Judd wrote a book of poems about these three women. "The art of dying a slave is / one for those who know the lash to be a kiss on your will . . . "

One hundred years later, there was Henrietta Lacks, whose body was used by a doctor who took her cells and reproduced them, a thousand times over, a million, whose cells solved countless mysteries of disease and inoculation, but who was given no pay and no credit and no chance to consent to this use of her body.

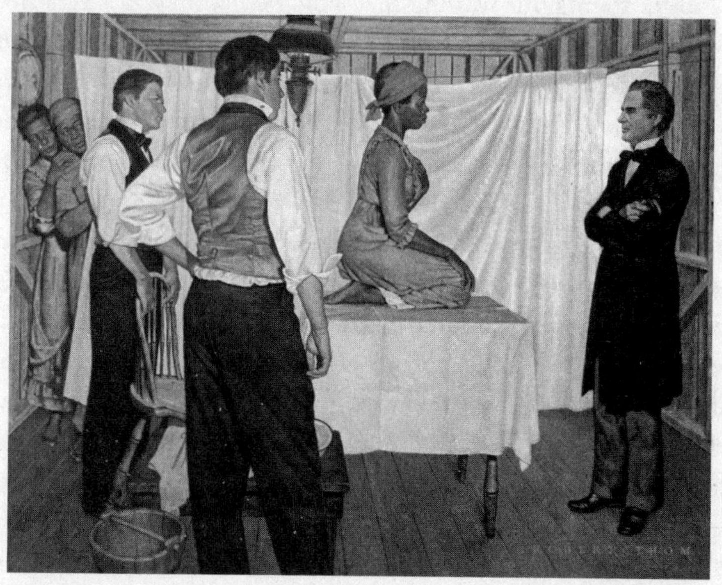

In between Anarcha and Henrietta Lacks, there were so many hundreds more. There was a man named Fed, an enslaved man, who was put into a hot pit—heated by fire from underneath, perhaps—and made to sit there until he passed out. The "doctor" gave him medicine to see what made him stay conscious longest. Fed was put into the pit "five or six times," and the products of his suffering were the medicine that other people were forced to take on the hot days out in the field, yielding to their owners their longest days, the highest pile of cotton or rice or indigo or tobacco. There were so many more enslaved people who were subject to experiments, whose names we don't know. Sick slaves were called for, and owners "donated" them, knowing they'd get them back healthy if they were cured, and that if they weren't cured, they wouldn't have to pay for their food and care as they ailed, useless, on their plantations, nor for their burials.

You know of the Tuskegee Syphilis Study, experiments performed by the US Public Health Service from the 1930s to the 1970s on black men who had syphilis. The doctors didn't prescribe the necessary medications, so that they could see how the men fared as the disease progressed. For forty long years. I think of how long my own lifetime, forty years, has felt, and try to imagine waiting that long. Penicillin was discovered in 1928 and used for syphilis in the late 1940s. For decades, black men were denied by white doctors and scientists the antibiotics that would save their minds and lives. I think of the days I spent sitting through long school years—each season passing out a window, winter's piles of snow and mornings we shoveled out, spring's slow green in New England, hot summers in the woods with July blueberries, and then those orange falls—each year, each season, men were sick and getting sicker, watching their children from their beds as they died. Instead of being so easily cured, as they could have been, the doctors experimenting on them allowed them to suffer and die. Instead of having the chance to watch their children grow up, instead of coming home to their wives after work each day in the '40s, instead of watching the civil-rights era bloom and fight in the '60s, instead of singing along with Nat King Cole and Ella Fitzgerald on the record player, instead of seeing Katherine Dunham dance or, for the most talented dancer who might have been among them, trying out for Alvin Ailey's new company, instead of applying to Howard University for the medical degree so that *he* could become a surgeon, instead of talking about the Selma march and celebrating the Voting Rights Act, instead of making eggs sunnyside up for the children each morning, kissing their heads as they walk out the door to school, playing catch in the backyard on a Saturday, holding their wives as they fell asleep each night. Instead, these men slipped into—were made to, allowed to slip into, by those white doctors—delirium, then insanity, losing what they did not need to lose, leaving behind their beloved wives and lovers and children and parents and siblings. For forty years. For what?

Tuskegee was based upon a long tradition. A century earlier, the bodies of enslaved black people were being stolen from cemeteries in the night for dissections, at the behest of white doctors and administrators. Enslaved people were subjected to experiments, which they endured day after day, and once these procedures were perfected, as was the case with Sims's vesicovaginal fistula fix, then the treatments were offered to white women, who could choose to submit to the treatment or not. Those women profited from the pain Anarcha, Lucy, and Betsy endured under Sims's knife. "Lucy's agony was extreme," Sims wrote of his experiments. "She was much prostrated, and I thought that she was going to die; but by irrigating the parts of the bladder she recovered with great rapidity."

Irrigating the parts of the bladder, he wrote. This without anesthesia, antibiotics, or the painkillers that welcome us when we emerge from surgery today. Doctors do all they can to keep us—some of us—from pain today, asking when we enter the office for a routine exam, "Are you in any pain?" or when we come in for an injury or sickness, "What's your pain on a scale of one to ten?" They administer numbing agents to the skin before injections or incisions, they inject novocaine before working on our teeth and their tender nerves. I think of doctor women who provided herbs and medical assistance on plantations, of the countless midwives who "caught" babies—people whose enslavement couldn't prevent them from caring for one another and finding cures that white doctors, like Hasell, would come to use themselves. Hasell's medical notebooks include "homeopathic" treatments; many of the herbal recipes and tinctures he learned at medical school were discovered and developed by Native Americans and African Americans.

African Americans are still, today, perceived by white doctors to feel less pain than whites. Scientists published a study that reveals how racial bias still affects blacks who are treated in the US medical industry:

> A young man goes to the doctor complaining of severe pain in his back. He expects and trusts that a medical expert, his physician, will assess his pain and prescribe the appropriate treatment to reduce his suffering. After all, a primary goal of health care is to reduce pain and suffering. Whether he receives the standard of care that he expects, however, is likely contingent on his race/ethnicity. Prior research suggests that if he is black, then his pain will likely be underestimated and undertreated compared with if he is white. The present work investigates one potential factor associated with this racial bias.

> Specifically, in the present research, we provide evidence that white laypeople and medical students and residents believe that the black body is biologically different—and in many cases, stronger—than the white body. Moreover, we provide evidence that these beliefs are associated with racial bias in perceptions of others' pain, which in turn predict accuracy in pain treatment recommendations. . . .

Black patients, say the researchers, are "less likely to be given pain medications" than white patients, and if they're given any, they're given "lower quantities." This could be because doctors fear that black patients won't comply with treatment or medication instructions, or it could be because they believe black people to be biologically different, more capable of enduring pain, stronger, with "thicker skin." The researchers write that "many people insist that black people are better athletes—stronger, faster, and more agile—as a result of natural selection and deliberate breeding practices during slavery." The idea that blacks and whites are different has been perpetuated since before our nation's founding, by people who needed to defend and maintain the system of enslavement—people who profited from it. "These beliefs were championed by scientists, physicians, and slave owners alike to justify slavery and the inhumane treatment of black men and women in medical research." They cite Samuel Cartwright, who wrote in 1851, that black people didn't feel pain when they were being punished. And, they say, "Today, many laypeople, scientists, and scholars continue to believe that the black body is biologically and fundamentally different from the white body and that race is a fixed marker of group membership, rooted in biology." People don't believe that race is a fiction, in other words, but believe that blacks and whites are fundamentally, biologically, different. People still buy into the myths that were spread by both public figures like Cartwright and average middle class people like Winthrop, Susan, and Hilton, to keep enslavement in practice.

It wasn't so long after emancipation that African Americans founded their own medical schools—the first in 1870 in Pennsylvania just six years after slavery was abolished. Long before that, in 1837, James McCune Smith earned his medical degree, the first African American to do so. His mother had bought her freedom—and therefore ensured her children would be free, too—and, as a child, he went to the African Free School in New York. When he was rejected by white American college administrators because of his race, he raised the money he needed to go abroad, to Scotland, to earn his degrees at the University of Glasgow. Another decade later, David Jones Peck earned his medical degree at a college in Chicago, becoming the first African American to earn a medical degree in the United States.

James McCune Smith, bust portrait, engraving by Patrick H. Reason

Twenty years after him, in 1864, Rebecca Lee Crumpler became the first African American woman to earn a medical degree; she attended a medical college for women in Boston. After she retired, she wrote the first book on medicine by an African American; her *Book of Medical Discourses*, published in 1883, was directed toward women and children: "treating the cause, prevention, and cure of infantile bowel complaints . . ." and "miscellaneous information concerning the life and growth of beings; the beginning of womanhood; also, the cause, prevention, and cure of many of the most distressing complaints of women, and youth of both sexes." By the time she wrote the book, she'd gone back to Boston, and then moved to New York, after treating "freedmen," formerly enslaved people, in Virginia during the Civil War.

No images of Rebecca Lee Crumpler exist, though some are misattributed as portraits of her online. This image is of Carol V. Still Wiley Anderson, who graduated from the Woman's Medical College of Pennsylvania (which later became part of Drexel University) in 1878, about fourteen years after Dr. Crumpler. Dr. Anderson's parents were Philadelphia abolitionists.

Doctors Crumpler, Anderson, Peck, and McCune Smith must have known this history of white doctors and medical students experimenting on enslaved people in medical colleges. What must it have been like to walk through the college doors that first day, the first to enter a system that systematically abused African American bodies? At the medical college, Hasell most certainly performed experiments on the corpses of people of color, and, based on that *Charleston Mercury* ad of 1838, likely on living enslaved people as well. My mind turns from Susan witnessing Hasell's medical exams with pride at his performance, to follow them on their walk home, down dirt and cobblestone streets, chatting about the day's questions, how he fared in front of his examiners, how they'll move to the island this summer for his practice—what a lovely summer it will be, they must have imagined. And as they approach their house by the bay, I see Eliza hanging wash on the line in the backyard, Juba peeling carrots in the kitchen, and Minerva jostling baby Hasell in the upstairs bedroom, shooshing him to sleep so she can set him in his crib and finish beating the rugs clean before Susan and Hasell return. There are Susan and Hasell's feet on the stones outside the house now, their idle chatter, the rise and fall of their voices that Minerva would have come to recognize from afar, hustling to ready the house, prepare for their approach, tend to their needs, maybe hiding whatever she was working on for herself or her children, or quieting her daughter, two year old Cecilia if she was fussing or playing too loudly. I see Susan and Hasell approach the house. And I feel a darker sense of trepidation, wondering if he performed experiments on Minerva, Eliza, and Juba, in addition to those people on whom he experimented at the medical college.

He may have been a "reluctant" slaveholder, a researcher told me, because he inherited his enslaved people and couldn't easily free them. He gave a speech on the "necessary evils" of slavery. But he did take the time to go to court and claim his "half" from his brother. Even if he saw enslavement as a "necessary evil," he was nonetheless thoroughly engaged in it. He didn't go back to court to fight to free his enslaved people, as he could have done. He went to court to *claim* them, to divide them as his and Charles' inherited property.

There's nothing to say whether he did or did not perform experiments on the women he owned. Jimmy, the man they rented with the island house that summer, might have been as unlucky as Fed, Eliza as unlucky as Anarcha. I think of Fed enduring the heat of that pit, and the present-day researchers who write that, "Research suggests that people even believe that black people are more likely than white people to be capable of fantastical mental and physical feats, such as withstanding extreme heat from burning coals" and that, "in one study, white participants who believed black people can tolerate extreme heat more than white people can, for example, were more likely to think that black people feel less pain than do white people." And there is a thread of time that doesn't palimpsest or fold in on itself but is drawn taught between then—Fed's days, when he was subjected by a white man to that hot pit—and today, when doctors under-treat black people's pain because they think that blacks are more capable of enduring it. The black man, the white doctor thinks, is capable of enduring pain because his body is different, stronger. "Well into the twentieth century, researchers continued to experiment on black people based in part on the assumption that the black body was more resistant to pain and injury." What Hasell did at the medical college wasn't unusual. It was de rigeur, part of the dailiness of his life.

I think of Fed, and Anarcha, and Eliza, too, if she faced the same fate, and imagine that they must have found ways to evade the doctor's treatment some days, to resist the experiments to which he would have tried to subject them. When Hasell went looking for Eliza, maybe she was nowhere to be found. When Susan needed an errand run, Eliza could have been the first to wait for its doing, her pass ready in her hands. Maybe Eliza feigned a different kind of sickness than the one Hasell wanted to cure, so her body was unavailable to him. Maybe she made herself throw up with ipecac when he wanted to examine her teeth. Maybe, when she couldn't stand it anymore, or simply because she felt like it, she went to stay with a free friend of color, and slept in peace for three or four nights—maybe even weeks—until Hasell found her again. There were dozens of ways to deny him, Eliza would have found, and some days, they must have worked. This was her agency.

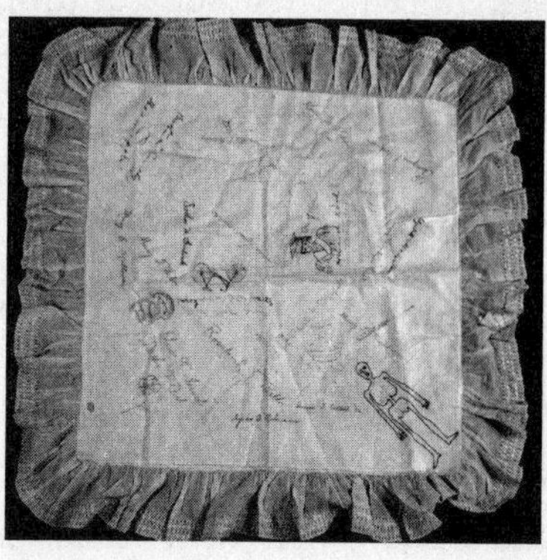

Dr. Eliza Grier ca. 1897. She earned her medical degree from the Woman's College of Pennsylvania, where, in the 1890s, female medical students embroidered this pillow sham, simultaneously proving and subverting their domestic training.

It was just a couple of years after Hasell finished his medical degree when they lost their little son. They were in pain. They waited all afternoon to bury him, waiting out the rains that went on for two weeks and made Hasell fear for the health of the city. They knew that rains brought on sickness, but not why. They didn't yet have the connection between mosquitoes and sickness. One night, Winthrop wrote home from Columbia, saying he was swarmed by mosquitoes and bitten all over. He was lucky then, that he wasn't struck by malaria or yellow fever, but he never knew that.

They went back to the city to bury Little Hasell, at the grand St. Philip's Church in the center of Charleston, a few blocks from the seaside at the southern end of the peninsula where all the oldest buildings still stand. They waited until the rain passed; Susan said it was the worst she'd ever seen. Once the storm moved off, they went to the graveyard and buried their baby beside Hasell's mother, who died at twenty-one just a month after Hasell Sr. was born. Maybe, if you believe in these sorts of things, you'd have thought that Hasell's mother, Little Hasell's grandmother, would take care of him in that afterlife some call Heaven. Susan and Hasell believed that, at least, their child's pain had eased now that he'd passed onto the eternal afterlife.

They must have carried him to Charleston across the bay on one of the packet boats, perhaps already in a coffin made on the island, or perhaps just wrapped in a blanket, carried in Hasell's arms. It must have been a somber crossing, stepping onto one of those sailboats, Susan taking the hand of the captain with her baby, Emily, nestled against her chest, held tight. She set foot into the hull, took a seat on the bench that ran along one side. Hasell came in after her, tucked himself beside her with their son in his arms, pale-faced and still. *He has found peace*, Hasell and Susan told themselves. *He is in that better place.* Hasell must have felt this was a failing, though, not to have been able to save his own child with his new doctoring skills. Wasn't that his job, to save and to heal? Hadn't he studied while others around them attended balls and made light of the world? Hadn't he taken such careful notes of all the tinctures and treatments? And yet, here he was with his own dead child, and his sorrowful wife beside him.

They spent the days after talking about how their child died, conjecturing. *Worms? But it didn't seem to be—No, remember how he fell first from the crib six months ago and ceased talking? How he was less playful, less active, and wanted to sleep more? He didn't speak, and he was almost three—he should have spoken by now.* Hilton noticed, when he visited, that the boy didn't speak yet, and he called him backward. But Susan and Hasell, delighted with their child, didn't notice. He was still a happy enough boy. All was well. There was a second baby coming, there was Hasell's practice, and so much—always—to be done.

But after his death, Hasell pieced it together, maybe with the help of the doctor who helped him treat Little Hasell at the end, who administered the useless potion for the stomach sickness, which was not stomach sickness but a head injury.

The damned crib, they must have thought. That goddamned crib. Did they punish Jimmy for making it too tall? For following their orders? For failing to prevent the accident of Little Hasell's death? In the days and weeks after, Juba would have made the meals and Eliza and Minerva would have brought them to Susan and Hasell in their bedroom, taken the baby to be nursed, and slipped back to the kitchen as quietly as possible, avoiding the tender grief. There was Juba, maybe sorry to see Little Hasell suffer, and sorry for Susan, but how did the sorrow mingle with her resentment of them? How did she make space for empathy when they were her owners? Little Hasell had called her "Mammy," and maybe she considered herself something more akin to his mother, lately, than Susan, who was so preoccupied with the baby, Emily. Maybe she resented little Hasell for keeping her from her own children, for taking time from the boys she needed to raise, having always to tend to the boy who sought her out, calling her "Mammy" as if to claim her. Maybe she was Emily's nurse, too, the "good nurse" Susan referred to in her letters. Or maybe it was Minerva who nursed Emily; with a toddler of her own, she could have been Hasell's and then Emily's wet nurse, breast-feeding Emily into chubby, healthy babyhood, into the adulthood that would permit her white body to own enslaved people.

On the day they buried Little Hasell in Charleston, Susan's sister Emily, namesake of Susan and Hasell's infant daughter, was getting married up north. She'd accepted Mr. Harris's proposal; after he'd been denied by sisters Susan and Eliza, Emily said, "Thank you kindly, sir," and off they were, into this new life. His stepfather, Moses Brown, attended the wedding, even though his Quaker faith dictated that he should stay away from such celebrations. It was quite an honor to have had him there, Winthrop wrote. He wrote to his sister Eliza, back in their father's house in Providence, relaying the news he'd had from Charleston about Little Hasell's death, and wishing to taste a bit of Emily's wedding cake. He was still in Columbia, working as a clerk at the store, and longing to see again some of his family—at least, his sisters, if not his brother, Hilton. He found Hilton weak, annoying, troublesome.

Nursemaid with child, ca. 1855, likely from Arkansas.

July 10, 1836

. . . I received a letter from Hilton a day or two he wrote in good spirits but complained of too much, he wrote that Susan would like to see you this summer. Why do you not come on, you will be as safe on the Island as if you were at the North. She must be very sad since the death of little Hasell. I feel very sorry for her. Hasell must miss him very much.

I congratulated Mr. and Mrs. Harris [his sister Emily] *on their entrance to the wedded state and wish them all the happiness imaginable and a long life of harmony with "thumping luck and big children." I have not received a piece of the cake yet but I suppose if I ever visit you or even Charleston again I shall be able to obtain a piece of it as I understand it is very rich so there is not danger of its spoiling. I might have known as a matter of course it would be rich if it was Emily's cake for she never made anything poor in her life and I don't think she will now that she has married Mr. Harris.*

Yours very truly,
WB Williams

"You will be as safe on the Island as if you were at the North," Winthrop promised his sister Eliza Williams, meaning she need not fear the summer diseases that claimed the lives of "strangers," or tourists (and sailors and other workers), visiting Charleston. At this time, diseases were still divided by the classes, as certain diseases, like malaria and yellow fever, affected the poor and the enslaved disproportionately. The wealthy could afford to leave the city—and the mosquitoes and fetid water—and the poor and enslaved could not, unless they were taken along with the families for whom they worked or by whom they were owned. The poor and enslaved people were trapped in the "lowly" neighborhoods by the docks, sleeping in close and dirty quarters, while the middle class and wealthy had cleaner living conditions and better food. When cholera struck, it struck a whole neighborhood. They didn't know that it was probably an infected well that was making everyone sick. There was so much they didn't know, I can say now, though in a hundred, two hundred years, someone will say the same of us. We'll have cures for Zika and HIV/AIDS and cancer, and people will look back on this time with a sense of wonder and pity, that we just didn't *know*.

In the 1830s, a person's fate was constantly in flux due to sickness and disease. One never knew when an outbreak of influenza or smallpox or any one of the fevers would strike, without much to do but offer the patient tinctures and palliatives and simply wait. Hasell's notebook is full of recipes for cures, but for his son, there was nothing then that could have helped.

I think of Eliza Williams, widowed when her husband died after two months of marriage, and how it must have felt to watch him succumb to smallpox, that most painful of diseases. During the Civil War, when an African American regiment had been felled by the disease, they isolated themselves on an island where they couldn't contaminate others. But when they ran out of food, those still strong enough left the island—and others who came in their wake found hundreds of dead men sprawled across the ground, the living still moaning and raising their arms for help. At the end, their skin would come off when they rolled over. They would feel as if they were dying of thirst, but if they swallowed, their throats would burn with fire. The blisters would coat their skin and eyelids and throats and noses. They'd run high fevers. They were extremely contagious, by touch or by air; even the bodies could infect others.

There were variolations for smallpox by the time of the Civil War, but the problem was how to perform them. A variolation was an early form of inoculation and involved making a small cut in the skin where a similar virus—usually a cowpox virus, which was less severe than smallpox but still provided protection—was introduced. Around the site, the blisters would pop up and then, as the patient fought off infection, she built immunity to smallpox.

The cowpox virus came from cows, but how to transport it across the miles between cities and across battlefields? The answer would be refrigeration, which wouldn't come for many more years. In the meantime, they tried putting the diseased cells onto strips of cotton, which sometimes worked, but more often the virus died. Travelers in England came up with such brilliant ideas as bringing along on voyages twenty orphan boys and inoculating them one by one as they traveled across the sea. The virus was passed along slowly enough, through each boy's body, that by the time the passengers arrived, they'd have a newly infected person from whom they could variolate the citizens of the country in which they'd arrived. Genius. Except for the uprooted, guinea-pig lives of those orphans, who, supposedly, were rewarded with educations and foster families in their new lands. This experiment was part of the dramatic changes in medicine in the mid-1800s: "[The industrial revolution and] spread of democratic institutions helped to provide the required economic, social, and political environment for the astonishing revolution that took place in medicine in the middle of the 19th century."

The blame for diseases in the 1800s fell to the victims if they were poor or people of color. Middle-class whites, they told themselves, had their cleanliness and high moral standing to thank for their evasion of diseases like cholera that Susan wrote struck the "negroes and poor whites" of Charleston in 1835. They didn't know that cholera was caused by a contaminated well that infected a whole neighborhood. No, it was people's moral failings, their inferiority, that killed them. Whites continued to perpetuate the myths that reified their supposedly superior status; the Industrial Revolution's impact on medicine did not make the practice more egalitarian nor just. We know that smallpox was often used as a weapon *against* Native Americans, African Americans, and opposing troops—one of our first biological weapons, the deadly infection that killed swiftly and painfully—and that experiments on African Americans were done by white doctors and researchers "well into" the nineteen hundreds.

The more I learn, the more my perception of the world around me changes. I sit in the waiting room at the doctor's office now knowing this history, thinking about Anarcha when I slide up onto the crinkling paper of the examination table, thinking about how afraid a person of color must have been to come to a white doctor in the nineteenth century. About how blacks are treated differently by white doctors today, given by white doctors less medicine for pain, treated by white doctors as though their bodies are made to endure more.

Everywhere I go, I think about how these stories seem to live under the layer of life in which we exist, in the past that can seem invisible. How do we make these stories public? Where do we recognize our histories and the people whose lives shaped the world we know today?

We have new museums that honor African American history—the National Museum of African American History and Culture in Washington, D.C., a similar museum in Charleston, South Carolina, coming in 2020, and the Whitney Plantation in Louisiana, whose whole story is of the enslaved people rather than the wealthy whites and the big house.

Shana Adams, who invited me to her family's plantation, Wavering Place, works to tell both sides of her family's story. She and her husband Robert Adams called Nkrumah Steward to invite him to visit the plantation, upon hearing that Steward is a descendant of enslaved people who were owned by the Adams family. Robert told Nkrumah that they are in fact related—"cousins," as Steward explains it. Several of the plantations regularly host similar reunions of the descendants of people enslaved on the plantation with the descendants of those who enslaved them, and of course, their family trees are linked. Middleton hosts a "family reunion" every year, including white and black descendants. One woman I met said she hates that term *family*, as if the blacks and whites are family—"No," she said, "We were the product of rape; this wasn't family."

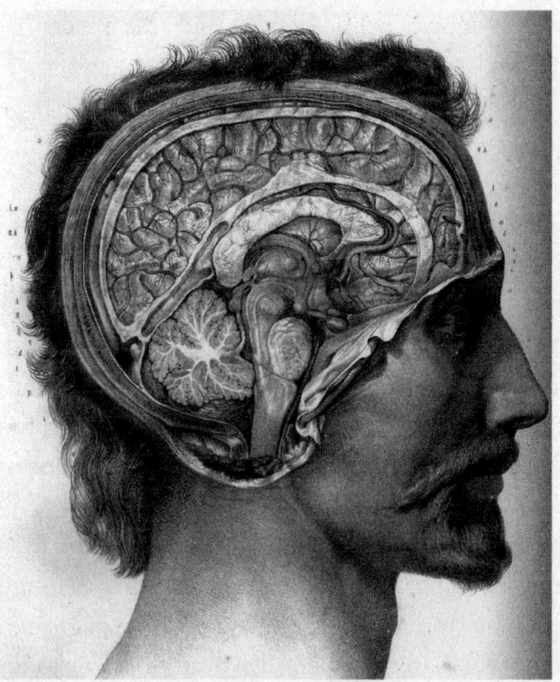

In the 1950s, when Franklin was recording and cataloging the story of the Crouch-Cushman family, slavery was within living memory. There were people who had been born enslaved, now free, witnessing the beginning of the civil-rights movement, having grown up with stories of their parents' and grandparents' survival of slavery, and living through the Jim Crow South. There are strings through time that bind the past to the present, ever-unwinding, tangling, spinning back with the sound of a bobbin whirring. Nkrumah Steward feared the Adamses might want to keep secret the fact that he and Robert are cousins and says he was thankful to learn Robert wanted to connect. While Steward is able to trace his ancestors, many of us don't know our whole pasts, don't know the stories and names of those who came before us; and of course, many Americans will never be able to know the entirety of the story because blacks were not considered human. They were property.

While stories of African American people have been obfuscated, erased, and suppressed in archives and government records, the story of Little Hasell's death is repeated over and over again in the archive, and distorted over time. Franklin, the grandnephew, writes in 1951 that Little Hasell was kicked in the head by a horse. Susan's letter says he fell from a crib. Another note from Franklin says he was dropped on his head. Emily, who was an infant when Little Hasell died, might have relayed the story to her nephew Franklin as she remembered it told by her mother. Maybe Susan rarely talked about it and Emily was left to her own imagination to conjure up the incident that caused her parents so much pain. Maybe Susan retold it wrong on purpose—absolving herself of guilt or shifting the blame, making it an easier memory.

How did Little Hasell die? The nurse had just left, Susan said. The nurse was an enslaved woman, unnamed. This could have been Minerva, who, with children of her own, could have been a wet nurse, or Eliza, who was in her thirties (with no children recorded as living with her, she may have been a nurse if not a wet nurse, or she could have been a wet nurse who had just lost her own baby or had a child sold away from her).

Did Susan scream for one of them to come and help her when she found Little Hasell on the floor after his second fall from the crib? Did she blame Eliza and Minerva? Did she ask for their advice about what to do for him in those moments after? She was a new mother, twenty-three and lonely. Did she rely on Minerva and Eliza to comfort her? I wonder how Minerva and Eliza felt when Little Hasell died, and Juba, who was called "Mammy" by Little Hasell, as her own children called her. Her children must have played with Little Hasell, and helped raise him, too, pulling him away from the great kitchen hearth when he got too close, spooning smashed peas into his mouth, wiping clean his face. Susan wrote that when she and Hasell lived with Hilton, they had six people helping them—*helping them*, she said, as if it were their beneficence that inspired their help—including a six-year-old and a three-year-old.

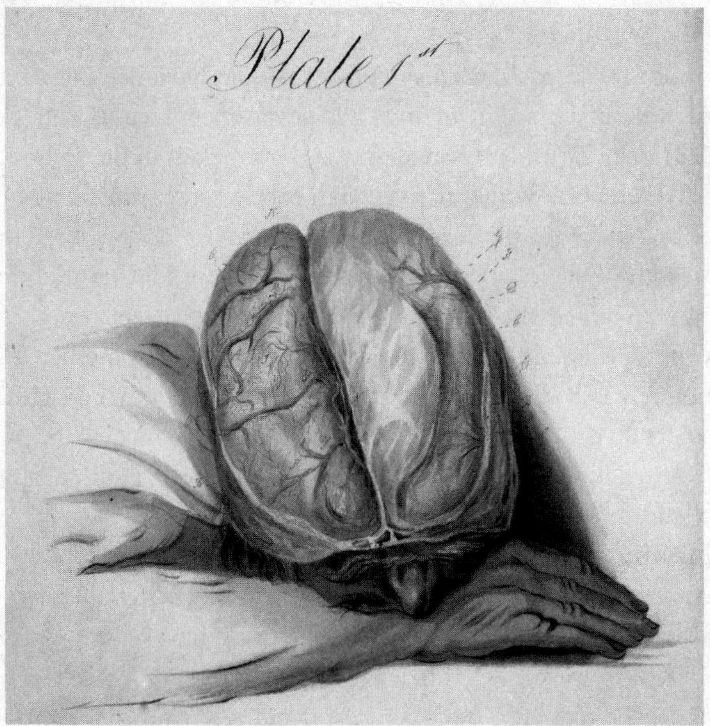

Brain head down, Charles Bell, 1802.

Susan must have wondered, all the rest of her life, if she might have done something differently to save her son. She might have saved him, she must have thought. He might have lived—because this grief was followed so quickly by another: Months after Little Hasell died, Hasell the doctor died, too, leaving Susan twice-bereaved.

A letter from Winthrop (who has just recovered from the dangerous "typhus fever," he says, and is getting up and about again) on December 2, 1836, reveals Hasell's state of health (and mind) seven months after Little Hasell's death.

> *Hasell has been unwell ever since he came upon the island. He took cold and as he was very bilious he was compelled to take medicine, since which he has been imagining he was going to have all sorts of diseases—the fact is he is very much reduced by fasting and being physical so much so that he has got the Hypo. And the Doctor says, too—there is not much the matter with him. He might be up and well in a week if we could make him think he was getting better. We are all at Charles' yet, where we shall stay until Hasell gets up . . .*

The "Hypo" that Winthrop refers to might have been hypothermia, the chills and fever caused by being too thin and overworked. While the doctor said there wasn't much wrong with him, maybe today he'd be diagnosed with a disease that's curable with antibiotics. Maybe he'd be referred to a therapist to deal with the death of his son. Maybe he was wracked with guilt at not having been able to save him, or traumatized by watching his boy seize repeatedly before death. He could have lost faith in his profession, or his ability to help his other patients; he might have lost his faith in God. He was almost certainly deeply depressed. In the sole remaining scrap of the letter Susan wrote home about his death, she said that Hasell was never right after Little Hasell's death, and that she believed he died not of yellow fever but of heartbreak.

Hasell never got up. He died a few days after Winthrop wrote this letter, on December 6, 1836. His cause of death on the death certificate was listed as yellow fever, which he could have caught treating patients in Charleston before he went to the island or from someone who had come to the island from the city.

Why were they on the island in December? They usually went in the summertime to avoid yellow fever and for Hasell's medical practice. Maybe this December they needed an escape and they longed to be back where their son had last been alive. Or maybe Winthrop misspoke and they'd just come from the island.

Maybe the doctor Hasell died because he'd been too long away from Charleston during his college days at Brown, or maybe it was because he'd never developed immunity as a child if he left Charleston in the summertime as his father had. Only strangers were susceptible to yellow fever, or those who had left the city for too long a spell. Many years later, in a sermon preached by Rev. Fiske in honor of Susan upon her death, Fiske notes that the doctor Hasell "died, a martyr to professional duty and sacrifice, in an epidemic of yellow fever." Did Hasell go out to help someone when he knew he might fall prey to the disease? Was he being heroic, intentionally making himself a martyr, or are these the flourishes of a man trying to make sense of Hasell's death for Susan's sake? The inscription on Hasell's grave, probably written by Susan and her brothers, as well as, perhaps, Hasell's uncle Charles, at whose house they stayed after Hasell's funeral, reads:

> SACRED TO THE MEMORY OF HASELL WILKINSON CROUCH, M.D. A NATIVE OF THIS CITY, AND GRADUATE OF BROWN UNIVERSITY, PROVIDENCE, R. I. WHO DIED THE 6TH OF DECEMBER 1836 IN THE 28TH YEAR OF HIS AGE AN INTELLIGENT PHYSICIAN RAPIDLY INCREASING IN USEFULNESS AND REPUTATION A JUST & GENEROUS MAN WHOSE AMIABLE DISPOSITION AND EXEMPLARY DEPORTMENT SECURED THE ESTEEM AND CONFIDENCE OF ALL WHO KNEW HIM A SINCERE FRIEND AN AFFECTIONATE HUSBAND AND FATHER, HIS PREMATURE DEATH IS TO HIS FAMILY AND FRIENDS INDEED A BEREAVEMENT. BESIDES HIM LIE THE REMAINS OF HIS ONLY SON HASELL CHARLES CROUCH WHO DIED AT MOULTRIEVILLE SULLIVANS ISLAND ON THE 26TH MAY 1836 AGED 2 YEARS & 10 MONTHS.

Hasell was twenty-eight when he died, but the women in his life, Susan and Emily, would live long lives. By the following year, Susan's baby daughter, Emily, would be living in Providence with her parents and sister, and Susan was eager to follow. Until her estate was settled, they stayed at Charles and Eliza Crouch's house. Susan was now a widow with an infant daughter, heading into years of financial depression caused by the falling cotton prices. Susan sold off all of Hasell's belongings—except for the quilt they were making together and his dental forceps—including the enslaved people they owned.

Winthrop bought Eliza and John for $530 and $570, respectively. W. or Mr. Greer bought Minerva (spelled Manerva here) and her two children Cecilia, listed here as Celia, and Samon for $870 total.

She must have told herself—if she considered it at all—that she had to sell "the slaves" in order to survive as a widow in the recession. She wouldn't be able to go north, Winthrop told the court to petition the estate sale, unless she sold Hasell's goods, including "seven" enslaved people. Minerva, Eliza, Juba, and their children would be sold away, their lives forever changed by the changes in Hasell's and Susan's lives. This was the reality of enslavement, in which nothing was certain and the threat of sale always loomed, taking a mother farther from her children or husband, sisters, friends.

The estate sales for Hasell's goods were private, meaning the women were advertised to be sold not on the public auction block but at the family home, 6 Cumberland Street. The enslaved people were sold on three different dates: on May 11, 1837, "the boy George," who was listed in the inventory as sixteen years old, was sold. On May 23, 1837, "the negro girl Jane," said to be about twenty in the inventory, was sold. (The discrepancy in their reported ages is to be expected, as owners did not know their enslaved people's birthdays.) On January 30, 1838, Eliza, Minerva with her children, Cecilia and Samon, and John were sold. John was seven. He and George may have been Juba's sons in addition to Sorenzo.

George was sold for $700 plus the cost of advertising and commission ($6.93 and $7.50); Jane was sold for $560. Eliza was sold for $530, John for $570, and Minerva and her children for $870.

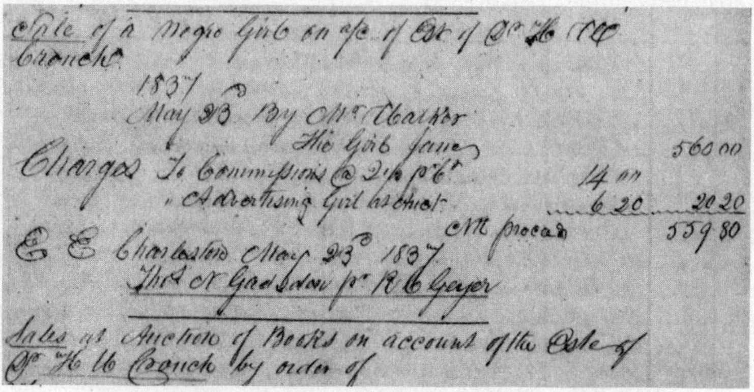

Sale of a Negro Girl on a/c of Est of Dr H W Crouch

1837
May 23 By Mr Walker
The Girl Jane 560 00
Charges To Commissions @ 2½ p ct 14 00
" Advertising Girl at auct 6 20 20 20
Nett proceeds 559 80
E E Charleston May 23d 1837
Thos N Gadsden pr R C Geyer

Sales at Auction of Books on account of the Este of Dr H W Crouch by order of

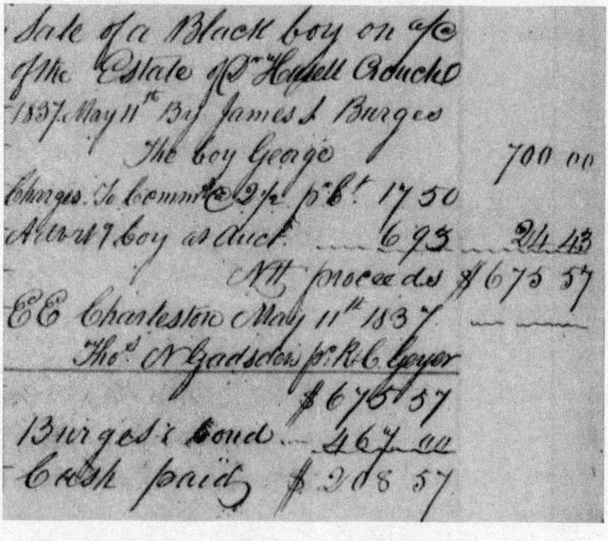

Sale of a Black boy on a/c of the Estate of Dr Haszell Crouch
1837 May 11th By James S Burges
The boy George 700 00
Charges. To Commn @ 2½ p ct 17 50
Advertg boy at auct 6 93 24 43
Nett proceeds $675 57
E E Charleston May 11th 1837
Thos N Gadsden pr R C Geyer
$675 57
Burges's Bond 467 00
Cash paid $208 57

W.S. Walker bought "the girl Jane," who was said to be twenty at the time, for $560. James S. Burgess bought George for $700.

I imagine Minerva, Eliza, and Juba watching the agents approach that day, setting down their accounting books in the living room, inviting people in to peruse the household items and the women. I wonder if, as Mary Ancrum Walker had done, Susan attempted to stipulate that Minerva be sold with her children (Walker noted it should be done "if possible"), and if it matters whether she did or not. Like Hasell, she might have thought slavery was a "necessary evil," but she helped perpetuate it by using the enslaved people she inherited and then profiting from their sale, with Winthrop's help selling them as trustee of Hasell's estate.

Minerva did get to stay with her children, as they were sold as a "lump sum," but George and John were sold away from Juba, who was likely their mother. I imagine the scene of their parting, Juba hanging onto her boys with all her strength, seeing in her son George's face his babyhood, remembering holding him as an infant. George might have sobbed, too, holding her, looking much younger than his sixteen years. I think of how sweet and innocent the sixteen year olds I know today look—how I always think, when I see them, that they look too young to drive, and far too young to enter a dangerous world. I can't imagine any of them being torn from their mothers and sold to work for someone else for the rest of their lives, knowing that at any moment they could be sold again, and again.

How amiable and exemplary could a man be who owned eight enslaved people (the record notes seven but there were eight people including Juba), including children, at the time of his death? How much do we forgive a person for living "in their time" and how much can we blame a person for not seeing clearly enough? In the case of the Holocaust, a person can still be prosecuted for killing Jews. We believe the soldier should have resisted. Descendants of the perpetrators carry that weight. Holocaust survivors carry that weight. We have a name for descendants who carry the trauma: "second-generation survivors." The Holocaust is within more recent memory, yes, but not so much more. Slavery was abolished only about eighty years before the Holocaust, a single lifetime. How do we cast ourselves in its light? And, if we can blame others for their part in slavery, then how do we assess ourselves for all we take part in today? I begin to think about all the things in which I'm implicated—every purchase, nearly every decision I make, I realize, has consequences in this global economy. Where are the supply chains for this paper, this computer, this lamp, this sweater? What am I wasting that I could reuse? What could I buy secondhand instead of new? How am I implicated as part of so many institutions—a university, a US citizen? I begin to ask myself what I'm choosing to see, and of what am I still ignorant? To what have I been blind?

This plaque stands at Fort Moultrie on Sullivan's Island, commemorating the thousands of enslaved people who passed its shores and, in the 17th and 18th centuries, were quarantined at the island's "Pest House" before being deemed healthy enough for transportation to their sale on the mainland. The pest house had long since moved by the time Susan and Hasell summered on the island, in a house near the fort. In the ad for its sale, Hilton listed the house as "pleasantly situated on front Beach."

6
Hickory Root

There is a balm in Gilead to make the wounded whole;
There is a balm in Gilead to heal the sin sick soul.

—African American spiritual

On a plantation, Christmas provides the smallest respite from work. There is, on this single day, a good meal, either gifted from the master or claimed for oneself. Chicken, bacon, flour or cornmeal for bread, molasses—maybe even sugar scraped off the cone in the big house pantry—to make a pie, collard greens, and maybe carrots or potatoes. Maybe the children picked vegetables from the gardens the family kept for themselves near the cabins, just as Juba and Minerva and Eliza might have picked and prepared their own vegetables on the holiday, if Susan and Hasell allowed them time for it. Maybe Juba saved what food she could from the kitchen—a slice of ham fat here, a handful of nuts there. Maybe she went to the meat market and bought a piece of ham earned with money she'd made from renting herself out. Juba, Eliza, and Minerva were often rented out; when Eliza was sold, Winthrop said he'd keep her for the man who rented her, if he wanted to buy her.

For enslaved people who had to secretly claim celebration at other times, there is open singing on Christmas, and talk and laughter and dancing. Except for the work of preparing the celebration, there is no labor on Christmas. There is rest—a nap after eating, the rarest indulgence. All the other days of the year are regular days, work from sunup to sundown, the body weary. The only other time to celebrate openly is if an enslaved couple has a wedding. And then, only if the union has been condoned by the master, "more chicken was fried" for dinner. If it is a private wedding, secreted in woods thick with leafy trees and Spanish moss and swampy undergrowth, then there are clothes made fancy by the seamstresses and mantua (dress) makers, and there's excess food taken from the plantation, and instruments handmade or claimed for oneself from the master's store, a celebration into the night, under a cloudy sky or stars with a sliver of moon, not too much light—to protect the group from unwelcome eyes or hostile ears. There are all sorts of ways to escape and resist.

In the wake of Hasell and Little Hasell's deaths, Susan was lonely. She was mourning. It was winter in Charleston, probably rainy, cooler than those summer days. She would have been back in the city, and having never really been accepted by Charleston's ladies, she was probably eager to see family and old friends. Her brothers kept asking for her sisters Emily and Eliza Williams to come down for a visit, to stay and help Susan in her grief.

Preparing to leave the city meant that she'd have to settle Hasell's estate—meaning, manage his property, the things that signified his membership in the master class, his citizenship in the country. In practical terms, Susan, a widow, had nothing without that money. She would not be able to leave without at least some of it, and would now be dependent on her brothers and parents again.

While Hasell's whole estate wouldn't be settled for a year, in May 1837, five months after Hasell's death, Susan's brothers petition the courts to allow Susan to sell the estate goods so that she can "return to the north." Once permission is granted, they set to work selling Hasell's books, the furniture he and Susan must have so carefully moved back and forth to the island each year, his medical tools and supplies, and the pots and pans and stove and all the things she'd requested to be sent down by her family as she made their home, hoping to become a part of this new city with her husband and young children.

These must have been sad days, and busy days, too, with infant Emily at her side, being nursed perhaps by Minerva, who had a two-year-old and was pregnant with another child. Eliza and Minerva, Jane, George, William, Juba and her children, would have been responsible not only for the daily chores of running the household and tending to Susan in her grief, but also the preparation for Susan's move—knowing all along that this would mean their own sale, too.

The house on Sullivan's Island, which Hasell had only recently bought with the profits from his now-busy practice, with all the hope of their future bound up in it, was put up for sale, as were all their goods. The advertisement for the furniture ran in the *Charleston Courier* on May 2, 1837, and, just as estate sales organizers do today, the family tried to entice people with some of the items they would find:

Estate Sale of Furniture.
BY T. HEYWARD THAYER.
On THURSDAY, the 4th inst. will be sold, at No, 6 Cumberland-street, at 11 o'clock, by order of the Adminitrator,
A variety of genteel Household and Kitchen FURNTURE, belonging to an Estate,
CONSISTING IN PART OF
Straw bottom and Windsor CHAIRS
Dining Tables, Carpets, Fenders, Shovels
Crockery and Glass-ware, &c.
Conditions cash, before delivery.
Unlimited articles will be received until the sale.
Ma 1

Crockery, glass-ware, straw bottom and Windsor chairs, a variety of genteel Household and Kitchen furniture. Genteel, the sort of goods one might like if one were, like Susan, trying to make their way as ladies who had gone to housekeeping, building parlors that proved their statuses. The estate sale was on May 4, and the public would have wandered through the house—just as we do at estate sales today—grabbing what served their own purposes.

In the handwritten list from the estate sale, marking to whom each item had been sold and for how much, there are double-columned sheets detailing the medical texts that Hasell had so carefully collected during his days in school, and of all the things they'd acquired as a young couple in the master class. *Dutch oven, frying pan, tin kitchen*—the tin kitchen, a cooking contraption, that Hasell had had Susan's father send down by schooner from Providence. *Pots and kettle, sifter, warming pans.*

And in the midst of this list, there are the names of his enslaved people sold at auction, on different dates, along with these goods. Eliza, Minerva, Juba, and Jane would have seen this day coming with a sense of dread. To whom would they be sold? Would they be separated from their children? Eliza might have watched people tour the house and buy goods, the same delight crossing the white peoples' faces when they found a delightful chair as when they decided to buy her—another possession claimed. Maybe, in the days leading to the sale, Minerva begged Susan to let her choose her new masters, to keep her with her children, to keep her in the neighborhood near friends and family. They had stayed together through Mary Ancrum Walkers' death, having been brought from North Carolina and Walkers' thousands of acres there, probably leaving behind family and friends they'd known for decades. They'd endured the uncertainty that Sophia Jane Withers, Hasell's mother and their trustee, had brought, and now, they waited again with trepidation to see what would happen when their owner Hasell, whom they'd likely known and cared for since he was a child, passed away, too. Maybe Juba made finer meals, trying to persuade Susan to sell her to a master of her choosing, or to keep her with Sorenzo and her other children. Minerva must have been relieved at Little Hasell's death if she was his wet nurse. Maybe she saw his death as justice for Susan and Hasell. Maybe, even as she resented him, she wept for Little Hasell's passing, too, having come to love the child she'd fed and nurtured. She must have felt the easing of a burden, with one less child to raise, slightly less labor for her—less laundry, fewer emotional obligations to soothe and sing for and entertain someone else's baby when her own children needed her. Maybe she and Minerva were related—their mothers Judith and Dianna could have been sisters, or cousins. Maybe Juba helped with Minerva's baby Cecilia. Maybe they were simply close friends, having lived together for so many years.

I can see the women side by side in the kitchen with its great fireplace, the cast iron pots and pans hanging and perched around the hearth, their feet dusty with the dirt that Minerva swept back into the yard three times a day. Did Susan and Hasell give them shoes? Were they barefoot? Minerva must have had Cecilia nearby; I see little Cecilia in a cotton dress of the same material as Minerva's, that red teakettle print, let's say. She toddles over to Minerva with something in her hands; they're clasped together hiding a secret. Minerva holds out her hands, and Cecilia drops into her mother's palms a small pile of straw she's gathered from the floor. She's helping her mother clean. Minerva smiles, says thank you, and pulls her close for a long moment, trying not to cry with the thought of losing her daughter. She feels Cecilia's chest rise and fall against her shoulder. She takes a deep breath.

As the date of the sale approached, she must have tried to stay calm for Cecilia's sake; she must have tried not to alarm her.

Thomas Gadsden, the agent for the sale, had an office "north of the Exchange," in the market area of the city, where people could call to see the enslaved people and make offers. Here, he advertised two people who were most likely George, whom he called "a likely young fellow, 17 years old," and "Jane, A Girl, 18, A complete seamstress. These Negroes are all of warranted characters, and sold for no fault." In other words, there was nothing they'd done that had instigated their sale—they were of "good character" and were not runaways or otherwise "troublemakers," or people who had found their way to resistance—though certainly, these people had resisted in other ways.

George could have been Juba's son, and Jane was "a complete seamstress." This news strikes me. I had known of Eliza, Minerva, George, and "the girl Jane" from the estate sale inventory, but I hadn't seen the ad for the peoples' sale before. Knowing she was a seamstress, that she had the skill to make dresses and suits and that fine quilt Susan was working on makes me wonder if it was her hand that made some of those perfect stitches that bind the hexagons together, and not just Susan's. Did Jane help make—or make entirely on her own—the dresses Susan had cut from patterns in the North for her own use? Students in Prof W.'s class studied those dresses and found Susan to be a talented seamstress with fine, even, tiny stitches. But maybe they weren't only hers. Women enslaved on plantations were more likely to stitch alongside the mistress than women enslaved in the city, but Susan would have known how talented Jane was, and probably made use of her skills as she made use of Juba's talents as a cook and one of the women's talents caring for children as the "good nurse" who tended to little Emily.

She was a seamstress. A *complete* seamstress, meaning she could make whatever a person required. If Jane and Jenny are the same person (the genealogist tells me that the names were considered interchangeable—and I know from reading these records how often masters misspelled enslaved peoples' names, calling, for example, Minerva "Minnon" in the ad for her sale), then she was sold to Mr. Walker in May 1837. Maybe this is a relative of Mary Ancrum Walker, and Jane went to live with enslaved people whom she knew. Perhaps she stayed in the city, working for another woman in a house in Charleston. Perhaps one day, like Elizabeth Keckley, she bought her freedom with her stitch work. Keckley would make some of the most renowned dresses in the country in thirty years' time, when she went to the White House to serve and sew for Mary Todd Lincoln.

George was sold that day in May, and Jane would have come back to the house alone, as yet unsold. She was advertised again, this time as "a likely young WENCH, 18 years old." A "wench" was an enslaved woman of childbearing age. A part of enslaved women's labor was reproduction—making the labor force the cash crops required, making a profit for their masters. Deborah Gray White explains that West African societies valued motherhood as an important "rite of passage" for women, and that mothers "lived with and nurtured their children in a hut separate from their husbands," and often most "cherished" their relationships with their daughters. In the "antebellum" communities, "motherhood was still the black girl's most important rite of passage, and mothers were still the most central figures in black families." Furthermore, White explains, women and men who produced many children for a plantation would be kept, and kept together, while women who didn't reproduce, and all men, were "more likely" to be sold. On the other hand, an enslaved woman's resistance might come in her refusal to bear children. Thavolia Glymph explains that a woman named Cynthia "used abortifactients" to avoid having children, and though her owners threatened to sell her, she was kept.

While Susan and Hasell owned enslaved people in a small, urban household, not a plantation, the same rules would have applied, with reproducing and skilled people being more likely to be kept. Since Susan and Hasell rented out at least Eliza and maybe also Minerva, Jane, George, and the rest of their enslaved people, they were assured of making a profit from the people's labor even when the couple didn't use them themselves.

I see Jane, Eliza, and Minerva walking to the market together, side by side, their long skirts billowing around them, the fabric kicking up in front as they swing a leg forward with each step. They move quickly. They're going away from the house, up Cumberland Street, chatting with each other in tones that won't raise questions from the whites around them. Quiet. Hushed. Enslaved people aren't permitted to gather in groups without a white in attendance, to prevent the organizing whites fear results in revolts like Denmark Vesey's in 1822 or the rebellion in Haiti in 1791. The women talk about the way out, making plans. Eliza and Jane, maybe having both lost babies of their own, are helping Minerva find ways to keep Cecilia beside her. They know that a woman in the neighborhood is looking for a wet nurse, and suggest Minerva ask Susan to sell to her. They tell Minerva about the people of color in the city who can help send her north to freedom with her baby. Maybe Minerva has a husband nearby whom she doesn't want to leave behind, or maybe, in April 1837, she reveals to Eliza and Jane that she's three months pregnant, and can't run with an infant and a swelling belly. In October, she'll have a baby boy, Samon.

Estate Sale.

BY THOMAS N. GADSDEN.

TO-MORROW, 30th inst., will be sold at the North of the Exchange, at 11 o'clock, by permission of the Ordinary for Charleston district, belonging to the Estate of Dr. H. Crouch, dec.

Five Valuable SLAVES, viz:

ELIZA, about 33 years old, a Market Woman and House Servant.

MINNON, about 31 years old, a complete Cook and House Servant, and her two Children, one three years old, and the other six months.

AND,

JOHN, about 8 years old, a House Servant.

Conditions—half cash; balance in one year, by bond and mortgage of the property. Purchasers to pay for bills of sale. **Ja 29**

Franklin writes that Susan had moved to Providence by the spring of 1837, probably just after the estate sale. A year later, she came back to Charleston for a visit, going back and forth between north and south as she'd done when she lived in Charleston. Her brothers were still there, after all, with their children. From Charleston, she writes, in November of 1838, to her sister Eliza back in Providence, asking after her daughter Emmie—"Mr. Harris mentioned in his letter that Little Emily had a cold was it anything like the lung fever? Does she get uncovered in the night? I think she had better have a flannel nightgown but you can do as you think best. I intend to send by the vessel a bundle containing some things belonging to Emily." Franklin writes that Susan and Emily returned to Charleston whenever they wanted to, often for a winter visit when the South provided a warmer respite from northern snow.

A year earlier, in October 1837, Susan was still living in Charleston but biding her time until she had enough money to move north, and the birth of Minerva's baby boy Samon would help provide the money Susan needed to leave. Susan was so worried for the little girl she left behind in the fall of 1838, but months earlier, she'd sold away all of her enslaved women and their children, separating them from each other. Hilton reveals Samon's birth when he writes from Newport, in the midst of his honeymoon; he had just married Harriet Thorne, a widow who was older than Hilton and, as Franklin describes her "of the lack-a-daisacal type." She came from a wealthy family and brought to the marriage several enslaved people who were also from Mary Ancrum Walker's estate in North Carolina. We don't know exactly how Harriet was related to Sophia, Hasell's mother, nor to Sophia's mother Mary Ancrum Walker, but their enslaved people were probably related, or at least knew one another, too, having lived together in North Carolina. Harriet and Hilton's marriage wasn't a happy one, but Hilton seemed hopeful at first and treated Harriet's stepdaughters as his own. In Newport, Hilton is out of money and asks for some to be sent to Newport immediately. He also writes, on October 8, 1837:

"Minerva has got a fine boy, quite an addition for Susan."

And a few weeks later, on Halloween, Winthrop writes:

> *Minerva has had a fine boy and is quite well. She has not gone to work yet. Eliza* [Crouch] *has not named her baby girl. We were all together last evening. Saw Mr. Smith a few evenings ago—he is the same "Yankee" as ever.*
>
> *Cotton is very brisk, chief sales from 11 ¾ to 12 ½ for new crop, old from 8 to 11 ½*
>
> *+ Rice is selling @ $4 ¾ but little coming in; I was in the market this morning.*

Reading this letter, I see Minerva holding a sweet new baby boy in her arms, swaddled in a blanket, her daughter Cecilia leaning against her and peeking in at her brother's face. Cecilia must have wanted to help take care of him—or maybe she was jealous of her mother's affections and competed for her attention by doing all her chores more quickly, or singing for her mother the whole song she'd just learned from George. Maybe Samon squirms in the blanket, getting hungry, and Minerva knows she'll have to feed him after giving little Emily her fill.

How did Minerva feel, holding her baby in the company of Winthrop and Eliza Crouch and her baby girl? How did she feel, knowing she was about to be sold with her babies, or that little Cecilia might be sold away from her?

As always, Winthrop is preoccupied with the markets and the price of the cash crops, chronicling his movements in business and his prospects. Mentioning Minerva's baby here is just another aspect of business for him. Hilton notes that the birth of Samon is "quite an addition for Susan," meaning that she'll make quite a profit from the boy's sale. When Winthrop says, more than two weeks later, that Minerva has not yet returned to work, it's evident that she was given some time off to recover from the child's birth. Deborah Gray White notes that slave owners were constantly trying to balance preserving an enslaved woman's health, and getting as much work out of her as they could. Winthrop and Hilton—or maybe Susan, if she was still in Charleston—are erring on the side of caution, or perhaps offering Minerva a respite since she is to be sold so soon. They probably waited until she'd had the baby before they sold her, knowing they'd get this "increase" if they did so.

Whether Minerva had a husband or lover isn't known. Maybe, as white owner Mary Chesnut and formerly enslaved couple William and Ellen Craft noted was so common, she was raped. Perhaps she was in love with a man in the neighborhood whom she wasn't allowed to marry. She likely attended church on Cumberland Street, the closest to the Crouch house. It's also possible that she attended St. Philip's with Susan and Hasell; the Crouches had inherited a pew from Hasell's grandmother, just as they'd inherited enslaved people. This pew was one of the items sold when Susan moved north. Minerva could have attended the church and sat in the gallery, along with other enslaved people.

Mother Emanuel Church might have continued to hold meetings in secret after it was razed to the ground by fire, and then banned in 1834, in response to Nat Turner's 1831 rebellion. Mother Emanuel, the first African Methodist Episcopal (AME) Church in the South, is where Denmark Vesey staged his rebellion in 1822, and was later hanged for his resistance. It's where Martin Luther King Jr. spoke during the civil rights movement. Today, of course, it's infamous for the tragedy that struck its minister and members when, in 2015, they were murdered by a white supremacist. In the days after that murder, I was in Charleston searching the archives, and walked past the memorial around the church most days on my way back to the hotel. The church leaders talked about forgiveness, not retaliation, and I thought of its burning in 1834, how the members of the church who were enslaved, lynched, harassed, and beaten did not succumb to that oppression, how the leaders of the church turn to the world now with forgiveness after such a horrific act, when they'd opened their study group to a white stranger. "We are a forgiving people," Joseph McGill told me when we met at Magnolia Plantation.

Minerva didn't live like people enslaved on plantations but was in close proximity to her owners, either alongside them in their home, or in a separate cabin in the backyard. Living within the house might have given her access to slightly better living conditions but certainly subjected her to more surveillance by her owners, and therefore fewer personal freedoms.

I think of my first encounter with slave quarters in Charleston, and how I didn't know then that it was important that my classmate had named them as what they were; she didn't erase that history. It seemed we weren't able to talk about it, but, looking back, I was never able to ask, plainly and without suspicion or anger, how it felt to have inherited a legacy of enslavement, the legacy of owning other people. By the time I got to Charleston back then, I had heard too many things from students about the North versus the South, had heard too many racist comments, too much about how northerners had no roots and no history, to approach a conversation with anything but self-righteousness. I still believed that I had come from a place that was free of enslavement and that it was only the South that had embraced and defended it.

On February 3, 1838, Winthrop, raised in the North, writes home from Charleston to tell his brother-in-law that he's sold Susan's enslaved people.

> *Susan's negroes were sold last Tuesday, I bought Eliza for $530 and John for $510, Minerva was sold with her two children @ $298, all round making $870 for the three making a good average sale, they certainly sold for all they were worth. I bought John for Hilton and Eliza for the man that employs her who was out of town. If he does not take her I shall put her up again when I will make her dress herself better and she will bring full as much if not more she looked like the dunce when on the Block.*

Minerva's baby Samon was about four months old (though he's listed as six months old), and her daughter, Cecilia, was either two or three years old; she's listed as two, but Susan had said she was three in an earlier letter. Minerva must have held her children close that day, and comforted them through the terrifying ordeal of leaving the only house they'd ever known, and being sold, and taken away to a new home, full of strangers.

Winthrop bought Eliza for the man who rented her, which tells us that she'd been rented out frequently, either since Susan left or since she and Hasell had come to own her in 1835. Eliza was bringing in income for them, and likely got to keep a portion of her rent. Winthrop kept Eliza, and, as of 1846, still hadn't paid her off completely; this means that he hadn't paid Susan for the cost of her property. Meanwhile, Hilton had borrowed from the estate. Her brothers were not good managers of her funds. As a widow whose husband's estate was in their trust, she was at their mercy to manage her finances and send her an annual stipend on which to support herself and Emily.

On the day of the sale, historian Beverly Morgan-Welch told me, it's possible Eliza didn't dress well on purpose, so that she wouldn't be sold away from family in the area, or away from her own husband or beloved. Such acts of subversion and resistance were common. In Boston, I met with Morgan-Welch, who was then Director of the Museum of African American History in Boston, to ask her advice about how to tell this story. It was a few days after the shooting in Charleston, and a conversation that I'd expected to take half an hour went on for hours. She shared with me her grief over the shooting; she told me stories about people from the nineteenth century free black community in Boston, which was in Beacon Hill, the neighborhood where we sat. Down the street, I visited the African Meeting House, where Frederick Douglass spoke. When I told her about Eliza's sale, she told me that I had to remember that enslaved people were not people waiting for life to happen to them, but were constantly resisting. "Plantation tools were always breaking," she said. "Wouldn't they have wondered why the tools weren't made very well?" She smiled, knowing: the tools were broken by the enslaved people, of course, in an act of resistance that would mean they didn't work that day, that the master's business would suffer an economic blow, that they had their autonomy. Eliza might have made sure she wasn't sold out of the city, that no one would compete with Winthrop's bid. Maybe she ensured she'd stay near her children, or her husband, or her sister.

Where did Minerva go? To whom did she belong after she left the Crouch household? Did she have to go farther south, where her life would have been even more difficult? Did she remain in Charleston, enslaved in someone else's house? Did she have more children? Did she make it to freedom in 1863?

What *is* the story? Magnolia, like every other plantation, is an archive, a site that's been preserved by the people who value this story, who are descendants of the white family who owned it in the first place. Within this place, tourists can learn the first and last names of every white resident, can see the chairs upon which they sat and the clothes they wore and the dishes they used. Can study the bed frame and its design, the chamber pot, the floorboards polished to a sheen over which each white person walked. The cabins where enslaved people lived are empty, shells of places that were used constantly for decades, the materials within their walls used and reused until they were transformed into something else and eventually fell apart or disintegrated. Joseph McGill's role at Magnolia, along with other guides who lead the tours of the slave cabins, is to tell the story of the people who lived within those walls, whose labor sustained the plantation.

Joseph's work is activist; he uses The Slave Dwelling Project to push people to reconsider the stories they've been told and perpetuate, stories that silence enslaved people and erase their contributions from our culture. When we visited a plantation in Wisconsin, Joe asked the guide, "Is there a back stairway in this house?" And he said, when we saw a section of the house exposed to reveal hand-hewn beams, "This is what I was looking for. See how these are hand-hewn and left rough? See how they look different than the smooth outer beams?"

This part of the wall was cut away to reveal what was underneath, and it became a metaphor for the entire community that existed behind the plantation's façade and for the way the story of the place was told. The people polishing the floor, emptying the chamber pots, climbing the back stairs with food and tea and clean linens washed in the kitchen and dried hanging over the lawn in the garden—these were the people whose lives have been ghosted. Joe is engaged in a *hauntology*.

Joe goes to places where once-enslaved people slept and worked and lived with their families and mourned the people they lost; this is how he makes visible the lives that have been rendered invisible, voiceless, by plantations and cultural institutions and historical societies and towns and states and the nation-state we call the United States. He invites people to join him on sleepovers, to have conversations with him about the stories of enslaved people, and the story of race in America, the issues we face today. Along with another faculty member, I took a group of students from my new home of northern Michigan down to Illinois, to travel with Joe and Mr. L, a high school history teacher, and his students. We went to towns in the Midwest where enslavement had once been alive and well; we stayed in a cabin built by enslaved people, where enslaved people had slept. I'd always been told these were the free states, that this part of the country, like the North, was abolitionist. But even into the 1830s, enslaved people lived in Illinois.

I asked Joe if he communes with his ancestors during his sleepovers, and he says no, because he's not ready to bear their suffering, to feel the suppressed anger he says they must have felt each day.

We can imagine a quiet evening in 1837, and Minerva has just had her baby. Eliza and Juba have been helping her with the baby and taking care of her tasks at the house since Minerva's had two weeks off. She's still sore from labor, during which she was probably attended by a midwife, a woman of color who lives nearby and takes care of all the delivering women. Minerva wouldn't have had the luxury of the dressing gown that Susan sewed before Emily's birth. But maybe Jane sewed her a memento for the baby—a small cloth doll, a blanket made of scraps that she transformed into an embroidered blanket, stitched with Samon's name.

Maybe, in the days after, Cecilia sits with her mother and the baby, uncertain of Samon yet. Now that the first frost has come, they'd be safe from yellow fever. Minerva must have looked down at her baby and swelled with love, adoring his every coo and murmur, nestling her face into his soft hair just as Susan had done with Little Hasell in his infant days. Minerva must adore this child and grieve for the life Samon would have to lead. She must have hoped for freedom, for an escape to a better life for her two babies. She must have done all she could to ensure their safety and keep them from the hardships she knew.

For Eliza and Minerva and Jane, medicine was arrowroot and "black-snake root, furrywork, jimpsin weed, one that tie' on the head which bring sweat from you like hail, an' hickory leaf. If the hickory leaf is keep on the head too long it will blister it." These are the words of Henry Brown, who also went by Toby. He's one of the people interviewed as part of the Works Progress Administration. The language as it's transcribed is fraught with the social tensions and racist stereotypes of that era, the 1930s. Almost all the interviewers were white. How could a formerly enslaved person reveal everything to a white person about enslavement in the racist Jim Crow days? They knew that, just as in the days of their enslavement, if they said the wrong thing, they could be lynched, and the murderer would not be prosecuted. Henry couldn't say everything in the interview. But the archive remains with testimonies to that time, full of valuable information about what enslavement entailed, and echoes we can hear today, of the voices of peoples who had lived through enslavement.

In Eliza, Minerva, and Juba's days, older women were respected for their wisdom and knew about the herbs that were harvested for medicine and steeped in tea, and about superstitions, too, like burying an ax underneath a woman's bed during childbirth to "cut the pain." They'd have known about "gypsum weed, which was boiled into a tea and drunk. Thread-salve buds was picked and strung on 'thread like a necklace, den put around de neck to keep off chills.'" Herbs were grown in the plantation and city gardens and harvested in the forests. When someone got sick, they'd have "made hot teas from herbs dat dey got out of de woods. One was a bitter herb called "rhu." It was put in whiskey and drunk to prevent sickness. This was *Ruta graveolens*, a bitter plant with a yellow flower.

Women of color—free and enslaved—would catch the babies and help mothers deliver. They were called upon for every birth and for every death, too, Deborah Gray White tells us. Sara Brown, trained as a nurse after the Civil War, describes being trained to work as a midwife: "My white folks give me to de doctors in dem days to try en learn me for a nurse. Don' know exactly how old I was in dat day en time, but I can tell you what I done. My Lord, child, can' tell dat. Couldn' never tell how many baby I bring in dis world, dey come so fast. I betcha I got more den dat big square down dere to de courthouse full of em. I nurse 13 head of chillun in one family right here in dis town. You see dat all I ever did have to do. Was learnt to do dat. De doctor tell me, say, when you call to a 'oman, don' you never hesitate to go en help her en you save dat baby en dat mother both. Dat what I is always try to do." Save the baby and the mother both, she was taught to do. She learned midwifery from a doctor, and delivered an astonishing thirteen babies from the same family.

There were white doctors, too, of course, like Hasell, trained in the new so-called "medical profession." When an enslaved person was sick, owners might call a doctor to protect not the person but their property, which was an investment, as they saw it. What must an enslaved person have thought on seeing a white man approach to treat him with those sharp shining instruments—prods and even saws—knowing the doctor was responsible for torturing enslaved people while studying in school? On the street, in their homes, this white man was given license to kill the black man whenever he desired; how could he be trusted to administer medicine, to heal, when his hands were the ones that whipped, burned, slapped, punched, and tightened the rope for the lynching?

Saidiya Hartman writes, "Why risk the contamination involved in restating the maledictions, obscenities, columns of losses and gains, and measures of value by which captive lives were inscribed and sometimes extinguished? Why subject the dead to new dangers and to a second order of violence? Or are the merchant's words the bridge to the dead or the scriptural tombs in which they await us?"

As soon as I found the words *probably for slave gowns* in the fabric notebooks while examining the quilt, and later, the words in the letters about Minerva, Eliza, Jane, Boston, and other unnamed enslaved people referenced in Hasell's letters; as soon as I encountered in Winthrop's letter the story of the black man who was stepped upon and then murdered by a white man who would likely be set free; as soon as I saw in the archive stories with the word *negroes*, and all the racism that came with it, I began to wonder if I could rewrite those words to tell a story. How does my re-presenting those words change the narrative, the story of these people's lives, the echoes that reverberate through time—if at all? How will I quote problematic language and stories without reifying racism and hatred? How can I reimagine people's lives with all the knowledge of history we have now? I wonder, throughout the start of the project, if it's better to reimagine the women who were enslaved by Susan in the 1830s, or to let them remain undefined for your own imagination to fill, untouched by my hand, which might be clumsy, or an unconscious product of its culture and time.

Eliza, Minerva, and Jane lived in Charleston, but before and after they came to the city, they had probably lived in North Carolina with Mary Ancrum Walker, or in Abraham's or Charles's houses in Charleston. Because Minerva was not as common a name as, say, Jenny, we can be fairly sure that she is the Minerva listed as having been owned by Mary Ancrum Walker; a missing record makes it impossible to know if it's this same Minerva who was owned by Mary and by Susan.

There was a boy named George, about sixteen years old. A woman named Eliza, about thirty-three years old, who was sold in 1838, but there was no Eliza listed in the extant, incomplete record from Mary Ancrum Walker's enslaved people. Did she, like Bishroom, have a beloved somewhere in the city? Was she hoping to stay in town to be near relatives and friends? Did she have children in a nearby household? Hilton and Hasell and Winthrop seemed to buy and sell their enslaved people from whites of the same class as they were—the middle-class businessmen—who lived nearby. Maybe the people they bought and sold had kin connections around 6 Cumberland Street and the neighborhood that buttressed the battery. Maybe they met in the mornings as they ran errands for their masters, or took their children to see one another, or went to see the circus or the scam "balloon ascension" man whom Winthrop once noted was in town.

There's no record of Hasell buying anyone; he's listed only as having petitioned the court to split the inheritance of people that came from Mary Ancrum Walker, in 1835, when he and Susan went to housekeeping. So, while his purchase records could have been lost, it's likely that all of Hasell's enslaved people came from the estate of Mary Ancrum Walker, Hasell's grandmother, who owned a large plantation in Wilmington, North Carolina, and then, after 1808, lived between Wilmington and Charleston.

Juba is named in Mary's marriage settlement (prenuptial agreement that ensured the wife's property was protected and would be passed to their children) as "Jouby Ann," the daughter of Judith. Maybe Juba was born in North Carolina, and came to Charleston with her mother in Mary Ancrum Walker's early days in the city. Maybe Juba was born in Charleston. She is at one point referred to as "Juber." Because, the genealogist tells me, Juba is a unique name, at least in Charleston from 1821 to 1960, when only "six entries for Juba and its variants" were listed, we can be almost certain that this is the same person whose name appears in the paper trail.

Six people listed in one hundred forty years. Certainly, many people were missed; enslaved people were not always counted, either as living or as having died. But the rarity of her name makes her easier to find. Juba means she was born on a Monday, and might come from the Ashanti people of Ghana, where the name Juba originated. I learned from Tammy Denease that the Ashanti people were warriors. These were the people from whom Belinda Sutton the African was descended, too. She had that spirit of a warrior, Tammy told me, and so I begin to imagine that Juba might have been born with the same sense of empowerment.

In 1837, Juba was sold in a separate sale to Aaron Caraway Smith, and—the news that delights me—she made it to see emancipation, and took the last name Simons after the Civil War.

Juba Simons.

She's the only enslaved person in the archive who leaves an archival trace to the years after the war, the only person whose chosen last name I see (Bishroom is listed as Bishroom Vale, but he may have been given his owner's last name, Vale, without his consent). When I asked the genealogist who found Juba for me if we could find her descendants, she said there's no record of Juba Simons in the Freedmen's Bureau records, which marked marriages, births, and deaths after the war, and that she couldn't find any record of her in the census. There is only this, her death certificate.

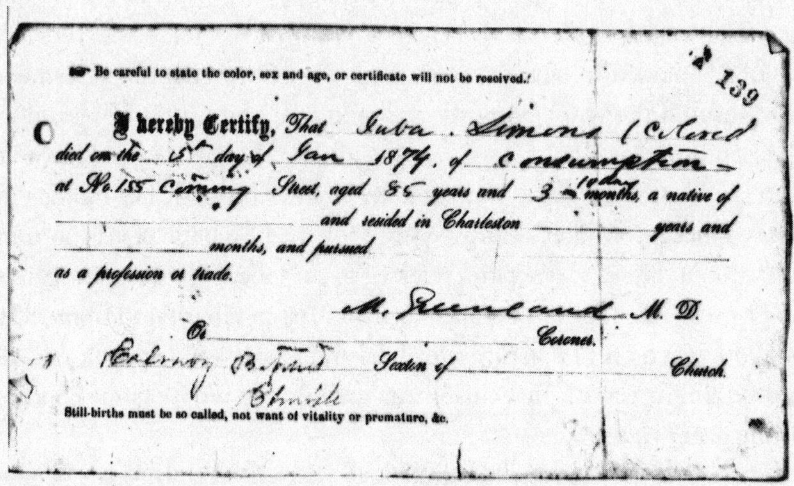

Be careful to state the color, sex and age, or certificate will not be received.

139

I hereby Certify, That Juba Simons (Colored
died on the 5th day of Jan 1874. of consumption
at No. 155 Coming Street, aged 85 years and 3 10 days months, a native of
and resided in Charleston years and
months, and pursued
as a profession or trade.

M. [illegible] M. D.

Or Coroner.

Calvary B[illegible] Sexton of Church.

Still-births must be so called, not want of vitality or premature, &c.

Juba Simons was a member of Calvary Baptist Church and lived at 155 Coming Street in 1874, when she died of consumption, what we'd call tuberculosis. She still lived on the peninsula, just a couple of blocks from where Denmark Vesey lived in 1822, and a mile and a half from the Crouch home at 6 Cumberland Street. She was eighty-five years and three months old when she died, having raised her children and then seen them sold away from her, and likely raised and cooked for many other people's children in addition to Little Hasell and the infant Emily. She was buried at Calvary Baptist Church.

What happened to her in the years from 1838 to 1874? More than three decades of a life lived, perhaps all on this small peninsula? Did she witness the war? Flee to Union camps for her freedom, or was she seized by the Union army to live as so-called "contraband" of war in a contraband camp? Did she help enslaved people escape? Find the children who had been sold away from her?

I know more about Juba than I do Eliza or Minerva. And yet, the only certainties are Juba died January 5, 1874, and lived, from approximately 1835 until 1838, at 6 Cumberland Street. Her death certificate notes that she was "85 years, 3 months," and what appears to be "10 days" old.

Juba Simons, or someone close to her, must have ensured that her death, and therefore the date of her birth, was accurately marked. Most enslaved people in Charleston were not given tombstones and historians note that most enslaved people and their owners did not know their exact dates of birth. These careful notes on her death certificate may signify her insistence on commemorating her birth and life. Thus, we know she was born September 25, 1788, twelve years after the American Revolution. She had a son Sorenzo and a mother named Dianna. She may have had a son named John, if the seven year old boy sold in 1838 was also her son. The Crouch house was small compared to the urban plantation preserved in the Aiken-Rhett House up on Elizabeth Street, or the Calhoun Mansion with multiple stories and marble floors and cabinets of silver in perpetual need of polish. At 6 Cumberland Street, there were eight enslaved people, though Winthrop petitioned to sell seven people in 1837. This we know. They lived together near the water, until 1838, when Winthrop sold them to support Susan. And Juba lived to the old age of eighty-five and three months and ten days.

Over and over, I listen to Mahalia Jackson and Paul Robeson sing "A Balm in Gilead," a black spiritual that was probably written in the nineteenth century. Robeson's voice is deep and slow, rolling over the word "there," up and down. He's accompanied only by a piano. *He died to save us all.* The afterlife will bring ease. When Mahalia Jackson sings the song, she starts out more slowly, lingering on the words *wounded* and *whole.* Behind her voice, there's a piano and an organ. I imagine a church service, Eliza and Minerva and Juba standing in a room with their neighbors and family and friends, singing this song.

We can imagine that Eliza, Minerva, and Juba knew different forms of escape possible only in the city: moments spent away at church on Sunday mornings, or at Bible study in an evening; they might have stayed late—long after they'd bought all the goods the family required—at the Saturday-night market, gossiping with friends. This market was for people of color only—free and enslaved—and Minerva or Eliza and Juba and Jane could have visited this market and been welcomed, at ease, for no one was looking over their shoulders to check for their passes, no one was waiting for them to make a misstep or looking for an opening into an accusation. "Slaves held a market every Saturday night, coupling fun with work. Slave women largely presided over this anchor of the city economy, peddling everything from sweet-grass baskets and baked goods to produce." Here, they could laugh at, say, a neighborhood woman's gaffe in church the week before, a master's vanity, a child's silliness—a funny face, the imitation of a parent dancing, or witnessing the sweet bumbling attempt of a baby taking her first steps. Here, they could laugh as boisterously as they wanted without anyone's reproach; they didn't have to feign humility or shame or submit to anyone else's whims or furies.

Religious meetings, too, offered some refuge. At church services, at study groups, Eliza, Minerva, Bishroom, Juba, must all have found solace in the songs, in the community, in the moments they had to escape the slave system for a time, and exchange valuable news and information with one another. They'd have heard from sailors who came into the port, gleaned information overheard at the market or on the battery, and, if they were able, glanced at newspapers and pamphlets distributed around the city—and they shared all the information they gathered with one another as they walked and met in the neighborhood.

> *If you cannot preach like Peter, if you cannot pray like Paul, You can tell the love of Jesus and say, "He died for all.*

A couple of blocks away, there was the harbor, where ships came and went, bringing with them the news from the North and South and the Caribbean, Europe, Africa. Sailors came ashore, black men and white men whose lives were counted more equally on board a ship. They sailed in on brigs, barques, and schooners, bringing with them what had been traded and bought: silks and spices and tea from China and India; sugar and molasses from the West Indies; chocolate, silk slippers, dried fruit, pots and pans made in the North; red wine from Madeira, and of course, more enslaved people, no longer from Africa or the Caribbean now (unless brought illegally) but from farther south in the States, hubs like New Orleans and Birmingham where the trade moved as quickly as ever. The domestic slave trade was booming.

Sometimes I feel discouraged and leave my fear away
In prayers the Holy Spirit revives my soul again

On a wooden schooner, there was the wind flapping at the cloth sails on a still day. More wind, and the ship could heel with full sails, riding the coastline, the sounds of the crew calling to one another from the masts and the crow's nest. On a dull day, there was no wind, just a hot sun bearing down, and the listlessness of the sails.

"How can narrative embody life in words and at the same time respect what we cannot know? How does one listen for groans and cries, the undecipherable songs, the crackle of fire in the cane fields, the laments for the dead, and the shouts of victory, and then assign words to all of it?"

These are Saidiya Hartman's words. She's speaking to the problems of an archive that absences black people's voices. I thought of this on my way home from Clermont Farm, listening to the radio as I wound through dark fields. A musician was telling the story of "Amazing Grace," a song written by a white man who used to be a slaver, based on the melody he heard enslaved people singing from the hold below. Singing together was a way through sorrow, and a way of conveying information; hymns could communicate stories, news, and plans for resistance.

We know "Amazing Grace" as the song written by a slaver who gave up the business and sought redemption for his past, but Wintley Phipps, in telling the story of this hymn, plays the pentatonic scale, and says, "You see? This is the 'slave scale,'" and shows the audience how the song shows evidence of having been made by West African people. Any "negro spiritual," says Phipps "can be played on the black notes of the piano," which make the pentatonic scale. "The slaves didn't come to America with *do re mi fa so la ti do.* That's somebody else's scale, okay?" he says in a talk I watch later. The audience, which looks to be mostly white people, laughs. Phipps expertly gets them on his side with humor. White spirituals, he says, are often built on the slave scale or pentatonic scale. Then, he plays as an example, "Amazing Grace," which he says sounds so much like a "West African sorrow chant." He "set his words to a slave melody," and Phipps says that he believes he wrote that song "exactly as it should be written, so that we would be reminded that whether black or white, we're all in this together." He says that wherever the song is printed, the words are attributed to John Newton, the former slaver, and the melody is written by "unknown." He asks how many people's lives have been changed by that person called "unknown."

Whether truth or myth, this version of John Newton's life, this story of the pentatonic scale, is what I hear as I wind through dark roads, away from a plantation where enslaved people lived and worked all their lives, most of their names never finding their way to a record we can read today. We have to read the story of their lives in the objects that remain, in the spaces and silences. "How can narrative embody life in words," Hartman asks, "and at the same time respect what we cannot know?" How do we listen for the "groans and cries," the "fire in the cane fields," the "undecipherable songs," the "shouts of victory." How do we "assign words to . . . all" this?

The men who came to Charleston's port with news of the world would have lived in what Susan called the "lowly" neighborhood, where free blacks and enslaved people who were being rented out in the city lived in boarding houses down by the wharves. Those sailors would have encountered women like Minerva, Eliza, and Jane at the Saturday market. They'd have, we could imagine, chatted, gossiped, and talked about the news that came down from the North. Would Boston's or Charleston's residents have heard about the Great Moon Hoax, published in a New York newspaper in 1835? It was a fiction, a story about an astronomer discovering creatures on the moon—humans with bat wings, unicorns, goats. The man-bats soared in the sky above the river, swam with their wings peeking above the water, while the unicorns jousted onshore. People believed this story for weeks after its publication. They believed that these creatures were perceptible by a giant telescope, and why not? It wasn't much stranger than the notion of inoculations, swiping one person's pus with another's blood to prevent infection, nor, for that matter, of enslavement—the bondage of a human as if an animal.

Enslaved and free blacks in 1830s Charleston must have talked about the abolitionists in Boston, the latest play put on at the Odeon, the establishment of the New England Anti-Slavery Society, a talk at the African Meeting House, or the construction of the Abiel Smith School in Boston in 1834; the institution had been teaching free blacks since the turn of the century and was located in the Beacon Hill neighborhood, one side of which was inhabited predominantly by free blacks. This is where I met with Beverly Gordon-Welch, who told me about The Great Prince Hall. The Abiel Smith School was founded by Prince Hall, who also founded a black Freemasonry society that's now named after him. He spent years teaching children in his home before building the school with the help of his son Primus Hall, among many others, and funded by a wealthy white donor as well as the black community's fund-raising. From the late 1700s on, Boston's black community fought for equal education in the city, and against segregation—a fight that's ongoing today; the founding of the Abiel Smith School was an attempt to create equal opportunities. The building for the school was constructed in 1834–35, alongside the African Meeting House, a church built in 1808, where Frederick Douglass would later advocate for abolition.

When Beverly Morgan-Welch told me about Prince Hall, who was declared a free man after the Boston Massacre in which Crispus Attucks died, she said he was called *The Great* Prince Hall, and was "no longer Reckoned a slave, but [had] always accounted as a free man." So, while he might technically have been, according to legal records, enslaved, Morgan-Welch said he was "always accounted as a free man, meaning he was walking around as if he were free—he *claimed* his freedom long before it was supposedly given to him." He claimed freedom, lived his life with the actions of a free man, so he had always been free. Prince Hall later petitioned the Boston school system to open public schools to black students, and helped set in motion the court cases that would come in the twentieth century, like *Brown v. Board of Education*.

David Walker, a Boston resident, gave his life to the cause for abolition. White, free people of color, and enslaved people would have known of him in Charleston, and they'd certainly have heard about his murder in Boston in 1831. He wrote *Appeal to the Coloured Citizens of the World*, which was banned in the South for its compelling abolitionist argument. It was considered a dangerous book that could incite the rebellions that whites worked to suppress. Resist, Walker told African-Americans, a message for which he was murdered, though his words would live on after he passed.

In 1828, a man named James runs away in Natchez, Mississippi. Running away is another form of rebellion, resistance, a refusal to submit. James is a sailor, and his owner imagines he is heading for the sea.

> 150 Dollars Reward. Ranaway from the subscriber, on the night of the 6th Inst., a certain negro man, named JAMES; about 5 feet 8 inches high, brown complexion, well made, the little finger of (perhaps) [sic] the left hand, crooked at the first joint and stiff, has marks of a blow or two on the head, none of his front [teeth] were missing, has some mark made on the arm with powder as sailors some times have, (the figure of an anchor or something else;) [sic] about 25 years of age, a smart, intelligent fellow, reads, writes and ciphers some; will probably try to pass for a free man; has worked at the mill and gin wright trade for the last seven years. It is thought he may make his way to the seaboard, or Richmond Virginia. Captains of vessels, steam boats, barges &c., are warned against taking him on board. For apprehending said fellow and confining him in jail so that I get him, a reward of Fifty Dollars will be given, if taken in the parish; One Hundred Dollars if taken in the state, and out of the limits of the parish; or One Hundred and Fifty Dollars beyond the limits of the state. WINDER CROUCH Bayou Boeuff, Parish of Rapide, La.

I reread the words, “has some mark made on the arm with powder as sailors some times have, (the figure of an anchor or something else;).” This is a description of a tattoo given by one sailor to another. Bind together needles, dip the needles into “Indian or Chinese Ink (lampblack mixed with animal glue, sold in solid rolls or cakes), laundry bluing, or vermilion (artificial cinnabar, i.e., alpha mercuric sulfide, ground with white wine and then mixed with white of egg),” then “stretch . . . the subject’s skin as tight as possible in the area to be worked on,” and pierce the skin with the needles, over and over, “until the design was completed or the subject could no longer stand the pain.” Then comes the cleansing with urine, “rum or brandy,” fixatives, they believe, and the tattoo will endure.

This is what James must have endured to get that tattoo of an anchor on his arm. He must have chosen this tattoo because his life on the sea means so much to him, or his camaraderie with the men on board, or it is a reminder of a sort of freedom he found there. Maybe, like the origins of so many tattoos today, he was drunk one night and did so out of foolishness, or was pressured by his friends to do it.

He is a “smart, intelligent fellow,” who found a way to learn the forbidden skills (maybe from a free person of color he encountered at markets just like the ones Minerva, Eliza, and Juba attended) of reading and writing. He is skilled, too, with the knowledge of the “mill and gin wright trade,” which he’s done for “seven years.” Maybe he is like Boston, who works at Hilton’s lumber mill in Charleston, pressing through the machinery logs for planing, risking his life against the whirring of the great roaring blades, each of the wheels propelling the mill weighing one thousand pounds and three thousand pounds, wheels that Hilton brought down from Providence. He “will probably try to pass for a free man . . . It is thought he may make his way to the seaboard, or Richmond Virginia. Captains of vessels, steam boats, barges &c., are warned against taking him on board . . .” And why wouldn’t he try to pass for a free man? I think about what Beverly Gordon-Welch said about The Great Prince Hall, about the free black community in Boston, about temperance societies and the African Methodist Episcopal Church, and all the places where free people of color crafted their lives, developed community, propelled their families forward.

⁂

In 1830, Charleston's total population was 30,289. Of those people, 2,107 were free blacks, and 15,354 were enslaved people. The remaining 12,828 were whites, encompassing the wealthy, the working class, and the poor. That was a black majority: 17,461 people total. Free people of color mingled in white society. They attended St. Philip's Church, alongside Susan and Hasell. They'd have sat in sight of free people of color who wore the same fine clothes—corseted waists and puffed sleeves, cravats and tailored jackets, top hats—maybe even made by the same tailors and dressmakers, as so many of those skilled sewers were African American: "Women of color and white women together dominated the clothing trades [in Charleston] . . . In 1848 free women of color comprised 46 percent, white women 43 percent, and slave women 11 percent of the 534 female artisans laboring in the sewing trades. Mantua makers and milliners crafted the latest European fashions for Charleston's wealthy women to display at balls, horseraces, plays, and concerts." So, women of color, free and enslaved, made up 57 percent of all skilled sewers in the city. Mantua makers were dressmakers, milliners were hatmakers.

Women's hats in 1835 were bonnets that shielded the side of the face, with an exaggerated brim embellished with flowers and ribbons. Sometimes of straw, sometimes of silk, depending on the occasion and a woman's class and means. What could she afford? To what did she have access? Her station was evident in her clothing. Everything was stratified—whites into classes of poor, working, and elite, and people of color into the categories of the enslaved, free working person of color, and elite brown person. The higher a woman's class, the more tightly she was corseted, the more embellishments and buttons and pleats on her clothes. A house slave was supposedly more elevated than a field slave, and had access to, for example, the clothes the master discarded, scraps from the master's meals, maybe even (illicitly) books in the master's library.

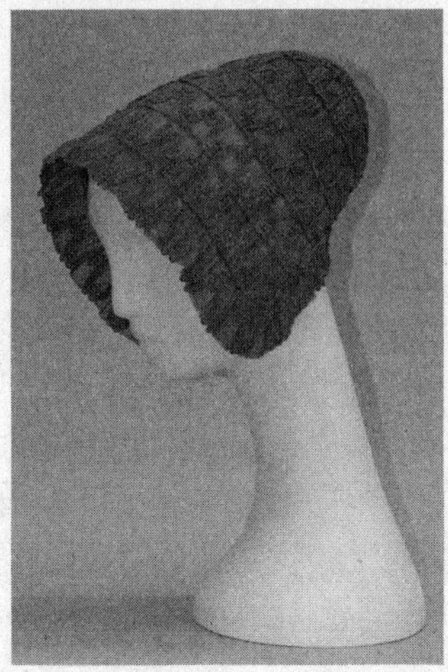

The sort of bonnet Eliza, Minerva, Jane, and Juba might have worn.

African-American women, Kennedy writes, were artisans, skilled in crafts in which they'd been, effectively, apprenticed by their mothers and the women with whom they lived. "Women of African and European descent labored in these trades, with the former controlling the mantua-making business and the latter dominating millinery. All had mastered skills that warrant their classification as artisans, not merely laborers." African American women dominated dressmaking, while most hatmakers were of European descent. And all women of the elite classes wore the finest hats and clothes, eyes shielded from the world, as if to blind them from what they didn't want to see.

It's likely Eliza would have worn a head tie, but perhaps she wore a bonnet like this, probably of white cotton with a simple tie that hangs down at both sides. As she walks from the house down to the port, two blocks away, does she swing her head to either side of the street to make note of the hustle, to see the men hauling baskets and crates from the ships? To look for a sailor she's become friendly with on his visits to the city? To greet the women she hopes to pass as they run errands for their own mistresses? Maybe she fingers the tin tag that hangs around her neck, the marker of her momentary freedom from Susan's house, the marker of her enslavement. Maybe, for a moment, she closes her eyes to feel the sun on her face before setting off again over the dirt road and then the cobblestones, her long heavy dress swinging against her legs, the whispered sound of cotton moving across her body with the motion of her steps.

The second bonnet is from 1837, described here in dramatic terms: "1837 was a pivotal year in fashion, when the large sleeves collapsed and the shoulder greatly decreased in size. Bonnets also gradually changed shape after that date, their exuberance giving way to more demure bonnets with narrow close-fitting brims that hid the face." "More demure bonnets . . . that hid the face." The gigot sleeves "collapsed." Fashions changing to reflect a changing world. This bonnet was worn by Elizabeth Hawes Russell for her wedding, and we can see that the "exuberant broad brim attractively framed the face and echoed the drama of the voluminous wing-like sleeves of the period's ankle-length, full-skirted dresses. Sometimes referred to in contemporaneous writings as a Victoria bonnet, this particular shape was appropriate for wearing in public in the afternoon." Maybe one of the elite brown women Eliza could have passed on the street wore a more elaborate bonnet like this one, embellished with flowers and silk. She wouldn't have described the brim as *exuberant*, but maybe dramatic. Maybe she'd have seen that woman with a sense of envy, longing for the tight corsets that signified that elite woman's freedom. Or maybe she'd have seen her in secret at the woman's house, as the woman was friendly and Eliza was taking the opportunity to learn to read. Literacy could offer escape. Maybe, like Frederick Douglass, who outsmarted white children by getting them to teach him to read by identifying one word at a time, she was able to take what she needed.

Brown silk damask dress, c. 1830, with full skirt and huge sleeves. It closes in back with hooks and eyes.

Did a woman of color wear this dress, housed at the Charleston Museum? It dates to the 1830s. The puffy sleeves are leg o' mutton, the style both elite white and elite brown women wore in the 1830s. Did a woman of color make this dress? Eliza, Minerva, and Jane probably weren't mantua makers, or else Susan would have had them cut and sew her dresses; instead, she asked for her dresses to be cut by the woman she knew in the North, and she probably sewed them together herself or had Jane sew them for her. If Eliza, Minerva, and Jane did any of her sewing, she didn't say as much in her letters. Maybe she wouldn't have wanted to admit to having her enslaved woman, Jane, do the sewing that Susan was supposed to do as a white "lady."

There were so many stratifications, so many distinctions between the races—*free brown person, wealthy white woman, poor free woman of color, poor white woman, "mulatto," "mustee," "negroe"*—when we know, today, that it was all a fiction. Today, we have critical race theory—Frantz Fanon and W.E.B. Du Bois and Hortense Spillers and Claudia Rankine and Ta-Nehisi Coates. We have Michel Foucault to teach us about the power of institutions. In this 1830s society, the one-drop-dictum hadn't yet been articulated but ruled. And even if a woman of color were free, she was still trapped by the social dictates of racism as well as sexism, even if she was no longer formally enslaved. Christy Clark-Pujara writes that "*free* was a terribly relative term," and that "Free blacks . . . had to cope with the legacies of slavery . . . being free did not mean having rights. Legal losses . . . retracted these newfound gains." Clark is referring to free African Americans in Rhode Island who were emancipated under the gradual emancipation laws that took years to free all enslaved people in Rhode Island. The same social restrictions held true in Charleston, of course, with the attendant laws that ensured "economic discrimination," and the denial of full citizenship, including the right to vote.

I imagine Eliza, Minerva, or Jane stitching in the latest hours of the day. Maybe Jane is making a jacket for Cecilia, say, Minerva's daughter, from Susan's stack of calico scraps, the remainder of what was sent down from Providence. The fabric may also have been cut from cast-off dresses and pants that Susan and Hasell no longer wear, as Susan herself makes Little Hasell's clothes from the hand-me-down clothes her parents send her from the North. Fabric is never wasted. But maybe Jane has traded for new fabric with someone at the market, making a shirt or a dress for a woman in exchange for fabric she's handwoven or for factory-woven fabric she'd bought. Is the fire warm when Jane sits beside it at night, working through a pleat in a dress, setting in the sleeves of the jacket, cutting away the most worn parts of the cloth that have been dulled to white, so she'd have a brilliant blue coat?

"Is it possible to construct a story from 'the locus of impossible speech' or resurrect lives from the ruins? Can beauty provide an antidote to dishonor, and love a way to 'exhume buried cries' and reanimate the dead?" These again are Saidiya Hartman's words. She is questioning the archive.

She is telling us about Jacques Derrida's *hauntology*, which he says is what happens when writers speak to a ghost.

This is what M. NourbeSe Philip has done in her book, *Zong!*, in which she gives voice to one hundred fifty enslaved people, from an archive that had rendered them voiceless. Philip reinvented the archive so it spoke not the voices of the slaver but the enslaved, who were murdered. It is a heartbreaking and tragic story. The slave ship *Zong*, full of kidnapped people, sailed from the west coast of Africa and lost its way. People held in the ship's hull began to starve to death, and as they died or were deemed to be dying, or were perfectly healthy but worth some insurance value, as the crew determined, the captain and crew pushed them overboard. Living and dead. Pushed into the sea. It was, of course, not uncommon for slave ship captains and crew to push dead and dying people overboard. The high number of casualties during the voyage was part of what made the process so "risky" as an investment and what prompted Christine Mitchell to think of the waters leading to the old site of the Sullivan's Island "pest house" as a burial ground. Sailors pushed the bodies of enslaved people overboard as they came into port, Mitchell told me, and you could smell those ships before you saw them, for all the stench of excrement and rotting flesh. It's impossible to visit the shores of Sullivan's Island, today, and not to feel that history, to look out on those waters and not to see that story, the horrific brigs sailing toward shore, the terror people onboard must have felt.

Philip is a lawyer and a poet. She went to the archive, and read and reread and reread the document, which consists of a couple of pages chronicling the court case. And from these words, she extracted those that would speak the story she wished to tell—of the enslaved people murdered by the ship captain, drowned at sea. This, says Patricia J. Saunders, is a *hauntology*. "These conversations take very seriously the question of the absence, or some would even say the impediments, in the work of mourning the millions of dead in the aftermath of slavery."

When I talked to Philip after reading *Zong!*, she told me that the sea is a tombstone, a marker for this tragedy. She went to visit the site marking the murders in Jamaica, where the *Zong* came ashore after the captain's atrocity, and she felt these people there. Her book was written in collaboration with the people from that ship who drowned, and she has named these collective voices "Sataey Adamu Boateng." At the bottom of each page of the book, there are listed the names of the people who drowned. These aren't their *real* names, since we can never know their names, but they are the names Philip has heard and given them, markers of their humanity. This is how she's upended the archive to speak—to hear, to voice—the people within it.

This woman, Mary Brice or Bryce, of Virginia, was photographed ca. 1853, later than Eliza and Minerva and Jane's time in the Crouch household on Cumberland Street. But Mary offers a hint of what these women's lives might have looked like—what they might have worn, how they might have portrayed themselves had they had the chance. She holds a fan in her hand. She wears a white tie on her head, and has fastened with a gold pin a wrap around her neck. I wonder if someone gave her that pin as a gift—her husband, maybe—or if she bought it or bartered for it herself. Maybe there are tintypes of Eliza, Minerva, Juba, and Jane somewhere, in an archive I've never seen, and maybe their names are inscribed on the back or in a note accompanying the photographs, and maybe someday those images will be united with their whole stories, wherever their whole stories may be.

On April 5, 1834, Charles W. Crouch bought a "mustee slave named Jane and her son William." He bought her from William Rice. In 1823, there was a William Rice in the New England Society membership listings in Charleston. Maybe this was the same man, affiliated, therefore, with the family through their northern connections. He might have simply been a neighbor, or a man who brought his enslaved people Jane and William to auction that day, and Charles bought them by chance. A "mustee" person was of both African and Native American descent.

Jane and William lived together at Charles's house, along with Susan and Hasell and Winthrop when they first moved to Charleston. This may or may not be the same Jane as "the girl Jane" who was sold in 1837, though people listed as "girls" were not old enough to have children. This is, more likely, the same person as the woman also called "Jenny," described earlier.

Jane and William were bought at about the same time as Susan described the woman who was probably Juba as being lazy, as having stolen things. And then, two years later, this was the same Juba who joined the Crouch household along with her children and was met with Susan's approval.

Don't ever feel discouraged, for Jesus is your friend; And if you lack for knowledge, He'll never refuse to lend.

In President Obama's eulogy for the Reverend Pickney and the eight other people murdered at Mother Emanuel, the church that, he says, continued to hold meetings in the 1800s even when they were prohibited from doing so by "unjust laws," the President ends on the song, "Amazing Grace," which he sings accompanied by the congregation. He talks about the original sin of slavery on which our nation was founded. He talks about how each of us can be granted grace, without deserving it. He says, "For too long, we were blind to the pain that the Confederate flag stirred in many of our citizens. It's true our flag did not cause these murders, but as people from all walks of life, Republicans and Democrats, now acknowledge . . . , the flag has always represented more than ancestral pride—" and the congregation cheers and claps, "For many, black and white, that flag was a reminder of systemic oppression and racial subjugation. We see that now. Removing the flag from this state's capitol would not be an act of political correctness . . . it would simply be an acknowledgment that the cause for which [the soldiers] fought, the cause of slavery, was wrong." And again, the crowd cheers.

And I think of all those Confederate flags I saw when I was in school, in North and South Carolina, and the flags I've seen in the Midwest, too, usually in the form of a sticker on a truck's back window or rear bumper.

"If we can find that grace, anything is possible . . . everything can change," President Obama says—and then he sings.

Minerva, Cecilia, and Samon, just three years old and four months old, respectively, were sold together for eight hundred seventy dollars; John was sold for five hundred seventy dollars; Eliza was sold for five hundred thirty dollars.

I wonder how young John fared out on his own, what the lives of Minerva and her children were like in this new household. Did Eliza want to stay near her children, or loved ones, or the community of friends in the free and enslaved populations around her, or simply the only place she'd ever known?

Inspired by Harriet Tubman's story, I begin to imagine a different life for Eliza, one in which she escapes to freedom. With no children to tie her to Charleston, she has nothing to lose now that she has been parted from Minerva and Juba. She befriends that sailor whose eye I've imagined she catches. She learns the ropes and knots and names of the sails, learns *port* and *starboard*, learns the dialect of a sailor, learns, hidden in darkness beside her friend on the ship, to haul ropes and walk the deck and climb masts. She learns to lick her finger and hold it in the wind to feel which way it blows—*offshore breeze*, she says. I imagine that soon, she'll barter for cloth to make sailor's pants, with vegetables from her garden. Soon, she'll cut off her hair. Slip out in the night. Fail to return. Succeed in undermining Winthrop one more time, getting hired onto the schooner her sailor friend has assured her needs another hand (her friend will get the captain drunk, *The captain will be incapacitated*, he assures Eliza). I imagine her stepping onto that boat, pulling at the mainsail to tighten it against the wind, and watching the moon as the men around her shout and hustle, as the captain hollers orders at her, as she feigns her way into a new life—a life that, like Prince Hall—she takes for herself.

7
The Leonids: A Sermon in Patchwork

In 1833, the stars are falling. It's November, a clear night in Georgia, where Harriet Powers's parents work, enslaved in the field. Imagine stepping out of the cabin in the middle of the night, maybe woken by a nightmare, maybe to relieve yourself, and seeing hundreds of stars raining down above you from a deep blue sky. The sky's almost-purple hue is lit up by streams of white and gold, star after star coming at you from a center of fire, so stunning and so frightening that you'd holler out to your wife sleeping in the cabin to *Come look! The world's ending!*

There are Geminids in December, North and South Taurids in early November, Lyrids in April, Orionids in late October, Draconids in early October, Perseids in August, and in mid-November, there are the Leonid showers that Harriet Powers depicted in that central square in her quilt. The Leonids emerge from a single point in the sky, so that as you watch them "fall," you might feel as though you're racing through outer space as in the opening *Star Wars* credits, or, as people recounting the 1966 Leonids described them, as if you were driving into a snowstorm with your headlights on, the stars making a cone around you. In 1966, the Leonids fell in the thousands per minute.

If it was that powerful a visual spectacle in 1966, when we understood what a meteor shower was, imagine what we would have made of it one hundred and thirty years earlier, in 1833, before we knew what meteors were and what caused them. Imagine that you have a strong faith in God and in Jesus' second coming, and that you rely on word of mouth and secondhand news from someone who's able to read the papers and pamphlets that make their way around the countryside. Imagine that you've come from a long day working in the fields and your shoulders ache; that you and your wife chuckled at the man in the next-door cabin as he sang to his homemade guitar in a tone-deaf ditty; that the two children who aren't your own but who need some love fell asleep nearby, and your wife hummed to them and rubbed her hand in circles on the little girl's back; imagine that you recognized in her motion the grief she held for the daughter you both lost a year ago. That you kissed the back of your wife's neck, in that gentle spot that makes a divot around her spine. This would have been an ordinary night, until the Leonids began when the sun went down—and then they are an incredible surprise, something you'll talk about the next day and the next and the next, surprised to see the world go on after you'd been so certain it was over.

Harriet Powers was born four years after the 1833 Leonid meteor shower, in 1837, but she'd have heard stories about them from the time she was a toddler harvesting creek shells for her family "to use as spoons," and then as a young girl working in the fields while her mother cooked for the master's family. The showers were legendary, and changed the way scientists understood meteors. There wouldn't be another one that powerful until just after the Civil War. In 1895, almost sixty years after the shower Powers had heard about, this is how she described the central square in her quilt: "The falling of the stars on Nov. 13, 1833. The people were frightened and thought that the end had come. God's hand staid the stars. The varmints rushed out of their beds."

A man named Basil Hall, son of the Reverend Charles Cuthbert Hall, was eventually gifted Powers's quilt. Laurel Thatcher Ulrich notes that "unlike Smith [who bought the quilt from Powers] . . . , Hall avoided dialect in reporting Harriet's descriptions, but in many ways the account he preserved reveals a view of the world even richer and more complex. . . ." When Jennie Smith recorded Harriet's descriptions in dialect, she was able to "keep her at a distance," Ulrich writes, (after all, white Jennie Smith couldn't have considered herself to be anything like African American Harriet Powers, no matter how much she supposedly valued the woman's art); Smith infantilized Powers, Ulrich tells us, making her view of the all-powerful God seem childlike.

In the square that depicts the shower, I see rabbits and mice (or a cat?), its tail curled around its body. And God's hand in the sky, great and all-powerful in the top left corner. Harriet Powers made the men, in pant-legs, distinct from the women in their dresses. She created the people with their arms in the air, alarmed by the falling sky, rushing to find each other, to pray at the end of the world.

Why does the man at the forefront stand with one hand on his hip, the other raised? Is he preaching? Praying? Greeting God? Trying to help the people around him?

All over the world, people witnessed those Leonids and were stunned by it. This engraving was made fifty years after the showers, and became the most famous image of the event. It was made from a thirdhand account: Joseph Harvey Waggoner saw the Leonids in 1833, when he was thirteen; as a Seventh-Day Adventist in 1887, he told the story of the Leonids to Karl Jauslin, who painted an image of the scene, from which Adolph Völlmy made this engraving. The image was meant to convince believers that the end of the world was nigh, as foretold in the Bible. Waggoner said of witnessing the stars: "It appeared so grand and magnificent as to be truly exhilarating . . . It is not possible to give in a picture a representation of all the stars falling at all points of the compass at once. But they *fell* in myriads to the north, east, south and west. . . . The stars of heaven fell unto the earth."

This is how we remember an event not just in the first generation but in the second, how an event can be passed down from person to person, creating collective memories, so that this image—the *best-known* image of the 1833 Leonid shower—was made fifty years after the shower, by a man who hadn't witnessed it himself but had been shown a painting, which was made by someone who had been told a story about how the shower looked that night. It is an example of how memory slips between us, how we take it on and change it, how we understand ourselves and our families and even our nations (if we believe in nations) generation to generation, memories building on each other, legends growing, shared memories culminating in events that may or may not resemble what they "really" looked like, how they felt, what they were. Harriet Powers's quilt is an amalgamation of Biblical stories and natural events witnessed by people who came before her. She called it *A Sermon in Patchwork.*

This quilt is held at the Smithsonian and is the first quilt Powers made.

In 1891, Harriet Powers sold her first quilt of Bible stories, the quilt held by the Smithsonian, for five dollars, encouraged by her husband to take half the price she'd asked because of the "hardness of the times." She sold it to a white woman, Jennie Smith, who exhibited it in the Cotton States Exposition in 1895. Smith had tried to buy it a few years earlier, but Powers wouldn't sell until 1891, when she apparently needed the money. Smith said that Powers described to her each square, and "has been back several times to visit the darling offspring of her brain." When a group of Atlanta University wives saw Powers's quilt at the exposition, they commissioned Powers to sew this second quilt as a gift, now held in Boston's Museum of Fine Arts.

". . . the darling offspring of her brain."

There's condescension in the line. The word *darling*. That word minimizes a piece of art, which Smith must have understood it to be since she made such an effort to buy the quilt (though she ended up underpaying when Powers was obligated to sell). Gladys-Marie Fry writes that "pictorial tapestries like these have been called 'living history books,'" because they include so many references to local and national events—the meteor shower, the coldest day in 1895. Powers described her images: "A woman froze while at prayer. A woman froze at a gateway. A man with a sack of meal frozen. Icicles formed from the breath of a mule. All blue birds killed. A man frozen at his jug of liquor." She described the "dark day of May 19, 1780," when fires in New England blocked out the sun. And in between these historic moments, there were Bible scenes: "Job praying for his enemies," and "Adam and Eve in the garden. Eve tempted by the serpent. Adam's rib by which Eve was made. The sun and the moon. God's all-seeing eye and God's merciful hand." There is God's merciful hand in the 1833 Leonid shower block, when He "staid the stars," and kept the world from burning. There is God "creat[ing] two of every kind, male and female." Smith also reported that Powers loved animals and wanted to see the circus when it came to town. She didn't say whether she was able to attend or not.

Did Harriet Powers see a circus? Did Eliza, Minerva, Jane, and their children see a circus in Charleston? Did they attend the annual horse races, another public festivity that Winthrop wrote about in 1838? He describes the "Balls, Parties, Concerts, Diorama, Theatres and Exhibitions," that made the city "unusually gay." Did the women celebrate alongside the free blacks, the poor whites, and the master class? The races were one of Charleston's major social occasions, and Cynthia M. Kennedy writes that "slaves did join those who thronged the racecourse, and took advantage of the socially sanctioned leisure time. Family and friends of the slave jockeys attended as a show of support or solidarity," and, Kennedy notes, some enslaved women combined work and play by bringing their white charges to the races with them. While the races gave wealthy whites an opportunity to reassert, or reify, their superior position and "quite literally facilitated reproduction of the master class, because social functions showcased young debutantes who married during a subsequent season," African Americans found a measure of power in watching the participation of black jockeys in the races. Lisa K. Winkler writes:

> For blacks, racing provided a false sense of freedom. They were allowed to travel the racing circuit, and some even managed their owners' racing operation. They competed alongside whites. When black riders were cheered to the finish line, the only colors that mattered were the colors of their silk jackets, representing their stables. Horseracing was entertaining for white owners and slaves alike and one of the few ways for slaves to achieve status.

Was the freedom to gallop on a thousand-pound animal in a race run by both blacks and whites "false" at a time when enslaved men weren't allowed to ride a horse in the street, for whites' fear of what they might do if given access to four legs and such speed? Think how it must have felt to sit atop a horse and push the animal as hard as it could go, around the track, wind in your ears, hands shifting with the motion of the horse against its rough mane, the sound of its hooves and its breath coming hard through flared nostrils, the feeling of its legs gathering and reaching underneath you, the blur of the audience alongside the track, the sound of their hollers. Imagine being able to scream for the jockey of your choice in a city where your voice and body would have always been monitored for obedience and subservience, how good that must have felt to let your voice go, to call out, and to laugh with friends when *your* jockey—maybe even a friend or relative—had won.

What a triumph that would have been, even if it *was* for a master's profit, at a time when your body was still considered chattel. You were in control of that animal, working with the horse to reach the finish line first. This was your talent, to know an animal well enough to work with it, to know when to ease the reins and when to lean forward or sink lower into the saddle, to read the ear spinning and twitching, to have spent years learning how to let your body move with the horse's until you and the horse were as one. You were responsible for the victory. And you, in the audience, were able to move and shout and laugh in those moments, watching the race, as engaged as everyone else. This is not to say that enslaved people at the races had the same rights and freedoms as the white and free blacks around them, but to think about the ways they could have created—*created and claimed for themselves*—freedom and autonomy, within the constraints of the racist law. The chance to ride a horse, and fast, the chance to cheer and celebrate and laugh together at the races when blacks were prohibited from gathering, the chance to see friends and take one's children out for a celebratory event—this was a way for enslaved people to claim autonomy in Charleston, in ways that people enslaved on plantations or in more rural towns could not do.

People claimed moments of time as their own, in the moments before and after church services (the only time they were permitted to meet as a group), or at public events like the circus and the races. They'd have stood to holler at the races, or chatted for a few claimed moments at the general store owned by a woman of color, as they bought a treat for their child or loved one with money they'd earned from their own extra labor or crafted goods.

In Harriet Powers's quilt, she placed the hand of God in the block that describes the story of Adam and Eve, with the legged snake, before it evolved into the legless creature we know today. Adam and Eve hold hands, and we can see Adam's rib, alongside the all-seeing eye in the sky beside God's merciful hand. And there is God's hand again in the square at the bottom, second from the left. Powers described these scenes, "The red light night of 1846. A man tolling the bell to notify the people of the wonder. Women, children and fowls frightened by God's merciful hand caused no harm to them." Was this Comet Biela, with its streaking tail, which they say split into two in the 1850s? There's Moses lifting "the serpent" that I myself thought was a scythe when I first saw the quilt, and there are the animals, "two of every kind, male and female," boarding Noah's Ark, and the freezing day "10 of February, 1895," and the "rich people who were taught nothing of God" enduring "everlasting punishment." There's a multiheaded sea monster, and Jonah being swallowed by the whale. This is an artful melding of religion and local history, astronomical wonders and nationally recognized events like the darkening of the sky during the wildfires and eclipse, the Leonids, the coldest day, illustrated with the woman freezing at the well. Harriet Powers called her quilt "a sermon."

Were Eliza, Minerva, and Jane making story quilts like this? Maybe, and maybe not. They may have been making the detailed patterned quilts like the hexagon top Susan and Hasell stitched together, so popular at the time among the white Charleston master class, or maybe they made pinwheels, drunkard's paths, or great star quilts of hundreds of tiny triangles.

Harriet Powers was born in 1837, the year Susan moved back to Providence and left Minerva, Eliza, Juba, and Jane in her brother Winthrop's hands. Harriet Powers was far younger than the women who lived at 6 Cumberland Street those few years, and she lived on a small farm, not in the city. She was born into enslavement and, according to Jennie Smith, used to talk about the days before the Civil War.

But though Eliza, Minerva, and Juba's lives were shaped by different forces, they could have shared the same sense of history and faith as Harriet Powers—the combination of biblical stories that would have made up their childhoods, their days spent in city churches, Bible meetings, or at plantation services. They'd have heard of those legendary local events—deadly cold days, meteor showers, a comet streaking across the sky—that their mothers and elders had witnessed. And they, too, would have seen those falling stars in November 1833. People would have cried out in the streets, afraid for their lives, praying at the end of the world, and the commotion would have woken Eliza, Minerva, Juba, and Jane, and they would have emerged from their houses to the scene of falling stars that Harriet Powers drew in fabric fifty years later, herself only learning about the event from secondhand sources, like Jauslin. I think of Jane, whom I know now was a seamstress, and wonder if she ever made her own version of the meteor shower, since she might have seen it herself. Did she embroider or appliqué a scene as Harriet Powers did, making her own art inspired by those bursts of light racing toward the earth?

Eliza, Minerva, and Juba were likely religious, given their era, and affiliated with one or another of the churches in Charleston, perhaps the Cumberland Street church, or the Mother Emanuel AME. African Methodist Churches were hubs of black society, for both free and enslaved people. Free blacks could also be members of St. Philip's, where Susan and Hasell had inherited a pew, but people of color weren't permitted to be buried in the cemetery. This led "five members" of the church, "all men of mixed race and part of Charleston's 'brown elite'" to "foun[d] the Brown Fellowship Society" in 1790. Eliza, Minerva, Juba, and Jane, as enslaved women, were far from the elite brown class in Charleston; they were subject to the stratification of the city and the harsh limits put on the lower classes, including enslaved women. In 1803, free people of color founded the Minor's Moralist Society to "educat[e] indigent children of color;" both of these societies, like the master class' benevolent societies, included men only. These groups, Kennedy notes, built in the days after the American Revolution, were constituted of the "palest and wealthiest free people of color." When Sally Seymour, a baker who built her wealth through her business and came to buy four enslaved people of her own, oversaw the marriages of her light-skinned children, she made sure they "marry well, and in Charleston 'well' meant light-skinned."

At church, if they were able to attend, Eliza, Minerva, Juba, and Jane would have mingled with free people of color who, if they weren't the "elites," would have been a mix of middle- and lower-class free people of color. They'd probably have heard of Sally Seymour's success, as she'd transformed herself from an enslaved woman "manumitted" by her "white male owner, and likely the father of her children" in 1795, to a wealthy business owner, who was able to leave a $1,600 estate and four enslaved people to her children when she died in 1824. One of Mary Ancrum Walker's relatives freed an enslaved woman and her "mulatto" child, which likely indicates that the child was the master's. One of Harriet Thorne's (Hilton's wife) relatives married a free woman of color, and the couple had several children in Charleston. It's impossible to see, from here, where the lines between love and oppression lie. I don't know what was true for Eliza, Minerva, Juba, and Jane, if any of these women found love and partners who offered them solace in a world that treated them harshly, nor if any of them were raped by or chose to partner with white men.

It's very likely they found community, though, at church and at the Saturday-night market, for example, where they could have chatted with friends from the Sea Islands around Charleston; these people would have brought seafood to sell—shrimp, crabs, mussels, herring, sea bass, or grouper—and talked in a language unique to the Lowcountry islands; the Gullah Geechee people speak not a dialect but a language that's derived in part from the West and Central African languages that enslaved people brought across the Atlantic, and in part from English. The Gullah Geechee are descended from the enslaved people who were brought to the islands, and they've been able to sustain the culture's language, music, and religious practices as a result of the isolation of places like St. Helena Island, where sandy beaches stretch long and wide—tourists' enticements—amid fishing and farming communities that have been there for centuries. These farms are now threatened by development. On nearby Hilton Head, now heavily touristed, bargain travelers and those out for a splurge can relax at multiplex beachside hotels and golf resorts that are destroying the fishing and farming that once supported the Gullah Geechee communities there.

If we look closely at the falling stars in Harriet Powers's quilt (detail), we can see how the circles of the stars are made not of a single piece of fabric but of multiple small triangles. Powers cut out each triangle, one by one, and then sewed them—front side to front side, with running stitches along the edges, then folded out the triangles and pressed them flat in a process that took skill and patience. She'd have cut out a shooting-star shape in the blue backing fabric, and then set into the blue each orange shooting star, one by one. She'd had to have been precise in clipping away the backing fabric and fitting it to the stars—too much cut away and she'd have gaps, too little and she'd have lumpy stars. It took a great deal of skill to piece those small triangles and set the stars into the blue square. She used a machine—something Jane could have only dreamed of—in addition to working by hand. Maybe she sat near her stove so she'd be near the iron and could press each star flat after piecing it, before setting it into the fabric.

I imagine what Jane would think, if she could watch Harriet work on that quilt with a machine in the 1880s, zipping across seams that would have taken Jane hours upon hours, bent over her project in low evening light with the fabric in her left hand while her right wove the needle in and out. Jane may have lived to see the distribution of home sewing machines in the 1850s. Maybe she, too, experienced the thrill of pressing her foot on the lever at the bottom of the machine, over and over, and watching the magic of the needle rising and falling into fabric, drawing a stitch in its wake.

See how, in Powers's quilt, some of the stars have moon-slivered centers? And some are flowered? Powers was using what she had on hand—scraps and castoffs—and carefully coordinating the fabrics she chose with the spirit of the image—a night sky, a bloom of a shooting star, its white burst leading its streak.

In 1972, when Gladys-Marie Fry saw one of Harriet Powers's quilts for the first time, she was taken to the "museum's lower level," and watched, in awe, as the quilt was lifted from its box: "[The curator] took me to a storage facility on the museum's lower level. There I watched as she removed the quilt from a box and from its acid-free paper. I am not sure I was breathing while watching this process. But at last the quilt was spread out on a worktable and I was handed a pair of white gloves. Then the curator said, 'I have to return to make an important phone call. Do you mind staying here by yourself for a few minutes?' At that she left, and, alone now, I touched the quilt, felt the raw, unprocessed cotton inside, looked closely at the various pieces of calico and other types of fabric Harriet Powers had used, and examined her quilting stitches, which I observed were fairly large to accommodate the raw cotton in the middle layer."

The second quilt that we know Powers made, held in Washington, D.C., at the Smithsonian, was made with batting the unprocessed cotton that came from the fields where her family lived and worked, when they were enslaved by a small-scale farmer in Georgia. Cotton was picked in the fields and brought to the cabin, where the family plucked out the seeds by hand, and then laid the carded cotton onto the backing to provide a batting before the top was added; finally, it would have been quilted. Powers's mother would card and spin cotton into thread that the master's wife then wove into cloth. Batting—the cotton in the center of the quilt—was processed in the textile mills along with fabric. But for this quilt, the cotton was left unprocessed, sewn into the center of the quilt as close to the bolls from the field as one could get. The Boston quilt, Ulrich explains, has a lining but no batting in the center, and so it isn't formally quilted—the stitches that go through all three layers in the final process of making a quilt—because there's nothing that needs to be held together in the layers of the fabric. And its dimensions are all wrong for a bed quilt. This quilt, Laurel Thatcher Ulrich argues, was made to be displayed as art, not as a bedcover.

Fry was the first to make the connection between the Smithsonian's quilt and the Boston MFA's quilt, and the first to research Harriet Powers further, to learn about her life, finding her last name and then her photograph as well as the narratives she gave to Jennie Smith, who bought Powers's quilts. That day in the museum in 1972, she writes: "My thoughts tumbled over each other. Harriet Powers's hands had touched this fabric, composed this square. The connection I felt with her at that moment was mystical. Then the curator returned. As I left, I remember thanking her for agreeing to see me on an unscheduled visit, but my mind was in a daze. There are two of them! There are two of them!" She used to sit in the Smithsonian each week, visiting with the quilt just as

Powers used to visit Smith's house to see the art she had to sell to help support her family.

Laurel Thatcher Ulrich writes that this research on Harriet Powers's quilt that was "begun in the 1970s" spawned interest "among art historians, folklorists, collectors, and quilters themselves," and set these makers off in various pursuits. She notes that this research "is still bearing fruit today, in landmark exhibits like those featuring the quilts of Gee's Bend, Alabama, or in the establishment of community-based projects like the quilting collective at Tutwiler, Mississippi." Powers's quilt has become "an American icon," and the Smithsonian "recently displayed it in an exhibit of 'American treasures' alongside Thomas Jefferson's writing desk, Thomas Edison's lightbulb, and Dorothy's slippers from *The Wizard of Oz.*" When Alice Walker saw the quilt in the seventies, she wrote, "In the Smithsonian Institution in Washington, D.C., there hangs a quilt unlike any other in the world. In fanciful, inspired, and yet simple and identifiable figures, it portrays the story of the Crucifixion. It is considered rare, beyond price. Though it follows no known pattern of quiltmaking, and though it is made of bits and pieces of worthless rags, it is obviously the work of a person of powerful imagination and deep spiritual feeling." She writes that the quilt was made by an "anonymous Black woman in Alabama," as this was before the story had been unfolded by Kyra E. Hicks, Gladys Marie-Fry, and others. But like the historians tracing Harriet Powers's and her quilts' stories, Walker recognized artistry in the quilt. As Ulrich writes, Powers was the product of her time, focusing on "sunbursts" and other images that were popular when she made the quilt; Powers's work is the product of a decidedly American quilt-making tradition, with its range of patterns and styles, Ulrich emphasizes, concurring with Cuesta Benberry to dispel the myth that had been espoused earlier, that Powers's aesthetic is a Dahomian one, brought from Africa. Powers was part of communities of women who were making quilts with similar images, but Powers is unique, Ulrich argues, as an artist who "innovate[ed]" on the forms that were popular, making them singular, her own. The colors she chose, the way she portrayed the whale and giraffes she likely saw in a circus, and the people staring up at the stars in fear—these choices are distinctly hers. These quilts are evidence of Powers's aesthetic; her combination of fabrics and figures, her arrangement and ordering of stories make these "sermon[s] in patchwork" art.

It was a spring day, and I'd wanted to see the quilt ever since I first learned of it years ago, and then suddenly realized that it was here at the Boston MFA, just half an hour from my apartment. It was ten years ago, I'd just started quilting, and I was having a hard year. Working with the fabrics—the bright colors, the cotton in my hands—had been a saving grace. I came home from work, sat down at the tiny quilting sewing machine I kept at my dining room table, and I sewed—first quilts, and then, with the scraps, pictures. They were the only thing that made me feel better.

I went to the museum because this quilt had been on my mind for years, and I suspect I'd internalized it. I'd gazed at images in books for years, devoured Kyra E. Hicks' publication of sources connected to the quilts. I probably started making story quilts out of scraps because of my love for Harriet Powers's quilts. When I visualize her quilt and the stories of her falling stars in the Boston MFA quilt, I fall in love all over again with the colors that riff and fall together and make a sense of tension, a story, of their own. When Powers' quilt was shown at the Cotton Exposition in 1895, some people complained that her colors were too outrageous, that she must have been color-blind not to have seen the way they glared against each other. When I look at the quilts in a book, I love the colors, though I'm not seeing them as they would have been back then—vivid, saturated. Now they've faded under the years of sunlight they endured before they were bought by the museums.

I walked through the museum, winding my way between objects in the folk-art exhibit. The quilt was only on display for a few weeks at a time, to protect it from sunlight. This was a sliver of time, my chance to see it. Finally, at the back of the exhibit, on one of the side walls, there it was: Harriet Powers's work of art, and there, thanks to the work of Kyra E. Hicks and Gladys Marie-Fry, was Harriet Powers's name and birth date and photograph, along with a description of each of the squares.

The back of the exhibit hall was dim, and there was a glass door leading to a hallway to the right of the quilt. A family walked behind me and through the door. I squatted down on the floor, dropped my things, and sat down cross-legged in front of the quilt. I lost my breath, stunned to see it in person—the people looking at the stars, Job, the whale, the animals of Noah's Ark, the strip of stained fabric on the right side. I assumed the fabric was stained after the quilt was made, but as the stain is bound by the seams, it was made beforehand. "Why did she choose stained fabric?" asks Ulrich—questions to which we still don't have answers. I looked at the red stars against the black square, at Job's coffin, at the perfectly spotted giraffes, thinking about how she must have picked up that polka-dotted fabric from a pile, and settled on it with satisfaction, knowing it would become those creatures. How she cut the shapes out one by one, and then sewed them on, with patience, turning each square into a story.

I sat there for a long time, staring at the quilt, in the quiet space at the back of the folk-art section, thinking about the long trail, the many days, between Harriet Powers's birth in 1837 and this moment in what we call the new millennium. Now, almost another decade later, I think of that moment when I got to see the quilt firsthand, and I imagine Eliza, Minerva, Juba, and Jane, and the objects they could have made—sweetgrass baskets, inventively embellished clothes, quilts—that just haven't survived, or if someone, somewhere, cherishes something made by an unknown woman, her hands that created that piece, which will never be attributed to her. Maybe, as Alice Walker argues, these four women, like so many, redirected their artistic skills into "everyday" objects and practices—making a perfect loaf of brown bread each morning, keeping fresh-cut flowers she'd grown herself on the dining room table, pulling dead buds from the blooming flowers in the garden. Maybe the woman who made the objects isn't unknown at all, but is someone's great great great great great grandmother, and the stories of her life have been carried down orally through each generation. It's possible that somewhere, Eliza's, Minerva's, Juba's, and Jane's stories are still being told today, by their descendants.

I used to resent Susan and Hasell's archive, the hexagon quilt that's been so carefully preserved to tell the story of the white family, while silencing the stories of the enslaved women who made Susan's life function and helped build her family's wealth that carried her through her own personal tragedy. But I find myself turning now, as grateful for the archive as I am resentful of its erasures. Susan and Hasell, and Winthrop and Hilton, mentioned in their letters the enslaved people whose names might otherwise have been lost. They're there in the letters, and in the contracts and estate records, their bodies misappropriated, disrespected, objectified—but also, ironically, their lives are more fully described there, too. If it weren't for the advertisement of Jane's sale, for example, I'd never have known that she was a seamstress. If it weren't for Hilton's and Winthrop's hateful and dismissive notes about Minerva's new baby, I'd never have known that she had a child that October; I wouldn't have discovered his name unless he'd been listed in the sale alongside his sister Cecilia—a baby boy named Samon. I'm still angry at the ways the women are objectified by whites throughout the archive; in every instance in which Winthrop, Hilton, or Susan mention the women, and in every instance in which I find the enslaved women's names in contracts, they are being documented as objects and possessions. I'm frustrated that I can't find more about them because they were seen by Susan and Hasell, and the culture more generally, as *only* objects with prices and costs. I'm angry at Susan, Winthrop, and Hilton for betraying what I used to think were their abolitionist roots. But the mention of the names of the enslaved people offers an opening, to tell a different story than the one Susan and Hasell intended to preserve. The beauty of the tenderly preserved quilt tops is a frustration, too, in light of so much from the enslaved peoples' lives that was not preserved; nonetheless, the quilt tops provide an unexpected key to stories I wouldn't otherwise have known: Minerva, Eliza, Juba, Cecilia, Samon, Jane, William, George, John, Bishroom, and Boston. These are people we can come to know, even if ever so slightly. And with each detail, we learn that they lived full lives in spite of the conditions into which they were born.

8
Even There

The Fox, a sloop, *The Betsey, The George, The Polly, The Harvest, The Friendship, The Nancy, Trial, Washington*—all sloops except *The George*, which is a schooner. In 1811 and 1813 in Charleston Harbor, there are *The Rambler, The Cock, The Dolphin, The Leader, The Little Sarah, The Patty*—sloops and schooners, too. In 1835, there's a sloop called *Susan*, in 1836, *The Teazer*, in the 1840s, *The Bibilla, Eunice Ann, Mary-Gold, Abby, Northerner*, and *West Wind*; in the 1870s, there are *The White Star, The Whiz*, a steamer, *The Wild Goose II, The Wilful*, and the *Witch of the Waves*. This last sloop/schooner, *Witch of the Waves*, built in Edgartown, Massachusetts, in 1873; there's a renowned *Witch of the Wave* schooner that was launched from New Hampshire in 1851. I think of the lore of water witches, mermaids who could control the sea, and the busts of women set on the prow as if to push the ship forward; I think of James Fenimore Cooper's 1830 novel *The Water Witch*, in which a Frenchwoman is kidnapped by a pirate and then saved by her beau, who follows the ship to rescue her, a romance.

Small mercantile sea-craft building was big business, and every ship is traceable. The shipbuilders, owners, and ports all dutifully kept logbooks that can lead us to the stories of what was carried in their berths—what sort of cargo, and whether that cargo was sometimes human. Studies have been made of these ships, digital illustrations of the trips that slavers made across the sea, by decade, have been developed, so that we can see the scale of this trade. If you live on the East Coast of the United States, in any state, you can find this history along your shores. It takes only a little digging.

Did you know that the first slaving ship to sail from the United States was built in Massachusetts, the state we hail as one of our most progressive? It was built in Marblehead, a town built on rocks with darling colorful colonial houses that rise up from the shoreline. I learned this story from the work of Lisa Braxton and Alex Reid, journalists who describe the *Desire*'s entry to Boston Harbor in 1638, carrying the first enslaved people forcibly brought to these shores in an American-built ship.

In Marblehead and Salem, there's no marker about the *Desire*, no note about the salted cod that the fishermen caught there that was shipped to the Caribbean to feed enslaved people on the plantations, no marker about the enslaved people who must have worked along the shoreline and on the small farms in the area, tilling rocky soil to harvest food from the lands where Wampanoag people had always lived, or helping to build ships with their carpentry skills. Instead of marking these histories in Marblehead, there are white wooden plaques on all the houses with the dates the houses were built and the occupations of their builders. There are four yacht clubs, and every night in the summertime, two of them set off heart-stopping cannons at sunset, a tradition locals seem to cherish.

My mother grew up in the town next door, Salem, land of our witch trials, and I learned to sail with my grandfather at the "working man's" boat club that was in what used to be the French-Canadian neighborhood, where he grew up speaking French with other immigrant families; this neighborhood had become, by the time I was in high school, the Puerto Rican neighborhood. My grandfather would bemoan the changing neighborhood, the new violence he perceived the Puerto Ricans to have brought, forgetting that his parents, too, had come to this country from another place and spoken a foreign tongue. French was his first language. I recognized and challenged his racism, but I didn't know how deeply rooted racism was in that place. I didn't know, back in high school—nor was I ever taught—the history of enslavement that northerners own.

I drove over the bridge from South County, Rhode Island, out of the woods where my house had sat tucked into trees (and before that, when the woods had been clearcut, set between fields) for almost two hundred eighty years. Every hurricane and northeaster snowstorm, I marveled at its fortitude. It still had most of its old leaded glass windowpanes, and the original wide pine floor planks. I never lost power in that house, even when everyone around me had. Maybe it was luck; maybe it was protected, somehow. I find myself beginning to believe in spirits.

I wound up the coast, past stone walls in green fields, past sections of woods, and then the bushes and trees fall away for the great reveal of the sea to the east. It sparkles, a promise in the distance. I think of all the people who were carried across that sea, by their own volition and against their will. I drove east, over the bridge to Jamestown Island, following the same trails George Washington followed so long ago when he met with Rochambeau, and then over another bridge to reach Newport. I turned into the cemetery that lines the main road that tourists drive all summer; they idle at the stoplight beside the cemetery, waiting to get to the restaurants, bars, and sailboats on the harbor.

I emerged from the car into the humidity of a hot July day, and met up with three women, one of their daughters, and Keith Stokes, a local historian. For decades, Keith has been researching and documenting God's Little Acre, which he and his wife, Theresa Guzmán-Stokes, write about on their website, calling it "America's Colonial African Cemetery." On this afternoon, Keith told us stories of this place that you won't hear at the docks where people pay hundreds to hold their boats for a night, nor at the bars where a man working the raw bar knifes open oysters and tourists drink into the morning, nor at the glamorous hotels buttressed by blue hydrangeas that spill over white picket fences and meandering stone walls. This cemetery stands outside the old town, protected by an iron gate along that busy main road and up a sloping, grassy hill.

Keith Stokes has an archive. He does the work Franklin did in saving Susan's and Hasell's quilt top and preserving, documenting, and donating the family collection of letters and furniture; he is a careful curator. Keith's family has been in Newport since the 1800s, and he has photographs of his relatives sitting on great lawns, waists cinched in corsets, necks prettied up in ties, children in summer whites. He knows the stories of his ancestors who came from Jamaica, has visited the plantation where they were enslaved in the 1700s, has been made an honorary citizen of that country. He can hold photographs of his father and grandfather and great-grandfather. He is uncommonly lucky to know the whole of his past, to be able to hold the document that marked the 1770 "installation of Reverend Samuel Hopkins of the First Congregational Church in Newport," to show an image of his great-uncle, Newport's first "dentist of African heritage," who graduated from the Howard University College of Dentistry in 1896.

Few African Americans can so fully trace their genealogies, as Keith can, back to the days of slavery. It's often possible to trace to the Civil War, when the Freedmen's Bureau was established and kept records of formerly enslaved people. But before 1865, the trail usually slips away because, of course, people were treated as property, bought and sold, not permitted to take last names, not permitted to stay with their families—sold apart from each other, trails lost and broken. I followed Eliza and Minerva and Juba and Jane from their previous owner to the Crouches to—what at first appeared to be a blank space. Or an opening into what we can only imagine are the threads that lead to their descendants. There are no existing contracts for the women in 1837-8, but the people who bought them are listed in the inventory, revealing where the women next lived. We know that W or Mr. Greer, in either case a city resident, bought Minerva, Samon, and Cecilia—so Minerva was able to stay with her children for the time being. George was sold to James S. Burges, who died in 1850; there's no mention of George in Burges' estate records. George's trace in the paper archives ends. Jane was sold to Mr. Walker. Did she sew for his wife? Work as a maid or housekeeper? Winthrop appears to have kept Eliza for some time, probably continuing to rent her out to the man who had been renting her. John, age seven, was sold to Winthrop, and there's no record of Juba's sale. Maybe she got to stay with the boy who was probably her son, John, as well as Sorenzo, if Winthrop bought her and her sixteen year old son, too. I know so little about Eliza, except that she, Minerva, and George were allowed, when they were owned by Susan and Hasell, to rent themselves out and keep part of their earnings, the majority going to Susan and Hasell. Did they save enough to eventually buy their freedom, or that of their families?

When Keith and I first met, months earlier, at the Empire coffee shop (a fitting name for this story) in Newport, he told me he has a doll from his ancestors' days of enslavement. This doll dates to 1830. She wears a brown scarf on her head, a belt over her apron and skirt, a plaid shirt, and a pair of bright red shoes, which peek out from beneath the skirt like a song of hope. How have those shoes stayed so vibrant in the course of almost two hundred years?

She has two eyes stitched on either side of a nose that juts out from her face with the gift of stuffing, and two high cheekbones. Her shirt is fraying at the edges, a piece made to do for a doll's top, gathered at the neck, and tucked into the dirt-stained skirt and apron. This, too, is a raw-edged scrap, not like Harriet Powers's pride of an apron with its carefully hemmed edges and two sunbursts appliquéd or embroidered onto its crisp white surface. But in the doll's era, each piece of fabric would have been a treasure. The doll's bright red toes are worn, as though she's walked or danced in a child's hands, moving across the surface of a table or the ground. Maybe, at one time, this doll had a friend or a husband with whom she walked and played. Maybe this doll accompanied her child to bed each night, tucked under the child's arm to comfort her to sleep, comforts changing little from then to now. I think of Cecilia, Minerva's baby girl, who might have played with a doll like this one, made by her mother or by Jane, from scraps of her other projects. I imagine the tenderness with which a woman stitched this doll together, the same love that inspired the embroidery of a sack by Ruth Middleton, recounting her great grandmother Rose's gift to her daughter Ashley when the little girl was sold away from her.

Years after I saw a picture of Keith Stokes's doll, I encountered a doll from the same era, 1830, in Galena, Illinois, hundreds of miles from God's Little Acre and Newport, Rhode Island. I had followed Joe McGill to Galena, and found myself standing with a group of students in a house built in 1828. I was there to learn about the Kinzies, who came there from Missouri, and the enslaved people they brought with them. Of course, just eight years before the Kinzies arrived in Galena, in 1820, Missouri had been made a part of the Union through the Missouri Compromise, which permitted Missouri to join as a slave state, in tandem with Maine, a free state, and established the Mason Dixon line above which no slave states could exist. And yet, in 1828, the Kinzies brought their enslaved people to Illinois, a supposedly northern and free state, and their enslaved people remained enslaved.

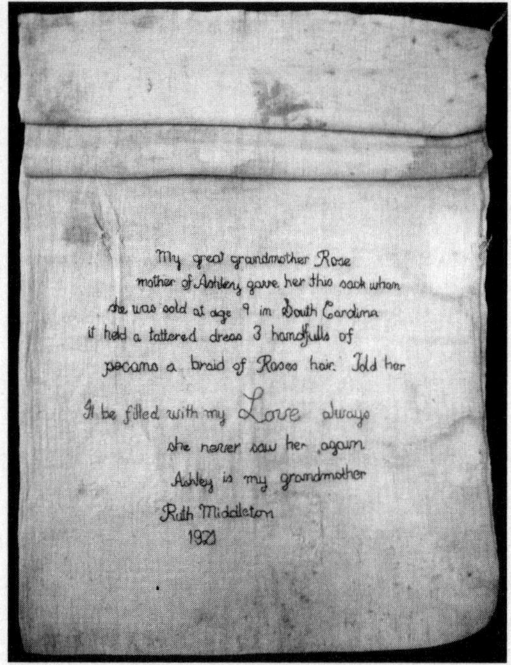

Cloth embroidered in memory of Rose and her daughter Ashley; this piece is from the Middleton Place in South Carolina and is now exhibited at the National Museum of African American History and Culture in Washington, D.C.

We visited Galena on a rainy April day, and the interior of the house felt even colder than the exterior. The group shivered through the tour, our arms crossed tight against our bodies. I imagined how a woman named Louisa, who lived and worked here, would have felt to have woken in the house early in the morning to light the fires, the chill she would have felt through her dress and petticoats, the wool shawl around her shoulders barely enough to stave off a piece of the chill.

On the floor of one of the front bedrooms, beside the small child's bed, there was a tiny four-poster bed, within which lay this doll with a walnut head, tucked underneath a tiny handmade quilt of one-inch hexagons whose pattern was similar to Susan and Hasell's quilt. These were calico hexagon flowers surrounded by white hexagons that made the "background" for the flowers. The calicos were flowered, red gingham, brown zigzags, so similar to the quilt I'd known these six years. A child must have made this quilt for practice, or her mother, teaching her child as she stitched for the doll, making her home the domestic space into which she'd have been proud to invite friends. This bedroom where the doll lay under her quilt was beside the front stairs, which led to the front parlor and front entryway.

Twenty yards away, toward the back of the house, there was another room under the gables, a room through which the chimney rose from the kitchen; this room was beside the back stairs, and Joseph McGill, the leader of The Slave Dwelling Project, who brought us here, had been waiting to see these stairs. Downstairs, minutes earlier, he'd asked our guide about these back stairs when she pointed out the fine front entrance and the fine front stairs and the piano that the lady of the house used to play.

Everything in this house is from the 1830s, when the Kinzies lived here, though these objects didn't belong to their family; they'd been gathered and installed here to replicate how the home might have looked then. John Kinzie was an Indian agent, sent to Illinois to "manage" the Sauk, Ho-Chunk, and Winnebago nations who lived in the area. John's wife, Juliette, wrote an account of her time in Illinois, describing the Native Americans in all the offensive language that was common then—they were drunks, savages, children to be tamed and tended to by her husband, John. She wanted to observe their burial rituals, she mocked what she called "a powwow," misattributing its purpose. She had nicknames for some of the people she respected least, and when we visited, the tour guide was eager to repeat these cruel nicknames for us, as if these were the names by which the people had wished to be known. When the guide told the names to us, she paused and chuckled, as if she was waiting for us to laugh with her.

That room under the gables and beside the back stairs held a bed, a simpler bed frame than the one in the white couples' room, and covering the bed was a quilt with great orange shapes against white.

"Who lived in this room?" we asked the guide.

"This would have been the servant's room," she said.

"What nationality was the servant?" someone asked.

"Well, we don't know."

"Was Louisa African American?"

"I think, probably, but I don't know," she said.

She was looking down, she didn't look at us. She couldn't acknowledge this and didn't know how to dodge it. She knew why we were there. We were there to see Louisa's room, to see where Louisa lived and worked and ate and slept and, I hope, loved and dreamed and found some happiness. We were there to know the lives of the enslaved people as much as we knew the lives of the white people who owned them. This guide worked for the Daughters of the American Revolution. I wondered if she'd ever questioned the cruel portrayals of Native Americans that she'd been taught to replay, if she'd tried to learn more than this slant of the story. Maybe she didn't want to acknowledge the truth to herself. Maybe acknowledging that the Kinzies held enslaved people would change this woman's perception of herself, her family. I didn't know. I didn't know anything about this woman. I only knew the story she was telling.

> "Newport Gardner arrived in Newport from Annanabo at twelve years and was enslaved by the Gardners. He learned French. He learned to read and write in English. He played music."
>
> —Keith Stokes

When I first met Joseph McGill three years ago, it was in Charleston, at the Old Slave Mart Museum, where he and Christine Mitchell worked as docents. In Charleston, I'd spent the morning at the Historical Society, scrolling through files to find mentions of the Crouches or Williams brothers, and emerged into the winter heat frustrated by how little I'd found, saddened by a document I'd sat with for an hour, and eager to wander. I left a snowy and cold January Rhode Island to come to warm Charleston, where the flowers bloomed and the palmettos blew in the wind; my friends had joked that this was the perfect time to research in the South. I thought of Susan and Emily, coming down to Charleston most winters for the rest of their lives after 1838. This was before I knew that Minerva and Juba died in the city in 1851 and 1874, respectively; they probably never left the state. I wonder, now, if Susan ever saw them again, on her returns south. I wonder if Susan knew the Mr. Greer who owned Minerva, if her brothers socialized with the Greers and saw Minerva at his home. I wonder how Minerva felt if she ever saw Susan again, if she and Eliza and Juba were relieved to have been sold away from Susan's family, if they despised her for breaking them apart from friends or relatives they might have known all their lives.

Released from the sterile air of the library, I walked through the city, down to the French quarter, past mansions with their iron gates and stone walls, all the way down to the battery, thinking of Eliza, Minerva, Jane, and Juba, who walked these streets almost two centuries before. I walked to the harbor, along the battery, thinking of Winthrop's daily dawn walks in the 1840s, resenting him his self-important letters about his morning, constitutionals when his daily work as a cotton factor came at the cost of so many peoples' lives.

I wandered inland again, until I found the narrow cobblestone street where the Old Slave Mart Museum sits in its original site, when it was called Ryan's Slave Mart. At the Old Slave Mart Museum, Joe and Christine welcomed me in and sent me through. I was nervous. The document I'd read for an hour at the historical society was a list of people enslaved on a plantation. It was handwritten, in that loopy nineteenth century cursive I'd come to know so well in all the letters and documents I'd find. That was my first encounter with such a document, the first such object I'd touched, and I read with sorrow each of the names listed in the plantation records. Mary, thirty nine years, Rose, seventeen, Diana, twelve, Jane, ten, and in the right hand column, Joe, sixty-five years, Isaac, thirty-seven, John, thirty-one, Betty, twenty-eight and "unsound." Labeled like a horse—sound versus unsound—Betty was injured, sick, or disabled. In vertical script down the column around Betty's name are the repeated words "Prime." I could see the wavering line of the pen in the scrawl of words, the loops of the *J* and *B*, the flourish on the *d* at the end of "unsound," and there was something in this particularity, in seeing the human hand in this list of peoples' names and ages, the sickening meticulousness with which this person recorded all the people who would be put up for sale. Seeing the document, I could see this era, could imagine this plantation and the people who lived there in January 1863. They were scheduled to be sold February 5th, even though they'd been declared legally free January 1st. I imagined as I read this list each person—a woman with a skirt blowing in the wind in the middle of a yellow field, a man walking across a field with two children by his side, a girl who walks into a cabin at the end of a long day, her legs and arm aching, and sighs as she sits down. I read this list, touch the paper, run my hand over each word. There is a little girl, two year old Eliza, marked as another object for sale, and I sink into this sorrow.

Inside the Old Slave Mart Museum, I wandered into a low-ceilinged room with brick walls. Three people could have spread their arms, touched hands, and spanned the length of the room. In this room, in the 1850s, dozens of people were crammed together each day, bodies naked or barely clad, waiting to be sold. Behind this building, there was a morgue, where all the dead were sent, and there was a kitchen, to feed the living just enough to keep them alive for the sale. Walking into this space, it was impossible not to imagine the people who waited here, who struggled to survive. It was impossible not to feel the weight of what happened here.

In the 1850s, enslaved people were still needed for the cotton trade, as well as for rice and tobacco cultivation. The cotton business continued to rise with more and more mills up north, and it was here in South Carolina and the other "cotton states" that it was grown. However, it had become distasteful to sell enslaved people from the steps of the Old Exchange Building and elsewhere in the market neighborhood, as they'd been doing until then. Abolitionists visited, foreigners visited, and looked with disdain upon the auction block where Charleston's slave traders made their sales loudly and publicly, hollering out each person's attributes and their prices, allowing those interested buyers to examine each man, woman, and child before making their purchases. From 1850 on, the Old Slave Mart saved the master class that embarrassment. Rather than using the public auction block, enslaved people were kept at Ryan's Slave Mart, and sold from storefronts in the neighborhood. Christine took me outside at the end of my tour to show me the houses that were storefronts.

"That one," she said, pointing to a pink-painted stucco house with a torch lit beside its doorway. It was the coziest looking house, I would have thought, before I knew it was a place for selling people. "That one was one of the storefronts," she said.

The lantern's flame becomes more ominous. Christine turned and said, "And that one, and that one up there," pointing on and on down the street.

We stood on the cobblestones that enslaved people carried from the harbor and set down here, laid into the mud and muck of the dirt road to make this pleasingly neat paved street where the master class and the brown elite could build their fine houses, where horses clomped, pulling carriages for hundreds of years. The stones under our feet were brought here because they were used for ballast, to balance the shifting weight of the people moving inside a brig; shipments of inanimate cargo wouldn't have needed such ballast. Ships came into the port after waiting out the quarantine at Sullivan's Island to be sure none of the surviving passengers were carrying a plague into the city, and the enslaved people who had survived that long passage were then forced to carry the stones used for ballast onto these streets. Now, when divers find shipwrecks with ballast in their holds, they know it was a slaver that sank, that within that hull what could not survive time and the ocean's tides and the scavengers therein were the bodies of people who drowned at sea, their graves the Middle Passage. I see some of these ballast irons at the National Museum of African American History and Culture in Washington, D.C., in the lowest level of the museum where objects tell the story of enslavement; a small room to one side is full of the sound of the ocean, with low ceilings, the feeling of a ship's low-lit hull.

John Potter and Family Served Tea by a Slave. The Rhode Island Potter family were involved in the slave trade. One of their family cemeteries was near my home in Kingston, formerly Little Rest, RI.

As always, in every part of this story, there is as much resistance and triumph as there is pain. Part of what made slave voyages so "risky" for the white traders was the ever-present threat of revolt, which often came to pass. By "ever-present threat," I mean the likelihood that a person would rise up to protest the abuse, the likelihood that people who had never met before, who spoke different languages and came from different regions of West Africa as ships traveled up and down the coastline to purchase people to fill their holds, would come to collaborate with one another—across these language barriers, and in spite of the trauma they were enduring. One of the most successful revolts was on the *Amistad*. It took place in 1839, within Minerva's, Eliza's, Juba's, and Jane's lifetimes. A group of fifty-three enslaved people, led by a man named Cinqué, rebelled aboard a schooner headed for Haiti. They had been captured and sold from Sierra Leone, sent across the sea for weeks in the ship's hold, and then sold again in Havana, Cuba, and loaded onto another ship, the *Amistad*—all this even though the international trade was abolished by European nations and the United States decades earlier. "You call us rebels we were spoons/in that ship for so long the wood/dark, drowned as the men who/made it from song sold on land/like ships like us christened/out of water," Kevin Young writes in his book of poetry, *Ardency: A Chronicle of the Amistad Rebels*. Young tells the story of the people who resisted. "one day we took/the wheel from men with eyes of/water we turned the ship towards/the rising sun . . . /that night the sailors turned us towards a Newborn/England . . ."

The people aboard this ship did not succumb to the torture whites doled out. They rallied together, in spite of their language barriers, and succeeded in killing much of the crew and taking control of the ship. Without knowledge of the sea or sailing, they couldn't control their passage without the crew to navigate them. The slavers steered the ship each night after the rebels, mostly Mendi men, Young writes, directed it during the day to head toward the sun, home, the African continent from which they'd been taken. The ship was discovered and captured off the coast of New York, and the prisoners were held until their Connecticut court case was resolved. Finally, they were released, and in 1842, abolitionists raised money to send those thirty-five people who had survived back home to Sierra Leone.

I wonder if Minerva and Juba heard of this case, if they saw stories about the people in Charleston papers, or heard about it from friends at church or at the market; I imagine that the story of the Africans' eventual triumph gave them hope.

When I leave the Slave Mart Museum, I go to the harbor and feel the breeze on my face. I look at the water with new eyes, remember what Christine told me, about how she sees these waters as a mass grave, as hundreds of enslaved people who were dead or dying were pushed overboard as the ships came to port. I walk through the park along the water, relishing the ocean breeze and the shade of palmettos. A ship is making its way to the open sea. I stop to read a sign that bears the picture of a black man. His name is Robert Smalls, and he's a sailor who stole a ship, the Planter, during the Civil War, navigating his family to the freedom the Union navy offered. I imagine how it must have felt to steer past the Confederate checkpoints, how his heart must have raced, and the sense of relief and triumph he must have felt when he and his family made it to safety.

> "Arthur Flagg employed other Africans. He was a leader. He had a factory on the outskirts of Newport, on Thames Street, where people worked as chord-winders, using hemp and heating it with molasses. He employed fifteen people, ten of them Africans. His son was a teacher in the school."
>
> —Keith Stokes

In the Newport cemetery, God's Little Acre, we wished for a breeze as we walked amidst the graves. The little girl and two of the women in the group—professors and writers—wore broad-brimmed hats to shield them from the sun; another held a piece of paper over her head. As we walked, Keith told us the stories of the people whose graves are marked in slate; these stones are interspersed with those made of granite or marble, the more durable materials that wealthier people could buy. Slate was cheaper than other kinds of stone, but the sadness is that it's the first to disintegrate, so the African and African American people's names are fading, the stones falling away in layers. When I asked Keith if they'd do something to preserve them, he said, no, that it seemed wrong to encase them in glass or plastic, that it would be better for them to have been recorded and photographed and to exist as they are, to return to the earth as they will.

Keith told us that in Newport in the eighteenth century, slaves were called "servants."

"We're genteel here," said Keith with a sly smile, and two women laughed, in on the joke.

I studied the grave of a child, William, son of Samuel and Animy, who died at thirty-four hours old on August 4, 1739, and that of Hector Butcher, servant to Ann Butcher; he died at thirty-seven years old, and came from Barbados. I study the gravestone whose top is stained in a drip of white, for Violet Hammond, the wife of Cape Coast James, who died Sep the 3rd, 1772, aged 20 years.

Keith reminded us that in the late eighteenth century, there were twenty-eight distilleries in Newport, cranking out the New England rum that was so beloved around the world that it was a necessary ingredient in the trade for human lives. Jay Coughtry writes, "As in other branches of Rhode Island commerce, the slave trade existed because a few enterprising colonial merchants found a profitable market for the colony's rum." Rhode Island was an important part of the triangle trade for its rum, and later, for the domestic slave trade with the textile mills that fueled cotton plantations in the South. The state produced not just the pretty calicos in Susan's quilt, and the slightly lower quality but still fine "teakettle" print that Minerva, Eliza, Juba, and Jane probably wore, but also the rough negro cloth, which enslaved people sewed and wore in the fields on the vast southern plantations where they picked more cotton to be sent to the North—this endless cycle that bound North and South and made the North just as culpable for nineteenth-century slavery as the South. No one was clean of slavery, not even Moses Brown. He was one of the backers of Slater Mill, the first mill that made use of the cotton gin in the United States. This would launch the American Industrial Revolution and spawn the founding of many more mills in New England. This was in 1790. And yet, in 1775, fifteen years earlier, Moses Brown converted to Quakerism, and had committed his life to ending slavery. He worked to pass the Gradual Abolition of Slavery act that would slowly—painfully slowly—free enslaved people in Rhode Island. He worked to ban the importation of African slaves to the United States—the work his family had been doing for generations. And yet, he helped found the mill that would help ensure the vitality of the domestic slave trade for many years to come by producing far greater yields of cotton cloth than had ever been produced before, requiring vast quantities of cotton to be grown in the southern fields, and the people to plant, tend, and harvest it. How did he live with this contradiction, of perpetuating slavery in the southern "Cotton States" when he'd worked so hard to disable it in New England? Did he see the effect of the mills in his lifetime on enslaved people in the South, or was domestic slavery a distant evil to him, disconnected from his own family's involvement in the international slave trade in Rhode Island? Was the allure of the money he knew he'd make from the mills too strong to resist?

> John Camino's father was a tribal chief in El Amina and asked a merchant to take John to America and educate him. Instead, John was enslaved, and then bought his own freedom with lottery winnings. He was recruited to educate and convert Africans to Christianity by the Congregational Quaker Community, and went on to become a Rhode Island privateer. He was killed at the Battle of Block Island.
>
> —Keith Stokes

In the seventeenth and eighteenth centuries, before the cotton gin's invention, our nation (before it was considered a nation and just after) was built in the northern colonies with the labor of enslaved people. In Newport, enslaved people lived in the same houses as their owners because there wasn't enough space for them elsewhere. If you've ever visited Newport, you know that the houses are nestled together in town, sometimes just a small gasp of a breath between one and the next. Their wooden siding is painted brick red, sky blue, brown, white, green—historically accurate colors. They've been carefully tended over the years, and carefully preserved. These houses rise up for blocks behind the shops on the main street that runs along the harbor, and then there's the top of the hill where the town levels out, and beyond, the mansions of the Gilded Age that line the other side of the shore. In the colonial houses, enslaved people slept in attics, small spaces that might be used today as a pantry—anywhere there was a nook—and worked as skilled laborers, cooking, sewing, raising children, firing iron, building houses, fishing, making chocolate.

Time passed, and the American Revolution unfolded, fought by soldiers white, native, and black. Years passed. Rhode Island passed the gradual emancipation laws. There were the compromises, the confrontations, and we were propelled into the Civil War, witnessed by Juba and perhaps Eliza. Keith told the story of Dinah, whose husband, Neptune, fought as part of the first black regiment in the Civil War. The Free African Society claimed that Neptune hadn't paid his dues and therefore wouldn't be given a sum for burial, but Dinah fought the society, sued them, and won. She was able to bury her husband.

Keith said, "Every spring, Newport Africans gathered to elect a governor. The whites called it 'Negro Election Day.'"

Kendall Moore, URI professor and documentary filmmaker, said, "That's so ignorant. [Many of] these people were royalty back home."

People who had been kidnapped from royal families in West Africa did not forget their histories. The annual elections were several days long and included a parade. In order to vote, one needed to own a pig. The election was held under the biggest fig tree in town, as was the tradition in Ghana. When disputes over property, marriage, or other issues arose, people were sent to the leader to resolve it.

I think of Abdulrahman Ibrahim Ibn Sori, whose story is narrated by Mos Def in the film *Prince Among Slaves* in 2006, based on the book by Terry Alford, and of Olaudah Equiano, who told his own story in *The Interesting Narrative of the Life of Olaudah Equiano, or, Gustavus Vassa, the African, Written by Himself.* Olaudah's father was "Embranche," a leader in the Benen community where Olaudah grew up; his father would have been one of those decision makers who heard cases under the tree. Olaudah was kidnapped and brought across the Middle Passage to England, then the West Indies—Barbados—and then Virginia, before being permitted to buy his own freedom by his owner, a Quaker man. Olaudah's autobiography, published in 1789, helped promote abolition and end the international slave trade.

He wrote about his time traveling the world aboard ships: "In twenty-eight days time we arrived in England, and I got clear of this ship. But, being still of a roving disposition, and desirous of seeing as many different parts of the world as I could, I shipped myself soon after, in the same year, as steward on board of a fine large ship, called the *Jamaica*, Captain David Watt; and we sailed from England in December 1771 for Nevis and Jamaica. I found Jamaica to be a very fine large island, well peopled, and the most considerable of the West India islands. There was a vast number of negroes here, whom I found as usual exceedingly imposed upon by the white people, and the slaves punished as in the other islands. . . ." Olaudah Equiano became a merchant and worked as a ship steward and captain. He recorded notes on his travels that became his autobiography, and then traveled to promote his book and the abolition of enslaved people. He's credited with helping to pass Britain's Slave Trade Act of 1807, outlawing the trade; the United States would follow with the Act Prohibiting Importation of Slaves, which took effect in January 1808.

Olaudah Equiano.

Keith says that people were "not slaves but enslaved people. We didn't come as blank slates. We came with our history."

Even in this earlier era of the eighteenth century, free blacks and people who had claimed their own freedom by running away from their owners, fought in the Revolutionary War, helping secure the United States' victory over Britain. The freedom we celebrate each Fourth of July is thanks, in part, to people like this man, whose name is unknown but who stands proud in a Continental Navy uniform, using his skills as a sailor and seaman to help win the war for a country that then, in 1776, didn't guarantee his freedom nor grant him citizenship as a voter and property owner. When he fought this war, the international slave trade was still alive and well, and after the creation of the United States in the Declaration of Independence, the domestic trade would carry on for another eighty years.

Attributed to James Martin, Portrait of a Gentleman, *ca. 1820.*

But Keith Stokes would want the focus of this story not to be on the slave trade itself, but on the accomplishments and what we knew about the inner lives of people who were oppressed, mistreated, tortured, and still prevailed. When I asked him and his wife, Theresa, if we should have markers of the slave trade down at the harbors in Newport and Bristol, to make this history known, they said, "No. That's not going to help our young people today. Our young people need to see the strength of their ancestors, to learn about all the talented people who came here and worked as doctors, skilled craftsmen, talented chocolate makers—these are the individual stories that can give a person pride and hope."

When we left the cemetery in Newport, I drove back over the two bridges—from Newport to Jamestown Island, to South County, the mainland, then through the woods to my house in Kingston, formerly known as Little Rest, where once George Washington stayed—in my very house—on his way to meet with Rochambeau in 1781. My house, like most in my neighborhood, was bordered by an old stone wall and sat amidst the forests of the Great Swamp, five miles north of the sea. In the late 1700s, it would have looked very different, with clear-cut rolling hills of the plantations that produced cheese that was sent to the Caribbean to feed enslaved people. This is the land for which our state is (still) named—Rhode Island and the Providence Plantations. When I take my dog to the Great Swamp, we follow the stone walls that run along the trails, converge in intersections, creating grids that have been erased by trees and brush and time. They

ALL IMAGES: The three Crouch quilt tops (Susan and Hasell composed the one in the middle image together), which began the author's investigation into the lives of Eliza, Juba, and Minerva, the enslaved women who worked for the Crouch family.

ABOVE AND BELOW: Detail of the back of the "hexies" of the Crouch quilt top.

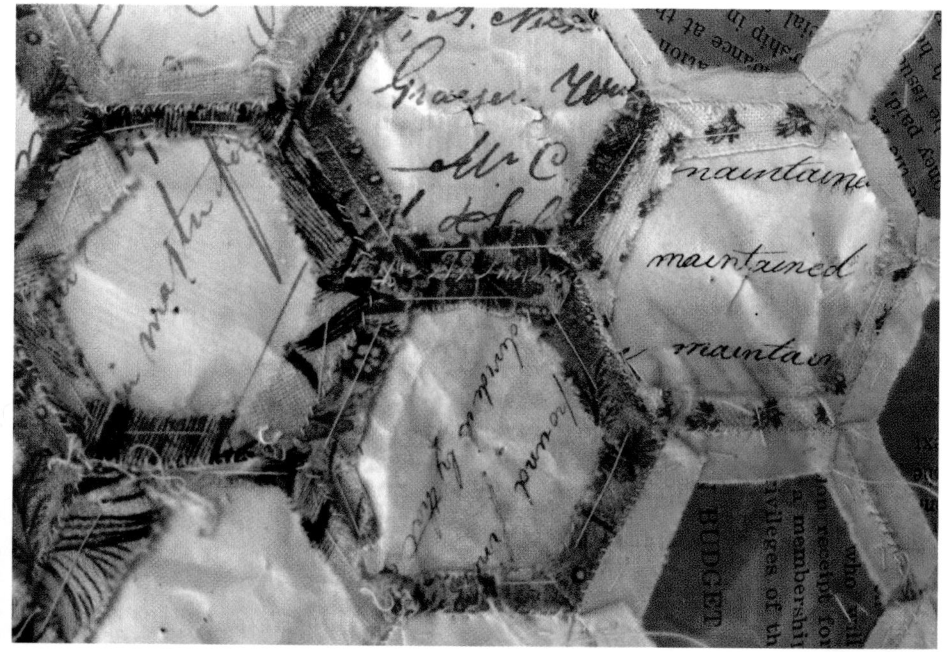

ABOVE: Older snippets, "maintained," and "master for" (probably referring to master for a ship, an oft-repeated phrase in the quilt top papers), enjambed with typed text on yellow paper, probably from the 1930s. BELOW: The three quilt tops. Susan and Hasell likely designed and assembled the one on the far left in the 1830s and prepared many of the hexagons for the other two, which Franklin likely designed and assembled with his family members in the 1930s.

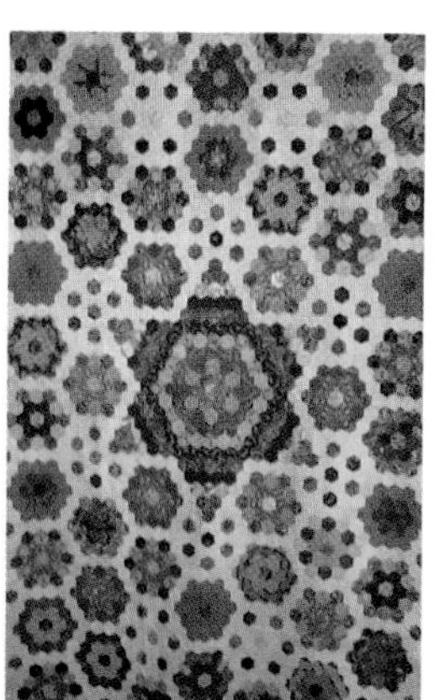

One of Emily Crouch's watercolors, ships in the distance.

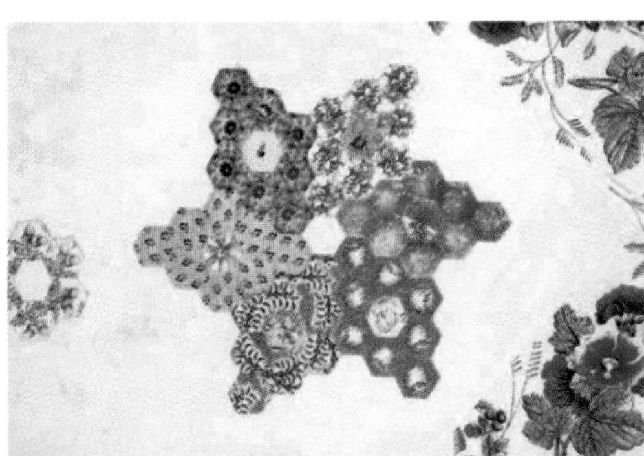

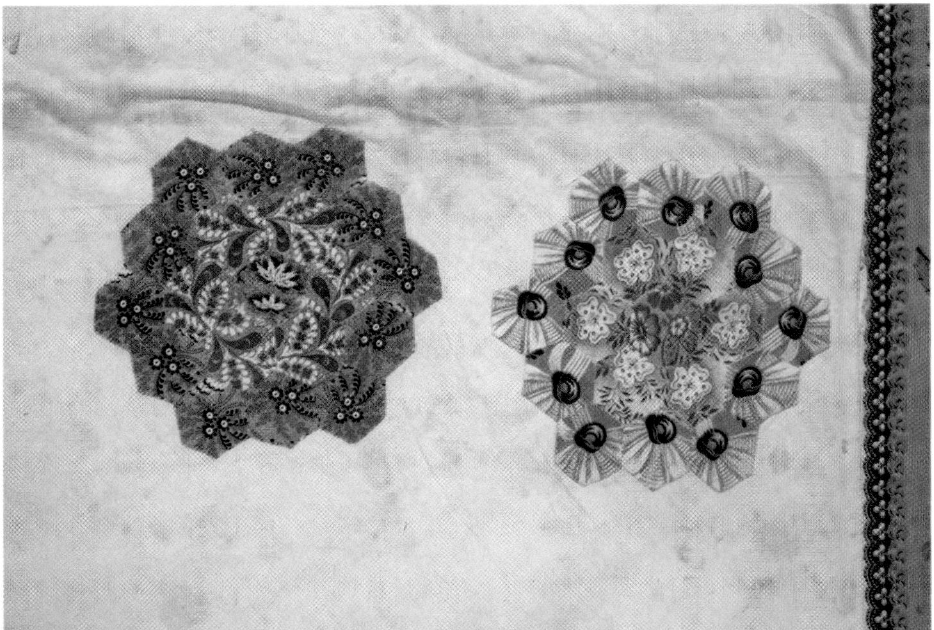

ALL IMAGES: Hexagon flower from quilt made by "a negro seamstress in 1780" on the Darsyton Hall Plantation, Charleston, SC. *Images courtesy of the American Museum in Britain.*

Anna Williams (American, 1927–2010). Quilt, 1995. Cotton, synthetics, 76 ¼ × 61 ½ in. (193.7 × 156.2 cm). Brooklyn Museum, Gift in memory of Horace H. Solomon, 2011.18.

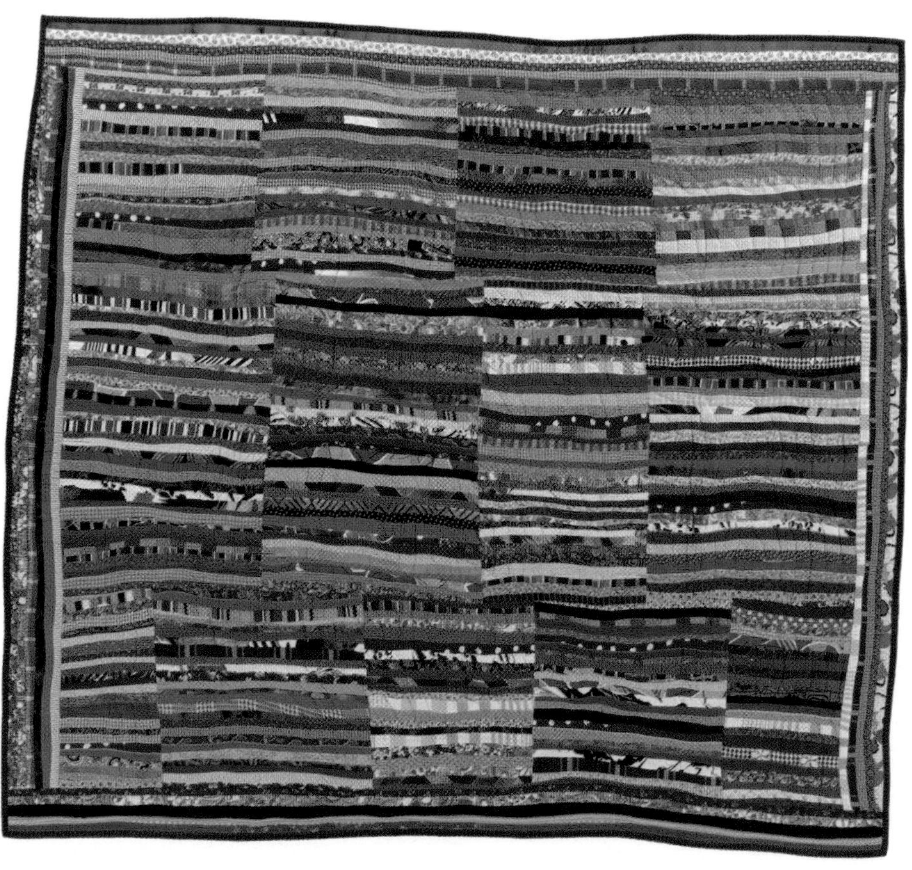

Anna Williams (American, 1927–2010). Quilt, 1995. Cotton, synthetics, 76 ¼ × 61 ½ in. (193.7 × 156.2 cm). Brooklyn Museum, Gift in memory of Horace H. Solomon, 2011.18.

From the Smithsonian's National Museum of American History: The embroidered inscription "Frances M Jolly 1839" graces the center medallion of this quilt top. This signed and dated silk-and-wool-embroidered quilt top came from an African American family, and the maker, Frances M. Jolly, was said to be an ancestor of one of the donor's grandparents. The family, of whom little else is known, is said to have lived in Massachusetts and moved to Pinehurst, North Carolina.

ABOVE: Cabin where enslaved people lived on the Wavering Place Plantation outside Columbia, SC, where the author visited at Shana Adams's invitation. CENTER AND BOTTOM: The ruins of the "slave quarters" and the great Ceiba tree at San Isidro de Los Destiladeros in Cuba.

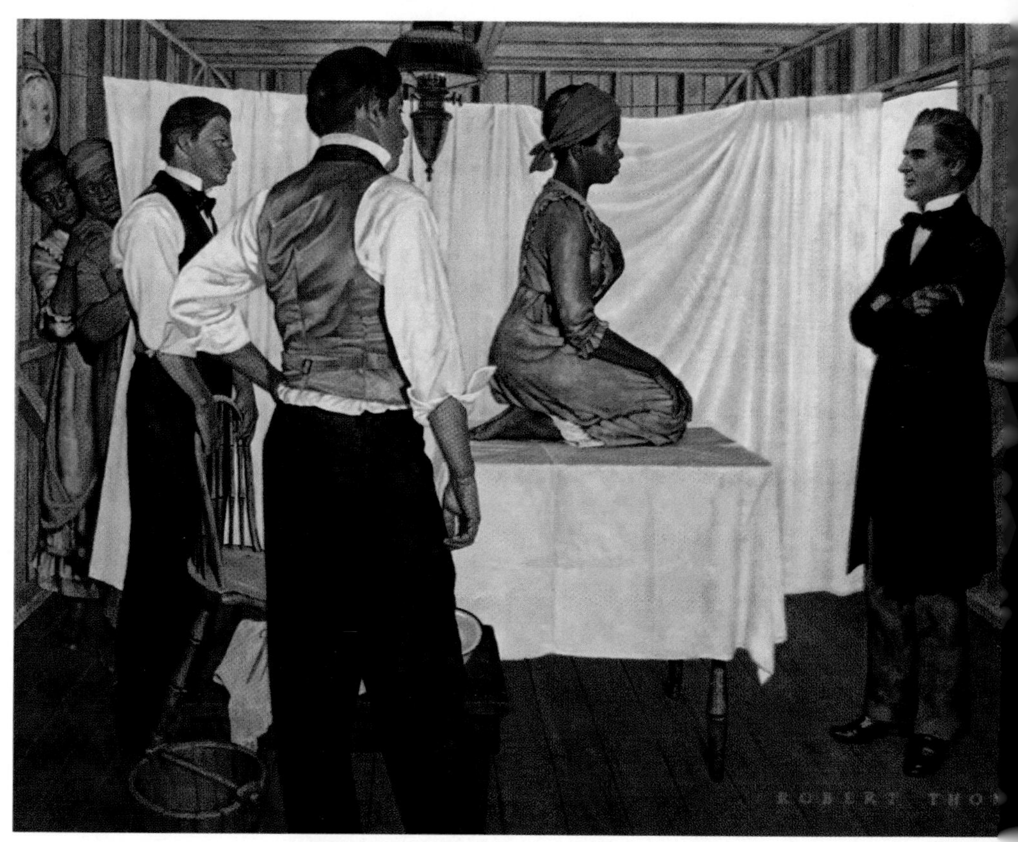

Anarcha, Betsy, and Lucy—enslaved women about to be subjected to medical experiments after they were taken to a plantation of Montgomery in 1845 to be the subjects of Dr. Marion Sims. *Illustration of Dr. J. Marion Sims with Anarcha by Robert Thom. Credit: Courtesy of Southern Illinois University School of Medicine, Pearson Museum.*

ABOVE AND BELOW: Dr. Eliza Grier ca. 1897. She earned her medical degree from the Woman's College of Pennsylvania, where, in the 1890s, female medical students embroidered this pillow sham, simultaneously proving and subverting their domestic training. *Image courtesy of Drexel University College of Medicine.*

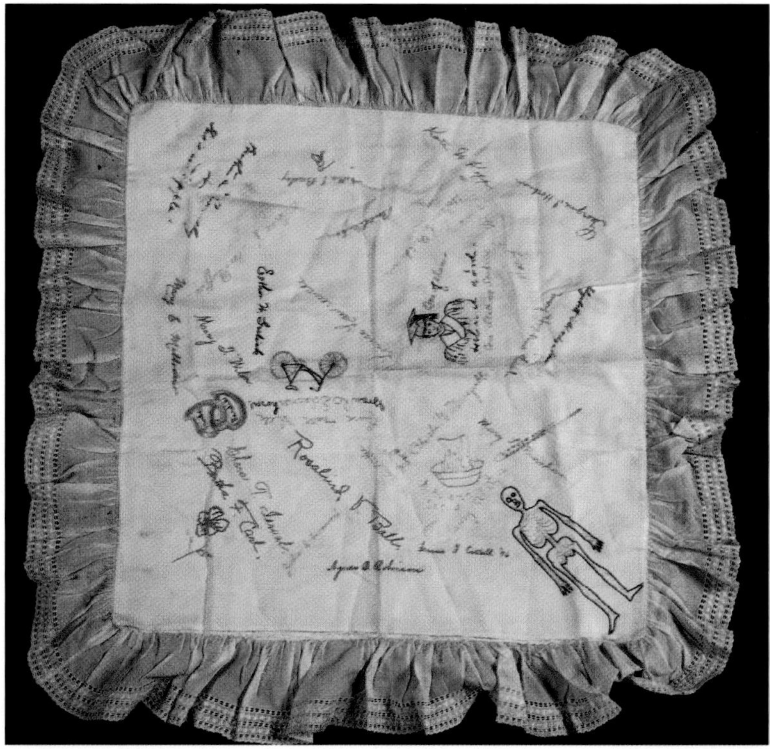

ABOVE: Detail of one of the squares of Harriet Powers's Pictorial quilt. Powers's description of this square is: "The falling of the stars on Nov. 13, 1833. The people were frightened and thought that the end had come. God's hand staid the stars. The varmints rushed out of their beds." *Courtesy of Bequest of Maxim Karolik. Photograph © 2018 Museum of Fine Arts Boston.*
BELOW: Harriet Powers's stunning Leonids Quilt. Harriet Powers, American, 1837–1910, Pictorial quilt, American (Athens, Georgia), 1895–98, Cotton plain weave, pieced, appliqued, embroidered, and quilted, 68 ⅞ x 105 in. (175 x 266.7 cm). *Credit: Bequest of Maxim Karolik, 64.619. Photograph © 2018 Museum of Fine Arts Boston.*

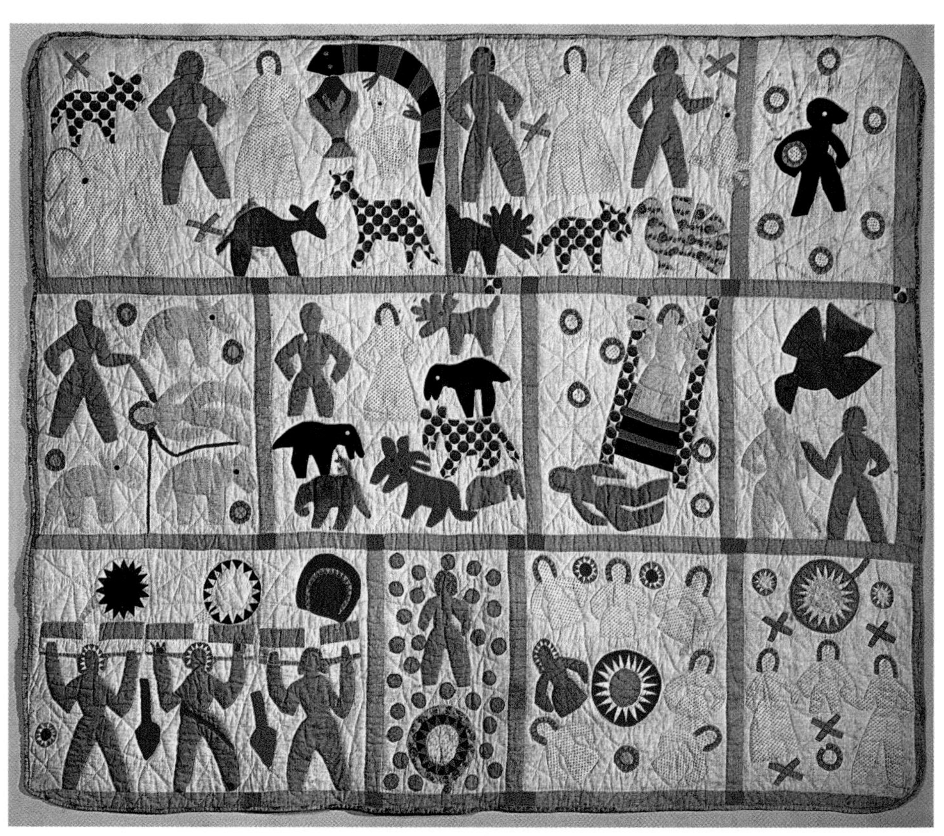

A Sermon in Patchwork by Harriet Powers. This quilt is held at the Smithsonian and is the first quilt Powers made. *Courtesy of the Division of Home and Community Life, National Museum of American History, Smithsonian Institution.*

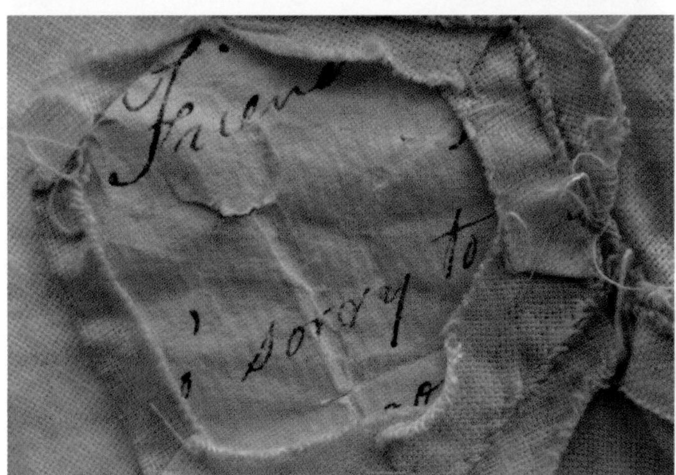

Details of the Crouch quilt top with the "Havana" backing, along with "knowledge" and "friend."

ABOVE: Interior of the slave quarters at Magnolia Plantation. BELOW: Joseph McGill in front of the Magnolia Plantations and Gardens cabin where enslaved and then free people lived.

A section of the "mosaic" quilt top with papers from the 19th and 20th centuries.

All images of the Crouch quilt top on pages 1, 2, 3, 14, and 16 of this insert are courtesy of the Historic Textile and Costume Collection, University of Rhode Island. Photos taken by the author.

meander back into the woods, then disappear to my eyes, their trails broken by a hill, by an ambitious cluster of trees. Here, in 1675, the "Great Swamp Fight" broke out when colonizers attacked the Narragansett and Niantic nations, who were led by King Philip; Mohegans and Pequots fought the British alongside the Narragansett and Niantic. The battle ended in the woods, when colonists burned women and children in their homes or forced them into the snow on a freezing night.

The more I learn, the more these woods change in my eyes, and I'm surrounded by that violence. I visit the site of the Great Swamp Massacre just once, in the summertime; it takes hours, and two trips with a local friend, to find the path that leads to the marker for the massacre. Half of it has been vandalized, removed. There's no marker along the road to tell us where to find this place. We find it only by searching several websites and old, printed maps, and asking my friend's family members. I think of the contrast between this history that's been nearly silenced in the landscape, and the history of the Revolutionary War that's well-marked and celebrated all over my hometown in Concord. The winter after we found the marker, I walked the woods nearby all winter long, and imagine the terror of being burned out of one's house into the snow, a baby nestled against a woman's chest as she raced toward safety.

Sometimes, I imagine people coming alive in the trees, clearing fields with hoes and oxen and donkeys, cutting trees, digging rows in the dirt in which to plant seeds. There's a woman carrying a pot to the well to make soup for dinner, and a boy bringing an ax to a chicken's neck on the chopping block in the yard, and a man setting stones onto a wall. The air is humid and thick in summer, heavy with flies that sting when they bite, and cold in winter with several feet of snow, a climate so foreign to western Africans who must have shivered come September, and so familiar to the tribal nations who lived here that they must have mourned the land's transformation under colonists' forced possession.

I think about Middleton Place, where enslaved people knew how to irrigate acres of fields into symmetrical pools of water and tributaries and sections that would flood with the tides. About the skill it took to irrigate land this way, and about Jimmy who knew how to build furniture like the crib he made for little Hasell and about the clothes and coverings Jane must have made with her skill as a seamstress. I imagine a seam embellished with an embroidered blue cotton stitch that looks like herringbone, around a seam from which a row of pleats rise. Let's imagine this is a neckline on a dress she made for Eliza when she heard they would soon be sold and separated, and that Jane kept it secret until the day they were to be parted. Before Eliza was taken by Winthrop to be sold, depressed all week as she saw the date approach, maybe Jane found her in the morning and slipped the dress into her hands. Maybe it was white with blue embroidery around every seam, and maybe Eliza took it with her and hid it in her room, and before she had to go to the man who rented her each day, she traced the marks Jane made to remind her she was never alone.

When I visited Charleston, I went to Sullivan's Island, to see if I could find the place where Eliza had once lived. I would not be able to find the site of this house, though I did find the site of the city house on Cumberland Street. Out on Sullivan's Island, at dusk, I drove to Fort Moultrie and walked to the beach, past the sign commemorating the tens of thousands of people who were brought across the sea against their will, to step foot onto this land. I stood on the beach, looking out at those seemingly peaceful waters, and I thought of Christine Mitchell's words about these waters that she sees as a graveyard, and I wept. "Places have power," a friend said later. "You can feel the past." Sunset approached, and I meandered slowly back toward the bridge, the city. On my way, I saw this marker, and pulled over on the side of the road.

The wooden crosses that once marked the graves have disintegrated, and all we know now is that the people who are buried there are of African American descent, and that they are the people responsible for "help[ing] to build the historic structures that have enhanced the fabric of the island." Fort Moultrie, which was used in the defense of the city many times over the years, including during the Civil War, is just one example of the places people buried here helped to create. They were "Carpenters, Cooks, Oystermen, Laundresses, Nursemaids, House Keepers, Midwives, Soldiers, and Seamen." I imagine a man heading toward the marshes and inlets around this island to gather oysters at low tide, a rake over one shoulder and a bucket in his other hand. I think about the ingenuity and the labor of people who helped build this country's wealth—John Camino, Newport Gardner, Arthur Flagg, Dinah—and the historians and activists I meet today who make sure their stories are remembered and heard, the people who make these markers to commemorate, to educate the public, to direct the stories of these places.

There's no such thing as "nice" slavery, no such thing as the "kinder" slavery of the North, no "genteel" slave owners. That myth, that northern slavery wasn't *as bad as* southern slavery, that some slave owners were *kinder* than others, persists. Who is retelling it? What did I learn in school? I only remember watching *Roots* in seventh grade, nothing about the history of New England slavery. No one ever told me that living alongside the transcendentalists in Concord, Massachusetts, were the descendants of enslaved people who settled in the 1830s, establishing communities of free people of color; I did not know that they had helped to build and sustain that town, the site of the "shot heard 'round the world," the American Revolution, cradle of liberty. Every year, when "Paul Revere" rode through our bucolic central square at midnight hollering, "The British are coming! The British are coming!" his horse's hooves clacking over pavement as we sat on the porch of the Colonial Inn to watch, someone should also have been proclaiming the other side of the story, the contradictions inherent in proclaiming a nation's liberty when people were enslaved here; this part of the story, the story of the people who worked to build this nation while they were owned and before they were given full citizenship, is now illuminated by the installation of the Robbins House—named for the Robbins family, free people of color who lived in Concord in the 1830s—at the site of the Old North Bridge, and told in the book *Black Walden*, by Elise Lemire.

ON Thurſday laſt arriv'd from the Coaſt of *AFRICA*, the Brig ROYAL CHARLOTTE, with a Parcel of extreme fine, healthy, well limb'd;

Gold Coaſt SLAVES,

Men, Women, Boys, and Girls. Gentlemen in Town and Country have now an Opportunity to furniſh themſelves with ſuch as will ſuit them. Thoſe that want, are deſired to apply very ſpeedily, or they will loſe the Advantage of ſupplying themſelves. They are to be ſeen on board the Veſſel at Taylor's Wharf.

Apply to *Thomas Teckle Taylor*, *Samuel* and *William Vernon*.

N. B. Thoſe that remain on Hand will be ſhipt off very ſoon.

Ad for slave sale from the June 6, 1763 Newport Mercury.

When I was a child, or even a high-school student, or a student in college, no one told me to read *Our Nig; Sketches from the Life of a Free Black, in a Two-Story White House, North, Showing that Slavery's Shadows Fall Even There.* Harriet Wilson's story was published in 1859; she was born in the "free" North at about the same time as Susan, in the 1820s, and her story reveals the depths of racism that were prevalent in the decades that followed, answering, in part, the question I began with when I first found myself confronted with the words *probably for slave gowns.* Why did Susan, a northerner, so easily slip into the slaveholding culture of Charleston? Because she was raised with the racist beliefs that had perpetuated slavery in the North and South, because she probably always believed that people of color were inferior. And yet—her two younger sisters, Sarah and Eliza, were opposed to slavery. What would divide a family this way? What would make Susan and her brothers so easily embrace it while their sisters could not?

Susan and Hasell would join the same church as the Grimkes, St. Philip's, in Charleston, and Winthrop would note the death of the elder Grimke, mother of Sarah and Angelina. Sarah and Angelina's parents were slaveholders, secessionists, and yet the two young women became abolitionists, exposed the cruelties of slavery with which they'd been raised, and moved north in the 1820s. They became Quakers, like Moses Brown and his stepson, William J. Harris, who married Susan's sister Emily. Emily and William's children would come to know Moses well, and one of them, Ava, would be raised by Moses on his farm. When Emily asked for her to be returned, Moses refused, and willed her a good deal of his property—much of it gained in connection with cotton and slavery. At the same time, Winthrop and Hilton sent many letters to William, using their connections with the North to negotiate the sale of the lumber and cotton that the brothers produced down South. So, William was a Quaker, his wife was opposed to slavery, and yet they, too, profited from the trade of goods harvested, tended, or produced by enslaved people.

Harriet Wilson's story, *Our Nig*, reinforces the truth of the North, that it, too, suffers from the shadow of slavery, both that which occurred on northern lands and that which was perpetuated by northerners with the trade of goods from southern lands and the West Indies. Her book was popular when it was released in 1859, but then disappeared from the record until it was recovered by Henry Louis Gates in the 1980s. If you didn't know Gates already from his work as a historian, you knew him by 2008, when he was invited for a beer at the White House after being arrested for entering his own home in Cambridge; he was perceived by the police to be a burgling black man breaking into a fine home near the Ivy League university where he teaches. Wilson's story still reverberates in our "free" North, the shadows still here.

There are other shadows, too, that I'd yet to learn. Tracing the story of the Great Swamp would lead me further back in time, to the founding of Rhode Island and the Narragansett and Wampanoag people who lived on this land before the colonists and enslaved Africans arrived.

9

Canuto Matanew

Havana, Havana, Havana. Barbados. Havana. West Indies, West Indies. Wes—. Indie—. Barbados. Carolyna. Havan—

In the shade of the porch at the house behind us, a group of men make concrete by hand in a wheelbarrow, restoring the old building to its original grandeur. It's a hot day, over ninety degrees and humid, and the men, sweating under straw hats, mix the concrete with shovels, a rhythmic scraping sound, and then they gather it up and smooth it with brisk arcing sweeps onto the wall.

This is the Valle de los Ingenios, just outside Trinidad, Cuba, and a young man named Gonzalo Alfredo López Turiño leads me through an old sugar plantation that was abandoned in the late 1800s. Guinea hens chatter and flee from us as we approach the ruins of the slave quarters in the shade of the woods; the restoration hasn't reached here yet, and the brick walls are only a few feet high, running in an even but dilapidated grid along the ground. Beyond, there's a great twenty-foot-high brick wall with two wide holes in it. There were no windows in the slave quarters, says Gonzalo, just small rooms eight feet by twelve feet, each holding six to eight enslaved people.

"It's basically a jail," he says. "They don't have any windows or beds. They just sleep on the dirt floor."

A windowless brick dirt-floored room in this heat. This isn't even a hot day, Gonzalo told me when I'd asked how he could wear jeans in this heat.

"It was a really hard life," he says.

He tells me that the man who's funding this restoration, which has been ongoing for fifteen years, wants to make an audio tour to teach people about each phase of the rum-distilling process, and about life here in the 1800s. The trick will be to limit the number of people who visit so they don't trample over it, he says.

There's a great black wasp perched on a branch near the ground in front of us. It's the largest bug I've ever seen, the size of a large mouse.

"Look," Gonzalo points, fascinated.

"What is it?"

"Spider wasp," he says. "I was stung by one years ago. The worst pain I ever had."

The tarantula wasp has a stinger half an inch long, and will kill a tarantula, carry it back to its nest, and lay an egg in the tarantula's underside so that the larvae can eat the tarantula's innards until they hatch into adults. Spider wasps, they're called. Gonzalo was in the army when he was stung by one of them, and it was one of the worst pains he's ever felt.

"I had a fever for days," he says. "It was terrible."

I'm here to learn about the triangle trade, but the more I learn, the more it feels like a tangled crisscrossed web of commerce—rum, from sugar and molasses, traded for goods from the east, and for enslaved people on the coast of West Africa and in the West Indies, and for cheese and salted fish, and crisscrossing back and forth again and again, a vision of threaded switchbacks and knots across the Atlantic.

I go back to the stories of how this began, or how it was perpetuated, since it had been ongoing for centuries by the time the Crouch-Cushman-Williams families became involved. Christy Clark-Pujara writes:

> By the mid-18th century, Rhode Island had become a permanent and prosperous colony, thanks to local investments in the business of slavery. Colonists supplied sugar plantations in the West Indies with slaves, livestock, dairy products, fish, candles, and lumber. In return, they received molasses which they distilled into rum. This trade began in the late 17th century but flourished after 1730, when rum became a major currency in the slave trade. The West Indian trade propelled Newport out of Boston's shadow and into the status of a major city and helped to establish Providence as a major port.

The rum that was made in Rhode Island was distilled from "West Indian molasses." Rhode Island was thus built upon the slave trade and the Atlantic mercantile system that interwove the West Indies with Africa and the new colonies. South Carolina planters could be supplied enslaved people from West Indian plantations, some of whom were owned by Rhode Islanders like the DeWolf family. The livelihoods of the San Isidro master sitting in his bathtub in Cuba, Winthrop and Susan in South Carolina, and their parents and grandparents in Rhode Island, were all tied up in this system that was built upon the exchange of goods from New England that supported the plantations in the West Indies—cod and meat and cheese to feed the enslaved in the West Indies, rum to trade for the enslaved people in Africa, and sugar to bring back home to make more rum. A tidy triangle, a messy tangle—a web of profits.

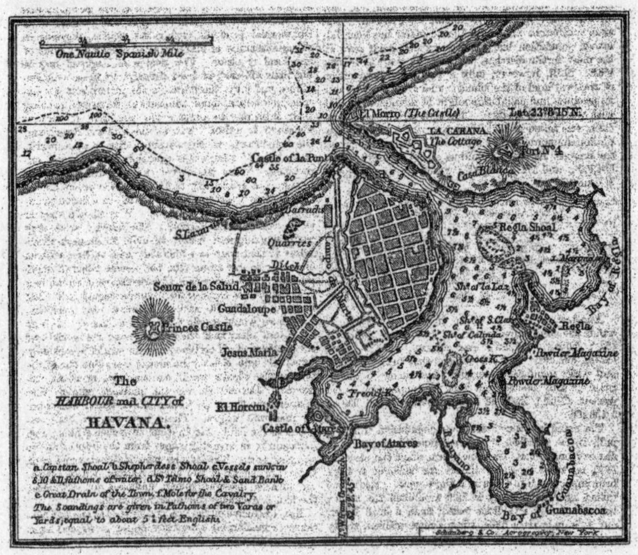

Susan's father and grandfather made their livelihoods, for a time, shipping to Havana, Barbados, South Carolina, and then Jason, Susan's father, lost it all in 1808. Until then, on their shipping manifests and accounting books, there are the words that span the globe, zigzagging with dollar signs trailing behind them like slug trails in the sea: Sugar, molasses, coffee, chocolate. Goods from the West Indies. Silks and tea and spices from China, traded for in the islands. And to trade with, from New England: Rum. Rum. Rum. Their currency. The currency of the slave trade. When I searched for diaries written by Providence women in the nineteenth century, many were written by women like Susan and her friend Sarah Hamlin, northern daughters of merchants who traded down the coast and in the West Indies. It was the course of trade then, an easy hop from the southern coast to the islands where enslaved people tended coffee and sugar, where plantation conditions were notoriously harsh and so many people were worked to death.

Before I get to Trinidad and the sugar plantations, I'm in Havana, and the music is just as they said it would be—boisterous, and on every street corner. Salsa, rumba, beats I'm learning only here. People in costumes dancing on stilts. Red and yellow and green fabric in strips that sway from their arms and legs when they groove and spin. They step forward and back, shift their hips, staying atop those six-foot stilts, I don't know how. A woman on the ground with big red circles painted onto her cheeks invites a tourist from the circle around them to dance. He tries to salsa with her, but he's awkward and brazen and gets too close. She plays the crowd, waves him dramatically away, fans her face.

The coffee here is better than it is back home. *Café con leche* and iced chocolate coffee with frothy milk and chocolate sprinkled on top. The rum is even better than they said it would be. Mojitos with handfuls of mint smashed in the bottom of the glass, frozen daiquiris, Cuba libres with sweet dark syrup that goes by the name Coke but isn't fizzy, white rum or dark rum in double shots at the club where the Buena Vista Social Club played.

It's three o'clock and raining, and I've retreated under the arches of a grand colonial building in the San Francisco plaza, part of the old city that's just a block from the famous Malecón where old cars wind along the shore. Four men play for the crowd—one man holds a set of cowbells lined up in front of him on a bar that hangs across his body, one plays trumpet, one plays a metal drum, and another man play the congas, a drum that, I learn, originated in Cuba. The men wear long white shirts and white pants. When it's time to go, the trumpet player leads the band out into the street and the crowd follows, a conga line. It's raining in the square, but the crowd moves into it, following the band across the cobblestone square and down a narrow street. In Havana, I come to love the sound of the trumpet. It fades down the wet street with the crowd that follows its blare.

I hold a list of enslaved people owned by James DeWolf for one of his three Cuban plantations; this one, Mary Ann, grew coffee. The handwritten list says: "103 negroes of both sexes, 96. from Affrica, 7. born on the [Journey]." There's a map of the plantation, with two large sections for plantains, two smaller for sugarcane, and the rest for coffee, coffee, coffee. I can read about these plantations in history books, can learn the story of these places, but it's still an awful abstraction—an idea of a world, an idea of torture and murder—until I see the maps and read the handwritten lists of tools, crops, and enslaved people, all of these "objects" side by side, property for the owner. I'm looking at copies of the originals, but still, I can see the stains on the paper, the tears and long straight marks of the long-folded sections, the slight variation of the capital *C*'s and *S*'s and *P*'s. Once it's material, it's real. Like the quilt tops and the papers they hold and the letters of the family.

I study the ink blots, those great misshapen stains that mark the imperfect hand and writing tools—the splash of ink with a long narrow tail and a smaller circle on the end, a word obliterated mid-sentence, the smear of a hand across the ink, a broken wax seal and the drops of red wax across the backside of the paper, or the way someone wrote in triangles across the folds of the sealed letter the way we did in third grade when we passed notes behind the teacher's back.

I think of the white cotton thread stitches in the quilt. I love the way these stitches look regular, small, precise—and then tilt slightly left or right. Almost perfect, but never quite. Marks of the hand, of the body, evidence of themselves that people leave behind.

What does it mean to know that 103 so-called "Negroes" were bought for the coffee plantation, most from Africa? To know that seven babies were born, delivered by seven laboring mothers, on the awful journey to Cuba? Can you picture 103 people in a group, looking up at once from the field? They're singular but nameless faces, a foggy crowd framed like one of those old black-and-white photos that blurs at the edges. I have a sense of collective grief and triumph over oppression that can't be made more particular because people are untraceable in the records. Then, I see the note about their sale handwritten in loopy cursive, and I see their names, and the story becomes more real, the fog burns off in ugly Technicolor magic: *Augustin, Hilarie, Crispin, Henrique, Sebastian, Frederico, Juliana, Lorenza, Beatriz, Margarita, Maria, Carolina.* Like the list I read in Charleston, the names of these people enslaved in Cuba are listed in that steady loopy hand that we'd call calligraphy today with wider lengths on the capital letters and dots at the ends of the J's and M's and A's. As I read each name, each person becomes singular, each with a distinctive voice, eyes, dreams, soul. Their bodies come into focus on the field and in the house; they walk down the dirt road that runs between the fields and make dinner for their families at night with a great cast-iron pot over a fire—a few beans, some plantains boiled in water. There's talk of the day, a brief chuckle and then a sigh; there's a boy playing, and a younger boy singing to himself as he nestles beside his mother. It's a hot night, and the older boy wails when he sees a great wasp fly through the open window. The boy was stung by one of these wasps weeks ago and was sick for a week, fevered and dizzy. His father jumps to kill it with the wooden spoon but only succeeds in shooing it out the window, its retreat a swift buzz. The father curses, knowing that one will be back. He curses because he can't protect his son's life.

From Fort Lauderdale, Florida, the flight is forty-five minutes long. When we land, it feels like we're a world away from that town, which looked antiseptic in comparison with Havana. Here, the streets are made of dusty cobblestone, the buildings are hundreds of years old with chipping paint in tropical colors—bright blue, candy pink, canary yellow—layered with dirt that's kicked up from the cars and bikes and mopeds and horses, like once-flamboyant young birds now showing their age.

The embargo has made Havana a sort of time warp, with bike taxis and 1950s cars for hire. People here are poor, having suffered for years under a ruler who keeps their grocery store shelves nearly bare, who educates every citizen but provides little in the way of job opportunities and bountiful food. At least, that's the story we heard from those we talked to in private, away from the public ear.

With the legend of Cuba's more recent history in our ears, it's hard to remember that Havana was once—a hundred years before Castro—just another stop on the merchant route, as interwoven in the capitalist path as any other city along the eastern seaboard. Havana was a stopping point for the Spanish trader who brought the fifty-three people from Sierra Leone and then boarded them onto the *Amistad*. Follow the U.S. coastline north for three weeks by sailboat and you'll reach Bristol, Rhode Island, not so far along the shoreline from Long Island, where the *Amistad* was captured. Bristol harbor is nestled north of the mouth of the ocean, a fifteen-minute drive and another bridge from Newport. This is where James DeWolf's grand white-pillared mansion still stands testament to the profits he built in part from these Cuban plantations, in combination, of course, with his trade of enslaved people who worked his land as well as acres and acres that belonged to others.

I wonder why I need to see all these places to understand the story. Why do I need the touch of fabric, the tactility of the quilt tops, the smells and sounds and sights of each place I visit in Rhode Island, South Carolina, Cuba? Say I'm an experiential learner. Say I need the sensory to understand a place, to know a person's story. In high school and college, I'd stare at the dates and names of battles and cities, trying to bore them into my memory without being able to *see* the story in my mind; without that story, history made no sense to me. I couldn't understand those places and people because no one had made them particular, singular, specific.

But maybe I need to see and touch all of this because I was indoctrinated in a culture that taught me that this history of enslavement, of the triangle trade, was so long past, and mattered so little now. I was told, back in elementary and high school and even college, that it was a blight on our history, when I had come to learn that it was our whole foundation, and that my sense of this country was shaped by the history books and stories of people who didn't see traces of enslavement everywhere, who didn't believe in palimpsests and legacies. Maybe it took me too long to find this story.

I latch onto DeWolf because he's so deeply connected to New England and the West Indies, in much larger terms but in similar ways as the Williams and Crouch families were. Leonardo Marques writes, in *The United States and the Transatlantic Slave Trade to the Americas, 1776-1867*, "It is unclear when Rhode Islanders started to purchase lands in Cuba, but by the very early 1800s, James DeWolf was already using his properties on the island as a strategy to deal with eventual unfavorable circumstances in the Atlantic trade. 'If the market [for slaves] in Havana slumped, and the Revenue Marine, as the Coast Guard was then called, made it risky to smuggle into American ports,' George Howe argues, James DeWolf 'could afford to wait. He owned three plantations in Cuba—the Mary Ann, the Mount Hope, and the Esperanza—where he could hold his stock until prices rose again, as they always did, sooner or later." Marques goes on to explain that the connections between American slave traders, "French expertise," and "Cuban plantations" were profitable as traders could, for example, buy slaves at cheaper prices in Charleston to use on their Cuban plantations, while a "very intelligent Frenchman" would "take care of & direct [their] plantation"

In Charleston, Joseph McGill leads tours that show people the fingerprints of enslaved people on the bricks that built the city's landmarks. The bricks were made on plantations, heated in ovens by enslaved people. Here is the print of a child or a young woman on a building; place your hand here, just as that child did. For a moment, you are walking in that person's shoes, so to speak, your body resting in the print their body left behind. Unless an enslaved person had children who survived, this fingerprint and the lasting works they created, are their signature, their legacy.

I learn from Joe to look for the fingerprints in the buildings, to find the quieted story in every master narrative; the people in that hidden story refuse to be silenced.

While Charleston feels like a community closed to outsiders, everything in Cuba seems to happen by word of mouth. "I have a friend," each person says when we tell them what we're seeking. The Airbnb woman knows a taxi driver who will take us to the city, the men at the bar know a guy who can give us a tour, the tour guide tells us to eat at this restaurant that his friends run; he promises we'll get the best mojitos in all of Cuba at this place. There's an underground market where we can buy anything we like with large American bills. We're told that the fifties and hundreds are easiest to hide behind the cell phone battery, for example, when a Cuban travels out of the country to buy goods to resell back in Cuba. Double the price, a quick profit. Cell phones bought for $50 in the States go for $200 in Cuba. One tour guide tells me I should have brought all my old cell phones to sell here, and I'd have paid for my whole trip, he is sure of it. When we go to change money at the storefront down on Calle Maceo in Trinidad, a man next door tells us his name is Ulysses and offers us a slightly better exchange rate for our large American bills. We can trade them for CUPs, the tourist currency, he says, no problem. He tries to lure us into his apartment, but we stick with the government bank.

When I'm looking for a tour guide to take me to the Valle de los Ingenios, where the sugar plantations were built, I go to the man who, the guidebook tells me, leads tours there on horseback. This man's wife invites me into their high-ceilinged home with nineteenth-century divans and rocking chairs and walls painted in period styles—rows of flowers in vases, curliqued vines. Hanging on the walls are dozens of photos of brides; the man is also a photographer, and he runs their home as an Airbnb. Like every Cuban we've met, he hustles with four or five different occupations, trying to supplement his modest government stipend. Cubans have only been able to do this—supplement their incomes—since 2008, when Fidel's brother Raúl took power. They've had Internet access for two years, thanks to a deal negotiated by the United States with significant benefits, another tour guide tells us, for the States. Of course, he says, it isn't entirely beneficent; your country is taking a profit, too. We nod, knowing that nothing a capitalistic nation does is ever simply beneficent.

She invites us, my friend and I, to sit down and wait.

We gaze up at the bridal photos, at the thirty-foot-tall ceilings and the wooden doors and shutters that are open to let in the light. There are no screens on the windows; dust from the road wafts in. An old man walks in with a cane. He doesn't acknowledge us but walks to the back with the wife and then returns, to sit on the windowsill. A big Dalmatian wags her tail and pants in my face while I pat her back; my friend gazes out the window. At last, a man comes up from the back, and says he's the one, the man who leads the horseback rides. "But, no, no," he says, "the Valle de los Ingenios is too far. The guidebook was wrong about that."

"Do you know anyone who could take me there, who knows the history of the plantations?"

"No," he says, shaking his head.

But then—"Oh!" he says. "Let me make a phone call. I have a friend."

Marques writes, "New England slaveholders improved their investment opportunities in Cuba by calling on French expertise in agricultural production and French business networks. Cuban planters and merchants, for their part, took advantage of the knowledge and skills related to crop production and slave trading brought by these individuals in order to create one of the wealthiest and most violent slave societies of the nineteenth century."

One of the wealthiest and most violent, I read. Life in Cuba as an enslaved person could be torturous and brief. New Englanders were not benign bystanders in this system, but active participants.

The day before, wandering through Trinidad, I noticed a restaurant with a wall of chains on display. I saw the chains on a glance through the doorway as I walked past and recognized them immediately as chains from the slave trade—the great loops that would encircle a person's neck, spaced five feet apart on a long cast iron chain. Smaller loops on another chain for peoples' ankles or wrists, or the necks of women and children. The iron balls that would weigh down a person's ankle to keep them from running. The whip and iron hook made for punishing, for a white man to enforce the power structure: *You are beneath me, and if you disobey, this will happen to you, too.* Make a display of oppression to keep the enslaved people subservient.

So that I would remember, I took pictures of this wall, and of the six-foot-wide stocks, a great wooden block with three holes for the head and arms, where a man or woman would have stood for hours.

"Were these for slaves?" I asked the waiter in broken Spanish. I know *esclave* in French, and he understood.

"Yes," he answered in English. "They're from the owner's collection. He wanted somewhere to display them."

Under the holes for the hands in the stocks, there were iron handcuffs hanging from chains on each side; one of them hung open, as if the person held hostage had begun to escape. To the right, a thick chain hung against the wall, its links wider than the wrists of the woman who cut her meal at the table below. Everyone ate in the midst of this display. No one seemed bothered.

The waiter walked me to another wall and pointed to a framed letter that he said was about freeing an enslaved person; it was framed alongside currency bills from the period that were lined up in neat rows, like the heavy locks and keys displayed on the wall, arranged in order of size, large to small.

Later, when I asked the guide who was found for me, Gonzalo, about this, he'd say yes, that's true, and that first, the owner of the restaurant had displayed a gun collection, but the government came and made him take it down; it was too dangerous to have that many guns hanging on the walls, they told him. So, instead, he put up this display of slavery paraphernalia.

Gonzalo works for Trinidad's historic commission, which conserves all the buildings in town, and his mother is a professor of historic architecture at the university. He and she usually bring people out to the San Isidro plantation together, so he's gathered all the information she has about the place, along with what his boss, the engineer of the excavation, has taught him.

"How did the restaurant owner come by it?" I asked.

"He's a collector. His family had all this stuff from their plantation, and they were going to get rid of it all, but he saved it."

"So he's part of the family who enslaved people?"

"Yes."

At the end of the day, when I talked to my friend about this back at the *casa particular* where we were staying, I was still incredulous that the man would display the tools of torture in his restaurant, for tourists to enjoy. Was this about colonialism? His family's success? What was it supposed to say?

"It's interesting," said my friend, "that the collector also displayed the letter that frees one of the enslaved people."

Is that an attempt to redeem his family, I wonder? To illustrate that they eventually did the right thing?

I ask people I meet if there is racism here in Cuba, tensions between whites and blacks. I tell a man, a man who's educated, that I've noticed that people seem to intermingle more than they do back in the States, that neighborhoods are mixed rather than segregated as they are in Boston or New York, for example.

"Do you have segregation, racism?"

"No," he says. "We don't have any of that. Everyone likes each other."

There's a pause.

Then he says, "The blacks are more aggressive, you know? You can see the blacks in the streets, you know, those black men who try to give you taxi rides? They're more aggressive, and lazy, too. They don't want to make just twenty-five CUPs more a month; they want to make twenty-five CUPs *a day*. They stand around talking about baseball all day. They don't want to work hard. The blacks, people who come from the slaves, they rise up with a bad feeling. I don't know why that is."

The view from the tower at a plantation near San Isidro; from here, overseers would watch for enslaved people attempting to escape.

James DeWolf was the renowned slave trader from Bristol, Rhode Island, whose story the average New Englander still doesn't seem to know.

DeWolf was not the only one; he was just the one to do it most frequently and successfully, the "preeminent merchant family." There were also: Briggs and Gardner, Clarke and Clarke, Cyprian Sterry, Vernon and Vernon, Jeremiah Ingraham, Bourn and Wardell. Often, because slavers were such costly and risky ventures (the journey was long, the crew and then the enslaved people needed food for the long crossing, there was the risk of contracting malaria and other diseases while traveling the West African coast to buy enslaved people, the crew might be overtaken by the people they'd captured, and the enslaved people might get sick and perish before they could be sold for profit), multiple investors went in on a single ship; thus, the names listed together in ventures. The story of the DeWolfs is known widely among historians and those interested in Rhode Island's involvement in the slave trade, but perhaps because it hasn't been commemorated anywhere publicly, it hasn't spread to those who don't seek it out. A tourist wouldn't just stumble upon the plaque that tells the story of his grand white mansion in the center of town; there's no mention of the slave trade at the port in Bristol, nor in Newport. The plaque in front of the DeWolf mansion reads, in part, "James and William De Wolf, of among the most prominent families in the town, constructed in 1797 what was to become DeWolf's Wharf . . . The brothers completed this wharf . . . to accommodate their thriving maritime business. It became a center for finance, foreign trade, and merchandizing, all activities which contributed to the wealth and architectural legacy of Bristol . . ." There is no mention, here, of their trade in human lives, and how that trade helped to build the family's and the town's wealth, but the descendants of the family are doing work today to make this history known. A plaque commemorating Bristol and Newport's part in the slave trade is now under way thanks to the work of Annie Chin's Middle Passage Ceremonies and Port Markers Project.

For a while, I thought that this was something I could do to make this story more public—I could help to install a plaque. When I asked at the Newport Historical Society if anyone had tried, they said no, that since the enslaved people were sold from private homes, there wasn't any public market to mark as the site of the trade. That sounded like a feeble excuse. I talked with Jennifer Rae Taylor, a lawyer who works for the Equal Justice Initiative, Bryan Stevenson's organization; they had offered to help me navigate the town bureaucracy and laws in order to erect a marker, as they had done in Alabama. I spoke with a prominent African American businessman in Providence who had erected a marker by the Providence bay; he said I should work to rehabilitate that Providence marker before creating a new one in Newport. I spoke to Keith and Theresa Guzmán-Stokes in Newport, who said that we shouldn't mark the trade but the important African Americans in town, that *those* were the stories young black men and women needed to hear, not that their ancestors were simply objects in the trade. I got overwhelmed, lost track of what was the right thing to do, fearing that this wasn't my story to determine; I gave up the idea of the project.

The story of the Bristol and Newport slave trade is one that tourists don't necessarily want to hear. They come here on sailboats in the summertime; they race on the bay, they stay in fine hotels on the water, historic colonial or Gilded Age homes transformed into hotels and restaurants. Rooms in these hotels go for hundreds to a thousand dollars a night. Many people return to old "family homes" where they've summered for generations. The weekly farmer's market, frequented by hipsters and yuppies and organic-leaning locals, abuts the low-income housing apartments, occupied predominantly by people of color. No one at the market notices the apartment complexes just behind the trees. People who summer in Bristol and Newport are, as they were in the Gilded Age decades before, wealthy and predominantly white. They don't want to hear about the dirty work that made these places opulent, beautiful, and ultimately, comfortable for them today. When I ask tourists, even longtime New Englanders, if they know how central Bristol was in the slave trade at the end of the eighteenth century, they say no. When I ask if they know who was the DeWolf family, of today's popular DeWolf Tavern in Bristol, they say no. I didn't know any of this history, either, before I stumbled upon this quilt. And the more I learn about the past, the more I notice about the present.

There's a spate of rum distilleries opening in Newport now, billing themselves as new iterations of those distilleries that were so important to the town—to the new nation that was still finding its capitalist legs in the eighteenth century. But do these new distilleries explain *why* rum was so important back then? Do they explain that New England rum was a critical element in the slave trade? That it was used to trade for enslaved people all along the western coast of Africa? That the sugar and molasses required to make rum came from the West Indies, where it was grown by enslaved people taken from Africa, or that, in the seventeenth century, the enslaved people in the West Indies included some from New England itself—that when Wampanoags and Narragansetts were defeated and captured in battle, they were sent there, to work as enslaved people for the rest of their lives? No. This isn't in their marketing scheme. They romanticize Rhode Island's rum distilleries and tell stories of the area's infamous pirates who lived off of goods they stole from boats that ran in and out of the ports. They perpetuate myths of the past that we like to hear—pretty pictures of pirates, without the stories of the captains and crews they murdered, the slave ships of which they took command, or the stories of who made the goods of which they took control, what it took to make those goods, whose lives were given to make the sugar, molasses, rum, cotton, silk, tea, chocolate, coffee.

Rum barrels at a factory outside Havana.

Infants shoes
Women's lee slips
Calf shoes for Winthrop
Shoes
Shoes
Shoes for wife
Cloth slipps
. . . *Goat skin slipps (Eliza* [Williams]*)*

Beef, calf's head, sugar, lamb, molasses, cotton, cambrics, calicos. These were the goods Jason Williams bought and sold for his store in the 1830s, when he was shipping items back and forth from his home in Providence to his daughter and son-in-law in South Carolina. Jason bought shoes for his wife and daughters, and goat-skin slippers for Eliza Williams, Susan's older sister who remained at home with her parents. These slippers were finer than her everyday shoes; they were probably long, dainty, and square-toed, suitable for parties and dinners and other occasions. Jason bought infants' shoes and an assortment of others that he likely resold at the store, along with dry goods, a variety of meats, tools, cloth, pots and pans and dishes—and anything else local residents required.

His life echoed, on a much smaller scale, a man who preceded him by a century, James Brown, a member of the prominent Brown family whom Christy Clark-Pujara describes in *Dark Work*. James's first journey to the West Indies on a ship he co-owned with his brothers "allowed him to open a shop in Providence. . . . His store provided Rhode Islanders with an array of everyday goods, such as salt, fish, beef, turnips, sugar, butter, lamb, mutton, iron pots, wood, cotton, linen, leather, looking glass, hoops for barrels, rum, wine, and brandy. Most of these goods were purchased from surrounding colonies with rum; however, cheese, pork, tobacco, and hoops for barrels were bartered for locally . . . Together, [he and his brother] supplied plantation owners in the West Indies with corn, cheese, tar, horses, shingles, and tobacco."

Clark-Pujara explains that Rhode Island plantations, as they were called, in South County, supplied meat and crops to the West Indies plantations, and that Rhode Island merchants, in turn, had "direct access to large populations of enslaved people as slave traders in West Africa and commodity traders in the West Indies." Between 1798 and 1809, Jason and his father Elijah invested in seven sloops, schooners, or brigantines that sailed from Providence to ports south, including Charleston, and beyond to the West Indies. There's no evidence that they ever bought or sold enslaved people from the West Indies. But they were a part of that mercantile exchange, running ships up and down the coast, trading goods from around the world in exchange for Rhode Island's produce, meat, and rum.

Molasses
Codfish
Nutmeg
Cloves
Molasses
Whiskey
Molasses
Apples
SC Sugar
Flour
Meal
Vinegar & Molasses
S.C. Sugar
W. Sugar

There is codfish. And molasses. White sugar. Refined. First grown in the West Indies or South Carolina, then harvested when it reached seven or eight feet tall. At the plantation outside Trinidad, I ask Gonzalo to stand next to the field of sugarcane planted at the old sugar plantation, San Isidro de los Destiladeros; he says they've planted it for effect, to illustrate how the land might have looked back then. As Gonzalo moves toward the stalks, I see how tall the stalks are. They loom far above his head. Their white feathered tips blow in the wind, thick stalks arching just slightly.

"They're much thicker than I expected," I say.

He nods. He says he'll show me the sugar mill at the next stop, so I can see how the grinding was done. At that mill, I see how many men it would take to press a great wheel around, crushing the juice from the cane. Sugarcane is not soft like grass, as I'd always imagined, but hard like bamboo. In December, when I visit, it's ten feet high.

Here, at San Isidro de los Destiladeros, whose name means roughly farmers of the distillery, founded in 1828 when Jason was buying and selling goods at his store and Susan was on the brink of a new life in Charleston with her husband, hundreds of enslaved people came to work at the hot fires of the Jamaican train, in the sweltering hundred-degree sugarcane fields, and in the master's house. In 1828, John C. Calhoun, that dastardly South Carolinian whose name would be uttered in the years preceding the Civil War, whose statue still looms over Marion Square, was protesting the tariff that, he believed, favored the industrial (northern) over the agrarian (southern) interests of the union. He threatened secession.

In 1835, Winthrop wrote to his sister back home that "people at the North were making trouble for the Southerners," by sending abolitionist pamphlets, and Franklin notes that this is the first intimation of Winthrop's becoming a "fire-breathing southerner," as he sides with Calhoun regarding slavery and secession, and wishes his sister could have such good "help," meaning slaves, of course, as they have in South Carolina. Ten years earlier, in 1825, Matanzas, north of San Isidro, experienced one of the largest rebellions of enslaved people, and thirty years before that, the rebellion in Haiti shifted the sugar plantations to Cuba. French planters got scared, and they moved away. Every rebellion altered the course of the story, intimidated the master class, disrupted the status quo.

beef
beef
tripe
beef
beef
Gallon whiskey
W. Sugar
Y.H. Tea
W. Sugar
Heyson Tea

Surrounded by sugarcane, I think about Kara Walker's *A Subtlety, or the Marvelous Sugar Baby*. And the way people posed for photos in front of her body, recorded, unbeknown to them, as part of the project. Walker installed the piece in the old Domino Sugar factory in Brooklyn, where sugarcane from the Caribbean was turned into the fine white stuff that Americans could consume, the stuff that, my friend insists, is killing us the way tobacco did before we knew it was rotting away our insides and causing cancer. The Brooklyn factory was built in the late 1800s, after San Isidro had shut down. The story Gonzalo tells me is that all the sugar plantations in the Valle de los Ingenios closed down as a result of the revolution that was under way. He says that all the people in the valley fled and sugar production ended here (when it picked up again, it was farther west). As a result, the plantations and all they contained were preserved. They became overgrown with trees and shrubs and weeds, wasps' nests and guinea hen grazing grounds.

San Isidro is being excavated by a group of archaeologists, and now the fear, says Gonzalo, is that too many tourists will flood the place and destroy all that it holds; buses will unload dozens of tourists all day long, as they do at Manaca Iznaga, another plantation down the road. They'll ruin it. He echoes the fear I've heard from several Cubans—that a flood of new tourism means both opportunity and the potential for destruction of Cuba—of the culture, the landscape, the values. Opening is a gift and, some people seem to fear, the beginning of the end, Starbucks and McDonald's where now the salsa bands play at the local cafés in the square and schoolchildren run their races around a row of cones and bottles.

The Jamaican train is a series of pots over a fire. It's an ingenious—*ingenios*—system for extracting molasses from sugarcane juice. Sugarcane stalks are brought to the mill area by two oxen hauling a cart; they're pulled into a bay area, where the cane is unloaded, then pressed at the mill. Once the sugarcane has been ground by two men pushing a wide rod around and around (all day long, pushing as they walk in a circle, on a machine whose metal parts were made in upstate New York), pressing the cane flat and extruding its juice into waiting pipes below, then the juice is siphoned into great iron vats over a fire. There are five brick pits built into an oven, a fire burning to heat the vats in the center. The fire gets weaker the farther to the left and right one moves. So that by the time the vats are moved to either end of the train, the sugar has burned into a thick paste that will be covered with ash and allowed to settle for a month. The *puntero*, says Gonzalo, was the enslaved man in charge of tending the fire and controlling the temperature.

Nothing is wasted. The animals are fed the mashed cane stalks, and whatever the animals can't eat is used as fuel for the fires.

As we move to the next phase of the rum production, Gonzalo points out the great Ceiba tree in front of us. It's taller than the tower that stands in the center of the field. The tower was used to survey the land, for the owner to keep the enslaved people under control, the all-seeing eye like Foucault's panopticon that reinforces institutional power. The tower had a bell that rang for breaks and mealtimes. The story of the Ceiba tree is that when enslaved people ran for escape, they asked the Royal Palm to hide them, and the palm tree said no. Next, they asked the Ceiba tree, and the tree said yes. So, this is a holy tree. In lightning storms, other trees might get struck, but not the Ceiba tree. Now, it stands dozens of feet higher than the tower, in triumph, I think.

He says this is the same sort of tree as in *The Little Prince*; do I know that story?

Yes, I say, and smile. The Baobab tree. That's where I recognize this trees' smooth bulging roots, strong trunk, cartoon-like branches that look like they're miles above us against the blue sky. The Baobab was Saint-Exupéry's symbol of Nazism taking hold of the earth; pull it up when it's young to prevent it from taking deep root. It's in the same family as the Ceiba tree, but in this culture, the Ceiba tree symbolizes good.

The top layer of the paste made in the fires is clear; that's pure liquor, tasteless—like pure tequila, Gonzalo tries to explain to me—*aguardiente*, fire water. That top layer would be exported and sold to others to store in drums, infusing flavor, and then bottling it into rum. The middle layer of the pot's paste is what will be made into rum here. It's dumped into a concrete bath poured into the earth thirty or forty feet from the Jamaican train. In the bath, the paste is combined with water that's diverted from the pond above via a dam and canals. Then the now-sweetened water is siphoned into a pipette and boiled. It will need to be stored in barrels to gain its flavor.

"Bees still come to eat the sugar from the floor of this bath when it rains," Gonzalo says. It sounds incredible, but one hundred years of sugar water still saturates the earth.

"When we look at the bath-shaped hole in the dam above," Gonzalo says, "we don't know exactly what that is, but we imagine that this is where the owner of the plantation took his bath, with a bottle of rum and a black woman, looking out over his plantation and all the enslaved people working. It's just a theory," says Gonzalo, like the big bang. He laughs. "But it's the most accepted theory."

I imagine the owner in this bath in 1835, seven years after buying the plantation. He bought this land at the same time Winthrop and Hilton were gaining their footing in Charleston, the year Susan knew she was pregnant with her first baby, the year Eliza, Minerva, and Juba were claimed by Hasell to live with him and Susan on Cumberland Street. In 1835, at San Isidro, the owner might have sat triumphant in his bath with a woman who was forced to lie beside him, while in Columbia, South Carolina, Winthrop wrote to Eliza Williams back home, settling into his indoctrination in the cotton industry of South Carolina. He was about to become a rich factor who brought bales of cotton from the plantations outside of Charleston to ship to the New England (and, sometimes, Liverpool) textile mills. I think of his father and grandfather trading in the West Indies in the early 1800s—the repetition of their words in the quilt's papers—think of his father's store and the mercantile connections that gave him ease of access to so many goods traded in the Atlantic waters that I see from the Manaca Iznaga tower later in the afternoon with Gonzalo.

"He must have been a jerk," I say of the owner in the bathtub. I ask Gonzalo whether "mulatto" women were often chosen as mistresses by white owners here as in the States, and does he know the term *rape*?

"Yes," he says. "Yes, I'm sure, like all the owners of the sugar industry, this man was a jerk."

We walk through the crunch of dirt and over excavated rocks to the slave quarters on the other side of the Jamaican train. The quarters are in the woods facing the big house, but the trees aren't very tall. This must have been cleared land in the 1830s, where the owners could oversee the enslaved people without the shade of trees.

"He was a jerk like most people who have a lot of money," Gonzalo adds.

What an ingenious bug, to kill the spider that will support all of its young until they become wasps themselves. It looks like deviance, what the bug does, pillaging the tarantula's belly, but it's a cunning way to perpetuate the species, isn't it? Can anything adaptive in the animal world be deemed deviant?

I mistake the wasp for a metaphor. What became adaptive for some humans, this exertion of power of one group over another, this racialized world they created, *that* is deviant. We have access to morals and ethics. We can't kill and profit without consequences. If those wise enough to point out the wrongs of the present—the people Winthrop admonished for distributing abolitionist pamphlets—aren't heeded, then we can rely on our descendants to try to correct for the future. Can't we?

I think of the building collapse in Bangladesh in 2013, where 1,134 people were killed and 2,500 more were injured. You probably saw the pictures of the concrete building, destroyed in the middle, a wreck of four stories piled one on top of the other. This was a building owned by a man who was warned of the possibility of collapse; the people who worked on the first two floors, in shops, were told not to come to work the next day, but the factory workers who made clothes whose brands you probably recognize (Walmart, Benetton, Mango, among others), they were told to come to work; they worked on the top two floors, which were never meant to be used for the heavy equipment a factory required. Most of them were women who needed their jobs to support their families. How could they say no when they were told to come to work that day?

Industrialization led us there, to the textile factories, to the poor working conditions, to the pollution of lands surrounding the mills with dyes and fixatives and cleaning agents, to the lands, in India and elsewhere, where cotton is grown, still, sometimes by enslaved people and almost always by people who have suffered at the cruel processes capitalism mandates: high yields, for example, require farmers in India to use a cotton seed that's been genetically modified to resist the boll weevil, which ended the production of Sea Island cotton in the late nineteenth and early twentieth centuries. But, like every creature, the boll weevil has adapted, and can still feed on that genetically modified seed. The farmers have to use more pesticides to kill the boll weevil. In 2005, five hundred farmers died from pesticide exposure; their only form of protection as they sprayed was "a piece of cloth covering nose and mouth," if any was used at all.

More rain is required to nurture that seed. Farmers are in debt from having to buy that seed, and many of them have killed themselves when their crops have failed, unable to fathom how they'll overcome the debt.

In 2014, India "produced forty million bales" of cotton. This was a "bumper year," which made for a surplus, and farmers weren't paid enough for what they grew. There was no way to pay the debt. Since the mid-1990s, 300,000 cotton farmers have died by suicide.

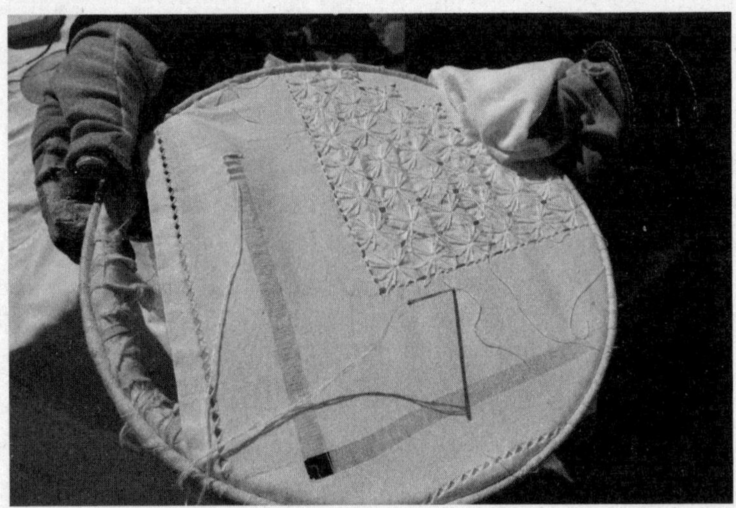

A woman's hand embroidery in Trinidad and a line of cloths for sale in front of a plantation. Women learn the art and sell goods to support themselves and their families.

I think of the people who produced the cotton that Winthrop thought would fund his retirement. I think of Eliza, Minerva, and Juba, and Boston and Bishroom, and William and Jane and George. I think of the women in the building collapse in Bangladesh, knowing that the conditions under which they lived and continue to live are fueled by capitalism, too. I look down to see what I'm wearing, who made it, and what it's made of, I look at the piles of fabric I've bought for quilting, and the stacks of pretty threads whose colors I love, and it's as if I hear the screech of brakes in my mind; I cannot buy these anymore. I think about the resistance to fast fashion—but, I read, conscientious buying is not enough. One person's pocketbook will not change this system. A friend says that the women working in those mills abroad *need* those jobs, and boycotting those brands means they could lose work that supports their families. I keep circling: What will change it?

In the main house, one of the men is still mixing concrete by hand in a wheelbarrow. They're restoring this house with all the traditional materials, making it historically accurate. The man points us to a corner where some artifacts have been found; it looks like a pile of junk from afar—broken bricks and vases, dirty screens with pebbles stuck in the grids. The engineer we met on the grounds, the man overseeing this project, tells us that the most important place for archaeologists to search is the "bathroom," as it's translated to me—the privy or outhouse—because that's where people threw away all their trash that we study today—broken pottery, discarded utensils, china plates, and chipped cups.

The men tell us they've just found the well—maybe it used to serve as the toilet—where they uncovered two guns. Gonzalo picks them up. They're Winchesters, he believes, based on the shape of the barrels. The metal is rusted and decaying, the barrel now fragile with age. The men tell us they also found this, says Gonzalo, translating for me. He gestures farther into the corner, where there's a stack of bricks.

"This is our lucky day," he says. "Oh, we're making history today!"

We stand in the corner where the sun comes through the open archway to my left. It falls on the red bricks stacked together. One of the bricks lies on its back, rough side down, and there, scrawled on its surface are letters. Gonzalo picks up the brick: *Canuto Matanew.*

Gonzalo lifts the brick and holds it in one hand. There are notches in the brick's side where four fingers must have rested.

"Put your hand here," I say. Fingerprints. A perfect fit.

Fingerprints, a name. Symbols of identity.

When I go home, I research and think at first this is Tagalog, a language from the Philippines. Filipinos came from their homeland to this similarly Spanish territory to work on tobacco plantations to the west of Havana, in Pinar del Río Province, once called New Philippines. But then I write to a scholar, Manuel Barcia, who tells me that someone who could write his name was probably not enslaved. He'd have been a local, most likely, he says, perhaps a plantation worker, an overseer. He was most certainly a Spanish speaker, so if an immigrant, he'd have come to the country as a child and acquired the language young, or as an adult from Spain. We don't know when the brick was made, Dr. Barcia reminds me; we can't come to any conclusions without more information.

I try to imagine the man named Canuto, the hot days he must have spent hunched over the fire where bricks were made, or standing at a pile of red clay, shaping the earth into rectangles. He'd have paused, that day, and picked up a stick or a piece of metal, and scrawled his name into the brick, his fingers pressed on its side as he held it steady. And then it went into the fire.

The brick will remain a mystery to me; I'll leave, my trip over, and Gonzalo and the historic commission will go on restoring this place, finding clues to the people who worked here, piecing them together, telling the story. This restoration has been ongoing for fifteen years, and it may take fifteen more to complete.

"That seventy years have rolled away, since she on the banks of the Rio de Valta received her existence—the mountains Covered with spicy forests, the valleys loaded with the richest fruits, spontaneously produced; joined to that happy temperature of air to exclude excess; would have yielded her the most compleat felicity, had not her mind received early impressions of the cruelty of men, whose faces were like the moon, and whose Bows and Arrows were like the thunder and the lightning of the Clouds."

—Belinda Sutton, from the petition for her freedom, 1783

Belinda Sutton stands before the house where she was enslaved by Isaac Royall. She wears a red cape and a brown dress. She takes off the cape before she begins speaking. It's warm this evening, in the seventies, too warm, even, for the bell-sleeved dress she's wearing. She'd have to have worn a long-sleeved dress no matter the weather. It's of brown and white calico, vertical stripes, with a corseted top that tapers towards her belly, and a long, gathered skirt. I think about the moments it would take to dress herself in the dark morning before the masters rose, the quiet of the house versus the clamor in the cooler slave quarters, where there are no thick blankets and fine silk curtains, no stacks of clothes from which to choose, no oil paintings on the walls, no carved mahogany desks and chairs on which to sit.

The slave quarters at the Royall House

The slave quarters are spare, with bare wide-planked floors and roughly carved chairs that don't hide their origins from trees—here a knot, here a set of asymmetrical legs—as many comforts as the enslaved people could afford to add, with innovation. Those hand-carved chairs, for example, and maybe a soft pillow for a child, made of flannel from the white family's last new batch of clothes, stitched with care by the child's mother. Likely, the fire always roars hot. This is where the cooking for the master's family is done. In wintertime Massachusetts, families must have nestled together close to the great hearth, trading places each night to give everyone a share of the heat.

The house where the Royall family lived, beside the slave quarters.

This is the house owned by Isaac Royall, founder of the Harvard Law School. In the 1700s, he owned a sugar plantation in the West Indies (Antigua) and lived in Massachusetts. He traded not only sugar but also enslaved people, and is another of those merchants whose lives and livelihoods zigzagged the colonial U.S. coast, including New England, and the West Indies, the Atlantic world.

In the house that's been restored to display fineries from the period in which the Royalls thrived, the house that stands beside the slave quarters where Belinda would have lived, there's a painting of the family, their hair curled up above their glossy finery, eager to document their wealth. Their hair was probably curled, in preparation for that portrait, by the enslaved people they owned, house "servants" who would have held the iron curler carefully so as not to burn themselves or their masters, tenderly twirling each strand of hair around the iron, then holding it tight, until a series of perfect spirals fell from the girls' heads. I imagine what a woman might have been thinking as she held a hot iron rod in her hands over her mistress's head, day after day.

In a room off the main hall, to the right, there's a room with a hearth and a cot where an enslaved woman slept and worked. Above the hearth shine hanging copper pots and pans, and perched on stands over the logs are cast-iron pots waiting to boil water, stews, and soups. This is where Belinda might have worked, hauling water in from the well, boiling potatoes or vegetables picked by the people who were enslaved to work in Royall's fields and gardens, on his five-hundred-acre farm.

At night, and in quiet moments between work, maybe Belinda or her children played with the beads and marbles and china shards that have since been found in the archaeological digs around the slave quarters. As historians documenting the site explain: "Finding evidence of 'games' and leisure in the archaeological record is more than quaint. In recreation, we see an active reassertion of humanity within the worst of dehumanizing conditions. The prevalence of such evidence on slavery sites across the country attests to its importance, as do the often creative ways enslaved people created and possessed these items." Games were empowerment, personhood, resistance.

With china shards—fragments of dishes broken by the family they served, perhaps—of two different patterns and a crisscross pattern on cloth or scratched into the dirt, people might have played Achi, a game similar to tic-tac-toe. Get three in a row first and you've won; complicate the game with four pieces and variations on the rules. Now, I watch two children play in my office at school, smiling before they make a move, tongue in a corner of her mouth, a quiet *hmm* from him as he decides where his chip will go next, her laughing on the next move when she's won.

Tammy Denease portrays Belinda Sutton, telling us her story. In 1783, with the help of Prince Hall, the Boston founder of the Freemasons society for African-Americans (now called Prince Hall Freemasonry), who claimed his own freedom, Belinda wrote her own story. Since she wasn't literate, Phillis Wheatley and Prince Hall likely helped set down what she spoke. The petition to the Senate and House of Representatives doesn't read as I'd expected—a dry legal document—but is a story told in beautiful, lyrical language, describing her life, the trauma she witnessed and experienced, and her home, which she must have missed her whole life.

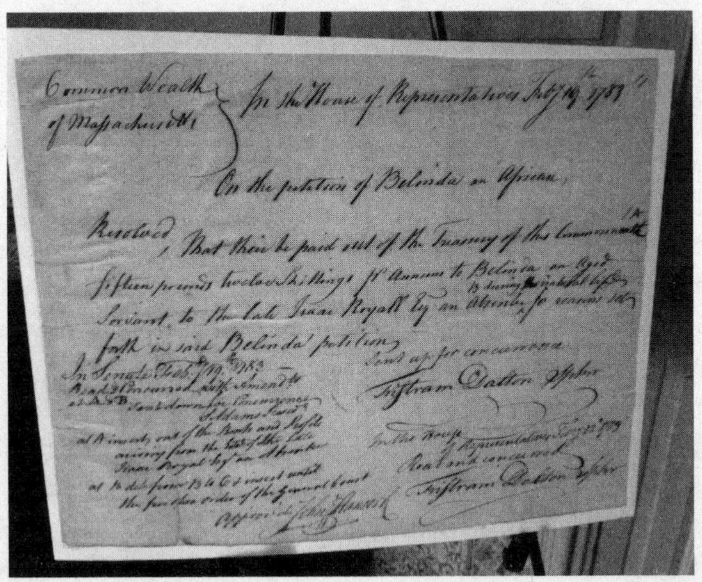

Common Wealth of Massachusetts

In the House of Representatives Feby 19th 1783

On the petition of Belinda an African,

Resolved, That there be paid out of the Treasury of this Commonwealth fifteen pounds twelve shillings pr Annum to Belinda an aged Servant to the late Isaac Royall Esq an Absentee for reasons set forth in said Belinda's petition

Sent up for concurrence

Tristram Dalton Spkr

In Senate Feby 19th 1783

Read & Concurred with Amendt

Tristram Dalton Spkr

Belinda's petition, 1789, displayed at the Royall House.

She refers to herself as "Belinda the African," proudly claiming her identity and history, and says she grew up "on the banks of the Rio de Valta" in Ghana, surrounded by those "spicy forests," "valleys loaded with the richest fruits," delighted with the world until she saw the Europeans with their "faces . . . like the moon, and whose Bows and Arrows were like the thunder and the lightning of the Clouds." No longer safe "with each hand in that of a tender Parent," and praying to "Orisa who made all things," before she was twelve, she was kidnapped, "ravished from the bosom of her Country, from the arms of her friends." Her parents were deemed too old "for servitude," and she was "cruelly separated from them forever." She was taken to "a floating world," above "sporting Monsters of the deep," and was surrounded by "three hundred Affricans in chains, suffering the most excruciating horrors." She goes on to describe her arrival to the continent and the life she spent serving Isaac Royall before he died in the Revolutionary War. The irony of a battle for freedom while she had none is not lost on her, nor is the fact that she was never given any of the money Royall earned with the help of her labor—not "one morsel of that immense wealth."

She asks, now that she's seventy years old and "feeble," to be granted an allowance from Royall's estate to help sustain herself and her daughter, Prine (she also had a son, Joseph, and both children were baptized). She was named as free in Isaac Royall's will in 1778; a condition of her freedom was that she be given an annual stipend, so that she wouldn't be a "charge" or burden, on the town of Medford. It was illegal in many states to free enslaved people because the governments feared they'd be responsible for them once their owners deemed them too old for work and requiring care. Belinda was awarded thirty pounds, for three years after Royall died, and then she began to petition for back pay. She petitioned in 1783, 1787, 1788, and 1793, winning "a year's allowance" in 1787 and a small sum of money from one of Royall's relatives.

She wasn't successful in getting the money, but her petitions have marked her place in history as she persisted in asking for her due. Like Phillis Wheatley, Sojourner Truth, and Ellen Craft, she wrote herself into the record when others would have attempted to erase her. This—her tenacity—is probably why Tammy Denease thinks of her as bearing witness to her Ashanti heritage.

Belinda's story was pieced together more fully in 2015, when the 1788 petition was found via a digital archive and revealed the fact that she'd been married, and was now a widow with the last name Sutton. As more digital archives are created—the runaway slave advertisements one among them—more stories might be pieced together, more threads connecting narratives of which we know parts.

10
An Abomination

Peace depends on cotton and negroes.

—Winthrop

In places, Winthrop's letters can be entertaining. In 1840, he accidentally shoots himself in the hand while bird hunting and tries to dispel the rumors that he did it from being spurned by a woman—that it was an unsuccessful suicide attempt. He misses home and the company of the boarders at his parents' house; he finds the ladies in Columbia wanting in looks but resourceful—unlike his sister Susan, who sends home for fabric and dresses to be cut by the Providence seamstress they know. (Columbia women cut and sew all their own dresses because the tailors and seamstresses there are too costly.) He writes about a failed hot air balloon "ascension" he'd paid to witness, and jokingly asks his family to demand a refund from the man when he brings this scam up north. He reveals a lot about his family and his adjustment to the south. He hopes a northern man will take the place of the clerk who's just left the store in Columbia; he can't stand Hasell's "disagreeable" brother, Charles Crouch, nor his wife, Eliza Crouch. He writes to his sister Eliza Williams for shirts, as his are about to wear out. He asks if the family has the same cow they had when he was home, and if she still gives milk, and writes about two local cows whose deaths he believes he expertly diagnosed.

> *There were two cows died here a few nights ago from eating of the wild cherry. The people could not find out just what killed them until I happened to see the cherry trees lying near the places where they died and told them that was what had killed them. They could hardly believe me for they had never heard of it before. Ask Father if it is not a fact that the leaves of the wild cherry will kill them.*

He's so invested in this diagnosis of the cows, so certain of himself. And the more I read of him, the less I can tolerate this sense of certainty, his bravado, his claiming authority on all things, even down to cow-milking, which he says, in the 1860s, he can do better than the people he'd enslaved, denigrating them in his anger that they've been emancipated. He is so invested in his sense of superiority as a white man and membership in the master class as, throughout the 40s and 50s, he acquires more and more wealth earned from enslaved people's labor. He is the most passionately racist member of his family. He and Hilton, who was less lucky in business but was served by his wife's inherited enslaved people even in difficult financial times, enriched themselves with the labor of enslaved people. They chose this life; Hilton bought and sold people for his mill, found and sold the man who ran away, sold Adam and George with the mill. Winthrop's son, Winty, inherited Patty and

Amelia from his mother's estate; those women likely served Winthrop until Winty came of age.

Winthrop writes about how he gained his wealth, working in the store, moving from the cotton building to the front where he had to serve the ladies and gentlemen in the shop, and then, to his relief, moving again to the cotton building and back of the shop. He writes that he "sees by the papers" that the infantry from Providence are traveling to Boston, and he asks for more papers to be sent south. He and Hilton say they've sent by the brigs *Commerce*, the *Mary*, a package of figs or hominy or peaches for the family, and later, Winthrop says he's sent bales of cotton north to be conveyed to his brother-in-law or to his father to sell for him. He relays to his northern family the news he's gotten in letters from Susan and Hilton in Charleston. But most interesting of all—to me, at least—he writes about the news of the North and South. As Franklin notes at the bottom of the pages on which he's transcribed these letters, Winthrop slowly becomes a wealthy cotton trader; he's for states' rights to sustain enslavement, but not secession. It's strange to watch from the distance of nearly two hundred years a person change over the course of his lifetime, to hear in his letters the shifts in voice—first ebullient and hopeful for his future, and then, by the time the Civil War begins thirty years later, he is weary, afraid, and tired. In those thirty years, he married, had four children, built a fortune and lost it all. It's hard not to despise him when he writes about how he built that wealth, the system he took so easily in stride as he adapted to the South, his complaints about his enslaved people and then about freedmen after emancipation. In the first letter in which he talks politics with his sisters, noted by Franklin as the beginning of his transition to conservative southerner, he begins to draw a line between himself and his sisters, the South and the North. He echoes a letter Susan sent to her parents, wishing they had more "help." He starts the letter by bemoaning the fact that his family in the North can't "get as good help," meaning enslaved people, as Winthrop has in Charleston. In Providence, Susan and her family hire domestic workers; those who are mentioned in his sisters' letters are Irish immigrants, but when Winthrop and Susan were still children living at home in 1820, their family had in their household a woman listed as "colored" and "servant."

> *. . . I wish you could get as good help as the people have here. The people at the North are making trouble sending incendiary publications among us. They had better be doing something else for there is no calculating what ever may result from them—I may say making trouble for themselves also for if this subject comes to an issue it will shake our country to its very centre. The people here have too much spirit to be humbugged or trampled on by any set of men.*

Those "incendiary publications" Winthrop refers to were the abolitionist pamphlets being sent from the American Anti-Slavery Society in the North, led by William Lloyd Garrison and Arthur Tappan. Garrison published *The Liberator,* an abolitionist newspaper founded in 1831, the year that Nat Turner led his rebellion in Virginia. Turner organized fifty to sixty enslaved people who left the plantations on which they were held, and protested, recruiting more enslaved people as they went through the county—murdering their enslavers and other whites they encountered, who had perpetuated their torture for years—until at last, the group was finally thwarted and murdered by a white militia.

Just two years earlier, in 1829, David Walker, an African American man living in Boston, published his *Appeal to the Coloured Citizens of the World*, a call to action for the immediate liberation of enslaved people. He writes: "The whites have had us under them for more than three centuries, murdering, and treating us like brutes; and as Mr. Jefferson wisely said, they have never *found us out*—they do not know, indeed, that there is an unconquerable disposition in the breasts of the blacks, which, when it is fully awakened and put in motion, will be subdued, only with the destruction of animal existence. . . ." Nat Turner's rebellion, like the Christmas Uprising in Jamaica in 1831–32, when sixty thousand enslaved people revolted under the leadership of an enslaved man named Samuel Sharpe, is evidence of a more public moment when enslaved people seized their freedom with careful planning and organization that came from skillful communication strategies and determination. Imagine how hard it would have been to set a time and place to gather when it was illegal to write, to walk anywhere without a pass, to gather without permission, or to buy anything that might help a person escape and survive. At the end of the rebellion, twice as many people of color, many of whom weren't involved in the rebellion, were murdered by whites in retaliation. Nat Turner's rebellion, like Denmark Vesey's in 1822, inspired fear in the white master class in Charleston and Columbia, as they saw the possibility of their lives and livelihoods overturned.

Those stricter laws that attempted to control enslaved people's lives were strengthened in the aftermath of The Stono Rebellion in 1739. This rebellion was led by Jemmy or Cato, outside Charleston. George Cato, great-great-grandson of Cato or Jemmy, was interviewed in about 1937 as part of the Works Progress Administration project—founded, of course, to employ those who suffered in the Great Depression—to document the lives of formerly enslaved people. There are thousands of stories from formerly enslaved people transcribed in volumes that anyone can read in text or online. In the 1930s, two hundred years after the rebellion, George was interviewed by a white man hired by the federal government to carry out the WPA project. Historian Mark Smith, who discovered the significance of George Cato's narrative, reminds readers that this is an interview from a person of color by a white person in the Jim Crow era, with all the inescapable power dynamics that would have been attendant at the time. Interviewees may not have felt free to tell—or may not have *wanted* to tell—all they knew to the interviewers. Scholars have noted that people may have not been as frank about the violence they witnessed and experienced when they were enslaved, or may not have wanted to implicate or denigrate their former owners in the face of a white interviewer who could so easily exact punishment. The note accompanying the narratives explains that in the 1930s, "white representations of black speech already had an ugly history of entrenched stereotype dating back at least to the early nineteenth century. What most interviewers assumed to be 'the usual' patterns of their informants' speech was unavoidably influenced by preconceptions and stereotypes." The documents therefore become evidence not only of the era of enslavement but also of the 1930s: "The result, as the historian Lawrence W. Levine has written, 'is a mélange of accuracy and fantasy, of sensitivity and stereotype, of empathy and racism' that may sometimes be offensive to today's readers." Smith explains that in spite of these complicated layers around the narratives, they're reliable, and hold powerful anecdotes and testimonies whose facts have been verified in other sources.

George Cato said of his ancestor Jemmy or Cato: "I thinks de first Cato take a darin' chance on losin' his life, not so much for his own benefit as it was to help others. . . ." George Cato went on to explain that Jemmy or Cato was elected captain and that the group conquered a place that had been designed to render them helpless: "How it all start? Dat what I ask but nobody ever tell me how 100 slaves between de Combahee and Edisto rivers come to meet in de woods not far from de Stono River on September 9, 1739. And how they elect a leader, my kinsman, Cato, and late dat day march to Stono town, break in a warehouse, kill two white men in charge, and take all de guns and ammunition they wants. But they do it. Wid dis start, they turn south and march on." Cato had been hiding for two months before he was found after the rebellion. "Commander Cato speak for de crowd. He says: 'We don't lak slavery. We start to jine de Spanish in Florida. We surrender but we not whipped yet and we is not converted.' De other 43 men say: 'Amen.' They was taken, unarmed, and hanged by de militia. Long befo' dis uprisin', de Cato slave wrote passes for slaves and do all he can to send them to freedom. He die but he die for doin' de right, as he see it."

Cato was taught to read and write by his master, and used his skill to help others, as George Cato explained; his great-great-grandfather undertook the rebellion to "help others," leading the group on a march to Florida to "join the Spanish," who had promised freedom to any enslaved people who crossed into their territory. The men who were found in hiding were taken unarmed, George Cato said, posing no threat, and then hanged by the colonists.

In 1740, in the wake of Cato's resistance, the colonists created the Act for the Better Ordering and Governing of Negroes and Other Slaves in this Province, a brutal law with a placid name. This would be an improvement, the law's name told the people, "better," and there would be safety in "order." Don't be afraid, that law said, for we are cracking down. The law stated that enslaved people could not own or carry weapons, nor walk in public without passes from their masters; furthermore, anyone who attempted to insurrect would be put to death. This law held for another 120 years, until the Emancipation Proclamation and the Civil War in the 1860s.

> *Cotton has been coming in rather freely for a month past . . . As the market is now up to former prices we may look this week for an increase in business.*

What does it mean that one of the best-known images of Nat Turner is that of his capture? In the sketch, he stands holding his sword, the weapon that came to symbolize his resistance, facing a grimacing white man holding a gun to Turner's face. They emerge from the woods. Turner's pants are torn at the knee, and he wears the same sort of light-colored, loose-fitting shirt open at the chest—though Turner's appears to have buttons, undone in a gap at the stomach—that symbolizes the enslaved men in the engraving that illustrates the "massacre" and contrasts with the white gun holder's buttoned shirt, neat jacket, and whole-cloth pants. The white captor is clean-shaven, wears boots and a hat. Nat Turner is pictured as barefoot, bareheaded, and with a beard.

The Confessions of Nat Turner were recorded—supposedly, as we don't know how precisely his words were transcribed—by Turner's white lawyer. How are we to interpret so many texts, so many images, made by colonists? How is a story of a person of color inevitably filtered in the hands of a white writer or painter or storyteller or lawyer? What does it mean to describe the images here, without reprinting them? Would it be better to reprint them? The forces of our culture, the ways in which we're indoctrinated, are inevitable and unavoidable. Something seemingly as simple as a drawing can be interpreted so many different ways, depending on who's looking at the image. The past, our institutions, are always present. How is my telling of this story shaped by who I am? How are the myths by which we live perpetuated by what we imagine ourselves to be, as individuals and as a nation?

In 1835, northern abolitionists Garrison and Tappan helped launch the country's first mass-mailing, which was possible only thanks to industrial printing machines; they harnessed industrial technology for an act of rebellion against its evils—the perpetuation of slavery due to mass production of cotton at the mills. The society sent more than a million pamphlets to southern slave owners and distributed them on sidewalks and at taverns. And southerners were enraged. The Charleston postmaster held the pamphlets when they arrived at his office, saying that he wouldn't distribute "such unpatriotic material." Alert to what was on hand at the post office, rioters in Charleston broke into the office and burned the pamphlets (which, incidentally, had been brought south via the *Columbia*, a ship that often took Winthrop's, Hilton's, and Susan's letters north) before they could be distributed. They weren't going to be, as Winthrop says, "humbugged or trampled on." In other words, they were determined not to be stripped of their way of life, notably the enslavement of others that made their lives possible.

Winthrop echoes the views of Andrew Jackson, who was now in his second term as president. Jackson was against the abolitionists, going so far as to say he "might call them monsters" who were inciting a Civil War. Jackson proposed a law stating that abolitionist material couldn't be sent by federal mail. John C. Calhoun, whose statue, today, stands stately in Marion Square in Charleston's downtown, was, like Jackson, a slave owner, but while Jackson did all he could to sustain the Union, Calhoun helped spawn secessionism. He didn't want the federal government to have the power to mandate what could or could not be dispersed, what could or could not be said; he thought it should be up to the individual states. So, Jackson and Calhoun, his vice president, agreed: The post office couldn't meddle with mail and hinder free speech, and the federal government would feign ignorance when they did so.

Winthrop would have heard about the mob burning abolitionist pamphlets in Charleston—either from Susan, Hasell, Hilton, neighbors who traveled back and forth between the two cities on business, or the city's newspaper, the *Charleston Mercury*, to which he'd have had access. He writes about the similar mode of law in Columbia.

> *There has been a Lynch Club formed in this town, their object is to punish and keep all persons of known ill fame out of the community also such pestilent ornery persons distributing Incendiary Tracts; they whipped a man by the name of Johnston a notorious counterfeiter, and sent him out of town about three weeks ago.*

Those who sent around "incendiary tracts," abolitionist papers and pamphlets, would be dealt with by the mob. Winthrop says he doesn't agree with this sort of law, as he thought the lynch mobs were "Dangerous to the Supremacy of Law," which was Andrew Jackson's argument. However, Winthrop goes on to say:

> *There may be some cases where there is no other way of administering summary punishment . . . for instance . . . the case of the Barber that was lately whipped and tarred and cottoned in Charleston. It seems he had been taken up and tried several times, but had managed either to evade the Law or pay the fine imposed, which the profit of his illicit trade afforded ample means . . .*

We don't know what his illicit trade was, but his punishment—being whipped, then having hot tar poured over his skin and covered in cotton—was a severe punishment, though surely not the worst the lynch club exacted.

The mail crisis of 1832 was one in a series of instances that illustrated the growing tension between North and South, which Winthrop chronicles in his letters and illustrates in his expressions of frustration with family members who represent his political opponents, and with his sisters Eliza and Emily who were opposed to slavery. In many of his letters, he mentions the current price of cotton, whether it's high or low, and often, also, the prices of "negroes," corn, and rice. In a letter from April 1835, he refers to a friend, "the first person I have seen from home since I have been here." He says they spoke of "home and bygone days," and that it "gave me much satisfaction" to spend time with an old friend. This friend, Leonard Hyatt, is adjusting to his newfound life as well: "He is very much altered since I saw him last. He has become a southerner throughout but no nullifier." Winthrop is referring here to the Nullification Crisis of 1832, just a year earlier, which also involved John C. Calhoun and was a dispute over the state's versus the federal government's power, and the balance of agrarian products in the South and industrial manufacture in the North. It almost resulted in a civil war, which, they couldn't have known then wasn't prevented but only postponed. Winthrop and Susan would find themselves on opposite sides of the battle lines. And yet, their ties between North and South would continue to serve them well, saving Winthrop's son when he served as a soldier.

In the early 1830s, when the Civil War was still in the future, distant and unknown, when textile mills churned out fabric in the hands of New England mill girls, when the Leonids fell, when Susan and Hasell were settling down in Charleston and Eliza, Minerva, and Jane were working to support them, when hundreds of people were picking the cotton that was slowly building Winthrop's fortune as a cotton broker, and just before Hilton bought Boston and Bishroom (who had by then lost the woman who was probably his wife, Mary) to work at his mill, there was a conflict between the North and South over that cotton. Three years later, it erupted as the Nullification Crisis, but its roots had been planted years earlier.

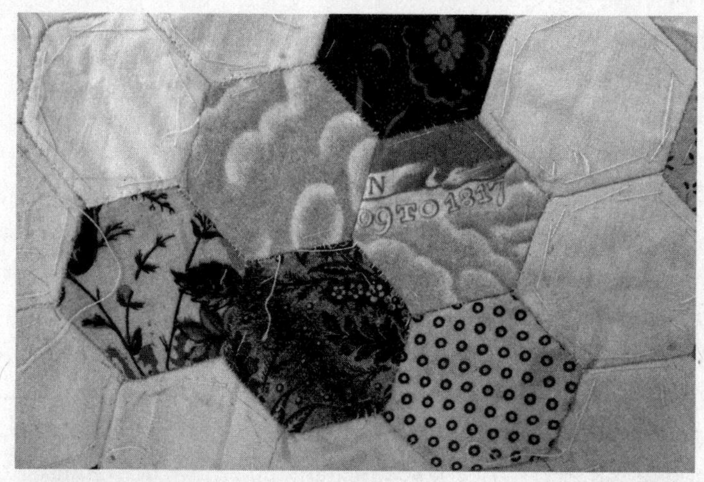

This commemorative fabric celebrates Jackson's inauguration. It was likely added to the quilt tops by Franklin; these stitches are not nearly as fine and even as others, which are likely Susan's.

In 1828, the federal government instated a tax on all imported goods, with the intention of preventing England from selling its goods at lower prices than those with which the industrial North could compete; this law followed those that had been passed years earlier, after the War of 1812, and echoed that Embargo Act of 1807 that would so cripple the business dealings of Jason Williams, Susan's father. I witnessed his losses as I flipped through folders with receipt after receipt in longhand as he slowly paid off his debts—the great sloping letters in black ink, splotches and smudges obliterating some of the numbers and words.

Andrew Jackson was a part of the War of 1812, as well, leading the battle at Horseshoe Bay in 1814 in Alabama, where he and his troops killed a thousand people from the Creek nation, who fought to defend their territory rather than be pushed west. Years later, as president in 1830, Jackson would sign off on the Indian Removal Act, which ruled that the federal government could send tribal nations to new lands west of the Mississippi River in a "trade" for the lands to which they held claim in the settled states. This would eventually lead to what's commonly referred to as the "Trail of Tears" in 1838, when people of the Cherokee nation in Georgia refused to cede lands illegally taken by the colonists; these Cherokee people, as well as Cherokees from other states and people from other southwestern tribes, were then forcibly pushed off their land and sent west of the Mississippi River, to "Indian Territory" in what is today the state of Oklahoma. This journey would kill between four and eight thousand people; some people died in the stockades before they began to walk, and others died on their way west, through exposure—as they were made to walk through the winter—starvation, or dehydration because they were given little food and water, and from the sicknesses and injuries that came from lack of proper shelter or medicine—all this in spite of the fact that John Marshall, Supreme Court chief justice, had ruled in *favor* of the Georgia Cherokee, judging that they held the right to their lands and should not be forced west. "This is the *only* time a president openly defied the Supreme Court," a scholar reminds us. Jackson ignored that ruling, and sent troops to move the nations off their land, which he wanted to repurpose for the planting of cotton.

Jackson was a planter himself. He owned enslaved people (as did some of the Native American people he removed). Jackson's first concern, he said, was to preserve the United States and protect its ability to trade products. But, he was driven by racism in his attempts to eradicate indigenous nations from these lands. In 1814, he was saved by a Cherokee chief, Junaluska, who had led 800 warriors to fight with Jackson's troops in the battle against the Creeks. And then, in 1830, in a speech to Congress about the progress of "Indian removal," he espoused the benefits of moving the nations west, one benefit that it would "perhaps cause them gradually, under the protection of the Government and through the influence of good counsels, to cast off their savage habits and become an interesting, civilized, and Christian community. What good man would prefer a country covered with forests and ranged by a few thousand savages to our extensive Republic, studded with cities, towns, and prosperous farms embellished with all the improvements which art can devise or industry execute . . ." Those who had fought and died with him, who had saved his life, were now "savages" who needed to be taught by white colonists to cast off their ways. He says the government is doing the people a favor by sending them to new lands and "support[ing] them for a year in their new abode. How many thousands of our own people would gladly embrace the opportunity of removing to the West on such conditions!" He goes on with his paternalistic comments and adds that the "wandering savage" can't possibly be more attached "to his home than the settled, civilized Christian." They were *saving* the people, he said in closing. This was a *kindness* for the General Government to "offer" them "a new home."

In 1835, he proposed his plan to the indigenous nations, betraying them, under the guise that he was trying to protect them from the violence they'd face in Georgia from whites. "I have no motive, my friends, to deceive you. I am sincerely desirous to promote your welfare," he says in 1835 when he urges them to agree to move west and sign away rights to their lands. He goes on to warn the Cherokee people that the "condition of the Creeks" provides an example for what will happen to the Cherokee if they don't move. "See the collisions which are taking place with [the Creeks]. See how their young men are committing depradations upon the property of our citizens, and are shedding their blood. This cannot and will not be allowed. Punishment will follow." He starts the speech trying to woo his "friends" into trusting him, and closes with the threat that if they don't, they will end up like the Creeks who purportedly do harm to *our citizens* and will be punished by the patriarchal US government as a result.

Winthrop wrote an account of meeting Osceola, a well-known man from the Creek and Seminole nations. There was no intimation then of Winthrop's desire to "exterminate" the "Indians," but his letter from 1836 reveals his beliefs:

> *It would seem that the predictions of many that there would be war if Gen. Jackson became President of the United States has been and is being fulfilled, the Seminole Indians are still in arms. Volunteers are collecting from all quarters of this State. I have been thinking about it myself, it would be fine fun to shoot one of the yellow rascals. War with France still seems to be undecided. I believe I will wait a short time and see if that would not be the best chance. I don't like the idea of having my hair taken off skin and all, perhaps Whiskers.*

His lines ring in me as an echo to that day on the lawn in college, when I heard similar sentiments, when I hear them now from America's leaders, including the president. Genocide, extermination, murder—acts against African Americans and Native Americans, sanctioned by the US government through its laws, its loopholes, its unwillingness to enforce laws.

As Jackson pressed for Indian removal, Jackson also believed he had to limit competition from the British for American goods. South Carolinian John C. Calhoun was Jackson's vice president. He was ardently opposed to the tariffs Jackson instated, because he thought they gave advantages to the North, who had ready local access to industrially produced goods—like cotton cloth made at the mills—that were available only at a high tax to southerners. And so the Nullification Crisis was born when southerners, with Calhoun leading the way, opposed the high tax on goods they couldn't get except from the British or from the northern industrial states. They resisted the tax, and said they had the right to nullify any federal law that didn't serve the state's best interest. They said this tariff was an abomination. The land Jackson believed was necessary for the success of the cotton industry, and thus the nation, was to be "cleared" of indigenous people who had claims to it, which would fulfill both his goals of genocide of Native Americans and large-scale profits from cotton production.

Winthrop chronicles the slowly roiling tensions between North and South as soon as he moves to Columbia, and then Charleston. He writes of a man visiting Columbia:

> *He is an engineer from some part of Massachusetts engaged out here* [near Columbia, SC] *to put a cotton factory in motion which is being built on a river about a mile from this place. It is to be operated by negroes instead of white labor, which has been found to answer very well indeed in several small factories in this state.*
>
> *They intend making very coarse heavy goods called "cotton usnaburghs," in which they think they can cut out the Northern manufacturers entirely, owing to the cheapness of slave labor and having the staple right at their doors.*
>
> *. . . He is a great advocate of the System as you may suppose . . . They were not aware that I was in favor of it. . . . They live in much style.*

Winthrop writes to his sister Eliza Williams, explaining that a factory for "usnaburghs," osnaburgs, commonly known as slave cloth or negro cloth—the rougher, lower grade fabric produced for people enslaved in fields to wear—was to be built along the river near his new home in Columbia. This, he says, would save money, since the cotton was being harvested so nearby. Like those who supported nullification, Winthrop hopes the building of the factory in Columbia will mean that they can cut out the northern mills and save the cost of shipping and buying the cloth back for the enslaved people to make their clothes with negro cloth on the plantations. The "staple," cotton, was being picked right there, and the enslaved people were wearing clothes made of cotton; he argues that it's senseless to ship the raw good north only to ship the cloth south again to be sewn into clothes by the people who labored to pick the cotton. Winthrop writes this letter just after the Nullification Crisis was dodged by the federal government, in a compromise with the state of South Carolina. The state had threatened to secede over the disagreement, so the federal government proposed lowering the import tax to which South Carolina opposed; the decrease would come gradually, over time (a promise later broken). Though they avoided confrontation in the 1830s, Winthrop continues illustrating the rising tensions between North and South in his letters home. The Nullification Crisis was a prelude to the coming attempt at secession—and the resulting war.

In November of 1834, Winthrop writes, "You would laugh outright if you should see the suit of clothes I wear they are of coarse negro cloth black mixed—the pantaloons and vest cost me 2.50$ all made. They answer very well for my business. Much better than anything very fine would because they would tear." He's speaking about working back among the "cotton bales and countrymen . . . instead of Dry Goods and the Ladies," a position to which he's happy to return in the spring of 1835: "I like the rough outdoor business better than the confinement behind the counter. We sell a great many goods and buy a good deal of Cotton."

In this letter, like so many others, Winthrop notes the prices of cotton, corn, and rice: "The cotton market is up—the article was sold here today for 19 cts—the highest we have paid is 18 cts for a small lot which we sold the same day for 18 7/8. Since October last we have bought about six thousand bales in both Houses."

Six thousand bales of cotton at about three hundred seventy pounds apiece is about two million two hundred twenty thousand pounds. At nineteen cents a pound, that's $422,000. This was 1835. Today, that would be nearly $6 million dollars.

Winthrop was in the thick of big business. He had hit the boom.

In the coming year, he and Mr. Ewart would enter into partnership together, one that benefited both men and took advantage of their respective connections in New York and Providence. By the time of the Civil War, Winthrop stood to lose what amounts to millions today. As he said, he was "in favor of the System" that made this business profitable—slavery. Like his brother, Hilton, and sister Susan, he slipped into the slave economy with ease. Hilton writes, in November 1834:

> *One of my negroes ran away during my absence and I caught him the day after my return. I have since sold him for $600. I gave $500 for*

> *him about seventeen months since, he was a great rogue, would steal from me every opportunity he had. I bought another fellow last week for $462 that I think will answer my purpose much better. Negroes are now selling very high—the other negroes behaved very well during my absence.*

Where Hilton sees a "rogue," we might see a man who was expert at resisting enslavement. Maurie D. McInnis writes, "There was little that made traders angrier than slaves who tried to run away, not only because an escape represented a significant financial loss, but also because such actions powerfully refuted the proslavery assertion that slaves were content." Hilton wasn't a trader, of course, but as an owner of enslaved men he was equally as furious that one of "his men" would undermine him by claiming his freedom. The man was likely intelligent and knew the land well, because he not only ran away but also seems to have kept that freedom for at least a few weeks. Maybe he was visiting a beloved, a friend, a family member—a child, a wife, a brother, his ailing mother. He took what he needed from Hilton, though Hilton calls it stealing. The man was supposedly worth $600, which was a high price for a laborer, and yielded a profit of $100 for Hilton. Powers writes that "Mill owners preferred using slaves in unskilled or semiskilled capacities," and notes that the "majority of workers employed at the Gibbes and Williams Steam Saw Mill" were enslaved men. So, the man who ran away was probably unskilled or semiskilled, meaning he hadn't been permitted to apprentice to a craftsman to gain skills that would allow him to do the "skilled labor" that other jobs (like carpentry, for example) required. But this doesn't mean, of course, that he didn't have skills and talents that were unrecognized by the whites who bought and sold him. Maybe each night, he carved intricate animals and dolls for his daughter who lived a few blocks away. Maybe he knew how to play violin, like Solomon Northrop, or banjo, and secretly made one for himself with scraps from the mill. Maybe he was a beautiful writer who would one day escape, for good, and tell his own story.

To whom did Hilton sell him? Where did he go?

Like Winthrop, Hilton comments on the markets, discussing the costs of buying enslaved people just as he would the cost of buying rice or cotton. In 1835, Winthrop was twenty-one and Hilton was twenty-six. They were young. When I walk around my university campus, I try to imagine my students—many of whom are here to swing themselves into upward mobility, just as Hilton and Winthrop hoped to do—in the brothers' places, heading to a new land far from their own home, and buying and selling people to build their businesses, propelling themselves upward in the stratification of the classes. This, Hilton and Winthrop must have believed, was their best hope for advancement in a world that hadn't guaranteed their father's wealth. They'd witnessed him paying off his debts for a trade gone bad since they were children, their mother tending a house full of student boarders attending Brown—the college their uncle had attended but which they, apparently, could not afford to attend. They seemed to have been willing to do anything to rise up, to—like Susan, striving to be part of the Charleston master class and the circle of fine ladies—enter the world in which their friend Hasell had been raised, surrounded by "servants" in a fine home by the battery.

But their sisters Emily and Eliza Williams, back in Providence, were, nevertheless, apparently opposed to the "System." Because so few letters in their voices survive, we don't get to hear them speak their stories. The women's stories are told, for the most part, through the lens of their brothers' responses. Here, Winthrop gives Eliza advice about coming south and reforming a man who might not live so differently than he does:

> *Believe me now it is a good place for them to come for there are unmarried men aplenty, but then you say they are slave holders, horse racers, carry dirks and pistols. Now, the best plan is to marry one and reform him. You will get double the merit for such an act, than to stay at home and marry a quiet, easy steady husband.*

He suggested she might find a "wild" southern man and "reform" him, gaining the benefit of the community for having done a social good.

Eliza seemed already to have chosen a man. Here, Winthrop calls him "your intended," and says the worst idea is to bring with her other women who might provide competition: "But the worst of it is to plan it so as to bring your intended other's company, you will have to make a visit to this place as he will not be able to have leave here this winter. But more of this anon." He suggests she visit Columbia soon so she can see him, as he won't be able to leave that winter. This was October 8, 1836, almost exactly two years after Eliza was widowed when her husband fell to smallpox, in September 1834. Now, she was perhaps in love again, or had at least found someone suitable to marry.

This is likely the match that her family opposed. Maybe the "intended" was a factor like Winthrop, who had moved south from Providence to make his fortune. Maybe he was a southerner whom she'd met when he traveled north. We never get to learn why the marriage was prohibited and her inheritance denied her, but after Susan returns from the south in 1838, Eliza moves in with Emily, with whose family she lives until she dies. Emily and Eliza would only go back to the George Street house where Susan and her daughter lived, Franklin notes, when Susan and her daughter had left to winter in Charleston with her brothers.

We never get to hear Eliza Williams's reaction to her marriage being blocked, nor even Susan's or Emily's. It seems to have been a quiet rift that grew between the sisters, perhaps deepened by Susan and Hasell's ownership of enslaved people while in the South.

Winthrop goes on to justify the need for enslaved people to build a person's wealth, as if trying to convince Eliza Williams of the System:

> *My friend Shrivers, who was a clerk with me at the upper store last winter, has made quite a speculation in the matrimonial line—he is engaged to a Miss Bynum, daughter of an old rich planter to whom it is said he will give 70 negroes. Is not that worth having? More especially when the said young lady happens to be accomplished, intelligent, and very amiable?*
>
> *I had the pleasure of selling her and her mother a large quantity of goods for the said purpose as I presume for the wedding was to take place immediately but in consequence of Mrs. Shrivers having a slight attack of fever it will be consummated soon.*

He sells her goods from the general store. His friend is making not a marriage but a "speculation," an investment. Winthrop asks, "Is not that worth having?" To Winthrop, the "negroes" represent wealth. Based on the way this paragraph is composed—the question posed in the negative, the list of benefits Shriver will supposedly gain—Eliza must have been morally opposed. The enslaved people are wealth, he seems to be saying to her, and, the woman whom his friend Shriver will marry is "accomplished, intelligent, amiable," so it happens that the woman is pleasant, to boot. It's all for the good, he seems to think.

I wonder again how siblings end up with such different politics, how families become so divided. The sisters had to marry, or face living with their parents under strained financial circumstances for the rest of their lives. They didn't have the option, as the mill girls did, of going to work on their own—but of course, the mill girls didn't have access to the education and other luxuries afforded Emily, Susan, and Eliza Williams. Eliza Williams was married and then consigned to living with her sisters' families for the rest of her life, as a widow. Their sister Abby married Mr. Elles and gave birth to many children, several of whom died, six of whom survived; she seems to have been in physical pain—back pain—that immobilized her much of the time. Franklin describes her as lazy, but she seems to have suffered from chronic pain and depression as a result of her children's deaths.

At one point in the 1830s, overwhelmed, Abby sends her boys out to board with a woman nearby, to ease Abby's workload. She could sometimes afford to hire a girl to help, and sometimes could not. She and her husband lived in upstate New York, and then, when they moved to New York City, they became wealthy with his printing business that included sales of "cambric" (cotton) notebooks. The cambrics were another product of the cotton and textile industries, of course, grown in the South and woven in the North.

Emily married a man who would help propel Winthrop and Hilton's trade and who profited from it himself, as the trader of their goods in the North. Did Emily see the contradiction in this, if she was also opposed to slavery? Did she have any choice in the matter, even if she did see it?

The microfiche machine whirred and paused, whirred and paused, as I scrolled through the pages to the section for ads. I was in Charleston, in the South Carolina Room at the public library, reading a year's worth of newspapers in search of an advertisement for the man Hilton said ran away.

That man resisted. Maybe he went to see his wife, or one of his children, at a home or plantation nearby. Maybe he spent those days of freedom eating hardboiled eggs gifted from a woman he knew at a neighboring farm on the outskirts of the city. Maybe he hid in swampland, or in the trees, or at a local grog shop where he spent time with friends. Maybe he looked up at the stars each night and, like Elizabeth Mumbet Freeman, thanked God he was free, at least for those moments: "Any time, any time while I was a slave, if one minute's freedom had been offered to me, and I had been told I must die at the end of that minute, I would have taken it—just to stand one minute on God's airth [sic] a free woman—I would."

I searched for hours, and then, it was closing time and I'd reached the dates when Hilton said he found the man and sold him. The man was not listed in the newspapers, so I had no more clues—nothing about his skills, how he might have looked, what he wore—anything that, even though given through Hilton's eyes, could have provided some clues as to who this man was, a blurry portrait from which I could piece together a part of his story.

Across town at the archive where paper contracts are held, I rolled apart great metal shelves and lifted five-pound books from the shelves, one by one, running my finger across lines of loopy cursive. There were no windows in this room. It was quiet, still. I searched, hoping for something that would lead me to this man's story. But, there was no listing of a sale by Hilton in that year. There was nothing that could tell me more about the man who ran away, who claimed a spell of freedom for himself. Frustrated, tired, my eyes aching from squinting to read small handwriting under fluorescent lights, I leave the library. As I emerge into the sun, I imagine that maybe it's meant to be that this man left no trace in these papers. I thought of a man moving in the early morning light, the sky blue at the edges of the world, holding in his movement, in his hands, a secret. He is walking to freedom. He never dies.

When we read accounts of Nat Turner's rebellion today, even in contemporary articles, the number of white people murdered by enslaved people is emphasized, while the number of enslaved people murdered by white people after the rebellion is listed secondarily, if at all. That second number is twice as large as the first.

Maybe you've seen an image of the rebellion. It's a woodcut titled *Horrid Massacre in Virginia*, and the white people are on their knees, begging for mercy from black men with raised arms; one of the attackers holds an ax, and the other, presumably Turner with his celebrated sword, raises his arm ready to murder a white man who kneels, wearing a suit, hair coiffed. The men of color are in shirts open to reveal their chests, their work clothes, osnaburg—not the fine suits of the white men. Behind the kneeling white man, a mother kneels with four children, her arm raised to a man with an ax. The children cling to their mother. Here, the white people are weak. The black men are powerful, dangerous, and violent. The caption reads, "1. A Mother intreating for the lives of her children. –2. Mr. Travis, murdered by his own Slaves. –3. Mr. Barrow, who bravely defended himself until his wife escaped . . ." On the right side of the image, a white man raises his sword against Turner's men, while a woman in the background escapes with her baby in her arms. Underneath the scene of the attack, the army—dozens of men on horseback and pulled in carriages—race after three men of color who retreat into the woods. The image is labeled "Authentic and impartial narrative of the tragical scene which was witnessed in Southampton County. [New York], 1831."

The white people are pictured as helpless, the black people as violent murderers.

This was fear, perpetuated: Prevent a rebellion. Enslaved people—black people—pose a threat. Keep them down.

Uprisings were the master class's worst fear.

Knowing all we know about Jackson, it's alarming to read the work of white historians who debate how he should be remembered—complicated, they say, both hotheaded and sensitive. *Hotheaded?* I ask myself. *Really? He tortured and murdered thousands of people, whom he told Congress were "savages," after promising those people that he had their best interests at heart—after the leader of the Cherokee nation saved his life.* I pull book after book about Jackson off the shelf in the library, dismayed. They say that because he was the first president to come from working-class roots and wasn't elite, the public could relate to him. His inauguration party became raucous and had to be shut down, because, they said, working-class people attended for the first time in the nation's short history. Jackson wasn't well educated. He defended democracy, say some. He did both wonderful and terrible things, they say. I want to ask, *And what were the wonderful things?* Roxanne Dunbar-Ortiz, in her book *An Indigenous Peoples' History of the United States*, casts white historians' assessments into perspective: "The continued popularity of, and respect for, the genocidal sociopath Andrew Jackson is another indicator . . . that the 'essential American soul' is a killer."

Genocidal sociopath. The essential American soul is a killer. Jackson left the Battle of Horseshoe Bend, for which he was valorized, with soldiers who made reins for their horses out of the "skin stripped from Muskogee Bodies, and they saw to it that souvenirs from the corpses were given 'to the ladies of Tennessee.'" Jackson had begun what Dunbar-Ortiz calls "career building through genocide," enacting what distinguishes the United States as a nation with the "willingness to eliminate whole civilizations of people in order to possess their land." How can anyone, no matter their political leanings, let Jackson off the hook by categorizing the genocide for which he fought, which he validated and supported and set into motion, as simply *horrible?* We don't give Hitler any qualifiers, no "but's," no excuses nor calls to look at "both sides" of his character and actions, as if he's redeemable. Jackson set the tone for the way the US government would treat indigenous nations and individuals, with violence both rhetorical and physical that resonates into the present moment, into every second of this present moment. The current US president cites Jackson as one of his heroes.

Jackson's actions and beliefs about enslaved and indigenous people resonated with Winthop. The nation needed land for the production of cotton, and Jackson was the man to get it. On his plantation, The Hermitage, lived 120 enslaved people he owned. Both he and Winthrop were decidedly "in favor of the System."

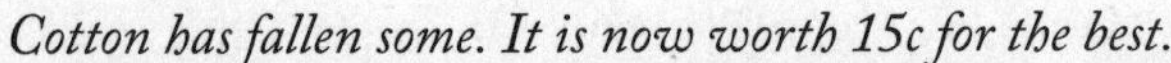

Cotton has fallen some. It is now worth 15c for the best.

Winthrop is making his way in Columbia, working at the store, welcoming in a new clerk when the old one leaves out of dissatisfaction with his salary. A circus comes to town in December of 1835, filling his boardinghouse, "Mrs. Gandy's," along with "countrymen who come in to sell their cotton and buy their necessaries." I imagine enslaved people and free people of color attending that circus alongside poor whites and the wealthy white master class. Circuses were moments of integration, a cause for celebration for all. Historians surmise Harriet Powers witnessed one in her lifetime, inspiring the animals pictured in her quilts.

Winthrop loves the southern air, and wishes his sisters would join Susan in Charleston for an easier winter than they'd have up in

Providence. At one point, he wishes for more rain so that the rivers will rise and the steamboats can come up with their goods, and a year later, in July 1836, just after Little Hasell died, Winthrop writes, "We have a thunderstorm nearly every day for a long time," and notes that there's so much rain that the weather is good for fruits and vegetables but bad for cotton and corn. While at first he thinks the ladies at Charleston who leave everything to the servants aren't as "smart" as the ladies of Columbia who have to do things for themselves, as he settles into South Carolina and acquires wealth from the work of enslaved people who pick and prepare the cotton he sells, he's quite comfortable buying enslaved people to do his own work, too, on land that was stolen from indigenous people.

In 1836, he longs to see his family back home but recognizes that he's in a better position to move up in class in South Carolina than he would be in the North: "Its inducements to settle [in Providence] are small to a young man without capital, are small indeed in comparison with other parts of our country . . . I am at something more than a competency . . . I am aware that a young man by close attention to business here can make a fortune in the course of ten years." Winthrop is middle class, not a man with "capital," but someone who will have to work his way up in class without a father's inherited wealth—though he does rely on his father's social capital and northern connections. He's ambitious, chasing after "something more than mere competency," which is all he thinks he'd gain in Providence. The South offers the land taken from indigenous people, now used for cotton plantations, as well as continued enslavement, and thus, for Winthrop, the hope of wealth.

In this letter in 1836, he describes his business plan, which includes five partners and will require him to "go to Charleston and open a commission house there for the transaction of the business of concern there, which is now done by Messrs Jas, Adger, & Co.," the sale of cotton, with the capital for the business furnished by Mr. D. Ewart, Winthrop's boss in Columbia. He'll "buy forward and receive goods and sell the Cotton purchased here [in Columbia]; it will be pleasant on account of being near Susan and Hilton and you if you visit Charleston as you contemplate," he tells his sister. He's to be a partner. He's awed by the chance: "This is an important period of my life. Whatever step I now take will influence the whole of my future life. It is my highest aim to keep in the path of virtue, it is my nightly prayer that I may not part there from and God grant that I may be so through life."

Virtue and honor. He's invested in the timocratic society that makes possible the System.

I have contemplated writing . . . but being engaged in taking stock, which when I tell you amount to $100,000 besides about $35,000 worth cotton . . . it is no small jot. It makes my head crack almost when it comes night so that I do not feel like doing anything but take a walk with my friend Barstow.

In Dodgeville, Illinois, it was late, and I was listening to the cacophony of snores—five people in various tones whistling and snorting around me—while I lay on the floor of the Henry Dodge cabin in Dodgeville, Illinois. My feet were pressed against a sleeping graduate student's head, and when I rolled over, careful not to jostle the student's head, there was my colleague beside me, creating the highest pitched sigh of the snoring chorus. The cold draft from the wall and window at my back chilled me. My neck hurt. My hip was sore from pressing into the hardwood floor.

This cabin was built in 1832 by Henry Dodge, according to the lore and pictures affixed to the wall, but in truth, it was the enslaved people who built this cabin; Henry brought his enslaved people with him to Illinois from Missouri. Toby is one of the men who built the cabin. I imagined how he would have felt, sleeping on the cold floor after a day of building.

Like the Kinzie house, one of the corners of this cabin had been cut away to reveal its shiplap and the mud that binds outer to inner layers. Joe McGill slept on the floor under the cutaway, and beside him were teachers Ms. C. and Mr. L., who organized this trip, and a man who filmed it all.

In the next room over, eight high-school boys were pressed into a room together in sleeping bags on the floor. They came on this journey with the teachers from the private boys' high school. The boys had been respectful all day, but just before bedtime, they were struck with giddiness and couldn't stop laughing, even when Mr. L. called out to them (once, twice—"Boys!") to be quiet and go to sleep. For a moment, the boys settled down. But then they couldn't help making jokes and whispering, and before long, they were in fits again.

I imagined how Toby must have felt if he slept in this cabin in the 1830s, if he was forced to overhear his master and mistress snoring through the night, or if he tried to quiet his own children so they wouldn't be punished for keeping the white family awake. How must it have felt to rise each day after sleeping through a cold night on a hardwood floor? How sore must his body have been as he set new logs in the fire, pulled his shirt or coat tighter, and started the work of the day? Meanwhile, at this same time, Susan and Hasell made their lives down in South Carolina, and Eliza, Minerva, Juba, and Jane must have borne similar dreams and plans for freedom as Toby surely did, hundreds of miles away.

While Toby was building Henry Dodge's cabin in 1832, John and Juliette Kinzie were in their fourth year at the Indian Agency House at Fort Winnebago in Illinois; this was the house our group toured. John's job was to "manage" people from the Winnebago and Sauk nations. The nations came to challenge the violation of a treaty made decades earlier with the United States, in what would be known as the Black Hawk War, named for the leader of the resistance. (Abraham Lincoln, the president we admire for ending enslavement thirty years later, served in the Black Hawk War, though he wasn't in combat. In 1862, Lincoln ordered thirty-eight Dakota men to be hanged in what remains the largest mass execution in US history. The men had defended their nation's rights in the face of starvation, acts of racism from local colonists, and the US government's violation of treaties. Dozens of colonists attended to watch the execution). At the end of the Black Hawk war, John and Juliette Kinzie moved to Chicago, and the US government tore the Sauk and Winnebago nations from their homelands, the place they'd always known and on which they'd subsisted for generations, and forcibly moved them west.

> *There has been 30 bales of new cotton brought into Market this week, the first this season. They were purchased by my friends, Chambers and Campbell for 20 ¼ cents per lb. The crop I expect will be pretty good as far as I can learn.*

In their views of enslaved people, Hilton is no different from Winthrop. When cholera strikes the city, Hilton writes that "nearly all of our negroes have had it. We lost but one, a very fine fellow, indeed." Hilton doesn't see him as a person; for Hilton, his death is a cost incurred—*but one*, as if the man is an animal in a flock, indistinguishable from the others. *We lost but one chicken to the sickness, one lamb.* "A very fine fellow, indeed," signifies that he worked well for Hilton, did not seem to cause him trouble. A *fine fellow*, but not a human who deserved his freedom. Hilton's not concerned with the people this man must have left behind—a wife, children, dear friends, who probably honored his memory at a funeral or memorial service at one of the churches, or at least in a prayer. They must have talked about who he was, whom he loved, all that he'd given the world in the form of kindness, skills, generosity, laughter, love for those around him.

While Eliza, Minerva, Juba, and Jane were forced to begin new lives in 1837-8, Susan, living back in the North, goes to visit her sister Abby in New York City. She visits the Astor House and marvels at the magic of cooking and bathing with water heated by steam. "I never saw anything so complete," she says. Abby and her husband became wealthy with his new printmaking business in New York.

In Charleston, Mrs. Thorne, Hilton's new wife, has two daughters, and though they declared bankruptcy in the 1840s when Hilton's mill went out of business, they were still served by the enslaved people Harriet Thorne inherited from Mary Ancrum Walker; in 1830, Lavinia was about twenty-two, and had a daughter named Jane; Chloe was about seventeen; Peter was about fifteen, and Cyrus was about thirteen. The genealogist who helps me trace these threads tells me that, ten years later, Harriet's daughter Henrietta inherited the people she'd owned. Henrietta's husband sold Cyrus "out from under" Henrietta; her husband was not allowed to touch her property, the enslaved people, as they were protected under her marriage settlement. Cyrus was about twenty-three at the time. Henrietta took her husband to court for selling a man she believed belonged to her.

Harriet's daughter Henrietta inherited Peter, Jane, Hager, Isaac, Louisa, Arthur, Anna, and Emma. So, many of the enslaved people who were first owned by Mary Ancrum Walker stayed together. These are the people who came with Mary to Charleston from North Carolina. In 1794, she owned twenty-four people who were listed as her property: Cupid, Felix, Hannibal, Tom, June, Alfred, Minerva, Statira, Cynthia, Roxana and her three children Nanny, Ned, and John; Venus and her three children Sarah, Diana, and Damon; Judith and her child Juby Ann (this is Juba); Hutt, or Huff; Minda and her two children Quash and Eliza. Of those people, Cupid, Felix, Hannibal, Tom, June, Minerva, Cynthia, Roxana, Venus, Cloe, and Hutt or Huff, were named in Mary's previous marriage contract, meaning they'd remained in her property and therefore remained together.

There are Juba and her mother Judith, Diana and her daughter Minerva. Roxana had three children, Nanny, Ned, and John, but I don't see them again in the contracts.

The genealogist was able to find people I was told we'd never find beyond the letters. *It is so unlikely*, historians had cautioned me years earlier when I set out to trace the enslaved people in the archive. But, the genealogist told me, Charleston is different. There are more records here; your odds are small, but slightly better than they would be in another town or city. And, after years of reading records and searching for another mention of these women, there they are—there is Juba, and a line drawn to her mother as well as her child Sorenzo; there is Minerva, with a line drawn to her mother as well as her children Cecilia and Samon. There are at least pieces of their family trees. It's both thrilling to see their names again, and disheartening to know this is the most I will find. But just as Bishroom's marriage offered a glimmer, so does Louisa's marriage to Isaac. When I learn that Louisa and Isaac have a child, Francis, who lives with her, I see them together as a family, enslaved and living apart, but united. Francis never had to say goodbye to his mother as Frederick Douglass had to say goodbye to his; he likely endured many traumas, but not that of being torn from his parents. His mother, Louisa, never had to see him sold away from her. Louisa was owned by Harriet, and Isaac was owned by Dr. Holmes. On September 22, 1843, when Francis was six years old, his parents had him baptized, privately, by Reverend W.H. Barnwell, who was Rector of St. Peter's Episcopal Church.

The picture of the (almost) united family—Louisa, Isaac, and Francis—dissipates with the death record from September 24 to October 1, 1843. Just a few days to two weeks after he's baptized, six year old Francis dies of scarlet fever, as does George Logan, a white boy, William and Henrietta's son, at two years old. Henrietta lived in the same house with her mother Harriet, which means that the two boys, Francis, who was enslaved, and George, who was part of the white owner's family, were in close proximity to each other, close enough for the disease to catch them both. They had different doctors; Francis' doctor was William's brother.

Six years later, in 1849, Isaac and Louisa lived together at 54 Coming Street, owned by Henrietta. Still enslaved, Louisa and Isaac were united in the same household, able to support one another in their grief over Francis' death, to nestle together at night and feel each other's chests rise and fall in sleep.

Eight years after that, in 1857, Hagar, Jane, Isaac, Anna, Juliet, and James were listed in Rosamond's house. Isaac lived there, without Louisa. Did she die? Was she sold? On Sullivan's Island, Hilton lived with

Rosamond, who was his stepdaughter, and her family. He must have known Isaac. Did he know what happened to Louisa? Was Isaac mourning her in 1857, or did she live in another house in the neighborhood (if she'd been sold by Rosamond)? Did Isaac now sleep alone, or did he find love again?

In 1863, Harriet owned ten properties around the city, and when she died that year, her daughters Henrietta and Rosamond sold most of them. When the enslaved people were emancipated that year—if the daughters followed the law to emancipate them—where did Hagar, Jane, Isaac, Anna, Juliet, and James go? Where did they make their new lives? I thought that Juba Simons was the only person I'd find after the war, but then I learn that Jane made it, too, and claimed the name Jane Jones. She was a member of Zion Presbyterian Church.

> *My business has been good of its kind for a month past. The great changes of late have put steamers and boats out of use . . . I have about 1500 bales cotton on the way down now—a part has been on the river more than two months. It has put me to great inconvenience . . . Cotton is very brisk, chief sales from 11 ¾ to 12 ½ for new crop, old from 8 to 11 ½ and rice is selling at $4 ¾ but little coming in . . ."*

In this letter, Winthrop notes, as a matter of course, between mentioning that Hilton is "in good health as well as his wife and her children," and that he himself is "quite hearty," and at the other end of the sentence, notes that his sister-in-law Eliza Crouch has had a baby girl, as yet unnamed—and, between these two comments he writes that Minerva, Susan's enslaved woman, "has had a fine boy." Winthrop doesn't name him here, but this is Samon.

Before our group snored through the night at the Dodge Cabin, we visited a cemetery in Galena, Illinois, where a local historian guided our group of university and high-school students. We learned that because so many people came to Illinois from Missouri, Missourians came to be called "pukes," and miners who lived on the side of the hills were called "badgers." We learned that people "played word-games" to illegally bring their enslaved people here, calling them *servants*, or *indentured servants* (just as Rhode Islanders called their enslaved people servants to appear more genteel). We learned that a man named John Hall and his wife Minerva were born enslaved in Tennessee, near Covington, and that they died enslaved in Illinois. When John's master was killed in the Civil War, John, who had been forced to accompany him, came home and married Minerva. She was the daughter of Moses Lester, who came to Galena, the town where we stood at the cemetery, to serve a family. John was a carriage driver and the city lamplighter. He lit all the gas lamps in the city and was charged with dealing with the loose animals in town—roaming or dead cows, dogs. It was John's job to round them up and send them home, or haul them off and bury them.

These are the stories told to us by Scott Wolfe. He told us that John wasn't always treated well. At least one incident of white boys throwing rocks at John occurred on his lamplighting nights. Probably, he faced worse than that.

Scott Wolfe is a white man, a war veteran. When I asked how he became so interested in the stories of enslaved people, he said it started with his interest in the Civil War, because he's a veteran himself. But, I persisted, so many people might not care about enslaved people, or to tell the stories of people of color, and here you are, a white man, doing that in a small town in Illinois. Why? Why do you think some people turn into these stories, and some turn away? Why would some people—from the same family—embrace slavery, while others would be disdainful of it?

He didn't have an answer.

The gravestones of John and Minerva, or Mernervery, as she was known, read: "John and Mernervery Hall." "Born and Raised in Slavery." John Barton: "Deprived of the rights of a citizen by odious and unjust laws, yet his whole life vindicated."

His whole life vindicated.

I think of Isaac and Louisa and their little boy Francis; I think of Minerva and Jane and Juba and Eliza. Of Bishroom and Boston and George and Adam. I imagine, for them, too, a life lived by this phrase *yet his whole life vindicated.*

The exposed corner of the Dodge cabin, perhaps the logs that Toby shaped and nailed.

Oblivious to the humanity and struggle of the enslaved people he and his family owned, in 1837, Winthrop keeps marking changes in business, focused on his acquisition of wealth. He notes the "great changes of late" that mark slower business and the financial depression.

> *Our cotton market has for the last week been in a very inactive and dull state . . . the market closed yesterday very heavily, the sales during the week were about 4,000 bales, the smallest week's business that has been done for many months. It is chiefly owing to the scarcity of vessels . . . This wet weather has operated very unfavorably on trade of all kinds during the week . . . Rice remains stationary . . .*

> *Invoice for six bales cotton shipped by Ewart Williams & Co., aboard Schooner Pacific for Providence, RI, consigned to William J. Harris for sale on account of the ship . . .*

Winthrop advises William J. Harris, whom he addresses as "Brother Harris," his sister Emily's husband, about which sorts of cambrics to send to the south. And then, at the end of this officious letter full of business news, he writes that the lives of Eliza, John, Minerva and her children are irrevocably changed, in what amounts to, for Winthrop, another business deal. He closes: "Money is confounded hard to (get) had, times are worse here." Susan has moved back to Providence, and her estate is managed by her brother Hilton, with Winthrop's help. As a woman, she isn't allowed to sell her own property, including enslaved people. He sells the people, and Hilton pays for a portion of the cost of Minerva and Eliza, why we do not know.

Maybe Hilton and Winthrop convinced themselves they couldn't change the women's fates by emancipating them because the law made it so difficult to do so. Maybe they told themselves they *had* to care for the "slaves" who could not care for themselves. Yet, hundreds of people were abolitionists by the 1830s. How did some people become abolitionists while so many others became slave owners and traders? Winthrop seems to have been blind to Louisa's and Isaac's lives. To Minerva's and Eliza's. He seems willing to do whatever it takes to propel himself upward.

> *I was very glad you sold the cotton at so good prices. You had better close the one bale J.H. at some price and send us sales and an a/c current of our transactions up to the 1st April, when we will commence anew just make up all your general charges against me in one general a/c current. I am sorry to hear that you do not find our cottons to work as well as Alabama and New Orleans the one bale January was of the finest quality of any cotton received here this season. Cottons have declined very much since the 1st July fully 1c per pound on all qualities the sales of the past week were 135000 bales at an improvement on the rates of the previous week—we now look for more steadiness in the market for the remainder of the season—shipping is very scarce so much so that the amount of cotton on shippers' hands amounts to about 2/3 of the stock in the city, say 25,000 Bales.*

The "finest cotton" was Sea Island cotton (among the sea islands are St. Helena and Hilton's Head), with its longer, finer fibers that made for softer cloth when it was woven. The Sea Island cotton's scientific name is *Gossypium barbadense*. In a 2015 study of the *G. Barbadense* genome, scientists showed that this cotton shows evidence of *domestication*, that it is "prized for its superior length, strength, and fineness of fiber," while other hybridized cottons are known for their "superior yield." This is a cotton that's the product of *selective breeding*, the "inter-genomic hybridization between an A-genome-like ancestral African diploid and D-genome-like American diploid." The scientists conducting this study have traced the genetic sequence of Sea Islands cotton and its progenitors, to understand how it came to develop its longer fibers rather than shifting into a high-yield but lower-quality crop. Winthrop is stockpiling the Sea Island cotton from the Lowcountry, along with the lesser quality cotton, to support himself and his family for years to come. By the start of the Civil War, he has tens of thousands of dollars in cotton bales stored in warehouses in Charleston and Columbia; this much cotton must have been picked by hundreds of enslaved people.

In the days leading up to the Civil War, the brothers still owned enslaved people. Hilton had one enslaved person in his name in 1860, and his house was kept by the people his wife Harriet, and then her daughter Henrietta, owned. Winthrop wrote about a couple he'd bought who were emancipated during the Civil War. Charles Crouch owned twelve people in 1860.

The price of enslaved people had steadily increased from the 1830s to '50s, and Winthrop, wealthy from the cotton trade by the 1840s, was buying. As one historian notes: "A serious-minded Scotch traveler in 1857 recorded the epigrammatic judgment: 'Niggers and cotton—cotton and niggers; these are the law and the prophets to the men of the South.' Southerners firmly believed, as one of them wrote: 'This alliance between negroes and cotton, we will venture to say, is now the *strongest power* in the world; and the peace and welfare of Christendom absolutely depends [*sic*] upon the strength and security of it." Winthrop, now firmly rooted in the southern way of life and cotton-trading business, believed in this, too. He often noted the rising cost of enslaved people in his letters north to Susan back in Providence; in fact, he noted the changing prices of cotton, corn, and rice in many letters home. In June 1856, he writes about settling his servants and enslaved people into his Sullivan's Island house:

> *Irish cook is pleased with the new kitchen, the cooking stove, and all new arrangements work well. Amelia* [the enslaved woman his wife inherited] *and Dianna have the wash room for their reception room. Amelia sleeps upstairs in the kitchen over the washroom and the Irish girl over the kitchen. Dianna and Sam have their old room under the last corner of the house. We have bought a house boy named William and* [sic] *proves a good quiet waiting man. He is 22 years old and cost $1000.00. He was Edwin P. Starr's house servant. We have all the help we have use for. Eve is hired out. . . . I am sorry to hear you have such hard times with servants but such things seem very common at the north.*

He emphasizes, again, how much more effective the southern slave-holding system is, how "obedient" and effective are his enslaved people at their work, while Susan has to contend with servants who don't always "obey." Around this same time, a cousin wrote to Winthrop, advising him that the best way to make a quick profit was to buy enslaved people in Washington, D.C. or Baltimore, and send them down the rivers to Alabama and Georgia, where, he said, slaves were always in high demand on the plantations.

In October 1860, Winthrop takes note of the impending conflict and is concerned about the future.

> *Politics look very alarming for the safety of the Union and from all I can learn of your city there are mad people there, as well as all over the North. But thank God there are some even in your state that are sound on the Constitution. Who is your ex-Governor (?) I never knew such a person in my day, don't know the family, but he is a man every inch of him. But politics aside, I am sorry to see this storm brewing and even more grieved because I was once a resident of the North.*

The separation between the families grows once the war is under way, but they remain loyal to one another in spite of their regional differences, Winthrop's beliefs that there are "mad people . . . all over the North."

He's sorry to see his world changing, sorry to see abolitionism growing in the land from which he came.

> *I have before me your letter date 17th March its contents being very acceptable except the fact of our being shared in the Bale Cotton $20. I guess I can make it up to you in this shipment now going on board the schooner . . . I have eight Bales Samples one [sic] bale and one small bale prime cotton for you're a/c and 9 bales for sale on my own a/c—I will send invoices BL by mail—the Brig Eagle sending this.*

In Illinois, our group visited another cemetery, this one on a hill that overlooked rolling farmland, a white house nestled into the hills that met below us. The sun was going down. It was the end of a long day, and the high school boys were restless. We pulled our small caravan over on the side of the road, and the boys spilled out of their van into the field, laughing. The light cast a glow on the greening fields. We were all grateful for spring after a long, gray Midwestern winter.

We walked through the cemetery, which held the bodies of people from the free community of color. This was Pleasant Ridge, founded by the Shepard family, who bought land from their former owner and later came to welcome, as the marker notes, "over 100 free and escaped slaves."

There was one gravestone here that looked different. It was glossier, newer, and made of mottled red granite. Scott told us that this stone was bought and set here by a man who's descended from the community, to mark the grave of his ancestors. There was an identical gravestone, this time, marking a new grave, not a memorial, which Scott found on a visit to that town. "People still want to be buried here," he told us. "Imagine loving a place so much that you ask to be brought back to be buried there."

This community thrived in the mid-1800s, until the start of the Civil War, when river traffic was halted and business suspended. Until then, town citizens worked as hotel staff, miners, and steamboat operators, building a strong community with its own school. Earlier that day, we saw a picture of a woman from this community; her name was America.

The boys wandered the graves, and two of them, unable to contain themselves, rolled down the great hill in the sunlight. I looked up to see them rolling, to hear their laughter, and beyond them, the great tree—still leafless yet—that stood at the top of the graveyard. The boys rolled seemingly without control, and they laughed at the simple thrill of it, just as boys in the 1830s must have done, maybe in this same spot. Mr. L. called out to them to be respectful, and they quickly got up and acted like proper young men again. But now, months later, as I sift through the ways this journey changed me, the sorrow of some of those places we visited, I remember the image of the boys' rolling laughter down that green hill, how full of life, how hopeful and carefree they seemed in that moment in the midst of the graves.

Back home in Michigan, resting after a sleepless night in the cabin, I called a historic preservation group in Charleston; they're planting a crop of Sea Islands cotton at McLeod Plantation. I talked to the organizer, who told me this was the first crop of Sea Island cotton to be planted in Charleston since the boll weevil infestation in the late nineteenth and early twentieth centuries, which sent cotton production overseas. For this crop at McLeod, locals have been invited to take part, to help plant and harvest the cotton, to experience the process. I wonder who will volunteer to harvest cotton on a modern mock-plantation.

When I talk to an instructor about organizing a trip to extant slave dwellings, she tells me that most African American students will not want to come on this journey. Why would they want to visit the sites of enslaved people? she explains. Had they lived generations ago, it would be them harvesting the field. And not by choice. School would be only a dream. She says that students of color can be made to feel like outsiders at the elite school they attend, and a trip like this would, they understandably believe, only make things worse.

I go to bed thinking about McLeod, those fields of cotton, and all that a simple plant seemed to cause. I think of the drawing "The Capture of Nat Turner," and I remember a dog snarling at Turner's legs. That doesn't seem right. I go back to look at the image again, and there is no dog. There's a gnarled tree stump; it is not a snarling dog. I confused the image with the myth, maybe, knowing that Turner had been found by a dog, and having learned, more recently, about the ways that dogs were trained to catch enslaved people. Enslaved people were told to run away from the dog, and the dog was made to chase them as a training exercise, and then the dog was rewarded for its pursuit. Imagine being told that your work for the day was to train the dog to track your friends and loved ones—to track the future version of yourself that would run away.

The original image caption reads: 'Turner was bent on getting to what was then Jerusalem, now the county seat of Courtland. He hoped other local slaves and those across the South would rise up with his band, but a full-scale rebellion never took hold."

This is the first image I'd known of Nat Turner's rebellion. I thought that I wouldn't need to include this image here, that I could simply describe it. Shawn Michelle Smith writes, "My argument proposes that visual culture is not a mere reflection of a national community but one of the sites through which narratives of national belonging are imagined. I suggest that photographic images not only represent but also produce the nation." If every image becomes part of the cultural conversation, produces our nation, then doesn't replicating racist images reify racism? But, describing it doesn't show what the image was, what it was attempting to *do*; we can't deconstruct it unless we look at it. This racism is already embedded. We can't see how deeply it's inscribed unless we look at all that's past—this archive, these letters, this history, the words and the images and the present they've created for us. At first, I thought I wouldn't replicate Winthrop's most racist writing. But then it seems I have to, to tell this story in its entirety. I hope that if I present these words, these images, in a "new context," as a friend suggests, their meaning will change.

This image tries to tell the viewer that the black body is a sign of danger. Uncivilized. Unpredictable. Violent. The men in field clothes hold knives and swords and axes. They threaten with their weapons the white people seated prostrate on the ground, those white people dressed in their fine European clothes. There is one white man who fights back with his sword. A white woman sits on the ground attempting to protect her children. It is all titled "horrid massacre," though the number of enslaved people murdered in the aftermath, again, was more than double the number Turner's group killed. And yet, here's another, very similar, image, this one of the Haitian Revolution 1791-1804.

This image of the Haitian Revolution tells the same story—that these are the violent men of color attacking the helpless whites.

And, this is the image that I initially misread, of "the capture of Nat Turner":

There is the "snarling" root at his foot, and the well-dressed white man with a gun pointed at Turner's head, while Turner wears rags—the clothes that signify his status as "slave" and field "hand," objectifying him—and his hand is on his famous sword, which he used to "slaughter" so many white people. He was the enslaved man who proved most dangerous, not for what he did but for the example he set: Enslaved people could emancipate themselves, could revolt and enact the violence that the master class always feared, could upend a system that had been carefully reinforced decade after decade, century after century. Winthrop and Hilton carefully created their own images as "masters" in contrast to this enslaved and supposedly "dangerous" black man.

Critical race theory has taught us that race is a fiction—I am not "white"—no one is white—but I've been culturally trained to think and act as if I am. White was an invention to make some people superior and to make people of color—whom the nation needed to work for free in the name of big profits, whom the nation murdered to take their lands—supposedly inferior; the system of superior and inferior was created so that the new nation would work to keep African Americans locked in chains. Ta Nehisi-Coates writes, in *Between the World and Me*, "Race is the child of racism, not the father. And the process of naming 'the people' has never been a matter of genealogy and physiognomy so much as one of hierarchy. . . . The belief in the preeminence of hue and hair, the notion that these factors can correctly organize a society and that they signify deeper attributes, which are indelible—this is the new idea at the heart of these new people who have been brought up hopelessly, tragically, deceitfully, to believe that they are white." And this belief in whiteness, he says, this elimination of each person's ethnicity to become white, came "through the pillaging of life, liberty, labor, and land . . ."

Was my misreading of this image, thinking the stump was a dog, rooted in the way that I've been inculcated by the white supremacy America was founded on? Was it rooted in my acculturation as someone who is supposedly white? Did I see the root as a dog because, on some level, I, too, believed this supposedly black man was a criminal who needed to be rounded up by a fierce beast?

If we don't think about how we've been bombarded by images, by language, that position us as different races, as superior or inferior to one another, how will we undo those subliminal messages that feed into our unconscious biases? These are powerful images, widely disseminated for nearly two centuries. Google "Nat Turner," and see what turns up. These images: in black and white. The murderer and the righteous.

Look at the words Winthrop and Hilton and Susan write. They are a part of this culture that positioned them as superior to enslaved people of color. Susan, Hilton, and Winthrop embraced that socialization. They bought and sold people. Eliza, Minerva, Jane, Juba, and William—and they rented Jimmy with their island house.

~

In her book *Citizen: An American Lyric*, Claudia Rankine includes the iconic image of a crowd of white people watching a lynching, only in Rankine's version, the hanging bodies have been edited out. All we see is the crowd, which is turned toward the camera, their pale faces lit in what I read as various forms of emotion—delight, vindication, anger; they all look engaged in this moment. A smile. A woman reaching to touch her boyfriend. One man toward the center of the image points up, to—in Rankine's version—an empty sky, a tree that's just a tree.

I walk around my university campus and imagine the groups of students walking from building to building in the hustle of moments between classes, being rounded up, captured—handcuffed, stolen from their families, sold on a block, robbed of their freedom, sent to work for the rest of their lives, far away, in a land they've never seen before, to work for others and to know their children will work for others and their children—always, forever.

Rankine says, "I wanted the reader to be engaged, visually, because racism is about a visual construction. You can have a phone call with somebody, and the phone call would seem quite innocent, and then you walk into the room, and spoken or unspoken is, *I didn't know you were black. Because now that I know that, things are going to change . . .*"

Racism is . . . a visual construction. What if, instead of being given so many images of people being enslaved, of people's backs scarred by whippings and torture, of people being sold on the block, of a black woman caring for white children (as I have included here to imagine Eliza's and Minerva's lives, wondering if I should)—if instead, we were always given the images of Sojourner Truth as she chose to construct it for herself, holding yarn and sitting in fine clothes and a bonnet that cues the domesticity from which women of color were previously excluded—of which Susan was so desperate to be a part—and on the table beside Truth, a book, presumably the one she wrote herself? Or the images of Frederick Douglass as he constructed them for himself? Each of them claiming their self-hood in the medium of photography that became available in the mid-1800s. In Shawn Michelle Smith and Maurice O. Wallace's anthology, *Pictures and Progress: Early Photography and the Making of African American Identity*, scholars write about the empowerment of people who had once been enslaved to subsequently shape their own identities. Sojourner Truth and Frederick Douglass were able to claim their representations, to create their images and to distribute that image in photographs—tintypes, daguerreotypes, visiting cards—to construct themselves in a society that had tried to shut them out. Now, they were public intellectuals to whom much of the country turned for leadership and guidance. The images Truth and Douglass produced and distributed, Laura Wexler, Augusta Rohrbach, and Ginger Hill argue, helped them reach and sustain that influence.

Sojourner Truth, Unidentified Artist, 1864, Albumen silver print, National Portrait Gallery, Smithsonian Institution.

In one of her talks, Rankine says to the crowd, that all of you, in this room, are responsible for this—pointing to the image of the bodies absent from what we know is the lynching photo (whether the bodies are there or not, the image has been culturally inscribed), the white crowd staring back at the camera. I play this clip for a class. And I pause it there, after

Rankine says we are all responsible, and I turn to the students, and ask, "How does it feel to be told this is our responsibility?"

There is silence, and I let that silence remain in the air.

Rankine says, "the removal of the scandal [of the bodies in the tree] just left the construction of whiteness that is implicated in systemic racism."

The construction of whiteness—the belief that some people are white, and therefore superior to others—not the *explicit* belief, necessarily, but the *implicit* belief. Taught by the actions of those around you. Family. Friends. What people say to one another. What we call today microaggressions. Taught with folklore and stories and pictures. Taught with evidence of who is given which jobs and who is given access to which communities and so on.

This is the answer to my initial question, why Winthrop, Hilton, and Susan so easily slipped into the System down South—because they had been trained, by their community, by their family, by the people who taught them their history lessons as children, by this new nation and all of its supposedly-white founders—that they were superior. This was the way things were. This was how they would advance in the world. Their father was part of the triangle trade by sending goods to the West Indies, bringing back molasses and sugar and tea and coffee and chocolate. He couldn't have been ignorant of that with which he was engaged. Elaine Freedgood argues that authors like Charlotte Brontë knew the implications of mahogany furniture that make up the setting of *Jane Eyre*. Those items were from the islands of Madeira and Jamaica, which were, Freedgood writes, deforested and planted with cash crops—sugar and Madeira wine—that were harvested by enslaved people. Brontë included mahogany furniture—the wood type explicitly noted—so thoroughly throughout the book to make evident the power of that trade of sugar and wine from the Caribbean islands, a trade fueled by the trade of enslaved people. Freedgood argues that we need to look more closely at the significance of objects that inhabit our world, inhabit our stories. *Jane Eyre*, which was published in 1847, was perhaps read by Susan and her sisters. We can find the story of the triangle trade in the letters, fabrics, quilt, and commodities of Susan's and Winthrop's and Hilton's families. They knew, all of them, where their sugar came from, where the cotton that was spun into their clothes was grown and by whom.

I keep wondering not only what happened to Eliza, Minerva, Jane, and their children after they were sold in 1837 and 1838, but also if Susan ever felt guilty for what she did to the women and their children? Could she have stopped her brother from selling them, or convinced him to emancipate them? Did she even consider this? Did she think about them on the day of their sale? Were they just commodities to her as well? And even if she *did* feel something, does that matter in the face of what she did? If I can understand why she did what she did, maybe I can understand how we all do what we do, how we keep living in a system that puts some above others, and that continues to put some so far below.

Bryan Stevenson notes that everyone asks how people could have been so callous to have owned enslaved people "back then"; everyone looks at the past and asks, *How could they have done that?* But, he says, we are living within a system of enslavement today—the for-profit prison industrial complex that sanctions the free labor black men, via the loophole left in the Thirteenth Amendment; no one shall be forced to labor without pay, "*except* as punishment for a crime . . ." *Except.* The loophole. And who is most often imprisoned in this country?

This black body is violent and is to be stopped, and this indigenous body must be removed, absented, our culture continues to teach us. This white body is innocent, victimized, and must be protected. This black body must be slayed. This indigenous body must be erased.

We have seen and perpetuated these same images, over and over, for centuries. Our police forces react with instantaneous fear of people of color, and aim, and shoot. This is the story the police have been told since even before Nat Turner's day, almost two hundred years ago. This is the story Winthrop tells in his hundreds of letters home, the stories he believes. He can't imagine the world to come, and the stories he's unintentionally preserved alongside his own.

11
Living History

The whole history of the progress of human liberty shows that all concessions yet made to her august claims, have been born of earnest struggle . . . Those who profess to favor freedom and yet depreciate agitation, are men who want crops without plowing up the ground. They want rain without thunder and lightning. They want the ocean without the mighty roar of its waters.

—Frederick Douglass

On an August day in 1844, imagine Frederick Douglass walks through the bucolic town of Concord, Massachusetts, a quiet wind blowing through oaks and maples heavy with humidity. He's on his way to listen to Emerson deliver his speech on the tenth anniversary of the liberation of the British West Indies (the law was passed in 1833 and went into effect in 1834). It's 1844, and the British Empire has been free of enslavement, according to law if not practice, for ten years. In the United States, people are pushing for abolition. People like Douglass and Sojourner Truth and Harriet Tubman and the dozens of people who claimed their freedom out of enslavement and wrote their own stories in the 1840s and '50s, and long before that, too—James Matthews, who ran away, Moses Roper, born in North Carolina, escaped north to New York aboard a packet boat, and "Aunt Sally," who dictated her story for the book *Aunt Sally, or The Cross the Way of Freedom: A Narrative of the Slave-Life and Purchase of the Mother of Rev. Isaac Williams, of Detroit, Michigan.* While she authors the book, a passage told from the point of view of her son Isaac recounts his memories of her spinning by the fire late at night after she'd worked in the rice fields all day; he thinks of how "weary" she was then, a mother at seventeen, and how she continued "sewing industriously to make or mend some needful garment, when so fatigued with the day's labor that she nodded between the stitches." Maybe Jane, a seamstress, was like "Sally," working late to sew pieces of clothing the family needed, making quilts and coverings, or a hat to keep a child warm on a rainy winter night.

> If your mother had been lost for twenty years, and you hoped to regain her through the remembrances of your childhood, how would you recall the birthday festival, and the prayers for you beside your little bed when your head was on her bosom, and the twilight walk through the rose-scented lanes when she told you a story of her girlish days, and that sad morning when, for an outbreak of passion, you fell in disgrace with your father, and she soothed and calmed you, and gently led you back to the path of duty and love!

This is a scene that many children might recall having had with a parent—one parent is frustrated with the child, and the other parent soothes and comforts and helps the child towards the "path of duty and love." Isaac, the boy who became a Methodist minister, eventually found his mother and bought her from her enslaver in 1852.

Frederick Douglass writes that he had few memories of his mother, as they were sold apart from each other when he was young. That day in Concord, he'd have walked over the dirt roads, past the colonial homes with their double chimneys, tidy rows of windows, and long, straight wooden siding that had been delivered from mills like Hilton's, planed by men like Boston and Bishroom and George and Adam, from trees into shingles and long narrow boards with perfect rolled edges. These shingled homes are some of the same houses I'd come to know 150 years later, as a child.

Did Douglass think of his mother as he walked through Concord that day? Did he wish she could have been there to see him now, having come so far? Look, he could say if she walked beside him that day, look how we changed our lives, and he would get to see the love in his mother's eyes.

Douglass would have been wearing a vest underneath a jacket with tails, narrow at the waist, and pants that seemed to billow slightly and then taper to his shoes. A tie cinched on his collar, a white buttoned shirt. Perhaps a top hat. These clothes signified his status as an important, respected, educated man—a man of relative wealth, a free man, a man who commanded crowds and led them toward abolitionism and suffrage. He may have been born enslaved, into a cabin like the one pictured above, which stands at Magnolia Plantation and Gardens outside Charleston, but he'd claimed his freedom and escaped. He'd gone north on a train, and now he helped lead the charge toward emancipation. Thirteen years later, he'd deliver a speech on this anniversary, and speak the words quoted above, articulating the need for struggle to create real change. The year was 1857, just a few years before the start of the Civil War, and now, looking back, his words seem to ring through the years that followed and led to those opening shots, the long battles and many deaths that were to come. Freedom does not come without agitation. We cannot have "the ocean without the mighty roar of its waters."

In Illinois, when we visited the so-called "Indian Agency House" and the Dodge cabin, Joseph McGill, our leader, wore his blue uniform from the Fifty-fourth Massachusetts Volunteer Infantry Regiment. The Fifty-fourth was made up of African American soldiers recruited after the Emancipation Proclamation was announced in January 1863.

The first Congressional Medal of Honor awarded to an African American man was given to Sergeant William H. Carney in 1900, for his valor on July 18, 1863. He fought in the Fifty-fourth Regiment, in a battle outside Charleston. Sergeant Carney rescued the American flag when its bearer fell, and is famously quoted as saying that the flag "never touched the ground," in spite of his injury in the battle. Frederick Douglass, who had been working for abolition since his escape north in the 1830s, saw two of his own sons off to the Civil War in the Fifty-fourth Regiment.

Maybe you saw the movie *Glory* in the late eighties, starring Morgan Freeman as Sargeant Major John Rollins, Denzel Washington as Private Trip, and Matthew Broderick as Colonel Shaw, the white man who led the soldiers into battle. Though that battle didn't win Fort Wagner, the Union prevailed two months later, in September, when the Confederates retreated.

Sergeant Carney in his younger and older years.

The Robert Gould Shaw Memorial stands on the Boston Common near the State House; one of the Crouch relatives called the Common "the lungs" of Boston, where people congregated to take air and walk together, just as Winthrop did each morning along the battery in Charleston. I've walked past that memorial in Boston Common many times in my life, but never took notice of what it illustrates. Now, I read every plaque on every monument I pass, in my home state and others. What do we publicly commemorate and what do we ignore or silence? This monument was erected in honor of Colonel Shaw and the men of the Fifty-fourth Regiment who fought even when they weren't granted full rights of citizenship and weren't being paid equally. The monument was originally proposed to be erected near Fort Wagner outside Charleston where Carney and Shaw died, but after residents protested to its installment there, it was finally completed and erected in 1897 in Boston.

Nearby, there's the memorial that includes a free man of color named Crispus Attucks, commemorating his part in the American Revolution, when he stood to face British soldiers and was murdered by them; Paul Revere's famous engraving, based on an image by Henry Pelham, helped demonize the British and spur the new nation towards war. Attucks was of African and Native American descent.

Growing up, I must have walked past these monuments countless times. In school, we learned about Concord as the place from which the "shot heard 'round the world" was fired, starting the revolution and our country's fight for freedom. I never learned about Crispus Attucks. In high school, I'd run over the Old North Bridge during cross-country practice, and then cross the street and cut into the woods to the marshy preservation land through which soldiers must have walked and fought, winding their way along the river. This is land that belongs to the Wampanoag and Massachuset nations, from whom Attucks was likely descended. I imagine how these marshlands along the river must have looked before colonists arrived, the waters full of migrating birds, those white cranes I loved to see moving as if in slow motion through water up to their knees. There would have been the hum and hiccup of frogs on summer nights, the skies filling with the sounds of honking geese as they moved north come spring. People must have pulled basketfuls of fish from those marshy fresh waters, and had access to the oysters, clams, and saltwater fish at the Atlantic shores, too. This is long before over-fishing, before the pollution that industrialization would bring, and decades of mill run-off that was toxic to these waters.

Emerson's house, Concord, MA. and a replica of Thoreau's cabin, built in 2009 at Walden Pond.

In all those years I moved through Boston's and Concord's landscapes, no one ever told me about Crispus Attucks, who was a hero of the revolution just as much as Paul Revere. No one told me about the Fifty-fourth and Fifty-fifth Massachusetts infantry regiments, made up of men of color who fought and died for a country that hadn't granted them full citizenship and paid them three dollars less than their white counterparts made, nor that the men had to keep fighting—and dying—for their rights to equal pay even after the war was won. Though I knew that Ralph Waldo Emerson and Henry David Thoreau were important thinkers who wrote and spoke and lived in town, I never learned that Frederick Douglass came to Concord to speak in 1844 and that he lived in Massachusetts, settling just after his self-emancipation in New Bedford, a whaling town. I was never taught that in the 1840s, Thoreau refused to pay his taxes in protest of slavery and the Mexican-American War. This was just before he went to Walden Pond in 1845 to live simply (with a little help from his mother's cooking and laundering services). No one told me about the African American women who worked to recruit men for the Fifty-fourth, who raised those infantrymen's families back home while they were away fighting, who sewed and knitted goods to sell, or worked in someone's kitchen, or taught someone else's children, to pay their own children's way to school or to buy their shoes for the year or to make enough for their dinner each night.

In school, I'd never learned that African American women worked as spies in the South—not only Harriet Tubman but also Mary Touvestre, who stole the plans for the battleship CSS *Virginia* from the man for whom she worked, and delivered the plans to the Union. There was also Mary Elizabeth Bowser, who worked with her former owner, a woman educated in Boston who returned to Richmond, Virginia, and became a spy for the North. Bowser was hired as a domestic by the Confederate White House, where she observed documents in the company of men who assumed she wasn't able to read or write and couldn't begin to understand their conversations and papers. She took advantage of the opening their racism and sexism created and sent the information she gathered to the Union.

Bowser and Touvestre were born to enslaved women, thus enslaved themselves, raised in city homes like the one in which Eliza, Minerva, and Juba lived in Charleston, or in cabins that looked like the one that opens this chapter. And now, by the 1860s, they'd been emancipated, at last, thanks in no small part to the work of abolitionists like Tubman and Douglass, who pushed Lincoln toward emancipation.

I try to imagine Eliza and Juba during the war, having learned that Minerva, mother of Cecilia and Samon, daughter of Diana, would not make it to hear the Emancipation Proclamation. She died on November 16, 1851, of "dropsy," or edema, probably caused by heart failure. Her last name was listed in 1851 as "Greer," so she was still owned by the man who bought her in 1838 when Susan and Winthrop sold her. Eliza may have still been owned by Winthrop, as there's no record for her sale after Winthrop bought her in 1837-8; he refers to her once in 1839, indicating that he must still have owned her then. Whether he ever sold her or not, I allow myself to keep imagining that she escaped. Then again, so many records are lost. She might have been sold to the man for whom Winthrop said he bought her, or sold to someone else in the years that followed Susan's departure. Maybe she found her way to the homes of sympathetic people on Beacon Hill, who took her in and helped her start a new life. Maybe she'd claimed literacy in the south, and eventually came to teach at the Abiel Smith School, lived nearby on Beacon Hill, and spent her early evenings before dinner walking and visiting with friends. Maybe she wrote her own story, as many former slaves did, and testified to her life in the south under Susan and Hasell's hands, to help promote the abolitionist movement.

I imagine her in 1870, walking in a cream-white dress that swishes around her ankles, in a straw bonnet decorated with artificial flowers that's set forward on her head, listening to a story her friend tells her as they walk uphill. Their bodices button up the front, with gold pins fastening lace at their necklines. The skirts, now, are flat in the front and gathered into bustles in the back. Maybe she's wearing a skirt with a pull in it that allows her to raise the hem when she's out walking, to avoid the wet and dirty ground. This creates the look of what I always thought of as a princess dress, with fabric gathered up in even waves around the skirt. It's late summer, and the evenings are cool; the trees around the Common have just begun to change color, revealing orange and yellow tips that will soon blossom into full-fledged fire. Eliza pulls her shawl around her shoulders, dodges a puddle, tucks a fallen piece of hair back into her braid.

If she was, indeed, able to escape, did Eliza hear of friends and relatives back in Charleston during or after the war? Did she know of Minerva's death?

In 1851, over a decade after Susan and Hasell sold her, Minerva was still in Charleston, likely walking to the market and along the battery, visiting with friends when she could, maybe seeing her children if they were still nearby. She may have been sent to the work house and strapped to that horrific wheel, may have endured beatings at the hands of her mistress and master, may have survived slaps and whippings and rapes. I wonder if she bore scars from her time under Susan and Hasell's ownership. And I hope that, like Bishroom, she was also able to live with her spouse, the father of Cecilia and Samon. That she was able to see her children grow up. That she got to watch Samon take his first steps, rushing towards his mother's arms as all able-bodied babies do, delighted in his ability to stand and walk.

Either at the time of her death or before, Dr. Michael tended to Minerva, providing what care he could offer, or simply arriving to declare her cause of death. Did Eliza or Juba Simons see Minerva before she died? Were they related, or friends? I think of Eliza and Minerva tending to Little Hasell and imagine the hundreds of times Minerva might have escaped or ignored Susan's demands to tend to Cecilia and Samon, to hug instead her own children, to sing to Samon when he woke late in the night, to teach Cecilia to weave as she was taught by her own mother, pushing the spoon into the straw to sew the basket tight.

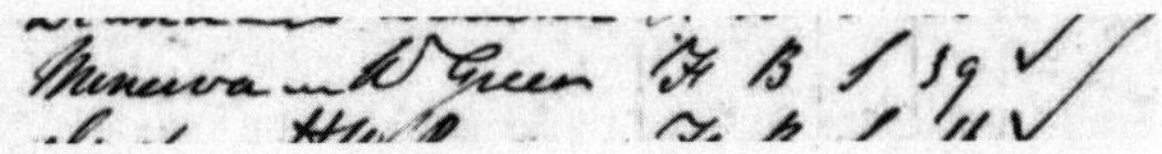

Maybe by the time of the war, Minerva's children were in Charleston, acting as spies; maybe Cecilia delivered messages from whomever she worked for to one of the Union sympathizers or Union troops around the city. Or maybe she and Samon and Eliza laid low until the victory they prayed for came about and they were at last free. Maybe they spent those worried and sleepless nights dreaming about what they would do and where they would go should the Union win—and then, when the time came, they stashed away the money they'd earned by being rented out by their owners, and they fled.

Did they see the battle at Fort Wagner? See the fire and hear the shots from the city? Did they hear about Sergeant Carney's bravery in upholding the flag during the battle? Maybe Minerva thought of her son, Samon, who would by then have been in his mid-twenties. Maybe she dreamed he'd made it to Union lines to fight with the Fifty-fourth regiment, or that he'd simply escaped north, to settle with a family, a wife. Maybe he escaped to live in the swamplands in which archaeologists are discovering evidence of the people who settled there. Deep in muggy, mosquito-filled wetlands, communities of people who had claimed their own freedom lived, fished, and farmed together, subsisting outside the bounds of the nation that mandated they live in bondage.

I imagined that Eliza might have dressed as a man, a sailor, and escaped north. Maybe, like Lizzie Hoffman and Martha Lewis, African American women who fought in the war, Eliza and Minerva disguised themselves and stood alongside their brothers, husbands, and friends.

Scholars estimate that nearly four hundred women fought in the Civil War as soldiers and spies. Imagine dressing yourself up to go undercover, donning blue pants and a blue coat, cutting your hair, setting that dapper hat on your head with the curled horn to signify your Union alliance. Imagine walking into battle with a new name, one adapted to cover your given gender. Imagine becoming friends with the men in the trenches, most of whom would never know your life-before, as a woman in a dress, a woman with fewer rights and choices. As a man, you could hold a bank account, find gainful employment, live alone, and choose your own mate, if you wanted one at all. This was the path that Jennie Hodgers chose, claiming the name Albert Cashier, and continuing to live as Albert when he left the army, taking advantage of the opportunity to vote.

Albert Cashier in uniform. A musical in Chicago recently commemorated Cashier's life and legacy as a trans man.

I think, too, of Cathay Williams, an African American woman who was born enslaved, disguising herself as a soldier to serve in the army from 1866 to 1868, under her new name William Cathay. Today, she's commemorated with a bust statue in Leavenworth, just outside Kansas City, keeping watch eternally out towards the horizon.

Before she made herself into William Cathay, Cathay Williams was born into enslavement and "forced to serve for the Union Army as a cook" during the Civil War, as journalist Miranda Davis writes, and then, after the war, became a Buffalo soldier, enlisting under the new name. She served for two years before being discovered. She was tall, at five foot nine, which worked in her favor. I think of a recent conversation I had with a fellow tall friend about being called "sir" when we're bundled up in our winter clothes and walking or skiing around town. With a hat, a heavy coat, and our height, people just assume. I think of William Cathay in her army uniform, the same one Joe McGill wears during his Slave Dwelling Project sleepovers today—the hat set down over her hair, the square-shouldered jacket, the pants that no woman would yet have worn. How must it have felt to slip into that uniform and claim that authority, hold her gun, and step up, ready for battle?

The bust of Willam Cathay/Cathay Williams, dedicated in Leavenworth, Missouri, in 2016.

This narrative has become, in so many ways, a story of images: those we choose to consume, those we seek out, those we choose to create, those we use or deride for our purposes. There is Nat Turner, in supposed defiance, and the white people, in supposed supplication. Just as one is supposedly black and the other is supposedly white, so the image is, like race, a fiction, perpetuated over and over, until people begin to think it is truth.

When I seek images of Bowser, I come to find that those that attributed to her online are not in fact of her; someone posted the image, and people copied and pasted and passed the image around, and this picture came to be known as a picture of her. When I go to research the painting of the "Black Sailor" from Rhode Island, I'm told by the historical society that this is originally a painting of a white sailor; it was transformed to represent a black man at some time, by whom they do not know. Maybe this was an effort by an artist to commemorate black mariners, to change the archive by changing the painting itself.

The same is true with the way we perpetuate stories. There are the stories I was told, and here, on the other hand, are the stories I seek out, the stories held in the gaps and silences of those earlier stories, the people and places and historic events that have always been there, told by people of color, activists, historians, writers—if only I'll find them, read them, and listen.

While I once thought that I'd be able to find descendants of Eliza, Minerva, Juba, and Jane, and could learn more about the women from family members, could ask the family for their advice, input, and permission before publishing this book, I have not been able to find anyone, even with the genealogist's help. Maybe someone will see these records and hear echoes of their own family stories here. As I've zig-zagged between archives to recollect the scattered letters, contracts, and objects that haven't yet been digitized, I hope that someday, someone else will take this information, and rewrite the story. If no text is ever dead but constantly changing and alive, then this is just one more fluid piece of an ever-changing narrative and archive, a thread that loops and tangles and then is pulled straight and taut through time, then and now, that *sshhhhh*-ing sound in my ears as the cotton thread comes up through the fabric—as it will be changed, re-pieced, re-stitched, again.

I keep asking myself: What should I be doing in a time when this history of racial oppression, our foundation, rises up again, fracturing in the daylight, evidencing what's always been there. I think of those days in North Carolina, when people said in front of me the things they'd never have said in front of a person of color, imagining I was "safe" because I'm white. I think of all of those arguments I had with them—what did they amount to? Did they change anything? I was so strident back then, so angry about what I was just coming to witness in explicit terms after seeing it in implicit terms around Boston and with my friends—and the segregation of a city I'd believed was "liberal," until I left and returned to see it with new eyes. Boston has been called one of the most racist cities in America. Now that I know the stories from Beacon Hill, of Prince Hall and Phillis Wheatley, Mumbet Freeman and Belinda Sutton an African, and of the Robbins family in Concord, I know that enslaved people built Boston just as they built Charleston, that enslavement is just as much the root of northern history as of southern. Educating myself is only part of it; still, after so many years, I ask myself how am I going to become better at these conversations and at living in this time?

"Those of us who teach, write, and think about slavery and its afterlives encounter myriad silences and ruptures in time, space, history, ethics, research, and method as we do our work. Again and again scholars of slavery face absences in the archives as we attempt to find 'the agents buried beneath' the accumulated erasures, projections, fabulations, and misnamings." This is Christina Sharpe quoting Hortense Spillers and writing about her own work as a black scholar of slavery, and the problems with doing this work in a society that exists in what she calls "the wake" of slavery, with systems that are still defined by those in which Eliza, Minerva, Jane, and Juba found themselves. She goes on to say that black scholars of slavery face the additional challenge of being "expected to discard, discount, disregard, jettison, abandon, and measure those ways of knowing [slavery and Black being in slavery]. . . ."

Tammy Denease as Belinda Sutton the African at the Royall House & Slave Quarters in Medford, Massachusetts.

I think of Tammy Denease, who portrays historic black women at schools and historic sites in New England; she says that by the end of every February, she's exhausted from having to present the Middle Passage over and over again. This is what white people want to hear about, she says. Like Keith Stokes, she also wants to tell not only the history of the Middle Passage and enslavement but also the stories of women who were inventors, teachers, pilots, soldiers—women descended from those who survived the passage and, against all the odds stacked against them, used their intelligence, talents, skills, and educations to triumph.

Abolitionists used to distribute the image you've probably seen a dozen times, which you'd recognize in an instant, of the enslaved or formerly enslaved man who is naked to the waist, his back to the camera. His back is covered in welts, his skin raised in thick scars that testify to abuse. You know from looking at this image and studying the layers of scars that this man survived years of abuse, in all its nefarious forms, including heavy beatings. This image was meant to illustrate the evil consequences of slavery and spurn people to action. Susan Sontag writes about how we're drawn to such images, and what it means to look: "One can feel obliged to look at photographs that record great cruelties and crimes. One should feel obliged to think about what it means to look at them, about the capacity to assimilate what they show. . . . Images of the repulsive can also allure."

We are drawn to these horrific images—for example, the picture of the lynching, which Claudia Rankine erased to focus our gaze on the white mob rather than the black bodies. You have seen that image a thousand times, too. When we see it, we recognize it as an icon, as something our culture created. As Euro-Americans, Sontag writes, we feel an obligation to look at these lynching pictures, at the images of enslaved people in the United States, in order to feel the "monstrousness of the slave system." And yet, she says, we don't look at images of people abused and attacked in wars of U.S. aggression around the world. We have national projects, national agendas, she says, and we remain true to those agendas; critiquing a war abroad would not be patriotic.

I think about Minerva in 1851. She died between October 26th and November 1st. It must have been cooler, and maybe rainy, in Charleston then. She must have heard the many church bells ringing around her home, marking the hours. She was said to be thirty-nine when she died, which means she was born about 1812, and was about twenty-two when she lived at 6 Cumberland Street, twenty-five when she had baby Samon. In 1851, if they'd survived, Samon would be fourteen and Cecilia would be sixteen. Were they enslaved at houses around Mr. Greer's where Minerva was enslaved? Had they been sold further away, or died of disease or beatings? Did anyone from

Minerva's household go and call for her children to come see their mother before she died?

In the last hours of her life, if they weren't able to stand beside her, she must have thought of Samon and Cecilia. If they weren't with her, she surely saw them in her mind's eye as she took those final breaths. Maybe it was the image of one of her children's faces she saw as she passed, that delight in Samon's eyes just before he fell into her arms. The warmth of her baby boy as she caught him and held him close.

Susan in her older years.

> *"Many years have passed since I have received any communication from you or any member of the family in Rhode Island," Winthrop writes in November 1864. "I have recently heard through* [my son] *Winthrop via Point Lookout where he is a prisoner of war that our Father and Mother are both dead and that you are living in the old Homestead at 51 George St. Though painful to have my son in captivity, I am grateful that his cousins have opened up correspondence with him, which will give him some relief in the way of sympathy."*

In 1864, while Juba found ways to navigate the war, and Eliza, perhaps, built a new life in Boston, the Crouch family lived on, suffering (as they perceived it) under financial strain and the trauma of the war unfolding around them, but otherwise unharmed. Winthrop bemoaned the loss of his fortune in the course of the war. Up until the Emancipation Proclamation, he and Hilton went on living their lives, raising their children, and buying and selling enslaved people.

Hilton was sorry to hear that his parents had died while the war between North and South raged around him. A year and a half earlier, Hilton writes home to Susan, saying that he hasn't had any news since May 1862, when their parents weren't well, and he hopes "this will find them alive with the enjoyment of health. I would very much like to see them. . . ." The more sensitive brother, Hilton is "very anxious" to hear from Susan "and to know how you have all got along. If you can let me hear from you even if it is only a few lines, it will be a great relief to my mind." Hilton was living then in Columbia with Winthrop and his family. Winthrop had managed to keep the cotton business running up to this point, and Hilton filled in for the bookkeeper, Mr. Ewart, the man who had hired Winthrop in his early days in Columbia. Mr. Ewart was killed in the Battle of Secessionville, Hilton reported.

Hilton's nephew, Winthrop's son Winty, was "still in the army and has grown to be a large stout man. He has been in a number of battles and thus far escaped all harm." His younger brothers, Henry and Trezevant, were still in school. Unlike so many wealthy southerners, Winty fought instead of paying a poorer man to fight for him; such common arrangements had come to make the war known as the "rich man's war, poor man's fight." Winty seemed to flourish in the army, at least according to Hilton, who says that "Camp life agrees with him," after seeing him on his trip to Columbia with "a detachment of Invalids."

A year and a half later, Winthrop writes to thank Susan for corresponding with his son Winty, and, having heard about conditions at the prisons, writes that he hopes Winty was being cared for by those northerners around him: "I trust that he has had his wants supplied from my old friends in New York." I wonder if, during the course of the war, Winty fought against people he knew from the North. Did he come up against friends, relatives? He made it through a dozen battles unscathed, and when he was captured by the Union and sent to Point Lookout, he was kept alive and well by his aunts and cousins in New York, who brought him food and clothing. Did they talk politics during those visits? Did Winty believe in the cause for which he fought—southern secession, the upholding of his father's way of life, enslavement? Or did he simply enlist and fight because it's what was done? Did Eliza and Emily talk to him about abolitionism? What happened on those visits, in those letters? Winthrop would write again, thanking Susan and Emily for their kindness to Winty. Though many in the prison camps succumbed to smallpox, Winty was lucky to return home safely. A list of "South Carolina Prisoners Died in Hospital" at Point Lookout, where Winty was housed, was published in the September 8, 1865, edition of Charleston's *Post and Courier*, with the names of hundreds of casualties. Other parents read that list and came upon their children's names with heartache, but Winthrop and Cassie were spared.

Meanwhile, Hilton's letters north to Susan are full of concern and longing to hear back; he writes that he sent several letters over the weeks and months and has gotten no reply.

> *Feb. 25, 1863: My Dear Sister, Your last letter that I have received was dated in May 1862 and came to hand in June, since that time I am totally unadvised respecting the welfare of our parents or any of the family. I have written you twice since the receipt of your letter but do not know that they have been received by you. I have been living at this place since August last and am now living with Winthrop. . . . His firm has moved their business up here.*

Hilton's wife Harriet, Franklin wrote, was never happy, nor were her daughters. They demanded too much, Franklin said. This must have been family lore. Harriet and her daughters were always wealthier than Hilton, having inherited the enslaved people passed down from Mary Ancrum Walker. Walker came from that elite upper-class, while Hilton was always struggling in the middle class. Maybe the family's resentment of Harriet, Henrietta, and Rosamond comes from that class difference, their perception that the women demanded more because they'd been given more. And yet, Hilton profited, and was served by those enslaved people until the war.

By 1864, Winthrop and Hilton and their families had been living in Columbia for three years. There's another silence in the correspondence, as Susan and Winthrop surely wrote back and forth to each other in letters lost or confiscated in the course of their transfer. It's not until June 1865, just after the end of the war, that the letters become more frequent again and Winthrop and Hilton are able to recount the full scale of their losses for Susan. Hilton write in June 1865, "Winthrop's warehouse and store were all burnt . . . they had a large amount of cotton on hand and six large warehouses all of which were destroyed. This will break up their business entirely." Winthrop didn't know "what he would do for the future," and Hilton writes that he's "in the same quandary." While Winthrop has his wife, Cassie, and three children in whom to take comfort, Hilton writes that he's "alone in the world, and feel that I have but a few years now to live." His wife died in 1863, and he longs to go back to the North and make his life there again. He lives in Columbia with his stepdaughters and their children, having made one of them, the little boy named Willie who suffers from epilepsy, his "pet."

> *He is now five years old last April and he has entirely lost his mind and does not speak. At two years old he was a fine promising child and talked but he has Epileptic fits and spasms which have reduced him to the state he now is in. The doctors say he cannot recover and that he may be taken away at any time. He is a very fine looking child and to look at him one would think him a very smart child. He is very fond of me, will leave his mother anytime to come to me.*

Hilton writes home about Willie in each of the previous letters, and continues to chronicle his progress for Susan. Winthrop writes that the child is "idiotic."

Thus, in the wake of war, the everyday aspects of life go on for the Crouch-Williams families—the child is brought to doctors, the mothers tend to their babies, the grandfathers dote. But they must also have been coping with the trauma of having witnessed the war unfold—what would have felt very different for Hilton and Winthrop as opposed to Sam and Dianna, the couple Winthrop owned before the war, or John, Juba, Eliza, and Minerva, if they were alive to see it. Now, the freedmen and women were rebuilding their lives, finding ways to make money when they had nothing, or relying on the little they'd saved from renting themselves out or selling their own vegetables, crafts, or wares.

Hilton writes about the family's evacuation of their home when "General Sherman burnt the place," but notes that "although the house was robbed and plundered, we were more fortunate than many. Winthrop's house was burnt and all his furniture; he only saved eight chairs and one mattress but was fortunate in saving a large portion of their clothes" because they'd packed up the day before to move to "our side of the city (they living on the western side) to avoid the shells which the enemy were favoring us with."

In February, after his renowned March to the Sea, Sherman directed his troops north to Charleston and Columbia. Hilton recalls that windy night when Columbia burned at the hands of the Union soldiers: "That night the 17th of February was a night of horrors and never to be forgotten. The wind was blowing a hurricane and we were surrounded by a sea of flames and expecting every moment that our House would be fired. About one o'clock, I sent Rosy [my step-daughter] and the children in the woods with only a change of clothes for them by which both Willie and Rosy took the cold and have suffered very much for it." And yet, the whole family survived.

Winthrop writes that "the House was burned by Sherman in February . . ." and "On the 12th of February last some of General Sherman's scouts or spies entered the city secretly and another warehouse was burnt to the ground containing Sea Island Cotton and an enormous amount of bagging, rope, and twine on storage and on the 17th February General Sherman swept the rest of our warehouses containing some 2500 bales cotton, all of my books, papers except my two ledgers, one day book and my two iron safes were rifled and then burnt. . . ." He lost two hundred bales of cotton, and notes that his warehouses were some of the largest in the city. He blamed not the United States Army but Sherman himself. "fortunately we saved one cow from Sherman's men," he says later in this same letter.

He managed to save his silver "by burying it, and after the Yankees left town I dug it up. My bonds, notes, and valuables were not discovered by the soldiers and escaped plundering." Of course, he says, so much of what he owned in stocks and notes is now worthless in Confederate dollars. "What my losses on Bank Stocks, Rail Road Stocks, Banks of the States, and Real Estate I cannot estimate. Then I lose $37,500 in eight percent C.S. bonds besides on half of the Confederate money Bonds&c. of Blakely & Williams [his cotton trading company] which was near $20,000. At present, I have nothing valuable I can sell, not even real estate." The amount of money Winthrop must have accrued before the war was vast. He says that he had been planning to retire, having enough Sea Island—the finest—cotton stored, and savings and investments made, to secure his income for many years to come.

Now, he prides himself on his great skill at milking the cow (as he tells it) that she yields enough milk and butter to keep the family afloat, in addition to the vegetables he got from his "small kitchen garden." (Later, in another letter, though, he says that their formerly enslaved man still milked the cow.) He writes about his new thrifty ways: "I buy a small piece Beef for ten or fifteen cents, make a soup or a stew for the whole family with a dish of rice and tomato sauce comprises our dinner nearly every day in the week. Our garden has yielded green peas, snap beans, lima beans, corn, cucumbers, watermelons, okra, and tomatoes but all the earlier vegetables are past. We are out of corn and flour. Fortunately, we saved one cow from Sherman's men," though he lost another cow and calf. He says that the milk and butter from the cow "is our chief living and the greatest luxury in such times as these. We make all the butter we use which is not much but we enjoy it more for not having it more than five days for breakfast out of the week. We have not had butter for any other meal than breakfast for the last three years . . ."

It's strange to read Winthrop's pride in his new methods of survival, which were the ways that his enslaved people survived for so many years before the war—with kitchen gardens, chickens or livestock they bought with money made from their own vegetables, eggs, baskets, or sewing. Scraps of meat, milk, and butter where they could get it. He continues to insist that he's superior even in doing the work they once did for him, for years, without pay.

Two people, who might be his formerly enslaved people Sam and Dianna, remained with him for a short time. Right after he recounts the details of buying butter, and having just a little for breakfast five days a week and none for other meals for three years—and just before he lists the amounts of money he lost and says that his wife, Cassie, would like some quince preserves and grape jelly (with apologies for the seeming extravagance but "we have not had any preserves for the last four years")—Winthrop writes: "We have but two servants left, a man and a woman. We hire a woman to do our washing. The man is house steward and milks the cow. The woman cooks. These will only remain with us until fall, when we return to Charleston."

He says that his wife will hire only "one Irish or German girl" when they get back home. "Our cook woman I bought seven years ago with her husband. He is an old man and a Methodist Preacher since the army occupied this town he obtained the College Chapel and has held services there regularly ever since. Although he lives in my yard he is a much more important character than I am and lives far better than I do. The loss by Emancipation [bears?] on me lightly. I suppose $12,000 in gold will cover it."

How cavalierly he writes off people's lives with $12,000 in gold. How flippantly he says the man lives better than he does, as if completely unaware of the figures he just listed, the prices of cotton and stocks and bonds he says he lost, the hopes he has of starting his cotton business back up again when he returns to Charleston. He tells Susan in 1860 that he sold John, who is likely the man he bought in the 1830s from Susan and Hasell's estate. At that time, John was only about seven; in 1860, he was about twenty-three. Winthrop sold John, whom he'd watched grow into adulthood alongside his own son, for $1,000 but says no more about to whom he was sold, nor what the man John was like, what he had done for Winthrop in those intervening decades. Did he sell Juba, who was likely John's mother, too, if he had bought her in 1837-8? More than two decades spent with a man and he can only say he sold him and made a tidy sum.

I described the man above—the man who revealed his back to show scars of abuse—an "enslaved or formerly enslaved man," and I think about a conversation I had with a friend the other night. She was talking about ticking off the boxes on a form to indicate whether she's single or married. She ticked off "single," but the automated form popped up and informed her she could not be single because she had once been married.

"That's right," said another friend, "now you're divorced. You can never be single again."

The condition of marriage defines her forever, no matter how far past it was—she's always known to have once been married, and now to no longer be married.

Am I defining that man by his condition of having once been enslaved, instead of simply seeing him as a man? Unlike marriage (at least, in my friend's case), enslavement wasn't a choice. Why should I define him as having been enslaved? Why not say that he's a man? A man, naked to the waist. Is that what I should have said?

When I began trying to understand how to tell the stories of Eliza, Minerva, and Juba, and met with Beverly Gordon-Welch in Boston, we sat in her office, which had a great window along one side that looked out to all the other offices. I could see the women working and talking on the phone while we spoke. And, when I started by saying that I was trying to write about "the slaves," she stopped me, and said, "*Enslaved women.*"

"Enslaved women," I repeated after her, like a child learning a language.

"That's right," she said, "if you say simply 'slave,' then you're objectifying her again. She was already objectified once, back then, as a woman who was treated as an object to be bought and sold, and now you're doing it again, in the present moment when you call her 'a slave.'"

"I see," I said, "thank you."

You have probably seen a man named William Casby in a photograph by Richard Avedon. The photo was taken in 1963, a century after these letters between Susan and her brothers were written, and Richard Avedon titled this piece, *William Casby, Born in Slavery*. In his book on photography, *Camera Lucida*, published in 1980, Roland Barthes labels the photograph, *William Casby, Born a Slave*. Laura Wexler writes that Barthes's analysis of the photograph keeps William Casby "frozen" in the era of slavery as Barthes does the looking-at-pain that Susan Sontag writes about: "the man I see here *has been* a slave; he certifies that slavery has existed, not so far from us; and he certifies this not by historical testimony but by a new, somehow experiential order of proof (a proof no longer merely induced). I remember keeping for a long time a photo I had cut out of a magazine . . . which showed a slave market . . . my horror and fascination as a child came from this: that there was a *certainty* that such a thing had existed: not a question of exactitude, but of reality: the historian was no longer the mediator, slavery was given without mediation, the fact was established *without method*."

Barthes says he kept that photograph tucked away safely, "keeping [it] for a long time." Wexler argues that Barthes continues to see Casby as only an enslaved man: "It is for Barthes as if Casby is *still* a slave, wearing the mask of that social station . . . Nor does Barthes think further about William Casby. He especially does not remark upon the tiny reflection of Avedon and his camera that the photograph reveals in Casby's eyes."

This image of the camera, Wexler says, allows Casby to turn back upon the viewer the truth of his objectification by the camera, "shooting back the objectifying gaze." Wexler writes that Barthes "ignores Avedon's remarkable reconceptualization of the power relations of photography" and instead "reproduces slavery's social relations by turning Avedon's animation of Casby's sight into a dead thing once again, 'outside of society and its history.'" Barthes, she says, denies him the power of refuting the gaze, and sees him, continually, as "a slave," an object, the "dead thing."

Just as people use the "selfie" and the Internet to distribute their own visions and representations of themselves, Wexler writes that Douglass used the new form of the daguerreotype, distributed widely in the late 1830s, to create his own images of himself, ones that show an educated, powerful man. Suddenly, with the daguerreotype, it was possible to make one's own image in ways that hadn't been possible before. There's one painting of Douglass, a portrait for which he sat (apparently with hesitation, as he was wary of painted and drawn portraits), but most of what we see of him, we see as photographs whose composition he alone controlled. "In this series, I propose, it is possible to discern decisions Douglass repeatedly made about self-representation and watch him holding firm to a particular interpolation into the American canon of 'illustrious' men." Wexler writes that while Douglass was born "socially dead" as an enslaved man, he now displays "signs of distinction assumed deliberately by a man who had formerly been denied it." She compares Douglass to Lincoln in his careful presentation of his portrait throughout time. The photo of him, above, wearing what Robin Hill calls "a luxurious tie, paired with a vest intricately embroidered with floral designs" illustrates the "rapt attention" to which he paid his clothes, "often wearing stylish yet somber suits, and well-pressed shirts and cravats, guarding a presentation of bourgeois respectability." Hill writes that his wife, Anna, "ensured that a freshly pressed shirt awaited his arrival at each destination." Having spent so long living as an enslaved man, and knowing that he faced the system to which Winthrop and so many others like him stubbornly clung, he used his clothes and pose to help ensure his reception as an educated, respected thinker.

> The coat and suit collars are raised high on the neck, a style common during the mid-nineteenth century and a sign of moral rectitude. . . . The head and shoulders fill most of the compositional space. The figure appears not only stately but imposing; even when viewed at eye level, the eyes seem to be looking down upon the viewer and commandeering the space between the image's surface and the point of the spectator.

Hill writes that Douglass used this same pose, over and over again, in the years and decades to come, in pictures that "helped to create and guarantee his citizen status, visually proclaiming Douglass' 'natural right' to own property and thus be said to be equal, which is to say autonomous and free."

Sojourner Truth, also an abolitionist and public intellectual, did this same photographic work. Augusta Rohrbach writes that "The success of her intervention [in the creation of her own image] relies on an idea about the relationship between the subject and its photographic representation that was common to 19th century viewers. Roland Barthes identifies the peculiar power of the photographic image, allowing that a photograph is 'somehow co-natural with its referent'; it retains a level of presence not necessitated by other referential systems. Indeed, as a signifier, the photograph documents 'the necessarily real thing which has been placed before the lens.'"

Rohrbach explains that Truth's portraits consistently feature her in a bonnet and white cape, holding white yarn in her hand as it unspools, employing the "trappings of femininity" she used in photographs she sold to support herself. She did this, Rohrbach argues, because "She knew that race mattered and that as a dark-skinned black woman she needed to find ways to make race work to her advantage." She understands the "complexities of agency within the context of visual and print culture" as she chooses different representations of herself. In the 1860s, she chooses the Quaker bonnet instead of the scarf that covered her head in the sketch that served as her book's frontispiece in 1850. In the 1860s photograph, she wears a buttoned dress with a full skirt, and a white woven shawl. The punctum—the detail Barthes would say catches our eye and stays with us even as we move away from the photo—is the book that often sits on a table beside her or rests in her hands. The book signifies her own autobiography, her claim to tell her own story (by dictating it to a writer, as "Aunt Sally" and other formerly enslaved people did when they had been denied literacy by whites); she distributed that story and her images widely in the abolitionist movement throughout the 1850s and '60s. This is the quiet, lasting presence of the photo that is the ultimate resistance. She has claimed her freedom, her identity as a formerly enslaved woman, and as a woman with access to the femininity that Susan sewed towards, *and* a woman with the right to not only own a book but to write her own—all rights she'd been denied as an enslaved woman. Wendy S. Walters reminds me that she'd have been killed for owning a book as an enslaved woman.

Truth copyrighted her own image and distributed it widely, which was, Rohrbach reminds us, part of her "reaction . . . against and interventions in a dominant white culture's production of her image."

For both Truth and Douglass, imagery went beyond a reclamation of self; photography also played an important role in their abolitionism. In 1861, the South was seceding and Lincoln gave a speech defending slavery as a legal system in the South. Douglass responded. Laura Wexler writes that "For Douglass, the temporizing of Lincoln's defense of the legality of slavery in the slave states was just as much a distortion of reality as the grotesque images that white artists made of black faces and bodies, rendering them unacceptable in the armed forces. Photographic seeing could help address that problem because it could correct the distorted representations of black manhood that put the Union at risk . . . Viewed correctly, black men could come to life in the white imagination, and Lincoln would find the soldiers the Union needed to win the war . . ." She goes on to say that Douglass believed that "Technological process could bring not only the external but also the inner nature of man more clearly to light; he believed that picture-making—'the process by which man is able to invert his own subjective consciousness into the objective form . . . was in truth the highest attribute of man's nature.'"

Technology—which had perpetuated slavery in the South with the proliferation of cotton mills in the North at the start of the nineteenth century—could also be harnessed for this greater good.

Wexler argues that Douglass adds "a fourth perspective to Barthes' more famous three: that of the revenant, or one who returns from the dead." So, as Douglass was considered socially dead, as an enslaved man, he returns alive into American society in his speeches and images. "Barthes was afraid of the specter but Douglass welcomed what came back from slavery's grave. The revenant is an effect of liveliness produced over time. It requires images that repeat, or return, to which we may return multiple times to try to comprehend the intentions of their makers." She goes on to say that these images belong as much to the past as to the future. "We project the persistence of the liveliness that inserts itself into the historical record."

In finally understanding this concept of the revenant, and how it relates to tangible objects, be it a daguerreotype or handicraft, the resistance of the objectification that Winthrop and his siblings enacted in the South, I returned to the archives I'd been studying, and the quilt, and the potential for the "liveliness of the people" who were silenced in these quilt tops.

In *The Pleasure of the Text*, Barthes describes what he calls "tmesis." He says that readers create "abrasions" in the text by skimming or skipping—as if the text, or *because* the text—is an object upon which we make a mark, we create "gaps or seams" as we read. He notes that the "erotic part of the garment is where it gapes." I think about Emily Dickinson and her shifts between writing and garment sewing, and the close relationship between sewing and writing for nineteenth century women, maybe for Susan, or Phillis Wheatley, or Jane, too. The "seam of the two edges, interstices of bliss. . . . occurs in the uttering, not in the sequence of utterances." This "seam or flaw" is called "tmesis." "It is the very rhythm of what's read and what's not read that creates the pleasure of great narratives."

In this case, the author of the quilt—Susan and Hasell Crouch—didn't intentionally create a narrative but have nonetheless left one that I've been trying to decode for the last six years, making my own abrasions as I read their stories and search for more. Others will come, just as I came after Franklin, to make abrasions of their own.

I think of all the markers of people's lives left behind—not just letters and diaries but dolls, baskets, fragments of dresses, and quilts. Laurel Thatcher Ulrich writes about the importance of recognizing women's work as thoroughly as we recognize the many documents and letters left behind by white men.

> We might begin with Anne Bradstreet's famous line: 'I am obnoxious to each carping tongue/ Who says my hand a needle better fits.' That sentence establishes a creative tension between pens and needles, hands and tongues, written and non-written forms of female expression, inviting us not only to take oral traditions and material sources more seriously . . . but also to examine the roots of the written documents we take so much for granted.

Ulrich argues for the importance of reading textiles as texts in and of themselves—like Harriet Powers's quilt with its creation of her world, the stories she was told and witnessed, or the scraps of fabric that Minerva and Eliza and Jane wore as dresses they might have sewn themselves. As I studied this quilt, it became evident that there was another story within these seams. We know snippets, pieces of an unseen whole. When Hilton petitioned to sell Hasell's seven enslaved people, the pew at St. Philip's that he'd inherited from his aunt, and the Sullivan's Island house, it was so that "the widow can return to the north." Susan made her choices in her time, and the result was the changed lives of the people she owned. We all make choices in our time. How will I tell this story? How will I find the people quieted in these seams and gaps? In what systems of oppression am I implicated? This has been my odyssey. I've followed trails

I'd never imagined, seen places that hold stories of people I needed to know. I see how much more I have to learn—all the books I've yet to read.

Every time I sit down to sew, now, I think of Jane. I buy little new fabric, now that I know the conditions under which it's made. If I can critique Susan for buying all the industrially-woven calicos for the quilt, which she knew were made from cotton picked by enslaved people, how can I buy clothes I know are made by people who work in conditions I would find abhorrent if I were to see them myself? I don't entirely avoid buying new cloth. The women who hold jobs at factories abroad need those jobs to survive. But I can at least try to live by my values, use and reuse all the fabric I buy, and speak out about working conditions here and abroad. Capitalism makes it difficult to live outside of its hold; when I buy a used couch and plan to reupholster it instead of buying a new couch made abroad, I find the only affordable fabric is made in China. I buy most of my clothes secondhand, on websites like ThredUp and in thrift stores, but when I need new shoes, the only ones I can find made in the USA are beyond my budget, even if these are the only shoes I buy for two years. I allow myself to do as a historian of slavery has advised—I do my best, buy most of my clothes and goods secondhand, buy fair trade and organic cloth as much as possible, and make exceptions when I have to.

I can pay attention, listen, speak when it's helpful, and keep educating myself. The version of this nation with which I was raised is not the truth. I grew up recognizing inequality, injustice, racism—but I hadn't plumbed down into its roots as I have since I met Minerva, Eliza, Jane, and Juba Simons. Researching this story, traveling and reading so intensively, searching for traces of these women, and for the contexts that shaped their worlds, has sent me into sorrow and rage, especially as our current world unfolds around us. I began to write this story when the case over Trayvon Martin's murder was decided; George Zimmerman was acquitted, declared not guilty of murdering Trayvon Martin, a child. At this same time, I read Winthrop's letter about the murdered "negroe" and the white man who would be acquitted. And I saw more clearly. This is not just the continued legacy of enslavement, not a straight and plodding line through time, but an overlapping, circling, ever-present reality; then is now. It has always happened. It has never stopped happening. As I finish this book, OJ Simpson is released on parole, and I think back to my earlier days in North Carolina, when students made racist jokes about his trial. About the controversies we face now over the Confederate flag and monuments to Confederate soldiers. On my travels, I look for the monuments to people like Denmark Vesey, who is honored in a park in Charleston, and Sargeant Carney, the Civil War hero who's honored in a plaque on the battery, and Robert Smalls, whose escape I read about that day I visited the Old Slave Mart Museum.

I look to the past and seek the people whose stories enliven a world I didn't know but can still feel in the present. I reach for the tactile—the clothes, a quilt, the thin paper on which loops of cursive huddle to fill the page. I visit historic sites and feel the give of wooden floors beneath my feet, imagine other peoples' feet on those boards, other people's breath and hands touching these walls. I hear what docents and tour guides are saying as well as what they're not saying; I ask them questions. I learn about the food people made in the past, their daily habits, the authors they might have read, speakers they'd have heard—and this past seems to exist around me in the present, informing my days, changing the places I thought I knew.

12

Portraits

Imagine: Juba Simons chooses her dress carefully that morning, trying to decide if it will be the blue calico or green and yellow striped dress she'll wear for her portrait. This is her first photograph, and she's considered every detail. She'll carry the Bible she bought from her white neighbor in the months after the war, when he was desperate for cash to feed his family. She's been saving for years for this moment, and celebrated every purchase that marked her freedom.

Each transaction was a triumph, signaling to the whites around her that they were no longer the masters and she was no longer enslaved. She is free. She works for whom she chooses, buys and sells what she chooses, establishes her own home apart from theirs, finally out from under their constant gaze and the constant threat of their punishments. Best of all, she chooses her own clothes, at last. None of that old red print Susan forced her to wear, in that plain print and simpler pattern than all of Susan's ruffled and buttoned dresses, cloaks, and gloves. She scoffs at the memory of Susan receiving that cloth from her family at the north, laying it all out on the table with the air of a religious touching sacred objects, running her hand down each folded layer of cotton, all those pretty calicos in blue and green and soft white and pink. And for Eliza and Minerva and herself? The drab print, that mucky brown Juba always despised, which Susan deemed good enough for the women she thought she could own.

Juba has three dresses now, each purchased with her own money or in trade for vegetables from her backyard garden or the baskets she expertly weaves. Maybe she becomes a washerwoman in the years after the war, living on twenty dollars a month—several dollars from each of the ten families for whom she took in washing. She's had to start making her own soap again, as she'd done in the 1830s when Susan and Hasell kept her at their house on Cumberland Street. Now, she's blocks from that neighborhood, closer to Marion Square and nestled in with friends and family around her.

So much for store-bought, she might think to herself as she sweeps ashes from the fireplace to begin the process of making lye. Her back aches as she leans forward to get the ashes at the back of the hearth. Soap is too expensive to buy readymade, but the whites who employ her won't pay for the soap she makes. She ends up with about twelve cents per pound of laundry in profit—a pittance for all the labor of hauling and boiling water, making soap, scrubbing out their damned sweat marks—and yet, it's all hers to keep. No portion of her pay goes, anymore, to greedy and abusive owners. It's hers.

As she gets ready for her portrait, maybe she pulls her hair back into a bun at the base of her neck, the part to one side of her face, her hair draping across her forehead. Maybe she dons a bonnet with a spectacular white feather. Maybe she ties her hair up a white head tie, just as she'd seen her mother Judith do in her older years. Does she wear a necklace or a ring given to her by her husband so many years ago? Does she bring her son Sorenzo, if he's living nearby, or in her own house, with his wife and children?

We don't have any known images of Juba, but I imagine she had one taken. I can see her in her bedroom that morning, facing a dresser she got from her former master's house, one of the few things she still has that was a hand-me-down; she's slowly replaced all those things given to her by her former masters with objects of her own choosing. On the dresser sits a small mirror, chipping at the edges. She leans towards it, pats the sides of her hair, secures the scarf tied at her neck with a round pin. Smiles. *Just right*, she thinks to herself, and then she turns from the mirror and walks out of the bedroom she shares with her sister, heels clicking over wide creaking pine boards, into the small main room where two of her cousins have left their beds made up and tidy, just as she prefers, and then out the front door into the bustle of Coming Street.

I wonder if, back in Providence or visiting Boston, Susan and her daughter Emmie ever saw Frederick Douglass or Sojourner Truth speak, in those years leading up to the war, or if Susan's sisters Eliza and Emily ever talked to her about abolition and their disagreements with the southern *way of living*. Were there tensions between them? Emily and Eliza Williams lived in another part of the city; Emily's husband, William Harris, who had helped sell so much southern cotton and lumber (produced by enslaved people) was the stepson of Moses Brown, the abolitionist. How did he reconcile himself with his stepfather's beliefs?

Did any of the women and men Susan had once enslaved travel through Providence and freedom before or during the war, or in the early days after? Maybe, as Susan was sewing and arranging her parlor, Eliza, the woman Susan once enslaved, had help from someone like

Harriet Tubman, who would have helped her eventually move north, where she could escape into the black neighborhoods in Providence. In Providence, people of color owned hotels and boardinghouses and could have secreted her farther north, to the elite black community in Boston, or New Bedford, that whaling town to which Douglass traveled in 1838, disguised as a sailor.

Between the 1840s and '60s, Susan and Emmie had settled into their old home back on Providence's George Street, where Susan made her samplers as a little girl and learned to sew from her mother. She helped her mother care for the boarders and took charge of the family finances. Franklin writes that she "kept a tight rein" over her parents' finances. I wonder if this is because she was severe, as Franklin describes her, or because she was so concerned about her welfare as a widow without the ability to get a job of her own. In the 1840s, many of the women working in Providence's textile mills, less than a mile from Susan's home, were immigrants as opposed to local farm girls who had worked in the mills when they first opened in the early 1800s. Susan didn't go to work at the mills, but used her fine stitching skills to support the family. For so long, I thought of her as the woman in the photo with the stern face, someone who must have been unhappy. But then, years later, I see the second image of her, still tightly corseted in her black dress, but smiling at the photographer.

"She certainly kept up with the fashions of the day," says Prof W. when she sees the latest photo.

She looks happier here, and kinder, too, and I think about how much my impression of her was shaped by Franklin's remembrances of her as a "stern" woman, and my own perceptions of her based on that first photograph.

This second photograph is accompanied by the sermon a preacher gave at her funeral. He describes her as generous and religious and devoted. She lived as a widow for sixty-six years, he says. She did a lot of volunteer work in the church. In the days after she moved north in the 1830s, she wrote to her brother-in-law Mr. Harris to ask for a recommendation about which Bible to buy.

Emily Crouch's watercolors; many are of Rhode Island landscapes and ports. It's Emily who painted the portrait of Franklin that's included in the beginning of this book; she lived with him in Providence in her old age, bringing with her the trunk of clothes and the quilt tops, prompting Franklin's conservation of the collection. Emily never married and supported herself by teaching painting at schools in Providence, including the Moses Brown School, the Quaker school he founded in 1784; the school continues to serve students from preschool through twelfth grade.

In Providence, she'd have cleaned the home and prepared meals, gone out calling, visited with friends, done the sewing and mending. I imagine her on a cold November day, bundling into her cloak—that shawl she'd so carefully directed to be made from South Carolina—and stepping into the narrow, cobblestone street alongside Brown. When the chill of Rhode Island's November air strikes her face as she steps into the street, she pulls her shawl tight across her chest, nods to her neighbor in passing, thinking of her husband and the warm fall days they spent together in Charleston, newly in love, sewing and dyeing a bonnet and picking roses for cordial. Those days were sweet, she must have thought. Maybe she was softer then, easier to laugh and more tender with her loved ones. But the death of her baby and husband would change everything. She lived to ninety, and never remarried, but her brothers often mention a male friend in their letters, asking him to send them the Providence newspapers. Maybe she fell in love again.

Her sister Eliza Williams, whose marriage had been "prevented" by the family, Franklin writes, never married. She lived to eighty-two and died in Boston. Susan took the furniture that had been left to Eliza in her parents' will. I don't know why, nor how they felt about each other. The majority of the letters saved are from Winthrop and Hilton, sending word north; those letters were saved first by Eliza, and later, presumably, by Susan. "My dear sister," so many of them begin. But who was she? I used to think there was another archive of letters held by the southern branch of the family—along with that letter from the Gaud family cited in the 1960s magazine—and I searched for that bundle, imagining that that was where Susan and Emily and Eliza Williams talked about all they felt and knew. That's where the women's voices would predominate, I imagined, as they appeared here and there a decade before, in the 1830s, when Susan wrote home and Eliza saved her letters. I called their descendants, whom I thought may have those letters, but I found that the letter from the 1960s is part of the collection in Rhode Island after all. As far as I could tell, there was no mysterious missing bundle, no more secrets waiting to be uncovered, as the quilt and its letters sat for so long before Franklin excavated them, and then I returned to them.

When the war struck, Susan reappropriated her skills, knitting and sewing for soldiers instead of for her Victorian-era parlor to establish herself as a lady. Maybe those dreams of rising up to the upper echelon of the middle class had faded, anyhow, now that she was back in her parents' house and laboring alongside them to care for students again. She'd bemoaned her mother's hard work when she lived down in Charleston, wishing her mother didn't have to work so hard when she had such "good help" (her enslaved women) to do her chores. Back at home, through the long depression years of the late 1830s to '40s, Susan brought in extra money with her handmade goods, which later became donations for the soldiers during the war in the 1860s.

I traced my fingers over her penciled letters and numbers—mittens and scarves and hats, all detailed with prices and names—the people for whom they were made. There weren't any dates. This was a small notebook, easy to slip into her pocket as she walked through town or sat at her fireside table at night after Emmie had gone to bed, knitting without having to think about the stitches, her needles moving as if on their own, muscle memory taking over while her mind drifted to Emmie's progress as an artist or memories of her chubby sweet boy, Little Hasell, thirty years gone.

Did she ever see the effects of the Fugitive Slave Act, passed in 1850? Did she witness or cause the capture of enslaved people who were then delivered back to their owners in the South? What did she make of the rising abolitionist movement that grew around her in the North, having owned people herself down South? Did she face recrimination from her siblings? Did Winthrop and Hilton?

I think of those famous sisters, Angelina and Sarah Grimké, whose family Susan knew when she was in Charleston. They lived in the same neighborhood as Susan and Hasell, by the battery, and attended St. Philip's along with them. They must have passed each other along the battery, strolling in the afternoon or walking back and forth to the market. When Mrs. Grimké passed away, Winthrop was sure to note her death in his letter to Susan. The Grimkés were a long-standing and powerful family in Charleston, and the girls' rejection of their parents' slaveholding was well-known. They moved north and became Quakers, like Moses Brown, turning away from their family's way of life and drawing a sharp divide between the two sides.

Susan was no radical, or what Sarah Ahmed would call a "killjoy," as Angelina and Sarah, and Harriet Tubman and Sojourner Truth, were feminist killjoys—those who see the problems with the status quo or resist their oppression and walk against the crowd. Susan's sisters Eliza and Emily might have been killjoys, as they were at least opposed to enslavement. The woman Eliza, who was enslaved and dressed poorly when sold on the block, might have been a killjoy, resisting her sale by posing as an unappealing purchase. In writing her essay on killjoys, Ahmed quotes Sojourner Truth's speech at the 1851 Women's Rights Convention in Akron, Ohio. Truth supposedly raised her arm at the end and said, "Ain't I a woman?" to proclaim her humanity in the face of the slaveholders who disavowed that claim.

It doesn't matter whether, as scholars once debated, Sojourner Truth ever spoke those words. She was said to have spoken those words, and later, she herself claimed to have done so. It was an erroneous history that struck a chord with the public and carried her message further. Why not embrace it? She used the misattribution for her own—for the abolitionist cause's—benefit, because she saw that it was effective. "I sell the shadow to support the substance," is the caption on one of Truth's own photos, explaining that the sale of this "shadow," the photographic portrait of herself, would support the abolitionist cause.

In the days after the war, everyday women and men fought to proclaim their freedom and status as citizens, with the agency to own their own homes and land, thousands of whites resisted—in the North and in the South. After so many years of the booming cotton industry, and thus the booming slave industry, it would take years to push closer toward justice. The people the Crouch-Williamses enslaved might have been able to take advantage of the chaos of war to claim their freedom, or, unable or unwilling to move for various reasons, waited for the moment they could leave. I imagine, in the early days of the war, the people enslaved in fields at Middleton around those symmetrical pools, and nearby Boone Hall, cultivating and harvesting rice and the fine Sea Island cotton that Winthrop bought and sold, their days in the hot sun, the sounds of battle reaching them at the plantations around Charleston. Some ran for freedom in the midst of the battles and fires and made it to Baltimore and then north, enlisting in the Union Army; others were made to work throughout the war, helping to build Confederate camps and forts, feeding the soldiers, digging trenches, doing the hard labor of battle behind the lines. Maybe William, the "house boy" Winthrop bought in 1856, worked for a time as one of the Confederates, forced to strengthen the army until he could escape—then went north, spending time first in a contraband camp outside of Washington, D.C., with hundreds of other formerly enslaved people, and then traveling to New York, where he enlisted and fought for the North. Almost 200,000 African American men fought for the Union, and nearly 30,000 of those men died. Some of those men, like Cathay Williams or William Cathay, were actually women, and others, like Albert Cashier, were trans men. Some enslaved men were forced to accompany their masters in the Confederate army while they fought.

It's likely that Juba was still in Charleston during the war, or somewhere nearby, since she was there in 1874. I wonder if she fled the city during the fire in 1861, if she met her children in the neighborhood—if George and John, if they were her sons, were still in the city as well. Maybe she sat in a church on watch night, New Year's Eve, waiting to hear of the emancipation proclamation. Maybe she heard those words in 1863 and celebrated with friends. And yet, her and her children's lives in the days of reconstruction would have been difficult, with white men like Winthrop resentful of her new freedom and continuously attempting to deny it of her.

Maybe, during the war, she escaped and became a Union nurse, wrapping soldiers' wounds, feeding them their medicine, helping with bloody amputations, comforting them. Maybe Minerva and Juba slipped away during the war, south to Hilton Head, to which many runaways fled, or to St. Helena Island, where the Gullah Geechee community continues to farm land they've lived on since their ancestors were brought from Sierra Leone. Just as African Americans were the abolitionists who propelled the country to emancipation, so they were the people rebuilding their own lives after the war. The Penn School, on St. Helena Island, was founded in 1862 and served to educate formerly enslaved people after emancipation. Today, the Penn Center serves as an education and history center on an island still protected from, but threatened, by development.

At a farm on St. Helena, a woman named Sara Green and her husband, Bill, teach young people to farm sustainably, hoping the love for this land, the desire to stay and to farm as they and generations before them have done, will resonate with these children and teens so that they can protect this place from the developments encroaching all around. If you've been to Hilton Head Island, you've seen the results of this development. It's a place full of hotels, along practically every inch of expensive shoreline. It, too, was part of the Sea Islands where Gullah Geechee people lived and fished and made their livelihoods in the years following the Civil War. In contrast, there's St. Helena Island, quiet, green, with a national park that protects long stretches of the shoreline, and small farm stands and restaurants on the way on and off the island. The residents of the island have worked hard to protect this place. In the 1860s, the Sea Islands were isolated, the communities insular. Charlotte Forten, a wealthy black woman from Philadelphia, was one of the abolitionists and writers (she was a poet) who worked for emancipation and the education of freedmen during and after the war. She wrote about her trip to St. Helena, to teach freed people of color:

> *. . . Some of the officers we met did not impress us favorably. They talked flippantly, and sneeringly of the negroes, whom they found we had come down to teach, using an epithet more offensive than gentlemanly. They assured us that there was great danger of Rebel attacks, that the yellow fever prevailed to an alarming extent, and that, indeed, the manufacture of coffins was the only business that was at all flourishing at present. Although by no means daunted by these alarming stories, we were glad when the announcement of our boat relieved us from their edifying conversation. We rowed across to Ladies Island, which adjoins St. Helena, through the splendors of a grand Southern sunset. The gorgeous clouds of crimson and gold were*

reflected as in a mirror in the smooth, clear waters below. As we glided along, the rich tones of the negro boat-men broke upon the evening stillness,—sweet, strange, and solemn—"Jesus make de blind to see, Jesus make de cripple walk, Jesus make de deaf to hear. Walk in, kind Jesus! No man can hender me.

Forten spent two years on St. Helena Island before she had to return to Philadelphia due to illness. She'd later marry Sarah and Angelina Grimké's nephew, Francis James Grimké, a white man; this turn of events would have been unimaginable to the southern slaveholding Grimkés, whose lifestyle Winthrop hoped to emulate.

As she walked down the sidewalk in 1870, Juba would not have to step aside for the white people she passed. She'd have set her own hours and days of work, or determined whose washing or cooking she would do. As Thavolia Glymph writes, "From 1866 through the 1880s, tasked work remained a visible hallmark of the strategies black women employed to institute free labor relations in domestic employment . . . Taking on jobs by the task and working part-time as day or casual labor allowed household servants precious time for their own domestic production and moved white women employers toward a new order in labor relations in the domestic sphere." While Juba, a skilled cook, might have taken full-time employment in a single household, she may have chosen, instead, to do some cooking, some cleaning, and some washing for people. Or, maybe she made her living by making baskets or selling other goods or food at the market. No matter what, her life was markedly better. She was free. And, the women in whose house she'd been enslaved—Winthrop's wife Cassie, for example—had to learn to care for their own homes and children. "For a time," Glymph writes, "the pedestal of white womanhood was cracked. Former mistresses worked, and black women suffered far less violence than previously."

Juba would have walked to the photographer's temporary or permanent studio, paid her fee, and decided which backdrop and objects she'd include in her portrait. Would she sit holding a fan, like Mary Brice or Bryce, pictured in a previous chapter? Would she hold a skein of yarn, like Sojourner Truth? A basket, like the woman pictured here? Maybe she was literate and wanted to proclaim her hard-earned skills by holding a book. Maybe she held something having to do with her skill as a cook, like contemporaneous occupational portraits of men holding the tools of their trades—a blacksmith holds a horseshoe, a chimney sweep holds what looks like a broom, a shoemaker holds a wooden shoe form. Maybe Juba walked to the studio wearing a beautifully embroidered apron, like the one Harriet Powers made for herself with starbursts. Maybe she carried with her the large copper pot in which she made her favorite dishes for her family and friends—sauces for brisket, grits, sweet potatoes boiled for pie.

Her work as a cook meant that she shaped people's lives. As Rebecca Sharpless writes, we remember the food we knew as children, those meals that comforted us when we were sad or struggling, the favorite foods we ate when we were young and now request for celebrations. We go back to what we always knew. We make for friends and family those dishes with which we grew up. "What humans eat at home," Sharpless writes, "and what they offer guests are general markers for their society. As cooks, African American women profoundly shaped the foodways of the South and, hence, its overall culture." Juba held this power. She was probably taught to cook by her mother, Judith, and in turn, continued to help shape what has become known as American food. She'd also have to have fought against the racist cultural inscriptions of black women cooks (the "mammy") that whites must have continuously tried to superimpose upon her—which are, Sharpless writes, continuously reified today with images like Aunt Jemima, "representing a reassuring tie with the Old South in which cooks worked happily for whatever came their way."

If Samon was able to live to adulthood, I imagine that when he thought of his mother, he must have thought of his days beside her in the kitchen, the smells of her cooking, the sight of her hands expertly chopping vegetables at the countertop, or sitting in the yard as she bent off the ends of beans with that sweep *snap*, or plucking a chicken or braising a ham. If she was able to claim literacy, maybe she risked her life and her son's by teaching him to read as Susan or her other mistresses napped in the afternoon or went out calling; maybe she held a book up for Samon and traced with her hand each letter on the page, while the smells of the stew she'd made for dinner that night rose up behind them on the stove. Maybe she was caught trying to teach her son to read, or to learn herself, and was severely punished at the work house or by her mistress or master—this could have been Susan or Hasell—a punishment she barely survived. In 1870, she'd have moved through this new world, free, able to determine how much she was paid for her work, and if her employers treated her poorly and she was unhappy with her circumstances, she could demand higher pay, refuse to do certain tasks, and, if she wasn't given what she required, she could leave.

Maybe Samon lived near or with her in Charleston, and they continued to share meals. Maybe Samon was married and he and his wife were able to offer meals to his mother, easing her work after long days piecing together her living. Maybe he took care of her in her old age, and she was able to stay home and do easier tasks as her body allowed.

In 1865, Hilton and Winthrop and their families moved back to Charleston, where Winthrop resumed his cotton trade and watched the city rebuild. He wrote, in October 1865:

> . . . *I find Charleston gradually improving and as it were rising from the ashes, stores are being put in order, repairs going forward in all directions, King St. is thronged morning noon and night but the negro race predominates, very few ladies (white) to be seen at any time. Negro soldiers throng the side walks and crowd along regardless who they jostle. Grace Church has been the only one of the Episcopal order open until last Sunday when Rev. Mr. Porter opened the Church of the Holy Communion. I attended and found all there to be the old citizens and their families, not a blue-coated Yankee to be seen, it seemed like old times. The Holy Communion was duly administered and received by all present in the most solemn manner, as became the occasion viz the reopening of this church permanently since the close of the late Civil War. . . .*

Winthrop continues using his connections in the North to make a profit, asking his brother, Hilton, who's visiting Providence and hoping to resettle there, about the price of soap. He says they live on "fish and schrimps [sic], which are now very abundant and cheap." The Crouch-Williams family continued to cope with their material losses and resist the upward mobility of "freedmen." Both men say they wished they could return north after the war, but that their business connections are all in the South; Hilton returns home for a spell, but Winthrop soon writes to say he'd better come back for a job prospect.

Winthrop's letters in the days after the war are a sharp reminder of the challenges of Reconstruction, the proliferation of lynch clubs; and a portent of the Jim Crow laws that would come. In November 1865, he wrote in response to the newspaper that Mr. Cross, Susan's friend, had sent:

> *. . . by which I notice many strange and peculiar, the most marked is the general tone of the reading, all showing strong radical anti-slavery feeling antagonistic to the south even to the perversion of truth and common sense: such a condition of public feeling prevails [in the] north resulting from the overthrow of the south in the recent contest and being so strong and we so weak can only be changed by time. The south is down trampled underfoot, we cannot raise hand or foot but by permission of our masters of the north. I see no chance at all for the south and regret the day I ever came here to reside.*

He'd continue with his cotton business, but struggled to make the same level of wealth he'd had before the war. In the days after, in 1865, he was sad to find himself celebrating a gain of ten dollars, as he'd lost more than $60,000 in cotton alone (not including his investments and properties), in the war. He says he has:

> *money due . . . from the Planters but never expect to collect much of it for they are all ruined in the emancipation of the negroes . . . The whole south will become of no value to the Federal Government. There can never be another large cotton crop made and each successive year there will be less and less made until finally there will be only small*

farms where formerly there were large Plantations and this state of things will be brought about by the mistaken philanthropy in the north toward the negro.

I think of James Baldwin's writing, the recent film made from his essays, *I Am Not Your Negro*, explaining that the creation of "the negro" is a fiction generated by whites to oppress people of color. *Why do you need this fiction?* he asks the white viewer. *What in you requires someone to be beneath you?*

In 1868, Winthrop wrote that with the upcoming election, he feared the "companies of negroes" who have "been drilling and outnumber us largely." He said he was "heartily sick and tired of this disturbed state of affairs," meaning, the struggle for African Americans to gain their rights and freedom.

He'd written in 1865 that "we are bound to have trouble in the South soon and it will be long years' trial to get rid of the negroes. I consider the question settled as to their fate, it can be none other than that of the Indian extermination and much more rapid than that of the Indian so far as this city is concerned. We may be safe from any rising here but the seaboard plantations will suffer."

Winthrop continues nonchalantly, to say he needs to write to their sister Abby, that he's delighted to have run into the author William Gilmore Simms (who would write the pro-slavery book in response to *Uncle Tom's Cabin*). How did Winthrop become this person? He came from Rhode Island, where Narragansett and Wampanoag people had been murdered and enslaved, sent to Europe or the West Indies to be sold; the European settlers attempted to "exterminate" Native Americans from their land in order to make way for farmers, who would come to make the cheese that was sent to those plantations to feed the enslaved people who grew the sugarcane that was turned into molasses that was shipped back to Rhode Island to make the rum that was shipped to the west coast of Africa to trade for people.

One long, breathless, exhausting, infuriating cycle that did not, of course, "exterminate" anyone. People from the Narragansett, Wampanoag and Massachuset nations continue to thrive in the northeast.

In the footnote of the 1865 letter from Winthrop, Franklin, transcriptionist, archivist, preservationist, writes, "Fortunately, I suppose, the dire prediction of extermination was not fulfilled." This was in 1952, almost one hundred years later, and on the cusp of the civil rights movement. Like Winthrop, Franklin couldn't have foreseen the radical changes that the 1960s and subsequent decades would bring. He was a vocational-technical high-school teacher but had money to invest, as evidenced by the many papers on investments that were cut up into templates in the back of the quilt from the 1930s.

Franklin would die in 1953, a year after transcribing these letters. He'd never live to see those social changes.

His phrase, "I suppose," stays with me. His reluctance. His ambivalence. Another ominous echo through time.

I imagine that Minerva, Jane Jones, and Juba Simons watched the Industrial Revolution and cotton boom with frustration if they were still in Charleston, wishing for the end of slavery, planning rebellions and subversions, attending church services and meetings, and raising their children. Perhaps one of Eliza's daughters was named Eliza as well, and was part of the same family that appears in the 1900 census of Hasell W. Crouch, son of Charles (nephew of our "original" Hasell, the doctor):

> Eliza E Jenkins [Eliza E Crouch], b. December 1856 in South Carolina, widowed, black, servant, 4 children born, 2 alive, parents born in Georgia

In 1838, after Susan returned home to Providence, her brother Winthrop said that he kept Eliza "for the man that lets her." The man who rented her. Perhaps that man didn't buy her but his cousin, Hasell W., did, and after emancipation, her daughter stayed on as the Crouches' servant. Maybe. It is remotely possible.

If the preacher Winthrop mentions in 1866, living in the yard with his wife, took a new name upon emancipation, he may have been Esop Smith, the first preacher of the Bethel African Methodist Episcopal Church in Columbia, which continues to hold worship services today. The church was founded in a sword factory in 1866, but Winthrop reported that the preacher was working in a church on the college campus. It's possible that the community first met at the college chapel and then, when Reconstruction began and the city was being rebuilt, they were pushed out of the chapel and sent to the sword factory. If he was, indeed, the same man, Sam, whom Winthrop owned in the 1850s, then he went on to thrive as a preacher. He set up churches throughout the South with his wife, and owned land in Georgia. This work of founding black churches was, like the founding of schools for free people of color, Richard E. Powers writes, crucial to black communities. Esop never learned to read, but he was a talented and impassioned speaker who was capable of winning over a congregation with his words. I imagine him on land of his own, his wife working with the women in the church to help the impoverished people around them develop new skills, find work, send their children to schools and educate themselves. They'd have helped to set up schools, to build houses and places for worship. I imagine what it must have felt like to board a train heading to a new town, side by side, helping to rebuild a country through which they could finally travel freely, even as they were still under constant threat from angry whites.

STATE OF GEORGIA, No. 226

COUNTY OF Thomas } PERSONALLY APPEARED before me this 13 day of Aug 1867, E. Smith who states that he resides in the 156 Election Precinct of Thomas COUNTY, GEORGIA, and who makes oath as follows:

"I E. Smith do solemnly swear in the presence of Almighty God, that I am a citizen of the STATE OF GEORGIA; that I have resided in said State for 12 months next preceding this day, and now reside in the County of Thomas in said State; that I am 21 years old; that I have not been disfranchised for participation in any rebellion or civil war against the United States, nor for felony committed against the laws of any State or the United States; that I have never been a member of any State Legislature, nor held any executive or judicial office in any State, and afterwards engaged in insurrection or rebellion against the United States, or given aid or comfort to the enemies thereof; that I have never taken an oath as a member of Congress of the United States, or as an officer of the United States, or as a member of any State Legislature, or as an executive or judicial officer of any State, to support the Constitution of the United States and afterwards engaged in insurrection or rebellion against the United States, or given aid and comfort to the enemies thereof; that I will faithfully support the Constitution and obey the laws of the United States, and will to the best of my ability, encourage others so to do. So help me, God."

The said E. Smith further swears that he has not been previously registered under the provisions of "An act supplementary to 'an act to provide for the more efficient government of the rebel States'—passed March 2, 1867—and to facilitate restoration," under this or any other name, in this or any other Election District; and further, that he was born in ______ and naturalized by ______ on the ______ day of ______, 18___ in the ______

Esop his X mark Smith

SWORN TO AND SUBSCRIBED before me 13 Aug 1867

O. T. Tyson

Register of the 17 *Registration District.*

Esop Smith's mark to denote his signature in the voting register.

I stopped on a street corner in Charleston known as the Four Corners of Law, for on each corner stands the post office, courthouse, city hall, and St. Michael's Episcopal Church, which Winthrop wrote was being rehabilitated with new glass after the war, in 1866. Here, today, a woman sat with her sweetgrass baskets displayed, working on one as she waited for passing tourists to buy. These baskets have long been made by women from the Gullah Geechee community, who, like the Gee's Bend quilters, learned the art from their parents and grandparents, an art passed down through the generations. Weaving takes hours and days. But when a woman in a documentary was asked how long a basket took to make, she said she didn't time it and didn't care to know; a basket simply takes as long as it takes, she said.

Some of the baskets I saw in Charleston had a single arched handle that twirled from one side to the other, and others were wide and flat with symmetrical handles on either side. The strands of grass—bulrush, in earlier times—were bound by wider palmetto fronds to form a thick sort of rope that wound around and around, like the coils that form a clay pot, to make the circular basket. A weaver slides a bone or spoon end into the rows of grass; looping the frond over to bind each cluster of grasses as she winds them. The variation in colors comes from stripes of pine grass. Museums now collect these baskets; like quilts exhibited in the 1970s, and the Gee's Bend quilts, this craft, too, is seen as an art.

I asked a woman where she got her grasses, imagining she'd say she gathered them. I thought I was asking her a question about the region—where the grasses grew—but she said that she bought them. In the past, people gathered the grasses from the marshes and wetlands along the shore, but now the sweetgrass is threatened by development; the areas where the grasses grew are impinged upon by great hotels and expanding roads.

I remember seeing Mary Jackson talk about her sweetgrass baskets years ago in an episode of *Craft in America*. This was two years before I'd begun studying the quilt, and long before I'd return to Charleston. I remember how Jackson talked about her baskets as pieces of art that were born out of necessity. She needed to leave her job to stay home with her young son, and was searching for a way to bring in some money, when she remembered the craft she'd been taught as a child by her mother. She sold her first baskets that year, and went on to become an acclaimed artist whose work is collected and commissioned. I remember her small granddaughter looking on and making a basket of her own.

Mary Jackson with one of her baskets.

In the episode, "Memory," she talks about how the baskets were used by enslaved people to winnow rice, in a process similar to that developed by Native Americans and Asians, she says, and makes the gesture, while holding the basket, of tossing the rice into the air to separate it from its husk, as if flipping an egg one-handed in a pan. The wind does the work of separation.

We call these fanners, she says.

Her feat was to make the basket, like the one she's holding above, from the design of the old fanner basket, but to add a top. It was difficult to fit her hand between the bottom and top, she says, but after some trial and error, it worked.

"It's called sewing," she tells the audience. "Binding the basket together is sewing."

The skill of basket making was brought from Sierra Leone and Senegal, by people who were kidnapped and carried across the Middle

Passage, carrying with them the muscle memory in their hands, the artistry in their minds and souls. Jackson says that the skill of basket making made her ancestors more valuable as enslaved people, and therefore helped to keep the family together—they worked together to make the baskets, so were kept together by slave owners. I wonder if this is a skill Eliza, Minerva, Jane, and Juba knew. I wonder if they spent evenings teaching their daughters—Cecilia, when she was older, learning from Minerva—how to sew a basket. I wonder if the boys were sent out with their fathers or uncles or older friends to gather up the sweetgrass and the bulrush and make the baskets used in the fields during harvest, to hold vegetables, fruit, cotton, and rice. That Carolina Gold rice.

Mary Jackson, holding a nineteenth-century basket, demonstrates how her ancestors would have held the basket on their heads as they carried produce to market, and I imagine Eliza and Minerva walking side by side with those flat-bottomed baskets balanced on their heads, their children swaddled against their backs or running beside them, the women chatting and laughing about something that happened in the kitchen that morning, or about the strangeness of the circus animals they'd seen the week before.

The giraffe! they might have declared. The oddest creature!

Their children might have asked when they could see the lions again, and roar at each other with raised hands like claws.

If they were from Charleston or the surrounding Lowcountry, they'd have spoken in the Gullah Geechee language, with its quick turns and the uplift and downfall of sound. When English becomes Geechee, it's almost indecipherable to my ears. This must have come in handy, to have a language that retained words from West African languages, that was difficult for people outside the community to understand. If one needed to tell a secret, if one needed to convey news of a relative who had been sold away, if one wanted to make fun of one's owner, maybe language made some degree of liberty—and resistance—possible.

> "Thus, these seemingly isolated episodes reaching back to the nineteenth century and carrying forward to the twenty-first, once fitted together like pieces in a mosaic, reveal a portrait of a nation: one that is the unspoken truth of our racial divide."
>
> —Carol Anderson, *White Rage*

One May morning in 2015, in Portsmouth, New Hampshire, it was sunny and cold, the taste of spring still new. A horse-drawn carriage sat at the top of a hill near the center of town, amidst colonial homes. In the wagon, handmade casks held the remains of thirteen people who were brought to the state in the 1600s, enslaved. There was a chief present from Nigeria, the native land of the enslaved people. He'd been invited there to perform a ceremony to rebury the bodies. They'd been exhumed twelve years earlier, in 2003, when they were discovered during construction in what had been an African burial ground. Instead of continuing with construction and destroying the burial ground as has been done in many other places, the team stopped to alert authorities. The bones were exhumed, studied, and identified. And so the citizens of Portsmouth, in New Hampshire, a small state whose motto is "Live free or die," a state composed of liberals and conservatives, the working class, middle-class city people, academics, and wealthy vacationers, chose to halt construction of the road and to build a memorial to the enslaved people there. They changed the plans they had for the city, dedicated those grounds for the memorial, and began a project that took more than ten years and changed the course of the place. On the morning I visited, hundreds of people gathered in the memorial square to witness the burial. A group of drummers played while men wearing black carried the caskets from a horse-drawn carriage, through the crowd, down to the memorial where the new grave awaited. The pine casks were made by a woodworker, fashioned to fit together in the shape of a heart in the new tomb. Hearing the drums, watching the pallbearers, the crowd was silent.

That sunny day, the chief stood before the crowd. “I will start with Igbo, because that is my mother tongue, which the departed would understand,” said the chief. He wore a long white robe and a red cap, and he blew through an elephant tusk.

“Is that okay, if I speak in Igbo?” he asked the crowd.

The crowd called back, “Yes.”

“I will speak in Igbo, and then I will translate. We are standing on a burial ground,” he said. “They were forgotten, as we say in Africa, ‘It is an abomination.’”

The crowd was hushed and listening. The morning air was cold, and a wind blew across our heads.

“People waited underground for hundreds of years for the action committee to take action—waited for the backhoe to come and dig them up—‘We have been stilled for a long time, and now thank you for finding us.’ We are not here to mourn them because they are mourned and grieved by those who knew them. We're not here to honor them as individuals but as our ancestors. In this tomb and grave, you will find peace, always. We will grant them a quiet resting place—that's why this road has been blocked off. When you want to be still and remember, you come here.

He asked the crowd to repeat after him, in Igbo. We did.

“These are elders and young people underground. We have some sense of their suffering from the research. We commit their graves to the ground. A grave is a ‘cave of honor.’ May God grant you everlasting peace.”

The grave where the caskets were set, before they were covered. Behind them stand figures engraved with phrases written by the memorial artist, Jerome Meadows, including, "I stand for the Ancestors Here and Beyond," "I stand for those who feel anger," and "I stand for those who were taken from their loved ones," "I stand for those who find dignity in these bones."

He blew again through the elephant tusk. He sprinkled soil that came from Nigeria and Zimbabwe and Portsmouth, the lands of the people whose bodies were buried there. He sprinkled it onto the caskets. As the crowd walked away, we walked over the engravings of petitions made by enslaved people for their freedom, as Mum Bett, or Elizabeth Freeman, petitioned for—and won—her freedom in Massachusetts in 1781. I think of Harriet Wilson's words that "slavery's shadow falls even there," in the north.

FLORA STEWART, LONDONDERRY, N. H.
Aged 117 years. Taken Nov. 5, 1867.

I think of Flora Stewart, born in 1750 in Virginia or New Hampshire, enslaved, who lived to be 118 years old. Her picture was published in the paper a year before she died. She wore fine clothes with ruffled embellishments, black gloves, a white ruffled collar, her hand on a cane. She lived through the American Revolution, the Mexican-American War, all of the so-called "Indian" wars, in which Native nations fought for their lands, and the Civil War. She died in 1868, six years before Juba Simons died in South Carolina, where we leave this story.

As we grapple with how we'll treat one another in a system built on genocide, the theft of lands, and enslavement, we're confronted by more hate, we're butting up against one another, never having had this conversation fully, never having had the sort of reconciliation that South Africa and Germany had to address their histories. Beverly Morgan-Welch said at the occasion of the burial in Portsmouth, "As we celebrate the country's liberty and freedom and justice in documents that are beautiful to understand and live out, we have to understand that that freedom has not been afforded to everyone. We must understand this history or we continue to be confounded by how we live together."

A section of the "mosaic" quilt top with papers from the 19th and 20th centuries.

How will we, as a nation, begin, walk through, this conversation?

This past continues to reemerge fully into the present. Those phrases I heard back in college—"Go home, Yankee!" "The South will rise again!" "The flag is my heritage, not hate."—are regularly in the news, as we begin to talk more openly about our collective history and to see that history emerge in pop culture. More Hollywood movies are being made about enslaved people and enslavement. Tammy Denease says this is a good thing but that she wants to see more varied representations of people of color, to see *many* black actors in Hollywood films and TV rather than just a few.

I reexamine my teaching, every semester, asking myself which stories I'm teaching in my classes, and which I'm omitting. Which stories do I seek, and what do I have yet to learn?

Pursuing the story of the quilt tops, interrogating this abrasion, has changed my life. I no longer see this country, these fabrics, the stories of the world around me, in the same way. I dive back into all the gaps in my knowledge of history, eager to listen, read, and learn more. I push myself to attend more events on campus and in my travels, to learn the histories of the places I visit as well as the nation I inhabit—and to keep learning it, knowing that history will never be static.

After learning about the Bangladesh collapse, and of Gap and H&M's horrific working conditions in Cambodian textile factories, I learn that Nestlé confessed to using enslaved people to fish in Thailand and tried to deny responsibility for using enslaved children to harvest cocoa on the Ivory Coast. I learn that the people who pick Florida tomatoes are, for all intents and purposes, indentured servants. I find that the region a few hours south of my new home in Michigan is the center of the US sex slave trade, and that, along the east coast, the sex slave trade now follows the same routes as the 19th century slave trade did, from Savannah to Charleston, up to Baltimore, then to Bristol, Salem. During a road trip one summer, when I stop at a rest area along Route 95, I close the bathroom stall door to find a sign that asks if I am being held against my will, tells me that if I am, I should call this number.

For me, learning this story will never be over.

When I get inoculations before traveling, which seem to most Americans like easy preventatives, I think of those epidemics of smallpox, the Williamses' fear of yellow fever, and outbreaks of cholera. I hear on the news that there's a new cholera epidemic in Yemen. I know that when I'm in Bali, a low-risk region for malaria, I can to protect myself with bug spray, and in higher risk countries, I can take pills to prevent infection. These pills offer me far better odds than people would have had in the nineteenth century, than many people still have today in countries around the world. In 2015, the CDC reports, 212 million people were reported to be infected with malaria, and 429,000 of those people died from the disease, most of them children.

Instead of buying more new fabric, I look for used fabric and unfinished projects. I recently bought a hexie quilt made from 1930s fabric and thought of Franklin, finishing his ancestors' quilt tops one hundred years after they'd been started. Now, I piece together a backing for the 1930s top, add new cotton batting, and machine-quilt through its layers, completing what someone else left behind. There are thousands of such unfinished projects leftover from sewers who ran out of time, leaving behind clues to their eras, cultures, and tastes.

I still feel the 1830s mosaic quilt and its papers in my hands, still hear the sound of the needle pulling through fabric—maybe Susan's, maybe Jane's. I see Jane's hands in the light of fires in the hearth and candles on the tables, the glow on her face as she thinks about, let's say, her brother who lives three doors down and shared fresh peaches with her this afternoon. How sweet they were, she thinks, as she directs the needle through the cotton and then back up again, drawing the thread through with that soothing *ssshhhh* sound. I think of the love between Boston and his wife Mary. The baptism of Francis, son of Isaac and Louisa.

I think of Juba Simons, and imagine her walking through 1870s Charleston, stopping at a bakery her friend owns at the start of her day, moving through the pre-dawn hours to get to work. She'd have seen the light come up over the bay, glistening at the horizon and then blossoming into pinks and blues as it spread across the sky. She'd have saved every penny she could to help her children make new and better lives. She'd have known how hard she fought to live to see this day. She'd have walked down streets she'd known for decades, have witnessed their destruction and slow rebuilding after the war, have helped her community by supporting her church and schools, have seen friends beaten and murdered at whites' hands, have seen friends emancipate themselves by fleeing or buying their freedom, have masterfully navigated an oppressive and ever-threatening system to make it to this day, and likely continued to work hard to support herself and her family.

I see the photographer setting up his camera as he asks Juba Simons to settle into her seat and find stillness. I see her fold her hands in her lap, sit up as straight as she can, raise her chin, stare into the lens, and wait those few seconds the wet plate needed to record her image. I see her in that pause, the suspended quiet before her life goes on, and wonder what she thinks about in those seconds.

I struggle to let go of these people from the past, to stop pushing to find more clues to their stories. I have found all that I can, for now.

In 1838, Minerva is still alive, and she holds her baby boy, Samon, in her arms. Imagine that we see Minerva and Samon in a church in Charleston on his baptism day, with little Cecilia beside them, and Juba and her children and Eliza and Jane in attendance, too. There, let's imagine, is the baby's father, Minerva's husband. It's a day for celebration. This is a day of hope, even though she knows she is soon to face her sale at Susan's and Winthrop's hands. For today, there is only Samon. Do you see the baby in the church, surrounded by people who love him? Think of all the hope they feel that day, watching the water run across their child's forehead. Here is Samon's baptism and Bishroom's marriage at a time when it is illegal for enslaved people to be married or to have a child baptized. Do you hear the voices singing behind Minerva, as she holds Samon in her arms and Cecilia leans into her legs? The whole congregation celebrates this day—mother and child survived the labor and birth, sweet Samon is healthy—and then, as the water falls across his head, he wails. What joy or relief or fear did his parents feel that day? They would know, with the baptism, that no matter what happens to him, he'll find heaven.

Here is the quietest moment, between Minerva and Samon. The world around them stops as she looks at her child. She is telling him, now, how much she loves him. She is urging him to know this, to remember her touch. And she tries to seal into her memory the soft nestle of his skin against her face as she bounces and shushes him back to sleep on her shoulder, soothing, the pastor and the people around her singing in words that become a blur; she closes her eyes and prays for her child.

Sources

The following sources directly and indirectly influenced the development of various aspects of this book. Sources are also listed by chapter, to more specifically cite information included in each.

Collections

The Cushman Collection & Accession Records, Historic Textile and Costume Collection, The University of Rhode Island, Kingston, RI.
Elijah Williams Papers, Rhode Island Historical Society, Providence, RI
MSS 9001-C Box 15, Crouch/Cushman, Rhode Island Historical Society, Providence, RI
Women's Diaries in the Manuscript Collection of the Rhode Island Historical Society, Providence, RI.
Papers of the American Slave Trade, Rhode Island Historical Society.
South County History Center (formerly Pettaquamscutt Historical Society), Kingston, RI.
South Carolina Historical Society, Charleston, SC.
South Carolina History Room, Charleston County Public Library, Charleston, SC.
South Carolina Department of Archives and History, Columbia, SC.
The Avery Research Center, College of Charleston, Charleston, SC.
The Smithsonian Anacostia Community Museum, "How the Civil War Changed Washington" exhibit, Feb. 2, 2015–Nov. 15, 2015.
New Bedford Whaling Museum, New Bedford, MA.
The Charleston Museum, Charleston, SC.
The Gibbes Museum of Art, Charleston, SC.
The Metropolitan Museum of Art, New York, NY.
The Museum of Fine Art, Boston, MA.

Historic Sites

American Textile History Museum, Lowell, MA (now permanently closed).
The Robbins House & The Old North Bridge, Concord, MA.
Walden Pond State Reservation, Concord, MA.
Royall House and Slave Quarters, Medford, MA.
Abiel Smith School & African Meeting House, Museum of African American History, Boston, MA.

The Nathan and Mary (Polly) Johnson House, New Bedford, MA.

The African Burying Ground Memorial Park, Portsmouth, NH. Slater Mill Museum, Providence, RI.

Tavern Hall / Elisha Reynold's House, Great Swamp, and Potter family burial plot, Kingston, RI.

God's Little Acre, Common Burying Ground and Island Cemetery, Newport, RI.

DeWolf Mansion, Bristol, RI.

Historic Indian Agency House at Fort Winnebago, WI.

Clermont Farm, Berryville, VA.

The Old Exchange & Provost Dungeon, Charleston, SC.

Fort Moultrie, Sullivan's Island, Charleston, SC.

Middleton Place, Charleston, SC.

Magnolia Plantation and Gardens, Charleston, SC.

Aiken-Rhett House, Charleston, SC.

Nathaniel Russell Middleton House, Charleston, SC.

Old Slave Mart Museum, Charleston, SC.

Saint Helena Island, Beaufort County, SC.

Manaca Iznaga & San Isidro de Los Destiladeros, Valle de los Ingenios, Cuba.

Primary Sources on the Crouch-Williams-Cushman families and enslaved people, in addition to the collections listed above

Admission to Zion: Zion (later Westminster) Presbyterian Church (Charleston, South Carolina, United States), Communicants' Roll Book, 1852-1861, p. 57-58, Jane Thorn, servant of Mrs. E. H. Williams, admitted on profession of faith, 6 March 1859; Historical Foundation of the Presbyterian and Reformed Churches microfilm MFPOS 1552, item 2, Presbyterian Historical Society, Philadelphia.

Admission as member of Rev. Jonathan C. Gibbes Organization: Zion (later Westminster) Presbyterian Church (Charleston, South Carolina, United States), Sessional records 23 April 1858-1 April 1866, p. 59-60, Members of Rev. Jonathan C. Gibbes Organization received as members, list includes Jane Jones (formerly Thorn); Historical Foundation of the Presbyterian and Reformed Churches microfilm MFPOS 1552, item 1, Presbyterian Historical Society, Philadelphia.

"At Private Sale," *Charleston Courier*, May 8, 1837, p. 3, col. 4; digital images, *GenealogyBank* (http://www.genealogybank.com : accessed May 22, 2017).

Birch, Charlotte Amelia to E. Hilton Williams, Trustee of Rosamond J. Walker and Children, Bill of Sale for a slave named Beckey or Rebecca, 12/13/1864, Series S213050, vol. 006F: 00040.

Chandler, George. *The Chandler Family: The Descendants of William and Annis Chandler Who Settled in Roxbury, Mass.* (Worcester, Ma: Press of Charles Hamilton, 1883).

Charleston County, South Carolina Directories, 1806, 1807, 1809, 1813, Abraham Crouch; Hasell W Crouch 1836 Supplement; Charles Crouch 1835–36, 1837, 1838 Directories, South Carolina Historical Society, Charleston, SC.

Charleston, South Carolina, death certificate no. 139 (1874), Juba Simons; digital image, "South Carolina, Death Records, 1821–1965," Ancestry.com (http://www.ancestry.com : accessed June 6, 2017).

Charleston, South Carolina, Probate Books, Returns, Vol. A, p. 14, Bundle 64, no. 2403, Dr. Hasell W. Crouch estate; digital images, *FamilySearch* (http://www.familysearch.org : accessed June 3, 2017).

Charleston County, South Carolina, Deed Book A10, pp. 64–67, William T. Thorne and wife to Martin E. Munro trustee, settlement deed, May 24, 1830.

Charleston County, SC Registry of Mesnes and Conveyances, Deed Book A12, pp. 177–178, John B. Irving, Esq. Sheriff to Jas. W. Gray, trustee for Eliza J. Crouch and children, conveyance.

Charleston, South Carolina, Deed Records, E14: 107–109, John Francis Walker and Rosamond Imogene Thorne to E. Hilton Williams, marriage settlement, Nov. 7, 1857; Charleston County Register of Mesnes Conveyances, Charleston.

Cohen, Hennig. "Preface" and "Historical and Descriptive Sketch," *The South Carolina Gazette*, University of South Carolina Press (1953): vii–9.

Crouch, Abraham, 1820, 1821, 1825 Federal Census, Charleston, SC, Ancestry.com.

Crouch, Charles, Nov. 29, 1880, *South Carolina, Death Records, 1821–1955,* Ancestry.com.

Crouch, Charles W., United States Federal Census, Charleston, SC, Roll M653_1216, Ancestry.com.

Crouch, Charles W. to William Rice, Bill of Sale for Mustee Slave Named Jane and her Son William, Purchased from John A. Fripp, 4/5/1834, Series S213003, Vol. 0050: 00438, South Carolina Department of Archives and History, Columbia, SC.

Crouch, C.W. to Thomas N. Gadsden, Bill of Sale for a Slave Named Phelix or Felix, 1/10/1837, Series S213003, Vol. 005T:00066, South Carolina Department of Archives and History, Columbia, SC.

Crouch, Charles W. to Court of Appeals, Petition to Practice Law, 2/24/1835, S137004, Box 0001, Item 00133, South Carolina Department of Archives and History, Columbia, SC.

Crouch, Emily H., Rhode Island Deaths, 1630–1930, February 23, 1926, Ancestry.com.

Crouch, Hasell C., South Carolina Death Records, 1821–1955, May 22, 1836, Charleston, SC Ancestry.com.

Crouch, Hasell W., Estate, Account of Sales "South Carolina Estate Inventories and Bills of Sale, 1732–1872," database and images, *Fold3* (http://www.fold3.com : accessed May 22, 2017) Sale account for Dr. H. W. Crouch; citing Charleston District, South Carolina, Inventories of Estates Book A 1839–1844, pp. 58.

Crouch, Susan McPherson, Rhode Island Deaths 1630–1930, 1 December 1902, Ancestry.com.

Cushman-Crouch files, MSS 9001-C, Box 15, Rhode Island Historical Society, Providence, RI. November 17, 2014.

Cushman Franklin R. Textile: Furniture Cloth Checks, Accession No. 19520278, Colonial Williamsburg, Williamsburg, VA.

Ibid, Bed Valance, blue and white, G52-13

Ibid, Fabric–Copper plate printed (blue and white), 1951-364, 1–2

Ibid, Quilt, woodblock print, 1951-01-01

"Commencement [Brown University]," *Rhode Island American*, September 3, 1830, p. 2, co. 1: digital images, *GenealogyBank* (http://www.genealogybank.com; accessed May 22, 2017).

Direct Deeds, 1898–1930, Direct Index to Conveyances and Miscellaneous Deeds, Charleston, SC.

Distillery Excise Tax Records, United States Treasury Department, Tax Accounts 1791–1802, MSS 232, sg3, Rhode Island Historical Society, Providence, RI.

Elijah Williams Papers, Rhode Island Historical Society, Providence, RI.

"Estate Sale," *Charleston Courier*, May 22, 1837, p. 3, col. 6; digital images, *GenealogyBank* (http://www.genealogybank.com : accessed May 22, 2017).

"Estate Sale," *Charleston Courier*, January 29, 1838, p. 3, col. 6; digital images, *GenealogyBank* (http://www.genealogybank.com : accessed May 22, 2017).

"Estate Sale," *Charleston Courier*, May 15, 1850, p. 3, col. 7; digital images, *GenealogyBank* (http://www.genealogybank.com : accessed May 22, 2017).

"Estate Sale of Furniture," *Charleston Courier*, May 2, 1837, p. 3, col. 6, digital images, *Genealogy Bank* (http://www.genealogybank.com: accessed May 22, 2017).

Grace Episcopal Church (Charleston, SC), Register 1847–1898, Deaths, April 10, 1862, Mrs. Harriet Williams' South Carolina Historical Society, Charleston, microfilm SCHS 50-336-1.

Grimke, John Paul VS Charles Crouch, Judgment Roll, 1768, Series S136002, Box 076B, Item 0080A, South Carolina Historical Society, Charleston, SC.

Harth, William to EH. Williams, Bill of slave for a slave named Boston, 2/17/1835, Series S213003, Vol. 0050: 00648, South Carolina Department of Archives and History, Columbia, SC.

"[In a notice . . .]," *Charleston City Gazette and Commercial Daily Advertiser*, September 13, 1830, p. 2, col. 2; digital images, *GenealogyBank* (http://www.genealogybank.com: accessed May 22, 2017).

Historical Catalogue of Brown University, 1764–1914 (Providence, RI: Brown University, 1914), 156.

James W. Hagy, Directories for the City of Charleston, South Carolina For the Years 1830–1831, 1835–36, 1836, 1837–8, and 1840–41 (Baltimore: Clearfield Company, 1997), 130.

Keith, C.C., Admix of Dr. Matthew Irvine to C.B. Moses, Bill of Sale for the Slaves Abby, Jupiter, John, and Betsey, 12/15/1834, Series 213003, Vol. 0050: 00595, South Carolina Department of Archives and History, Columbia, SC.

King, Wiliiam L., *The Newspaper Press of Charleston, S.C.: A Chronological and Biographical History, Embracing a Period of One Hundred and Forty Years*, Charleston, S.C., 1872, Chapter III: 21–23.

Limehouse.020.10, 20 Limehouse Street (Harriet Crouch House), Historic Charleston, www.historiccharleston.org.

"[Lumber Yard . . .]," *Charleston Courier*, May 4, 1832, p. 3, col. 5; digital images, *GenealogyBank* (http://www.genealogybank.com : accessed June 4, 2017).

Marriage contract Thomas Amers Walker and Mary Ancrum Withers, March 15, 1794. New Hanover, North Carolina, Deeds, 1734–1939, Book L1 1794–1797: 70–74, marriage contract, Thomas Walker and Mary Ancrum Withers, March 15, 1794; digital images, *FamilySearch* (http://familysearch.org : accessed 22 May 2017).

Marriage and Death Notices from Charleston Courier, 1806 (Continued), *The South Carolina Historical and Genealogical Magazine,* Vol. 30, 1 (January 1929): 60–68.

Marriage settlement, E. Hilton Williams and Harriet H. Thorne, May 16, 1837South Carolina Secretary of State, Marriage Settlements, 1785–1902, Marriage settlements Book 13, pp. 364–5, E. Hilton Williams and Harriet H. Thorne; FHL microfilm 22, 518.

Marriage Settlement Abraham Crouch and Jane Sophia Withers, July 15, 1806 South Carolina Secretary of State, Marriage Settlements, 1785–1902, Marriage Settlements Book 5, pp. 225–228, Abraham Crouch and Sophia Jane Withers; FHL microfilm 22, 515.

McCrady, Edward, Exor. Of Elizabeth Vale to E.H. Williams, Bill of sale for a slave named Bishroom, 2/17/1835, Series S213003, Vol. 0050: 00650, South Carolina Department of Archives and History, Columbia, SC.

Meeting .008.01, 8 Meeting Street, Historic Charleston Foundation, Property File, http://charleston.pastperfectonline.com/archive/A902D2AC-0826-4E00-970F-273654812631 & image owned by GIbbes Museum, Charleston, SC.

Moses, Charles B. to C. W. Crouch, Bill of Sale for the Slaves Abby, Jupiter, John, and Betsey. 12/13/1834, Series S213003, Vol. 0050: 00594, South Carolina Department of Archives and History, Columbia, SC.

Marriage and Death Notices from the *Christian Neighbor,* South Carolina Magazine of Ancestral Research, Vol. XXVII (1999): 170, 534–535.

Meeting Street (1-42), Charleston County Public Library, www.ccpl.org/content.asp?id=15675&action=detail&catid=6025&parentid=5747.

Peyre, Catherine. *Transactions of the Hugeuenot Society,* No. 79, Charleston, SC: Published by the Order of the Society (1974): 174–176.

Providence Gazette, June 21, 1799.

The Providence House Directory and Family Address Book was viewed for 1903, 1905, 1907, 1909, 1911, 1913, 1915, 1917, and 1920, 1921-1922; available at: cdn.providenceri.com. The house number had changed to 102 George Street, but no longer existed in 1921-1922.

"Providence, September 8," *State Gazette of South Carolina*, 10-18-1787, Vol. XLVI, Issue 3554: 2, Charleston, SC, American Antiquarian Soceity, 2004, http://infoweb.newsbank.com.

Return of Deaths within the City of Charleston, Sept. 22, 1832–June 10, 1854 and June 11, 1854–Sept. 18, 1870 and 1850–1912. Microfilm 45/326, South Carolina Historical Society, Charleston, SC.

"Return of Deaths within the City of Charleston from the 24 September to the 1st October 1843," deaths of George Logan, Dr. E. A. Benjamin, and [Francis] [servant of] H Williams; database and images," South Carolina Death Records, 1821–1965, Ancestry.com (http: // www.ancestry.com: accessed May 30, 2017).

Reuben Aldridge Guild, *History of Brown University, With Illustrative Documents* (Providence, RI: 1867).

Sale "A Young Sound Negro Woman Named Jenny," April 15, 1814, State of South Carolina, Charleston, SC.

Snowden, Yates, LL.D., "History of The New England Society of Charleston, S.C., 1819–1919, by William Way," reprint from "The News and Courier," Charleston, S.C. May 2, 1920.

Some Original Charleston Probate Records, *South Carolina Magazine of Ancestral Research,* Vol. 40, Folder p-180 (2012): 159.

South Carolina (1850 U.S. census, Charleston), slave schedule, St. Michael and St. Philip Parish, A. C. Smith; digital images, Ancestry.com (http://www.ancestry.com: accessed May 20, 2017); citing National Archives and Records Administration microfilm M432, roll 862.

South Carolina (1850 U.S. census, Charleston), slave schedule, St. Michael and St. Philip Parish, the Honl. Judge Rice; digital images, Ancestry.com (http://www.ancestry.com : accessed May 20, 2017); citing National Archives and Records Administration microfilm M432, roll 862.

South Carolina (1850 U.S. census, Charleston), slave schedule, St. Michael and St. Philip Parish, John M. Greer; digital images, Ancestry.com (http://www.ancestry.com : accessed May 20, 2017); citing National Archives and Records Administration microfilm M432, roll 862. The pages appear to be numbered using only odd numbers; this page is numbered 897.

South Carolina (1850 U.S. census, Charleston), slave schedule, St. Michael and St. Philip Parish, William Greer; digital images, Ancestry.com (http://www.ancestry.com: accessed May 20, 2017); citing National Archives and Records Administration microfilm M432, roll 862.

South Carolina (1860 U.S. census, Barnwell), slave schedule, p. 14, col. 2, lines 2–3, W. S. Walker; digital images, Ancestry.com (http://www.ancestry.com: accessed May 20, 2017); citing National Archives and Records Administration microfilm M635, roll 1229.

South Carolina (Charleston), Probate Books, Returns, Vol. D [E] 1849–1851, pp. 306–307, Box 58, no. 7, James S. Burges estate; digital images, *FamilySearch* (http://www.familysearch.org: accessed 23 June 2017).

South Carolina (Charleston), Probate Books, Returns, Vol. A, pp. 13–17, Bundle 64, no. 2403, Dr. Hasell W. Crouch estate; digital images, *FamilySearch* (http://www.familysearch.org : accessed June 3, 2017).

South Carolina Death Records, 1821–1960, databse and images, Ancestry.com (http: www.ancestry .com: accessed May 20, 2017); death of Boston [slave of] EH Williams, 1838; citing "Return of Deaths within the City of Charleston, from the 25th February to the 4th March 1838," line 8.

South Carolina Death Records, 1821–1960, databse and images, Ancestry.com (http://www. ancestry.com: accessed May 20, 2017); death of Hagar [servant of] Mrs. Williams, 1858; citing "Return of Deaths within the City of Charleston, from the 4th to the 10th of April, 1858," line 6.

South Carolina, Death Records, 1821–1960, database and images, Ancestry.com (http://www .ancestry.com : accessed May 20, 2017); death of Minerva [slave of] W Greer, 1851; citing "Return of Deaths within the City of Charleston, from the 26th of October to the 1st of November, 1851," line 24; below the entries for October 26–November 1, 1851 are the entries for November 16–22, 1851.

South Carolina Directory, 1813, 1809, 1807, 1806, 1835–6, 1836 supplement, 1837, 1838, South Carolina Historical Society, College of Charleston, Charleston, SC.

"South Carolina Estate Inventories and Bills of Sale, 1732–1872," database and images, *Fold3* (http://www.fold3.com : accessed May 22, 2017); Inventory of estate of H. W. Crouch, physician, April 10, 1837; citing Charleston District, South Carolina, Inventories of Estates Book H 1834–1846, pp. 256–7.

"South Carolina Estate Inventories and Bills of Sale, 1732–1872," database and images, *Fold3* (http://www.fold3.com : accessed May 22, 2017); Inventory of James S. Burges, 1850; citing Charleston District, South Carolina, Inventories of Estates Book C 1850–1854, p. 25.

South Carolina Estate Inventories and Bills of Sale, 1732–1872," database and images, *Fold3* (http: ///www/fold3.com: accessed May 22, 2017); Bill of sale, John G. Schoolbred trustee of

Joseph S and Amelia Sarah Gibbes to Messrs. Gibbes and Williams, citing South Carolina Secretary of State Miscellaneous Records Book 50 (1832–1836).

South Carolina Secretary of State, Mortgages (Charleston series), 1736–1869, Book 3X, p. 130, mortgage, Charles W. Crouch to John A. Fripp, May 10, 1833; SCDAH microfilm ST 0438.

St. Philip's Protestant Episcopal Church (Charleston, South Carolina, United States), Register, 1807–1810, p. 75, baptism of Charles Withers and Hasell Wilkinson Crouch and burial of Sophia Jane Crouch, 1809; SCHS microfiche no. 50-135A-7, South Carolina Historical Society, Charleston, SC.

St. Peter's Episcopal Church (Charleston, SC), Register of Baptisms 1834–1861, baptism of Francis, Letter F, line 9, September 22, 1843; South Carolina Historical Society, Charleston, SC.

St. Peter's Episcopal Church (Charleston, SC), "Register of Marriages 1834–1853," Williams-Banks Marriage (line 4) and Williams_Taylor (line 10); South Carolina Historical Society, Charleston. ("Winthrop B. Williams to Catherine Banks," November 15, 1842, and "Winthrop B. Williams to Carolina Taylor, March 16, 1848).

St. Peter's Episcopal Church (Charleston, SC), Register of Funerals 1834–1859, baptism of Winthrop Williams, September 8, 1843 (line 10) and Henry Taylor Williams, March 6, 1849 (line 17), South Carolina Historical Society, Charleston.

Trinity Methodist Episcopal Church (Charleston, South Carolina, United States), "Book C, Roll of Coloured Members, 1821–1868," p. 31, Class no. 2 list, line 20, Bishoom Vale; South Carolina Historical Society, Charleston.

White, Lorraine Cook, ed., *The Barrbour Collection of Connecticut Town Vital Records Vo. 1–55.* Baltimore, MD: Genealogical Publishing Co., 1994–2002. Connecticut Town Marriage Records, pre-1870 (Barbour Collection) record for Abigail Chandler, record for Jason Williams, record for Mrs. Abigail Williams, Ancestry.com.

William Harris Papers, Rhode Island Historical Society, Providence, RI.

Williams, Jason, 1820, Providence, RI, Federal Census, Ancestry.com.

William Logan Jr. and Henrietta R. Thorn marriage settlement, 7 July 1840, Charleston, South Carolina, Deed Records, C11: 423–425, William Logan Jr. and Henrietta R. Thorn to William Logan Sr., marriage settlement, 7 July 1840; Charleston County Register of Mesnes Conveyances, Charleston.

Zion (later Westminster) Presbyterian Church (Charleston, South Carolina, United States), Session minutes, 1866-1885, p. 200-205, 5 August 1869, List of 345 members dismissed to organize a coloured [sic] church, list includes Jane Jones; Historical Foundation of the Presbyterian and Reformed Churches microfilm MFPOS 1552, item 3, Presbyterian Historical Society, Philadelphia.

Additional Primary & Secondary Sources

Alexander, Michelle, *The New Jim Crow: Mass Incarceration in the Age of Colorblindness.* New York: The New Press, 2012.

Ahmed, Sara "Happy Objects," *The Affect Theory Reader*, eds. Melissa Gregg and Gregory J. Seigworth (Durham: Duke University Press, 2010), 29–51.

Ahmed, Sara. *Willful Subjects.* Durham: Duke University Press Books, 2014.

Allahar, Anton L. "Slaves, Slave Merchants, and Slave Owners in 19th Century Cuba." *Caribbean Studies.* Vo. 21, No 1/2 (Jan–June 1988), 158–191.

Allen, Paula Gunn. *Pocahontas: Medicine Woman, Spy, Entrepreneur, Diplomat.* New York: Harper One, 2004.

Anderson, Carol. *White Rage: The Unspoken Truth of Our Racial Divide.* New York: Bloomsbury, 2016.

Arnett, Paul and Joanne Cubbs, Eugene W. Metcalf, Jr., et al. *Gee's Bend: The Architecture of the Quilt.* Atlanta: Tinwood Books, 2006.

Auther, Elissa. *String, Felt, Thread: The Hierarchy of Art and Craft in American Art.* Minneapolis: University of Minnesota Press, 2010.

SOURCES

Bailey, Ronald. "The Slave(ry) Trade and the Development of Capitalism in the United States: The Textile Industry in New England," *Social Science History*, 14, 3 (1990): 386.

Baldwin, James. *Collected Essays*, ed. Toni Morrison. New York: Library of America, 1998.

Baldwin, James. *James Baldwin's Nigger: James Baldwin and Dick Gregory Talk about the Black Experience in America and Relate it to that of the Caribbean in Contemporary Great Britain.* Interview filmed by Horace Ové, 1968. Posted by Mikhael Moshe Dawid, Sept. 12, 2010, in three parts, https://www.youtube.com/watch?v=DeFpzp1pBjc.

Baldwin, James. *Civil Rights: James Baldwin Interview, Mavis on Four,* interview by Mavis Nicholson, Posted by Thames TV, Nov. 10, 2014, https://www.youtube.com/watch?v=3Wht4NSf7E4.

Baldwin, James. *Who is the Nigger?* clip from *Take this Hammer,* KQED Film Unit, 1963. Clip posted by twreflect, April 23, 2010, https://www.youtube.com/watch?v=L0L5fciA6AU. Full film: https://diva.sfsu.edu/bundles/187041.

Ball, Edward. *Slaves in the Family*, revised ed. New York: Farrar, Straus and Giroux, 2014.

Bamberg, Michael and Molly Andrews. *Considering Counter-Narratives: Narrating, resisting, making sense.* Amsterdam: John Benjamins Publishing Company, 2004.

Bancroft, Frederic. *Slave Trading in the Old South,* intro. Michael Tadman. Columbia: University of South Carolina Press, 1996.

Baptist, Edward E. *The Half Has Never Been Told: Slavery and the Making of American Capitalism.* Philadelphia: Basic Books, 2014.

Barber, Elizabeth Wayland. *Women's Work: The First 20,000 Years: Women, Cloth, and Society in Early Times.* New York: W.W. Norton & Co., 1994.

Barcia, Manuel. *The Great African Slave Revolt of 1825: Cuba and the Fight for Freedom in Matanzas.* Baton Rouge: Louisiana State University Press, 2012.

Barthes, Roland. *Camera Lucida: Reflections on Photography.* New York: Hill and Wang, 2010.

Barthes, Roland. *The Pleasure of the Text.* New York: Hill and Wang, 1975.

Bassett, Lynne Zacek. *Telltale Textiles: Quilts from the Historic Deerfield Collection* Deerfield, MA: Historic Deerfield, 2003.

Bassett, Lynne Z. and Jack Larkin. *Northern Comfort: New England's Early Quilts, 1780–1850.* Nashville: Rutledge Hill Press, 1998.

Beardsley, Edward H. *A History of Neglect: Health Care for Blacks and Mill Workers in the Twentieth-Century South.* Knoxville: University of Tennessee Press, 1987.

Beardsley, John, William Arnett, Paul Arnett, Jane Livingston, Alvia Wardlaw, and Peter Marzio, eds. *The Quilts of Gee's Bend*, Atlanta: Tinwood Books, 2002.

Beckert, Sven. *Empire of Cotton: A Global History.* New York: Vintage, 2014.

Berlin, Ira. *Many Thousands Gone: The First Two Centuries of Slavery in North America.* Cambridge: The Belknap Press of Harvard University Press, 2003.

Blackmon, Douglas A. *Slavery by Another Name: The Re-Enslavement of Black Americans from the Civil War to World War I.* New York: Anchor Books, 2009.

Boivin, Nicole. *Material Cultures, Material Minds.* New York: Cambridge University Press, 2008.

Bolster, W. Jeffrey. *Black Jacks: African American Seamen in the Age of Sail.* Cambridge: Harvard University Press, 1997.

Bolton, Ethel Stanwood and Eva Johnston Coe, *American Samplers,* Massachusetts Society of Colonial Dames & Harvard University, (1921, books.google.com): 242.

Bridenbaugh, Carl. "Charlestonians at Newport," *The South Carolina Historical and Genealogical Magazine*, 1767–1765. Vol. XLI, April, 1940, no 2.

Bridenbaugh, Carl. "Colonial Newport as a Summer Resort," *Rhode Island Historical Society Collections.* Vol. XXVL, January 1933, No. 1. (1–23).

Brown, Bill. "Thing Theory," *Critical Inquiry.* 28.1 "Things" (Autumn 2001): 1–22.

Brown, Bill. *A Sense of Things: The Object Matter of American Literature.* Chicago: University of Chicago Press, 2003.

Brown, Henry Box. *Narrative of the Life of Henry Box Brown.* Mineola, NY: Dover Thrift Editions, 2015.

Cady, John H. *The Civic and Architectural Development of Providence, 1636–1950.* Providence: The Bookshop, 1957.

Cameron, Dan and Richard J. Powell, Michelle Wallace, Patrick Hill, Thalia Gouma-Peterson, Moira Roth, and Ann Gibson, eds. *Dancing at the Louvre: Faith Ringgold's French Collection and Other Story Quilts.* Berkeley: University of California Press, 1998.

Camp, Stephanie M.H. *Closer to Freedom: Enslaved Women & Everyday Resistance in the Plantation South.* Chapel Hill: The University of North Carolina Press, 1994.

Cash, Floris Barnett. "Kinship and Quilting: An Examination of an African-American Tradition," *The Journal of Negro History.* 80: 1, Winter 1995 (30–41).

Clark-Pujara, Christy. *Dark Work: The Business of Slavery in Rhode Island.* New York: NYU Press, 2016.

Coates, Ta-Nehisi. *Between the World and Me.* New York: Spiegel and Grau, 2015.

Coates, Ta-Nehisi, "The Case for Reparations," *The Atlantic Monthly*, June 2014, https://www.theatlantic.com/magazine/archive/2014/06/the-case-for-reparations/361631/.

Coughtry, Jay. *The Notorious Triangle: Rhode Island and the African Slave Trade, 1700–1807.* Philadelphia: Temple University Press, 1981.

Craft, William and Ellen. *Running a Thousand Miles to Freedom.* Mineola, NY: Dover Thrift Editions, 2014.

Cromwell, Adelaide. *The Other Brahmins: Boston's Black Upperclass, 1750–1950.* Fayetteville: University of Arkansas Press, 1994.

Davis, Paul. "Unrighteous Traffick: Rhode Island and the Slave Trade," *The Providence Journal.* Special Report, March 2006. Pettaquamscutt Historical Society, October 18, 2014.

DuBois, W.E.B. *The Souls of Black Folk.* New York: Dover Publications, Inc., 1994.

Dunbar-Ortiz, Roxanne. *An Indigenous Peoples' History of the United States.* Boston: Beacon Press, 2015.

Edgar, Walter. *South Carolina: A History.* Columbia, SC: University of South Carolina Press, 1998.

Edmonson, Belinda. "Black Aesthetics, Feminist Aesthetics, and the Problems of Oppositional Discourse," *Feminism, Art, Theory: An Anthology 1968–2000.* ed. Hilary Robinson (Malden, MA: Blackwell Publishing, 2001), 325–342.

Eisler, Benita, ed. *The Lowell Offering: Writings by New England Mill Women, 1840–1845.* New York: W.W. Norton, 1998.

Fanon, Frantz. *Black Skin, White Masks.* New York: Grove Press, 1952.

Farrow, Anne, Joel Lang, and Jenifer Frank. *Complicity: How the North Promoted, Prolonged, and Profited from Slavery.* New York: Ballantine Books, 2006.

Franklin, RW. *The Manuscript Books of Emily Dickinson: Volume I.* Cambridge: The Belknap Press of Harvard University, 1981.

Franklin, Susan B. "Early History of Negroes in Newport, An Address Before the Union Congregational Church," Newport, Rhode Island. Pettaquamscutt Historical Society, October 18, 2014.

Ferrero, Pat, Elaine Hedges, and Julie Silber. *Hearts and Hands: The Influence of Women & Quilts on American Society.* San Francisco: The Quilt Digest Press, 1987.

Fitts, Robert K. "The Landscapes of Northern Bondage," *Inventing New England's Slave Paradise: Master/Slave Relations in Eighteenth Century Narragansett, Rhode Island.* Studies in African American History and Culture. Routledge, 1998. Pettaquamscutt Historical Society, October 18, 2014.

Fleming, E. McClung. "Artifact Study: A Proposed Model." *Winterthur Portfolio.* 9 (1974): 153–173.

Foner, Eric. *Gateway to Freedom: The Hidden History of the Underground Railroad.* New York: W.W. Norton & Co., 2015.

Fordham, Damon, Lecture on his books, *True Stories of Black South Carolina* and *Voices of Black South Carolina: Legends and Legacy,* January 21, 2015, Lecture Series at the Old Slave Mart Museum, Charleston, SC.

Foucault, Michel. "Discipline and Punish: The Birth of the Prison," *The Norton Anthology of Theory and Criticism*, Second Edition, Ed. Vincent B. Leitch. New York: W.W. Norton & Co., 2010. 1490–1502.

Foucault, Michel. *The History of Sexuality, Vol. 2: The Use of Pleasure*, trans. Robert Hurley. New York: Vintage Books, 1985.

Fry, Gladys-Marie. *Stitched from the Soul: Slave Quilts from the Antebellum South*. Chapel Hill: The University of North Carolina Press, 2002.

Galenson, David W. "The Atlantic Slave Trade and the Barbados Market, 1673–1723." *The Journal of Economic History*, vol. 42, No 3. Sept. 1982, 491–511.

Gaspar, David Barry and Darlene Clark Hine. *More than Chattel: Black Women and Slavery in the Americas*. Bloomington: Indiana University Press, 1996.

Gates, Henry Louis. "Talking Black: Critical Signs of the Times," *The Norton Anthology of Theory and Criticism*, Second Edition, ed. Vincent B. Leitch (New York: W.W. Norton & Co., 2010), 2430–2438.

Gilkeson, John S., Jr. *Middle-Class Providence, 1820–1940*. Princeton: Princeton University Press, 1986.

Glymph, Thavolia. *Out of the House of Bondage: The Transformation of the Plantation Household*. New York: Cambridge University Press, 2008.

Goloboy, Jennifer L. "Strangers in the South: Charleston's Merchants and Middle-Class Values in the Early Republic." *Southern Middle Class in the Long Nineteenth Century*. ed. Jennifer R. Green, Jonathan Daniel Wells, and Susanna Delfino. LSU Press, 2011. ProQuest EBook, created from NMich on 2016-11-18.

Gordon, Avery. *Ghostly Matters: Hauntings and the Sociological Imagination*. Minneapolis: University of Minnesota Press, 2008.

Gordon, Beverly. "Spinning Wheels, Samplers, and the Modern Priscilla: The Images and Paradoxes of Colonial Revival Needlework," *Winterthur Portfolio*, 33 no. 2/3 (1998): 163.

Hagist, Don N. *Wives, Slaves, and Servant Girls: Advertisements for Female Runaways in American Newspapers, 1770–1783*. Yardley: Westholme, 2016.

Hamilton, Ann. "Indigo Blue," *The Object of Labor: Art, Cloth, and Cultural Production*, eds. Joan Livingstone and John Ploof, (Chicago: The School of the Art Institute Chicago Press, 2007), 333–337.

Hartman, Saidiya. *Lose Your Mother: A Journey Along the Atlantic Slave Route*. New York: Farrar, Straus and Giroux, 2007.

Henry, Dr. Susan. "Exception to the Female Model: Colonial Printer Mary Crouch," *Journalism and Mass Communication Quarterly*. Dec. 1, 1985. Vol 62, Issue 4, 725–749.

Herbaugh, Karen J. "Needles and Pens: The Sewing Diaries of Four American Women, 1883–1920," Dublin Seminar for New England Folklife, 2006–2007.

Hesseltine, William Best. *Civil War Prisons: A Study in War Psychology*. Columbus: Ohio State University Press, 1998.

hooks, bell. "An Aesthetic of Blackness: strange and oppositional" and "Aesthetic Inheritances: history worked by hand," *The Object of Labor: Art, Cloth, and Cultural Production*, eds. Joan Livingstone and John Ploof. Chicago: The School of the Art Institute Chicago Press, 2007 (315–336).

hooks, bell. *Art on My Mind: Visual Politics*. New York: The New Press, 1995.

Horton, Laurel. "An Elegant Geometry: Tradition, Migration, and Variation," *Mosaic Quilts* (Charleston, SC: The Charleston Museum in cooperation with Curious Works Press, 2002), 14–15.

Hunt-Hearst, Patricia, "'Round Homespun Coat & Pantaloons of the Same': Slave Clothing as Reflected in Fugitive Slave Advertisements in Antebellum Georgia," *The Georgia Historical Quarterly* 83, 4 (Winter, 1999): 733.

Jaffee, David. *A New Nation of Goods: The Material Culture of Early America*. Philadelphia: University of Pennsylvania Press, 2010.

Jacobs, Harriet. *Incidents in the Life of a Slave-Girl, Written by Herself*, intro. Nell Ervin Painter. New York: Penguin Classics, 2000.

Johnson, Walter. *Soul by Soul: Life Inside the Antebellum Slave Market*. Cambridge: Harvard University Press, 1999.

Jones, Amelia, ed. *The Feminism and Visual Culture Reader*. London: Routledge, 2013.

Jones, Rhett S. "Plantation Slavery in Narragansett County, Rhode Island, 1690–1790: A Preliminary Study," *Plantation Society* II, no. 2, (December 1986): 157–170. South County History Center, Kingston, RI, October 18, 2014.

Joyner, Charles. *Down by the Riverside: A South Carolina Slave Community*. Chicago: University of Illinois Press, 1984.

Jung, Julie. *Revisionary Rhetoric, Feminist Pedagogy, and Multigenre Texts*. Carbondale: Southern Illinois University Press, 2005.

Kennedy, Cynthia M. *Braided Relations, Entwined Lives: The Women of Charleston's Urban Slave Society*. Bloomington: Indiana University Press, 2005.

Kincaid, Jamaica. *A Small Place*. New York: Farrar, Straus and Giroux, 2000.

Kingery, David, ed. *Learning from Things: Method and Theory of Material Culture Studies*. Washington, D.C.: Smithsonian Institution Press, 1998.

Kirk, William. *A Modern City: Providence, Rhode Island and Its Activities*. Chicago: The University of Chicago Press, 1909.

Kraak, Deborah E. "Early American Silk Patchwork Quilts," in *Textiles in Early New England: Design, Production, and Consumption, The Dublin Seminar for New England Folklife Annual Proceedings,* ed. Peter Benes (Boston: Boston University, 1997): 18–20.

Kruger, Barbara. *Remote Control: Power, Cultures, and the World of Appearances*. Cambridge, The MIT Press, 1993.

Lemire, Elise. *Black Walden: Slavery and Its Aftermath in Concord, Massachusetts*. Philadelphia: University of Pennsylvania Press, 2009.

Lemons, J. Stanley. "Rhode Island and the Slave Trade," *Rhode Island History* 60, no. 1 (2002): 101.

Manovich, Lev. *The Language of New Media*. Cambridge: The MIT Press, 1995.

Marx, Karl. *Capital: Critique of Political Economy, Volume I*. New York: Penguin Classics, 1992.

Matthews, Glenna. *"Just a Housewife": The Rise and Fall of Domesticity*. Oxford: Oxford University Press, 1982.

May, Rachel and Linda Welters, "The Cushman Quilt Tops: A Tale of North and South," *Uncoverings of the Research Papers of the American Quilt Study Group,* Vol. 38 (2017): 36–67.

Maynard, Barksdale W. "'The Best, Lowliest Style!' The Early-Nineteenth-Century Rediscovery of American Colonial Architecture," *Journal of the Society of Architectural Historians,* 59 no. 3 (2000): 338-357.

McBurney, Christian M. *A History of Kingston, R.I., 1700–1900: Heart of Rural South County*. Kingston, RI: Pettaquamscutt Historical Society, 2004.

McCandless, Peter. *Slavery, Disease, and Suffering in the Southern Lowcountry*. Cambridge Studies on the American South. Cambridge: Cambridge University Press, 2011.

McInnis, Maurie D. *Slaves Waiting for Sale: Abolitionist Art and the American Slave Trade*. Chicago: The University of Chicago Press, 2011.

Melish, Joanne Pope. *Disowning Slavery: Gradual Emancipation and "Race" in New England, 1780–1860*. Ithaca: Cornell University Press, 2000.

Miller, Daniel, Ed. Material Cultures: Why Some Things Matter. Chicago: University of Chicago Press, 1998.

Mitchell, W. J. T. *What Do Pictures Want?: The Lives and Loves of Images*. Chicago: University of Chicago Press, 2006.

Mitchell, W. J. T. *Picture Theory: Essays on Verbal and Visual Representation*. Chicago: University of Chicago Press, 1994.

Morgan, Kenneth. "Slave Sales in Colonial Charleston," *The English Historical Review*, 113 no. 453, (1998): 906.

Morley, Simon. *Writing on the Wall: Word and Image in Modern Art*. Berkeley: University of California Press, 2003.

Morrison, Toni. *Beloved.* New York: Vintage Reprint Edition, 2007.

Morrison, Toni. *The Bluest Eye.* New York: Plume Books, 1994.

Myers, Amrita Chakrabarti. *Forging Freedom: Black Women and the Pursuit of Liberty in Antebellum Charleston.* Chapel Hill: The University of North Carolina Press, 2011.

Olmstead, Frederick Law and Arthur M. Schlesinger, Ed. *The Cotton Kingdom: A Traveller's Observations on Cotton and Slavery in the American Slave States, 1853–1861.* Boston: Da Capo Press, 1996.

Parker, Rozsika. *The Subversive Stitch: Embroidery and the Making of the Feminine.* New York: I.B. Tauris, 2010.

Patterson, Orlando. *Slavery and Social Death: A Comparative Study.* Cambridge: Harvard University Press, 1982.

Philip, M. NourbeSe. *Zong! As Told to the Author by Setaey Adamu Boateng.* Connecticut: Wesleyan University Press, 2008.

Pinka, Sharon Fulton. "Lowcountry Chintz: The Townsend/Pope Quilt Legacy," ed. Lynne Zacek Bassett, *Uncoverings*, (Lincoln, NE: American Quilt Study Group) 2013.

Piper, Adrian. "The Triple Negation of Colored Women Artists," *Feminism, Art, Theory: An Anthology 1968–2000*, ed. Hilary Robinson (Malden, MA: Blackwell Publishing, 2001): 57–68.

Powers, Bernard E. *Black Charlestonians: A Social History, 1822–1885.* Fayetteville: The University of Arkansas Press, 1994.

Prown, Jules D. "Material/Culture: Can the Farmer and the Cowman Still Be Friends?" *Learning from Things: Method and Theory of Material Culture Studies*, Ed. W. David Kingery. Washington: Smithsonian Institution Press, 1996.

Prown, Jules D. "Mind in Matter: An Introduction to Material Culture Theory and Method," Winterthur Portfolio. 17.1 (Spring 1982): 1–19.

Rankine, Claudia. *Citizen: An American Lyric.* Minneapolis: Graywolf Press, 2014.

Rudisel, Christine and Bob Blaidsell, eds. *Slave Narratives of the Underground Railroad.* Mineola, NY: Dover Thrift Editions, 2014.

Savitt, Todd L. *Medicine and Slavery: The Diseases and Health Care of Blacks in Antebellum Virginia.* Champaign: University of Illinois Press, 1981.

Sebald, W.G. *The Emigrants.* New York: New Directions Publishing, 1997.

Sebald, W.G. *Rings of Saturn.* New York: New Directions Publishing, 1999.

Sedgwick, Eve Kosofsky. *The Weather in Proust*, ed. Jonathan Goldberg and Michael Moon. Durham: Duke University Press Books, 2011.

Sedgwick, Eve Kosofsky. *Touching Feeling: Affect, Pedagogy, Performativity.* Durham: Duke University Press, 2003.

Sharpe, Christina. *In the Wake: On Blackness and Being.* Durham: Duke University Press, 2016.

Sharpless, Rebecca. *Cooking in Other Women's Kitchens: Domestic Workers in the South, 1865–1960.* Chapel Hill: The University of North Carolina Press, 2010.

Shaw, Madelyn and Lynne Zacek Bassett. *Homefront & Battlefield: Quilts & Context in the Civil War.* Lowell: American Textile History Museum, 2012.

Smith, Shawn Michelle. *American Archives: Gender, Race, and Class in Visual Culture.* Princeton: Princeton University Press, 1999.

Sontag, Susan. *On Photography.* New York: Picador, 2001.

Sontag, Susan. *Regarding the Pain of Others.* New York: Farrar, Straus and Giroux, 2013.

Spillers, Hortense J. "Mama's Baby, Papa's Maybe: An American Grammar Book," *Diacritics*, 17, no. 2, "Culture and Countermemory: The 'American Connection'" (Summer 1987): 64–81.

Spivak, Gayatri Chakravorty, "Can the Subaltern Speak?" *The Norton Anthology of Theory and Criticism, Second Edition*, ed. Vincent B. Leitch. New York: W.W. Norton & Co., 2010. 2114–2126.

Spivak,Gayatri Chakravorty. "The Politics of Interpretations," *Critical Inquiry* 9, no. 1 (1982), p. 278.

Tandberg, Gerilyn G., "Field Hand Clothing in Louisiana and Mississippi During the Ante-Bellum Period," *Dress*, 6 (1980): 89–103.

The Charleston Museum, *Mosaic Quilts: Paper Template Piecing in the South Carolina Lowcountry* (Greenville, SC: Curious Works Press, 2002).

Trinidad, Cuba, Y El Valle De Los Ingenios. Guia de Arquitectura. Trinidad: Assamblea Municipal del Poder Popular de Trinidad, 2003.

Ulrich, Laurel Thatcher. *A Midwife's Tale: The Life of Martha Ballard, Based on her Diary, 1785–1812.* New York: Vintage Books, 1994.

Ulrich, Laurel Thatcher. *The Age of Homespun: Objects and Stories in the Creation of an American Myth.* New York: Vintage, 2009.

Ulrich, Laurel Thatcher. "Of Pens and Needles: Sources for the Study of Early American Women." *Journal of American History.* 77 (1990): 200–207.

Vlach, John Michael. "The Plantation Tradition in an Urban Setting: The Case of the Aiken-Rhett House in Charleston, South Carolina," *Southern Cultures* 5, no. 4 (Winter 1999): 52–69.

Wallace, Maurice O. and Shawn Michelle Smith, eds. *Pictures and Progress: Early Photography and the Making of African American Identity.* Durham: Duke University Press, 2012.

Walker, David. *David Walker's Appeal to the Coloured Citizens of the World.* Baltimore: Black Classic Press, 2013.

Ward, Jesmyn, ed. *The Fire This Time: A New Generation Speaks about Race.* New York: Scribner, 2016.

Wardrop, Daneen. *Emily Dickinson and the Labor of Clothing.* Lebanon, NH: University Press of New England, 2009.

Washington, Booker T. *Up from Slavery.* Mineola, NY: Dover Publications, 2012.

Weigman, Robyn. *American Anatomies: Theorizing Race and Gender.* Durham: Duke University Press, 1995.

Weiner, Annette B. and Jane Schneider. *Cloth and Human Experience.* Washington: Smithsonian Books, 1989.

Weld, Theodore Dwight. *American Slavery as It Is: Testimony of a Thousand Witnesses.* Chapel Hill: The University of North Carolina at Chapel Hill Library, 2011.

Welters, Linda. "Material Culture Theory and Methods," Textiles, Fashion Merchandising and Design, The University of Rhode Island, Quinn Hall, February 2012. Lecture.

Welters, Linda and Margaret T. Ordoñez, eds, *Down by the Old Mill Stream: Quilts in Rhode Island.* Kent, OH: Kent State University Press, 2000.

White, Deborah Gray. *Ar'n't I a Woman? Female Slaves in the Plantation South.* New York: W.W. Norton & Co., 1999.

White, Shane and Graham White, "Slave Clothing and African-American Culture in the Eighteenth and Nineteenth Centuries," *Past and Present,* 148, no. 1 (August 1995): 149–186.

Wilkerson, Isabel. *The Warmth of Other Suns: The Epic Story of America's Great Migration.* New York: Vintage Books, 2010.

William Harris Papers, Rhode Island Historical Society, Providence, RI.

Wilson, Harriet E. *Our Nig, or, Sketches from the Life of a Free Black,* ed. P. Gabrielle Foreman and Reginald Pitts. New York: Penguin Books, 2009.

Yetman, Norman R., ed. *When I was a Slave: Memoirs from the Slave Narrative Collection.* Mineola: Dover Publications, 2002.

Chapter 1: Piecing the Quilt

Notes

The Historic Textile and Costume Collection at The University of Rhode Island holds the three quilt tops: 1952.63.124 is thought to be the oldest, the one on which Susan and Hasell Crouch worked. The other two tops were begun by Susan and Hasell and finished by Franklin R. Cushman and his family members in the 1930s: 1952.63.125 & 1952.63.126. Franklin R. Cushman assembled the notebooks containing fabric scraps; he donated one and his colleague Grace Whaley donated the other to the University of Rhode Island. ACCESSION NUM 1952.64.127 & 1952.64.355.

SOURCES

My understanding of the family and history of the quilt tops was shaped in large part by the accession notes accompanying the collection, and Franklin R. Cushman's correspondence with Miss Mary C. Whitlock at The University of Rhode Island.

The Elijah Williams Papers and Crouch-Cushman folder (MSS 9001-C, Box 15) in the Rhode Island Historical Society's archives include hundreds of letters between Williams, Crouch, and Cushman family members, along with the notebooks of Franklin R. Cushman, who transcribed all the letters and commented with more information about the family, all of which contributed to my understanding of the family and this story.

Genealogical information was compiled from University of Rhode Island accession records, Ancestry.com, Findagrave.com, MSS 34, Series F, Vol. 1–8: Franklin Cushman's Notebooks (Elijah Williams Papers, Rhode Island Historical Society).

A letter from Franklin R. Cushman explains: "The work on [the two bed quilts] was begun by our grandmother's sister, a Charleston, S.C. bride in 1833. It is of block print calico with white borders. The color scheme was made by her husband, a young physician. After his death in 1936 [*sic*], the partly completed quilt was put away with all the pieces cut and ready to be put in place. The cut pieces were sewed in place in the summers 1930–1937, to make two quilts—twin bed size. Both Mrs. Crouch and her daughter had died leaving the quilts unfinished. Mrs. Crouch was in her ninetieth year, her daughter, an artist, had just passed her nineteeth birthday." Letter from Franklin R. Crouch to Miss Mary C. Whitlock, 8 March 1952, Cushman Collection, Accession Records, Historic Textile and Costume Collection, University of Rhode Island.

I'm grateful to Linda Baumgarten at Colonial Williamsburg for providing information about Franklin R. Cushman's donations to that institution, and to the American Quilt Study Group, for your support of our presentation at the annual AQSG meeting, 2017; special thanks to editor Lynne Z. Bassett. Thank you to the Robert and Ardis James Foundation and Jill Wilson, for your generosity as panel sponsors, and to Jill especially, for your kindness and encouragement.

Thank you also to Dr. Christy Clark-Pujara, for allowing me to read a pre-publication copy of your book, *Dark Work: The Business of Slavery in Rhode Island,* and for sending a list of sources regarding Rhode Island slave-trading families and black sailors.

Primary Sources

Beecher, Catharine Esther. *A Treatise on Domestic Economy*. New York: Source Book Press, 1970, c1841.

"Letter from Susan to her sisters," May 18, 1833, Series F: Franklin Cushman's notebooks, vol. 1: 120, (Elijah Williams Papers, Rhode Island Historical Society).

"Letter from Susan to her sisters," October 15, 1835, Series F: Franklin Cushman's notebooks, vol. 2: 42, (Elijah Williams Papers, Rhode Island Historical Society).

Randolph, Mary. *The Virginia Housewife, or, Methodical Cook: a Facsimile of an Authentic Early American Cookbook*. New York: Dover Publications, 1993.

Simmons, Amelia. *American Cookery: The First American Cookbook: A Facsimile of 'American Cookery,' 1796*. New York: Dover Publications, 1984, c1958.

Secondary Sources

Cady, John H. *The Civic and Architectural Development of Providence, 1636–1950*. Providence: The Bookshop, 1957.

Davis, Paul. "Unrighteous Traffick: Rhode Island and the Slave Trade," *The Providence Journal*. Special Report, March 2006. Pettaquamscutt Historical Society, October 18, 2014.

Fitts, Robert K. "The Landscapes of Northern Bondage," *Inventing New England's Slave Paradise: Master/Slave Relations in Eighteenth Century Narragansett, Rhode Island*. Studies in African American History and Culture. Routledge, 1998. Pettaquamscutt Historical Society, October 18, 2014.

Franklin, Susan B. "Early History of Negroes in Newport, An Address Before the Union Congregational Church," Newport, Rhode Island. Pettaquamscutt Historical Society, October 18, 2014.

Gilkeson, John S., Jr. *Middle-Class Providence, 1820–1940*. Princeton: Princeton University Press, 1986.

Ginzberg, Lori D. *Women and the Work of Benevolence: Morality, Politics, and Class in the Nineteenth-Century United States*. New Haven: Yale University Press, 1990.

Jones, Rhett S. "Plantation Slavery in Narragansett County, Rhode Island, 1690–1790: A Preliminary Study," *Plantation Society*. Vol II, No. 2, (December 1986) 157–170. Pettaquamscutt Historical Society, October 18, 2014.

Kennedy, Cynthia M. *Braided Relations, Entwined Lives*. Bloomington: Indiana University Press, 2005.

Kirk, William. *A Modern City: Providence, Rhode Island and Its Activities*. Chicago: Chicago University Press, 1909.

Melish, Joanne Pope. *Disowning Slavery: Gradual Emancipation and "Race" in New England, 1780–1895*. Ithaca: Cornell University Press, 2015.

Ousley, Laurie. "The Business of Housekeeping: The Mistress, the Domestic Worker, and the Construction of Class." *Legacy: A Journal of American Women Writers*. 23.2 (June 2006), 132–143.

Stankiewicz, Mary Ann. "Middle Class Desire: Ornament, Industry, and Emulation in 19th Century Art Education," *Studies in Art Education*. Vol 43, No 4, Summer 2002, 324–338.

Vicinus, Martha. *Independent Women: Work and Community for Single Women, 1850–1920*. Chicago: University of Chicago Press, 1985.

Chapter 2: Eliza, Minerva, & Juba

Notes

For more on Harriet Jacobs, please see: Yellin, Jean Fagan. *Harriet Jacobs: A Life, The Remarkable Adventures of the Woman Who Wrote Incidents in the Life of a Slave Girl*. New York: Basic Civitas Books, 2004; Sommers, Samantha M., "Harriet Jacobs and the Recirculation of Print Culture," *The Journal of the Society for the Study of Multi-Ethnic Literature of the United States*, Vol. 40, Iss. 3 (September 2015): 134-149; Thallam, Sarada, "African-American feminist discourses: understanding the writings of Harriet Jacobs and Adrienne Kennedy," *African Nebula*, no. 6 (2013): 21+.

Quoted descriptions of the women on p. 35, starting with, "She had two petticoats..." are from Hagist, Don N. *Wives, Slaves, and Servant Girls: Advertisements for Female Runaways in American Newspapers, 1770–1783*. Yardley: Westholme, 2016.

The address, 6 Cumberland Street, is taken from letters addressed to Susan and Hasell, Elijah Williams Papers, Rhode Island Historical Society, Providence, RI.

p. 36, "collectively defy white authority . . ." from Gaspar, David Barry, and Darlene Clark Hine. *More than Chattel: Black Women and Slavery in the Americas*. Bloomington: Indiana University Press, 1996.

p. 41, "Slave narratives frequently refer to the fact that slaves learned how to use plant dyes expertly." & quilt pattern names & p. 43 "A former Georgia slave" quote from Frye.

p. 44, "embodying a polyrhythmic . . ." Farris, Teresa Parker "Anna Williams," *knowlouisiana .org Encyclopedia of Louisiana*, ed. David Johnson. Louisiana Endowment for the Humanities, 2010. Article published September 12, 2012. http://www.knowlouisiana.org/entry/anna-williams.

p. 72, Susan's measurements and the analysis of her dresses were completed by students in Dr. Linda Welters' Textile Merchandising and Design 570 class, Spring 2017, University of Rhode Island: Ananís Rentas Vega, Elizabeth Beasley, Nicole Dee-Collins, and Sarah Gilcrease.

Primary Sources

"Letter from Hilton to Jason Williams," February 22, 1835, Series F: Franklin Cushman's notebooks, vol. 2: 112, (Elijah Williams Papers, Rhode Island Historical Society).

"Letter from Hilton to Eliza Williams," May, 7 1836. Series F: Franklin Cushman's notebooks, vol. 2: 56, (Elijah Williams Papers, Rhode Island Historical Society).

"Letter from Susan to Eliza Williams," July 2, 1835. Series F: Franklin Cushman's notebooks, vol. 2: 23, (Elijah Williams Papers, Rhode Island Historical Society).

"Letter from Susan to her sisters," May 18, 1833, Series F: Franklin Cushman's notebooks, vol. 1: 119–120, (Elijah Williams Papers, Rhode Island Historical Society).

"Letter from Winthrop to Eliza Williams," November 8, 1834, Series F: Franklin Cushman's notebooks, vol. 7: 52, (Elijah Williams Papers, Rhode Island Historical Society).

"Letter from Susan to her sisters," October 15, 1835, Series F: Franklin Cushman's notebooks, vol. 2: 41–42, (Elijah Williams Papers, Rhode Island Historical Society).

"Letter from Susan to Eliza Williams," December 10, 1835, Series F: Franklin Cushman's notebooks, vol. 2: 52–54, (Elijah Williams Papers, Rhode Island Historical Society).

Stoney, Peter G. *List and Memorandum Book: Names of Negroes at Calibogue 1829.* South Carolina Historical Society manuscript, College of Charleston. 34/707.

White, Alonzo. *List book of negroes for sale.* 1853–1863. South Carolina Historical Society manuscript. 34/0350.

Secondary Sources

Arnett, Paul and Joanne Cubbs, Eugene W. Metcalf, Jr. *Gee's Bend: The Architecture of the Quilt.* Atlanta: Tinwood Books, 2006.

Bancroft, Frederic. *Slave Trading in the Old South,* intro. Michael Tadman. Columbia: University of South Carolina Press, 1996.

Barber, Elizabeth Wayland. *Women's Work: The First 20,000 Years: Women, Cloth, and Society in Early Times.* New York: W.W. Norton & Co., 1994.

Beardsley, John, William Arnett, Paul Arnett, Jane Livingston, Alvia Wardlaw, and Peter Marzio, eds. *The Quilts of Gee's Bend*, Atlanta: Tinwood Books, 2002.

Camp, Stephanie M.H. *Closer to Freedom: Enslaved Women & Everyday Resistance in the Plantation South.* Chapel Hill: The University of North Carolina Press, 1994.

Clark-Pujara, Christy. *Dark Work: The Business of Slavery in Rhode Island.* New York: NYU Press, 2016.

Coughtry, Jay. *The Notorious Triangle: Rhode Island and the African Slave Trade, 1700–1807.* Philadelphia: Temple University Press, 1981.

Fry, Gladys-Marie. *Stitched from the Soul: Slave Quilts from the Antebellum South.* Chapel Hill: The University of North Carolina Press, 2002.

Hartigan-O'Connor, Ellen. "'She Said She Did Not Know Money': Urban Women and Atlantic Markets in the Revolutionary Era." *Early American Studies: An Interdisciplinary Journal.* Vol. 4, No. 2, Fall 2006. 322–352.

Johnson, Walter. *Soul by Soul: Life Inside the Antebellum Slave Market.* Cambridge: Harvard University Press, 1999.

Kennedy, Cynthia M. *Braided Relations, Entwined Lives: The Women of Charleston's Urban Slave Society.* Bloomington: Indiana University Press, 2005.

Matthews, Glenna. *"Just a Housewife": The Rise and Fall of Domesticity.* Oxford: Oxford University Press, 1982.

May, Rachel. *Quilting with a Modern Slant: People, Patterns, and Techniques Inspiring the Modern Quilt Community.* North Adams, MA: Storey Publishing, 2014.

Melish, Joanne Pope. *Disowning Slavery: Gradual Emancipation and "Race" in New England, 1780–1860.* Ithaca, NY: Cornell University Press, 2000.

Myers, Amrita Chakrabarti. *Forging Freedom: Black Women and the Pursuit of Liberty in Antebellum Charleston.* Chapel Hill: The University of North Carolina Press, 2011.

Patterson, Orlando. *Slavery and Social Death: A Comparative Study.* Cambridge: Harvard University Press, 1982.

Putzel, Christof. "Does the Long Shadow of Slavery Linger in Charleston?" America Tonight, Aljazeera America, June 28, 2015. http://america.aljazeera.com/watch/shows/america-tonight/2015/6/does-the-long-shadow-of-slavery-linger-in-charleston.html.

Register of Deeds Office, 101 Meeting Street, Charleston, South Carolina.

Robertson, Jean. "Oral History Interview with Nancy Crow," December 18, 2002. Archives of American Art, Smithsonian Institution, https://www.aaa.si.edu/collections/interviews/oral-history-interview-nancy-crow-13095.

Simmons, Amelia. *American Cookery: The First American Cookbook: A Facsimile of 'American Cookery,' 1796.* New York: Dover Publications, 1984, c1958.

Ulrich, Laurel Thatcher. "Of Pens and Needles: Sources for the Study of Early American Women." *Journal of American History.* 77 (1990): 200–207.

Walker, Alice. *In Search of Our Mothers' Gardens: Womanist Prose.* San Diego: Harcourt, Brace, Jovanovich, 1983.

Chapter 3: Warp & Weft: Agriculture & Industry

Notes

p. 81, Whit Schroeder notes that a piece of lumber in Rhode Island Hall is stamped "James A. Potter & Co.," a Rhode Island mill founded in 1838. Schroeder, Whit, "Chapter 3: "History of Rhode Island Hall," *The Transformation of Rhode Island Hall: An Archeological Perspective,* Joukowsky Institute for Archaeology & the Ancient World, Brown University, https://www.brown.edu/Departments/Joukowsky_Institute/about/rihalltransform/6500.html.

It's possible that Hilton's mill provided lumber for Rhode Island Hall that was not labeled, or not found to have a label, or perhaps they supplied lumber for other projects by the architects.

Information about Bishroom Vale's church membership gathered by Sarah Nesnow.

Primary Sources

Godey's Lady's Book, The Online Books Page, serial archive listing, University of Pennsylvania, http://onlinebooks.library.upenn.edu/webbin/serial?id=godeylady.

Godey's Lady's Book and Ladies' American Magazine, "The Lady's Book," Vol. 10–11 (1835), Philadelphia, PA: L.A. Godey & Co., 1830–1839 (original owned by Princeton University)."Letter from Susan to her sisters," May 18, 1833, Series F: Franklin Cushman's notebooks, vol. 1: 119–120, (Elijah Williams Papers, Rhode Island Historical Society).

"Letter from Hilton to Winthrop," March 15, 1833, Series F: Franklin Cushman's notebooks, vol. 1: 112, (Elijah Williams Papers, Rhode Island Historical Society).

"NB almost 24 yr," Franklin Cushman's note, Series F: Franklin Cushman's notebooks, vol. 1: 114, (Elijah Williams Papers, Rhode Island Historical Society).

"This very gentle self-reliant man . . ." Franklin Cushman's note, Series F: Franklin Cushman's notebooks, vol. 2: 121, (Elijah Williams Papers, Rhode Island Historical Society).

"Winthrop…was a very headstrong boy…a very gentle brother Hilton…always tried to restrain him," Franklin Cushman's note, Series F: Franklin Cushman's notebooks, vol. 1: 134, (Elijah Williams Papers, Rhode Island Historical Society).

"Letter from Winthrop to Eliza Williams," November 3, 1835, Series F: Franklin Cushman's notebooks: vol. 2: 45, (Elijah Williams Papers, Rhode Island Historical Society).

"Postscript, Letter from Eliza Williams to Sarah R. Williams," June 3, 1839. Series F: Franklin Cushman's notebooks: vol. 2: 138, (Elijah Williams Papers, Rhode Island Historical Society).

"Letter from Hilton to Winthrop," March 15, 1833, Series F: Franklin Cushman's notebooks, vol. 1: 114, (Elijah Williams Papers, Rhode Island Historical Society).

"Letter from Winthrop to Eliza Williams," November 8, 1834, Series F: Franklin Cushman's notebooks, vol. 7: 52–54, (Elijah Williams Papers, Rhode Island Historical Society).

"Letter from Susan to Eliza Williams," November 5, 1835, Series F: Franklin Cushman's notebooks, vol. 2: 46, (Elijah Williams Papers, Rhode Island Historical Society).

"Letter from Susan to Eliza Williams," July 2, 1835, Series F: Franklin Cushman's notebooks, vol. 2: 23, (Elijah Williams Papers, Rhode Island Historical Society).

"Letter from Susan to her sisters," October 15, 1835, Series F: Franklin Cushman's notebooks, vol. 2: 40–41, (Elijah Williams Papers, Rhode Island Historical Society).

"Letter from Sarah B. Hamlin to Susan," October 8, 1834, Series F: Franklin Cushman's notebooks, vol. 7: 49–52, (Elijah Williams Papers, Rhode Island Historical Society).
"Letter from Susan to her sisters," May 18, 1833, Series F: Franklin Cushman's notebooks, vol. 1: 119–120, (Elijah Williams Papers, Rhode Island Historical Society).
"Letter from Susan to her sisters," October 15, 1835, Series F: Franklin Cushman's notebooks, vol. 2: 41–42, (Elijah Williams Papers, Rhode Island Historical Society).
"Letter from Susan to Eliza Williams," December 10, 1835, Series F: Franklin Cushman's notebooks, vol. 2: 52–54, (Elijah Williams Papers, Rhode Island Historical Society).
"Letter from Susan and Hilton to Eliza Williams," September 11, 1835, Series F: Franklin Cushman's notebooks, vol. 2: 34, (Elijah Williams Papers, Rhode Island Historical Society).
"Letter from Susan to Eliza Williams," January 11, 1835, Series F: Franklin Cushman's notebooks, vol. 1: 145, (Elijah Williams Papers, Rhode Island Historical Society).
"Letter from Winthrop to his sister," November 3, 1835, Series F: Franklin Cushman's notebooks, vol. 2: 44, (Elijah Williams Papers, Rhode Island Historical Society).
"Letter from Winthrop to Eliza Williams," December 10 & 11, 1835, Series F: Franklin Cushman's notebooks, vol. 2: 49–51, (Elijah Williams Papers, Rhode Island Historical Society).
"Letter from Hilton to his sister," May 7, 1836, Series F: Franklin Cushman's notebooks, vol. 2: 57, (Elijah Williams Papers, Rhode Island Historical Society).
"Letter from Hilton to his sister," June 1, 1836, Series F: Franklin Cushman's notebooks, vol. 2: 59, (Elijah Williams Papers, Rhode Island Historical Society).
"Morning Dresses," *The Court Magazine & Monthly Critic and Lady's Magazine*, vol. 5: xiii (October 1834), London: Edward Churton, 1834. Google book: https://books.google.com/books?id=6qHNAAAAMAAJ&printsec=frontcover&source=gbs_ge_summary_r&cad=0#v=onepage&q&f=false.
Race and Slavery Petitions Project, Digital Library on American Slavery, University of North Carolina at Greensboro, https://library.uncg.edu/slavery/petitions/ PAR Number 21384008, 21384124. These are Charles Crouch's court cases, in 1840 and 1841, in which he represented "Simon Mathews and the five grandchildren of the late George Mathews, all free persons of color," to establish their freedom and handle property and inheritance.
William Hilton Williams' notebook, Elijah Williams Papers, MSS 34: Series D.

Secondary Sources

Beckert, Sven. *Empire of Cotton: A Global History*. New York: Vintage, 2014.
Cady, John H. *The Civic and Architectural Development of Providence, 1636–1950*. Providence: The Bookshop, 1957.
Clark-Pujara, Christy. *Dark Work: The Business of Slavery in Rhode Island*. New York: NYU Press, 2016.
Coughtry, Jay. *The Notorious Triangle: Rhode Island and the African Slave Trade, 1700–1807*. Philadelphia: Temple University Press, 1981.
Davis, Paul. "Unrighteous Traffick: Rhode Island and the Slave Trade," *The Providence Journal*. Special Report, March 2006. Pettaquamscott Historical Society, October 18, 2014.
Edward McCrady papers, 1787–ca.–1765, Description, South Carolina Historical Society, Charleston, SC.
Helsley, Alexia Jones. "McCrady, Edward, Jr." *South Carolina Encyclopedia*. University of South Carolina, Institute for Southern Studies, June 8, 2016: http://www.scencyclopedia.org/sce/entries/mccrady-edward-jr/.
"James C. Bucklin," Rhode Island Heritage Hall of Fame Inductee, http://www.riheritagehalloffame.org/inductees_detail.cfm?iid=673.
Johnson, Walter. *Soul by Soul: Life Inside the Antebellum Slave Market*. Cambridge: Harvard University Press, 1999.
Kennedy, Cynthia M. *Braided Relations, Entwined Lives: The Women of Charleston's Urban Slave Society*. Bloomington: Indiana University Press, 2005.

Melish, Joanne Pope. *Disowning Slavery: Gradual Emancipation and "Race" in New England, 1780–1895.* Ithaca: Cornell University Press, 2015.

Myers, Amrita Chakrabarti. *Forging Freedom: Black Women and the Pursuit of Liberty in Antebellum Charleston.* Chapel Hill: The University of North Carolina Press, 2011.

Schroeder, Whit, Chapter 3: "History of Rhode Island Hall," *The Transformation of Rhode Island Hall: An Archeological Perspective,* Joukowsky Institute for Archaeology & the Ancient World, Brown University, https://www.brown.edu/Departments/Joukowsky_Institute/about/rihalltransform/6500.html.

White, Deborah Gray. *Ar'n't I a Woman? Female Slaves in the Plantation South.* New York: W.W. Norton & Co., 1999.

Chapter 4: Mosaic

Notes

Hasell's grandfather, Charles Crouch, "printer," bought from Christopher Jenkins a man named Jack, February 8, 1771. Marriage and Death Notices from the *Christian Neighbor,* South Carolina Magazine of Ancestral Research, Vol. XXVII (1999): 170, 534–535.

Peter Timothy, the employer of Charles Crouch, issued an ad in the 1751 *Gazette* to reward anyone who could find him with "a small woodcut of a fleeing man . . . usually reserved for runaway slaves." Charles ran away again, and Timothy "discharged" him, saying that he "was 'very capable of the Business' but possessed 'an unhappy affection for Drink, Play and Scandalous Company.'" Hennig Cohen, "Preface" and "Historical and Descriptive Sketch," *The South Carolina Gazette,* University of South Carolina Press (1953): vii–9. (It's possible that Charles' grandson and namesake, C. W. Crouch, husband to Eliza Crouch, may have taken after his grandfather, as C.W. was described by family members as "slovenly," like his father Abraham. C. W. Crouch held many jobs over the course of his lifetime.) For more on Charles Crouch, printer, see also: William L. King, *The Newspaper Press of Charleston, S.C.: A Chronological and Biographical History, Embracing a Period of One Hundred and Forty Years*, Charleston, S.C., 1872, Chapter III: 21–23.

For more on the history of cooks and cooking: Lam, Francis, "Edna Lewis and the Black Roots of American Cooking," *New York Times,* October 28, 2015, *https://www.nytimes.com/2015/11/01/magazine/edna-lewis-and-the-black-roots-of-american-cooking.html;* Russell, Malinda. *A Domestic Cook Book: containing a careful selection of receipts for the kitchen.* Paw Paw, MI: 1866, Hathi Trust Digital Library, https://catalog.hathitrust.org/Search/Home?lookfor=russell%2C%20malinda&searchtype=subject&ft=&setft=false; Randolph, Mary. *The Virginia Housewife, or, Methodical cook: a facsimile of an authentic early American cookbook.* New York: Dover Publications, 1993; Simmons, Amelia. *American Cookery: The first American cookbook: A facsimile of 'American cookery,' 1796.* New York: Dover Publications, 1984, c1958; Tipton-Martin, Toni. *The Jemima Code: Two Centuries of African American Cookbooks.* Austin: University of Texas Press, 2015; Twitty, Michael W. *The Cooking Gene: A Journey Through African American Culinary History.* New York: Amistad, 2017.

p. 98, "Beginning in the last decade...," from Berlin, Ira. *Many Thousands Gone: The First Two Centuries of Slavery in North America.* Cambridge: The Belknap Press of Harvard University Press, 2003.

p. 99–102, information on Mary Ancrum Walker, the "feme sole," and enslaved people Walker owned, as well as p. 121–122 Abraham Crouch as trustee, was provided by Sarah Nesnow.

p. 102, "As well as extending . . ." & "acquir[ing] cultural capital . . ." from Stankiewicz, Mary Ann. "Middle Class Desire: Ornament, Industry, and Emulation in 19th Century Art Education," *Studies in Art Education.* Vol 43, No 4, Summer 2002, 324–338.

p. 107, "Between 1826 and 1836 . . ." from Beckert, Sven. *Empire of Cotton: A Global History.* New York: Vintage, 2014.

For more on Denmark Vesey and the planned rebellion, please see: Rasmussen, Daniel. *American Uprising: The Untold Story of America's Largest Slave Revolt.* New York: Harper Perennial, 2012; Douglas R. Egerton and Robert L. Paquette, eds., *The Denmark Vesey Affair: A Documentary History,* Southern Dissent (Gainesville: University Press of Florida, 2017); John Lofton, *Denmark*

Vesey's Revolt: The Slave Plot that Lit a Fuse to Fort Sumter, American Abolitionism and Antislavery (Kent, OH: The Kent State University Press, 2013); Edward A. Pearson, *Designs Against Charleston: The Trial Record of the Denmark Slave Conspiracy of 1822.* Chapel Hill: University of North Carolina Press, 1999.

Primary Sources

"Letter from Hilton to his sister," March 14 & 16, 1835, Series F: Franklin Cushman's notebooks, vol. 2: 6–7, (Elijah Williams Papers, Rhode Island Historical Society).

"Letter from Winthrop to Eliza Williams," January 12, 1835, Series F: Franklin Cushman's notebooks, vol. 1: 150, (Elijah Williams Papers, Rhode Island Historical Society).

"Letter from Winthrop to Hilton," January 11, 1835, Series F: Franklin Cushman's notebooks, vol. 1: 148, (Elijah Williams Papers, Rhode Island Historical Society).

"Letter from Susan to her sisters," May 18, 1833, Series F: Franklin Cushman's notebooks, vol. 1: 120, (Elijah Williams Papers, Rhode Island Historical Society).

"Letter from Winthrop to William J. Harris," March 3, 1838, Series F: Franklin Cushman's notebooks, vol. 2: 155 (Elijah Williams Papers, Rhode Island Historical Society).

"Letter from Susan to Eliza Williams," July 2, 1835, Series F: Franklin Cushman's notebooks, vol. 2: 23, (Elijah Williams Papers, Rhode Island Historical Society).

Middleton, Alicia Hopton. *Life in Carolina and New England during the nineteenth century, as illustrated by reminiscences and letters of the Middleton family of Charleston, South Carolina, and of the DeWolf Family of Bristol, Rhode Island.* Private printing, 1929. South Carolina Historical Society Rare Books. College of Charleston, Charleston, SC.

Receipt for Abraham Crouch burial, MSS 34, Series C: Jason Williams' papers (Elijah Williams Papers, Rhode Island Historical Society).

Godey's Lady's Book, The Online Books Page, serial archive listing, University of Pennsylvania, http://onlinebooks.library.upenn.edu/webbin/serial?id=godeylady.

Godey's Lady's Book and Ladies' American Magazine, "The Lady's Book," Vol. 1–17, Philadelphia, PA: L.A. Godey & Co., 1830–1839 (original owned by Princeton University), Hathi Trust Digital Library, https://catalog.hathitrust.org/Record/008920204.

Secondary Sources

Adamson, Jeremy. *Calico and Chintz: Antique Quilts from the Collection of Patricia S. Smith* (Washington, D.C.: Smithsonian Institution, 1997).

Bassett, Lynne Zacek. *Telltale Textiles: Quilts from the Historic Deerfield Collection* Deerfield, MA: Historic Deerfield, 2003.

Bassett, Lynne Z. and Jack Larkin. *Northern Comfort: New England's Early Quilts, 1780–1850.* Nashville: Rutledge Hill Press, 1998.

Beckert, Sven. *Empire of Cotton: A Global History.* New York: Vintage, 2014.

Berlin, Ira. *Many Thousands Gone: The First Two Centuries of Slavery in North America.* Cambridge: The Belknap Press of Harvard University Press, 2003.

Bolton, Ethel Stanwood and Eva Johnston Coe, *American Samplers,* Massachusetts Society of Colonial Dames & Harvard University, (1921, books.google.com): 242.

Bridenbaugh, Carl. "Charlestonians at Newport," *The South Carolina Historical and Genealogical Magazine,* 1767–1765. Vol. XLI, April, 1940, no 2.

Bridenbaugh, Carl. "Colonial Newport as a Summer Resort," *Rhode Island Historical Society Collections.* Vol. XXVL, January 1933, No. 1. (1–23).

Brown, Henry Box. *Narrative of the Life of Henry Box Brown.* Mineola, NY: Dover Thrift Editions, 2015.

Camp, Stephanie M.H. *Closer to Freedom: Enslaved Women & Everyday Resistance in the Plantation South.* Chapel Hill: The University of North Carolina Press, 1994.

Clark-Pujara, Christy. *Dark Work: The Business of Slavery in Rhode Island.* New York: NYU Press, 2016.

Coughtry, Jay. *The Notorious Triangle: Rhode Island and the African Slave Trade, 1700–1807.* Philadelphia: Temple University Press, 1981.

Craft, William and Ellen. *Running a Thousand Miles to Freedom.* Mineola, NY: Dover Thrift Editions, 2014.

Fitts, Robert K. "The Landscapes of Northern Bondage," *Inventing New England's Slave Paradise: Master/Slave Relations in Eighteenth Century Narragansett, Rhode Island.* Studies in African American History and Culture. Routledge, 1998. Pettaquamscott Historical Society, October 18, 2014.

Gilkeson, John S., Jr. *Middle-Class Providence, 1820–1940.* Princeton: Princeton University Press, 1986.

Glymph, Thavolia. *Out of the House of Bondage: The Transformation of the Plantation Household.* New York: Cambridge University Press, 2008.

Goloboy, Jennifer L. "Strangers in the South: Charleston's Merchants and Middle-Class Values in the Early Republic." *Southern Middle Class in the Long Nineteenth Century.* ed. Jennifer R. Green, Jonathan Daniel Wells, and Susanna Delfino. LSU Press, 2011. ProQuest EBook, created from NMich on 2016-11-18.

Henry, Dr. Susan. "Exception to the Female Model: Colonial Printer Mary Crouch," *Journalism and Mass Communication Quarterly.* Dec. 1, 1985. Vol 62, Issue 4, 725–749.

Horton, Laurel. "An Elegant Geometry: Tradition, Migration, and Variation," *Mosaic Quilts* (Charleston, SC: The Charleston Museum in cooperation with Curious Works Press, 2002), 14–15.

Jaffee, David. *A New Nation of Goods: The Material Culture of Early America.* Philadelphia: University of Pennsylvania Press, 2010.

Johnson, Walter. *Soul by Soul: Life Inside the Antebellum Slave Market.* Cambridge: Harvard University Press, 1999.

Kennedy, Cynthia M. *Braided Relations, Entwined Lives: The Women of Charleston's Urban Slave Society.* Bloomington: Indiana University Press, 2005.

Kenrick, W. (William). *The Whole Duty of Woman, comprised in the following sections.* Section IX: "Modesty." Philadelphia: Printed and sold by Joseph Crukshank, in Market-Street., MDCCLXXXVIII. [1788], Evans Early American Imprint Collection, University of Michigan, https://quod.lib.umich.edu/e/evans/N16488.0001.001/1:4.11?rgn=div2;view=fulltext;q1=Women.

Kincaid, Jamaica. "Sowers and Reapers," *The New Yorker Magazine.* January 22, 2001: 41–45.

Kraak, Deborah E. "Early American Silk Patchwork Quilts," in *Textiles in Early New England: Design, Production, and Consumption*, *The Dublin Seminar for New England Folklife Annual Proceedings,* ed. Peter Benes (Boston: Boston University, 1997).

Matthews, Glenna. *"Just a Housewife": The Rise and Fall of Domesticity.* Oxford: Oxford University Press, 1982.

McCandless, Peter. *Slavery, Disease, and Suffering in the Southern Lowcountry.* Cambridge Studies on the American South. Cambridge: Cambridge University Press, 2011.

McKinley, Catherine E. *Indigo: In Search of the Color that Seduced the World.* New York: Bloomsbury, 2011.

"Mrs. Abraham Crouch (Sophia Jane Withers)" & "Abraham Crouch," Gibbes Museum of Art, Charleston, SC, http://www.gibbesmuseum.org/miniatures/collection.

Murphy, Brian. *The Root of Wild Madder: Chasing the History, Mystery, and Lore of the Persian Carpet.* New York: Simon & Schuster, 2006.

Myers, Amrita Chakrabarti. *Forging Freedom: Black Women and the Pursuit of Liberty in Antebellum Charleston.* Chapel Hill: The University of North Carolina Press, 2011.

Parker, Rozsika. *The Subversive Stitch: Embroidery and the Making of the Feminine.* New York: I.B. Tauris, 2010.

Pinka, Sharon Fulton. "Lowcountry Chintz: The Townsend/Pope Quilt Legacy," ed. Lynne Zacek Bassett, *Uncoverings* 2013, (Lincoln, NE: American Quilt Study Group).

Powers, Bernard E. *Black Charlestonians: A Social History, 1822–1885.* Fayetteville: The University of Arkansas Press, 1994.

Robertson, David M. *Denmark Vesey: The Buried Story of America's Largest Slave Rebellion.* New York: Vintage, 2009.

Rudisel, Christine and Bob Blaidsell, eds. *Slave Narratives of the Underground Railroad.* Mineola, NY: Dover Thrift Editions, 2014.

Stankiewicz, Mary Ann. "Middle Class Desire: Ornament, Industry, and Emulation in 19th Century Art Education," *Studies in Art Education.* Vol 43, No 4, Summer 2002, 324–338.

Stansell, Christine. *City of Women: Sex and Class in New York, 1780–1860.* Carbondale: University of Illinois, 1987.

The Charleston Museum, *Mosaic Quilts: Paper Template Piecing in the South Carolina Lowcountry* (Greenville, SC: Curious Works Press, 2002).

Tipton-Martin, Toni. *The Jemima Code: Two Centuries of African American Cookbooks.* Austin: University of Texas Press, 2015.

Twitty, Michael W. *The Cooking Gene: A Journey Through African American Culinary History.* New York: Amistad, 2017.

Ulrich, Laurel Thatcher. *The Age of Homespun: Objects and Stories in the Creation of an American Myth.* New York: Vintage, 2009.

Ulrich, Laurel Thatcher. "Of Pens and Needles: Sources for the Study of Early American Women." *Journal of American History.* 77 (1990): 200–207.

Chapter 5: Medicine & Its Failures

Notes

Thank you to Matt Herbison, Archivist, Legacy Center: Archives & Special Collection, College of Medicine, Drexel University, for help with photos of the doctors who graduated from Drexel and for suggesting I look at the embroidered pillow sham.

For more on David Jones Peck's abolitionism and work with Frederick Douglass, see: Brown, Ira V. "An Antislavery Journey: Garrison and Douglass in Pennsylvania, 1847," *Pennsylvania History: A Journal of Mid-Atlantic Studies*, 67, no. 4 (Autumn 2000): 532–550.

For more on Gynecology/Medicine and Enslaved People, please see: Schwartz, Marie Jenkins. *Birthing a Slave: Motherhood and Medicine in the Antebellum South*; Roberts, Dorothy. *Killing the Black Body: Race, Reproduction, and the Meaning of Liberty.* New York: Vintage, 1998; Washington, Harriet A. *Medical Apartheid: The Dark History of Medical Experimentation on Black Americans from Colonial Times to the Present*; Owens, Deirdre Cooper. *Medical Bondage: Race, Gender, and The Origins of American Gynecology*; Ross, Loretta and Rickie Solinger. *Reproductive Justice: An Introduction.* Berkeley: University of California Press, 2017.

p. 147, "A young man goes to the doctor . . ." quotes p. 148, and p. 152 "Research suggests . . ." from Hoffman, Kelly M. and Sophie Trawalter, Jordan R. Axt, and M. Norman Oliver. "Racial bias in pain assessment and treatment recommendations, and false beliefs about biological differences between blacks and whites," *Proceedings of the National Academy of Sciences of the United States of America.* 113, no.16 (April 19, 2016): 4296–4301, Published online April 4, 2016: https://www.ncbi.nlm.nih.gov/pmc/articles/PMC4843483/.

p. 165–168, Sarah Nesnow gathered images of Dr. Hasell Crouch's estate sale and provided contextual information regarding the sale of Jane, John, Eliza, Minerva, Juba, and their children.

Primary Sources

Crumpler, Rebecca Lee. *A Book of Medical Discourses, in Two Parts.* Boston: Cashman, Keating, 1883. Open Knowledge Commons, US National Library of Medicine, https://archive.org/details/67521160R.nlm.nih.gov.

Denman, Thomas, M.D. *An Introduction to the Practice of Midwifery, Seventh Edition with a Biographical Sketch of the Author.* London: E. Cox, 1832. Google Books: https://books.google.com/booksid=ZNZNAQAAMAAJ&printsec=frontcover&source=gbs_ge_summary_r&cad=0#v=onepage&q&f=false.

"Letter from Susan to Eliza Williams," December 10, 1835, Series F: Franklin Cushman's notebooks, vol. 2: 52–54, (Elijah Williams Papers, Rhode Island Historical Society).

"Letter from Hilton to Eliza Williams," May 7, 1836. Series F: Franklin Cushman's notebooks, vol. 2: 56–58, (Elijah Williams Papers, Rhode Island Historical Society).

"Letter from Hilton to his sister," June 1, 1836, Series F: Franklin Cushman's notebooks, vol. 2: 59–60, (Elijah Williams Papers, Rhode Island Historical Society).

"Letter from Susan and Hasell to their sister," June 6, 1836, Series F: Franklin Cushman's notebooks, vol. 2: 61–63, (Elijah Williams Papers, Rhode Island Historical Society).

"Letter from Susan to Eliza Williams," November 5, 1835, Series F: Franklin Cushman's notebooks, vol. 2: 46, (Elijah Williams Papers, Rhode Island Historical Society).

"Letter from Winthrop to Eliza Williams," July 10, 1836, Series F: Franklin Cushman's notebooks, vol. 2: 69–71, (Elijah Williams Papers, Rhode Island Historical Society).

"Letter from Winthrop to his sister Emily," December 2, 1836, Series F: Franklin Cushman's notebooks, vol. 2: 116, (Elijah Williams Papers, Rhode Island Historical Society).

Secondary Sources

"Background on Providence Society for Abolishing the Slave Trade Minute Book," Special Collections and University Archives: UMass Amherst Libraries, scua.library.umass.edu/ead/mums935

Best, Stephen and Saidiya Hartman. "Fugitive Justice," *Representations.* Vol 92, No 1 (Fall 2005) 1–15.

Bolster, W. Jeffrey. "Putting the Ocean in Atlantic History: Maritime Communities and Marine Ecology in the Northwest Atlantic, 1500–1800." *The American Historical Review.* Vol. 113, No. 1 (February 2008) 19–47.

Brunelli, John. "McKisick Explores Different Treatments of Yellow Fever," January 26, 2017. *University of South Carolina.* http://www.sc.edu/uofsc/posts/2017/01/mckissick_museum_black_medicine_white_bodies.php#.W12A_7SpkW9.

Fenn, Elizabeth A. *Pox Americana: The Great Smallpox Epidemic of 1775–82.* New York: Hill and Wang, 2002.

Fett, Sharla M. *Working Cures: Healing, Health, and Power on Southern Slave Plantations.* Chapel Hill: University of North Carolina Press, 2002.

Hartigan-O'Connor, Ellen. "'She Said She Did Not Know Money': Urban Women and Atlantic Markets in the Revolutionary Era." *Early American Studies: An Interdisciplinary Journal.* Vol. 4, No. 2, Fall 2006. 322–352.

Hartman, Saidiya. "Venus in Two Acts," *Small Axe.* Number 26 (Vol 12, Number 2), June 2008, 1–14.

"History of Minorities in Medicine," Office for Diversity and Inclusion, University of Alabama at Birmingham, https://www.uab.edu/medicine/diversity/initiatives/minorities/history.

"History of the Medical College," Medical University of South Carolina, MUSC.edu.

Hoffman, Kelly M. and Sophie Trawalter, Jordan R. Axt, and M. Norman Oliver. "Racial bias in pain assessment and treatment recommendations, and false beliefs about biological differences between blacks and whites," *Proceedings of the National Academy of Sciences of the United States of America.* 113, no.16 (April 19, 2016): 4296–4301, Published online April 4, 2016: https://www.ncbi.nlm.nih.gov/pmc/articles/PMC4843483/.

Hughes, Warren. "Wavering Place Plantation," *Columbia Living Magazine,* (Nov.–Dec. 2016): Culture Posted online November 23, 2016, https://columbialivingmag.com/wavering-place-plantation.

Inglis, Brian. *The History of Medicine.* Cleveland: World Publishing Co., 1965.

"James McCune Smith," Consortium on the History of African Americans in the Medical Professions, University of Virginia, http://chaamp.virginia.edu/node/4028.

Jones, James H. *Bad Blood: The Tuskegee Syphilis Experiment, New and Expanded Edition.* New York: Free Press, 1993.

Judd, Bettina. *Patient.* Pittsburgh: Black Lawrence Press, 2014.

Lombardo, Paul. "Book Review: *Tuskegee's Truths: Rethinking the Tuskegee Syphilis Study," Bulletin of the History of Medicine.* 75.3 (2001): 616–617.

McCandless, Peter. *Slavery, Disease, and Suffering in the Southern Lowcountry.* Cambridge Studies on the American South. Cambridge: Cambridge University Press, 2011.

McGregor, Deborah. *From Midwives to Medicine: The Birth of American Gynecology.* New Brunswick: Rutgers University Press, 1998.

Morgan, Kenneth. "Slave Sales in Colonial Charleston," *The English Historical Review.* 113.453 (Sept. 1998): 905–920.

Morgan, Thomas. "The Education and Medical Practice of Dr. James McCune Smith (1813–1865), first black American to hold a medical degree," *The Journal of the National Medical Association*, 95, no. 7 (July 2003): 603–614, https://www.ncbi.nlm.nih.gov/pmc/articles/PMC2594637/.

Moskowitz, Milton. "The Black Medical Schools Remain the Prime Training Ground for Black Doctors," *The Journal of Blacks in Higher Education*, No. 5 (Autumn 1994): 69–76.

Murphy, Eliza, "Slave Descendant Unites with Plantation Owner for Heartwarming Dinner 181 Years After Families Lived There," ABC News, July 5, 2016. http://abcnews.go.com/Lifestyle/slave-descendant-unites-plantation-owner-heartwarming-dinner-181/story?id=40276632.

Myers, Amrita Chakrabarti. *Forging Freedom: Black Women and the Pursuit of Liberty in Antebellum Charleston.* Chapel Hill: The University of North Carolina Press, 2011.

"Rebecca Lee Crumpler," Changing the Face of Medicine, US National Library of Medicine, National Institutes of Health, June 3, 2015, https://cfmedicine.nlm.nih.gov/physicians/biography_73.html.

Savitt, Todd L. *Medicine and Slavery: The Diseases and Health Care of Blacks in Antebellum Virginia.* Blacks in the New World. Carbondale: University of Illinois Press, 1981.

Skloot, Rebecca. *The Immortal Life of Henrietta Lacks.* New York: Broadway Books, 2011.

Spillers, Hortense J. "Mama's Baby, Papa's Maybe: An American Grammar Book," *Diacritics*, 17, no. 2, Culture and Countermemory: The 'American Connection' (Summer 1987): 64–81.

"U.S. Public Health Service Syphilis Study at Tuskegee," Centers for Disease Control and Prevention, December 22, 2015. https://www.cdc.gov/tuskegee/index.html.

Vlach, John Michael. "The Plantation in an Urban Setting: The Case of the Aiken-Rhett House in Charleston, South Carolina." *Southern Cultures,* Volume 5, Number 4, Winter 1999, 52–69.

Chapter 6: Hickory Root

Notes

For more on women's roles, please see: Pease, Jane H. and Wiliam H. Pease. *Ladies, Women, and Wenches: Choice and Constraint in Antebellum Charleston and Boston.* Chapel Hill: The University of North Carolina Press, 1990; Gillespie, Michele and Susanna Delfino. *Neither Lady Nor Slave: Working Women of the Old South.* Chapel Hill: The University of North Carolina Press, 2002.

p. 171–176, p. 181–190, Sarah Nesnow found the estate sale ads that include mention of Jane as "complete seamstress," as well as Juba Simons' death certificate, and information on Mary Ancrum Walker, her North Carolina plantation, and the people she owned. She also found that as of 1846, Winthrop and Hilton still owed Susan money on her estate including the sale of her enslaved people. I'm grateful to Sarah Nesnow for several long conversations about this information, especially the likelihood that this is the same Juba who was owned by Hasell Crouch, as well as the laws of enslavement and inheritance in South Carolina.

p. 184, "blacksnake root, furrywork, jimpsin weed, one that tie' on the head," Interview with Henry Brown, 637 Grove St., Charleston, SC, *Slave Narratives: A Folk History of the United States from Interviews with Former Slaves,* 1936–1938, Volume XIV, South Carolina Narratives, Part I. Prepared by the Federal Writers' Project of the Works Progress Administration, Project 1655, interviewer Augustus Ladson, Kindle E-Book.

"gypsum tea, which was boiled into a tea and drunk . . ." Gillam Lowden, Greenwood, SC, June 23, 1937. Interviewer G.L. Summer, ed. Elmer Turnage, July 8, 1937. Project 1885, Spartanburg,

District 4. Federal Writers' Project: Slave Narrative Project, Vol. 14, South Carolina, Part 3, Jackson-Quattlebaum: 124. United States Works Progress Administration, Library of Congress, http://hdl.loc.gov/loc.mss/mesn.143.

[Gillam also says, "I 'member de old brick oven our marster had. Dey cooked lots of bread on Sad'day atternoons to last several days. Den we had corn-shuckings. de women had quiltings. Us chaps didn't play many games 'cept marbles, rope-skipping, and jumping high rope. We didn't git to go to school."]

"My white folks give me to de doctors . . ." Sara Brown, Marion, SC, June 1937. Prepared by Annie Ruth Davis. Project 1885-1. Federal Writers' Project: Slave Narrative Project, Vol. 14, South Carolina, Part 3, Jackson-Quattlebaum: 124. United States Works Progress Administration, Library of Congress, http://hdl.loc.gov/loc.mss/mesn.137.

p. 189, "petitioned the court . . ." This was one of the first documents I found on my journey to South Carolina, noting that Hilton had petitioned the court "on the estate of Dr. H.M. Crouch, late of Charleston, . . . that he may be empowered to sell and dispose of the property of said estate consisting of 7 Negroes, a House on Sullivan's Island, ½ pew in St. Philips Church & household furniture for the purpose of making a division . . . It is desirable that the small portions of both widow and child should be consolidated as much as possible, as it is the intention of the widow and child to reside at the North." April 10, 1837, Charleston, SC. "Some Original Charleston Probate Records," *South Carolina Magazine of Ancestral Research,* Vol. 40, Folder p-180 (2012): 159. My thanks to the librarians in the South Carolina History Room at the Charleston County Public Library, for helping me to find this and other information on the family and the people they owned.

p. 190, "Slaves held a market . . ." from Kennedy, Cynthia M. *Braided Relations, Entwined Lives: The Women of Charleston's Urban Slave Society.* Bloomington: Indiana University Press, 2005.

p. 191–192, Romeo Eldridge Phillips quotes Mary Ellen Grissom's *The Negro Sings a New Heaven*: "It is so easy for the Negro to swing from a major to a minor melody that his music is more often thought of as minor than major, whereas a large percentage of it definitely is major. This may explain the popular theory that he creates unusual harmonies. What he really does is to supply his own harmonies and harmonic background as he sings his melody" (42), Phillips, Romeo Eldridge, "Black Folk Music: Setting the Record Straight," *Music Educators Journal,* 60, no. 4 (Dec. 1973): 41–45.

Please see also: Shane White and Graham White. *The Sounds of Slavery: Discovering African American History Through Songs, Sermons, and Speech.* Boston: Beacon, 2005; "Index of Articles about Religious Music," *Black Music Research Journal,* 15, no. 2 (Autumn 1995): 214–218; Sharp, Timothy W. "Halleluja! Spirituals: America's Original Contribution to the World Sacred Music," *The Choral Journal,* 43, no. 8 (March 2003): 95–99; Jones, Arthur C. "The Foundational Influence of Spirituals in African-American Culture: A Psychological Perspective," *Black Research Journal,* 24, no. 2 (Autumn 2004): 251–260; Anderson, Iain. "Reworking Images of a Southern Past: The Commemoration of Slave Music After the Civil War," *Studies in Popular Culture,* 19, no. 2 (October 1995): 167–183; Peach, Douglas Dowling, "*Gullah: The Voice of an Island,* by Liz Kelly, Mark Kendree, and Tevin Turner (review)," *Journal of American Folklore,* 129, no. 511 (Winter 2016): 119–121; Johnson, James Weldon and Rosamond Johnson, *The Books of American Negro Spirituals,* Boston: DaCapo Press, 2002.

p. 195, "Indian or Chinese ink . . ." and subsequent description of tattoo application, Dye, Ira. "The Tattoos of Early American Seafarers, 1796–1818." *Proceedings of the American Philosophical Society* 133, no. 4 (1989): 520–554. Jeffrey W. Bolster cites Ira Dye in his explication of tattoos in *Black Jacks: African American Seamen in the Age of Sail.* Cambridge: Harvard University Press, 1997.

p. 196, "Women of color and white women together dominated . . .," from Cynthia M. Kennedy. *Braided Relations, Entwined Lives: The Women of Charleston's Urban Slave Society.* Bloomington: Indiana University Press, 2005.

p. 198, "1837 was a pivotal year . . ." from "Wedding Bonnet," The Metropolitan Museum of Art, Collection Records, Accession No. 2009.300.1560, https://metmuseum.org/art/collection/search/156289.

SOURCES

Primary Sources

Craft, William and Ellen. *Running a Thousand Miles to Freedom.* Mineola, NY: Dover Thrift Editions, 2014.

Douglass, Federick. *Narrative of the Life of Frederick Douglass.* New York: Dover Publications, Inc., 1995.

Douglass, Frederick and Harriet Jacobs, Austin Steward, William Still, and Booker T. Washington. *Slave Narrative Six Pack 3.* Enhanced Media Publishing Ebook, 2015.

Interview with Gillam Lowden, Greenwood, SC, June 23, 1937. Interviewer G.L. Summer, ed. Elmer Turnage July 8, 1937. Project 1885, Spartanburg, District 4. Federal Writers' Project: Slave Narrative Project, Vol. 14, South Carolina, Part 3, Jackson-Quattlebaum: 124. United States Works Progress Administration, Library of Congress, http://hdl.loc.gov/loc.mss/mesn.143.

Interview with Henry Brown, 637 Grove St., Charleston, SC, *Slave Narratives: A Folk History of the United States from Interviews with Former Slaves,* 1936–1938, Volume XIV, South Carolina Narratives, Part I. Prepared by the Federal Writers' Project of the Works Progress Administration, Project 1655, interviewer Augustus Ladson, Kindle E-Book.

Interview with Sara Brown, Marion, SC, June 1937. Prepared by Annie Ruth Davis. Project 1885-1. Federal Writers' Project: Slave Narrative Project, Vol. 14, South Carolina, Part 3, Jackson-Quattlebaum: 124. United States Works Progress Administration, Library of Congress, http://hdl.loc.gov/loc.mss/mesn.137.

"Letter from Hilton to Eliza Williams," October 8, 1837, Series F: Franklin Cushman's notebooks, vol. 2: 110, (Elijah Williams Papers, Rhode Island Historical Society).

"Letter from Hilton and Winthrop to Brother Harris," October 31, 1837, Series F: Franklin Cushman's notebooks, vol. 2: 111–113, (Elijah Williams Papers, Rhode Island Historical Society).

"Letter from Winthrop to Susan," February 3, 1838, Series F: Franklin Cushman's notebooks, vol. 2: 115, (Elijah Williams Papers, Rhode Island Historical Society).

"Letter from Winthrop to Eliza Williams," August 28, 1835, Series F: Franklin Cushman's notebooks, vol. 2: 26–29, (Elijah Williams Papers, Rhode Island Historical Society).

Prince Hall biography, Documenting the American South, University of North Carolina at Chapel Hill, http://docsouth.unc.edu/neh/bruceje/summary.html.

Secondary Sources

Best, Stephen and Saidiya Hartman. "Fugitive Justice," *Representations.* Vol 92, No 1 (Fall 2005) 1–15.

"Charleston Church Shooting," Special Section, NBC News, https://www.nbcnews.com/storyline/charleston-church-shooting.

Clark-Pujara, Christy. *Dark Work: The Business of Slavery in Rhode Island.* New York: NYU Press, 2016.

Clinton, Catherine. *Harriet Tubman: The Road to Freedom.* New York: Little, Brown, & Co., 2004.

Coates, Ta-Nehisi. *Between the World and Me.* New York: Spiegel and Grau, 2015.

Coates, Ta-Nehisi, "The Case for Reparations," *The Atlantic Monthly*, June 2014, https://www.theatlantic.com/magazine/archive/2014/06/the-case-for-reparations/361631/.

Cromwell, Adelaide M. *The Other Brahmins: Boston's Black Upper Class, 1750–1950.* Fayetteville: The University of Arkansas Press, 1994.

Derrida, Jacques. *Specters of Marx: The State of the Debt, The Work of Mourning & the New International.* New York: Routledge, 2006.

DuBois, W.E.B. *The Souls of Black Folk.* New York: Dover Publications, Inc., 1994.

Dye, Ira. "The Tattoos of Early American Seafarers, 1796–1818." *Proceedings of the American Philosophical Society* 133, no. 4 (1989): 520–554.

Elliott, Debbie. "How a Shooting Changed Charleston's Oldest Black Church," June 8, 2016, https://www.npr.org/sections/codeswitch/2016/06/08/481149042/how-a-shooting-changed-charlestons-oldest-black-church.

Fanon, Frantz. *Black Skin, White Masks*. New York: Grove Press, 1952.

Farrow, Anne, Joel Lang, and Jenifer Frank. *Complicity: How the North Promoted, Prolonged, and Profited from Slavery*. New York: Ballantine Books, 2006.

Fett, Sharla M. *Working Cures: Healing, Health, and Power on Southern Slave Plantations*. Chapel Hill: University of North Carolina Press, 2002.

Foner, Eric. *Gateway to Freedom: The Hidden History of the Underground Railroad*. New York: W.W. Norton & Co., 2015.

Foucault, Michel. "Discipline and Punish: The Birth of the Prison," *The Norton Anthology of Theory and Criticism*, Second Edition, Ed. Vincent B. Leitch. New York: W.W. Norton & Co., 2010. 1490–1502.

Foucault, Michel. *The History of Sexuality, Vol. 2: The Use of Pleasure*, trans. Robert Hurley. New York: Vintage Books, 1985.

Glymph, Thavolia. *Out of the House of Bondage: The Transformation of the Plantation Household*. New York: Cambridge University Press, 2008.

Gordon, Avery. *Ghostly Matters: Hauntings and the Sociological Imagination*. Minneapolis: University of Minnesota Press, 2008.

Hartigan-O'Connor, Ellen. "'She Said She Did Not Know Money': Urban Women and Atlantic Markets in the Revolutionary Era." *Early American Studies: An Interdisciplinary Journal*. Vol. 4, No. 2, Fall 2006. 322–352.

Hartman, Saidiya. "Venus in Two Acts," *Small Axe*. Number 26 (Vol 12, Number 2), June 2008, 1–14.

"History," Emanuel African Methodist Episcopal Church, Charleston, SC, http://www.emanuelamechurch.org/pages/staff/.

Horton, James Oliver and Horton, Lois E. *Black Bostonians; Family Life and Community Struggle in the Antebellum North, Revised Edition*. New York: Holmes & Meier, 1999.

Kennedy, Cynthia M. *Braided Relations, Entwined Lives: The Women of Charleston's Urban Slave Society*. Bloomington: Indiana University Press, 2005.

Levesque, George A. *Black Boston: African American Life and Culture in Urban America, 1750–1860*. New York: Garland Publishing, 1994.

McCandless, Peter. *Slavery, Disease, and Suffering in the Southern Lowcountry*. Cambridge Studies on the American South. Cambridge: Cambridge University Press, 2011.

McGregor, Deborah. *From Midwives to Medicine: The Birth of American Gynecology*. New Brunswick: Rutgers University Press, 1998. Myers, Amrita Chakrabarti. *Forging Freedom: Black Women and the Pursuit of Liberty in Antebellum Charleston*. Chapel Hill: The University of North Carolina Press, 2011.

Philip, M. NourbeSe, "Interview with Rachel May's Creative Writing Class," *The Ocean State Review*, The University of Rhode Island, Summer 2014; excerpt published online: http://oceanstatereview.org/2014/04/14/m-nourbese-philip-visits-rachel-mays-cw-class/.

Philip, M. NourbeSe. *Zong! As Told to the Author by Setaey Adamu Boateng*. Connecticut: Wesleyan University Press, 2008.

Phillips, Romeo Eldridge, "Black Folk Music: Setting the Record Straight," *Music Educators Journal*, 60, no. 4 (Dec. 1973): 41–45.

Phipps, Whintley, "Bill and Gloria Gaither: Amazing Grace Live," April 6, 2012, https://www.youtube.com/watch?v=qNuQbJst4Lk.

Powers, Bernard E. *Black Charlestonians: A Social History, 1822–1885*. Fayetteville: The University of Arkansas Press, 1994.

"President Obama Delivers Eulogy in Charleston," by Associated Press, posted online by *The New York Times*, June 26, 2015, https://www.nytimes.com/video/us/100000003767801/obama-delivers-eulogy-in-charleston.html.

Rankine, Claudia. *Citizen: An American Lyric*. Minneapolis: Graywolf Press, 2014.

Rudisel, Christine and Bob Blaidsell, eds. *Slave Narratives of the Underground Railroad*. Mineola, NY: Dover Thrift Editions, 2014.

Saunders, Patricia J. "Fugitive Dreams of Diaspora: Conversations with Saidiya Hartman," *Anthurium: A Caribbean Studies Journal*, 6, no. 1, Article 7 (June 2008), http://scholarlyrepository.miami.edu/cgi/viewcontent.cgi?article=1155&context=anthurium.

Savitt, Todd L. *Medicine and Slavery: The Diseases and Health Care of Blacks in Antebellum Virginia.* Champaign: University of Illinois Press, 1981.

Smith, Glenn and Jennifer Berry Hawes, Abigail Darlington, "Dylann Roof sentenced to death for Emanuel AME Church massacre," *Post and Courier,* January 10, 2017, https://www.postandcourier.com/church_shooting/dylann-roof-sentenced-to-death-for-emanuel-ame-church-massacre/article_3c24cc44-d729-11e6-9e5d-2f037e89bddc.html.

Spillers, Hortense J. "Mama's Baby, Papa's Maybe: An American Grammar Book," *Diacritics*, 17, no. 2, Culture and Countermemory: The 'American Connection' (Summer 1987): 64–81.

"The Limitations of the Slave Narrative Collection," and "Appendix II: Race of Interviewers," *Born in Slavery: Slave Narratives from the Federal Writers' Project, 1936–1938.* https://www.loc.gov/collections/slave-narratives-from-the-federal-writers-project-1936-to-1938/articles-and-essays/introduction-to-the-wpa-slave-narratives/.

White, Deborah Gray. *Ar'n't I a Woman? Female Slaves in the Plantation South.* New York: W.W. Norton & Co., 1999.

Chapter 7: The Leonids: A Sermon in Patchwork

Notes

The 1833 Leonids were also described in Lakota winter counts by Battiste Good, Lone Dog, The Flame, Major Bush, The Swan, American Horse, Rosebud, No Ears, and Cloud Shield, as described by Burke, Christina E. and Russell Thornton assisted by Dakota Goodhouse, eds. "Winter by Winter," in *The Year the Stars Fell: Lakota Winter Counts at the Smithsonian*, Candace S. Greene and Russell Thornton, eds. Washington, D.C.: Smithsonian Institution, 2007.

Scientist Agnes Mary Clerke described the showers as follows: "On the night of November 12–13, 1833, a tempest of falling stars broke over the Earth . . . The sky was scored in every direction with shining tracks and illuminated with majestic fireballs. At Boston, the frequency of meteors was estimated to be about half that of flakes of snow in an average snowstorm. Their numbers . . . were quite beyond counting; but as it waned, a reckoning was attempted, from which it was computed, on the basis of that much-diminished rate, that 240,000 must have been visible during the nine hours they continued to fall."

p. 216: Sarah Nesnow provided information about people enslaved by Mary Ancrum Walker.

For more on Harriet Powers' quilt, please see also: Gladys-Marie Fry, "'A Sermon in Patchwork': New Light on Harriet Powers," *Singular Women: Writing the Artist*, eds. Kristen Frederikson and Sarah E. Webb. (Berkeley: University of California Press, 2003); Anita Zaleski Weinraub, *Georgia Quilts: Piecing Together a History.* (Athens: University of Georgia Press, 2006).

Primary Sources

Clerke, Agnes Mary. *A Popular History of Astronomy During the Nineteenth Century.* London: Adam and Charles Black, 1902. Google E-Book, https://books.google.com/books?id=lvARAAAAYAAJ&printsec=frontcover&source=gbs_ge_summary_r&cad=0#v=onepage&q&f=false.

"Eyewitness Accounts of the 1966 Leonid Storm," Leonids: Leonid Multi-Instrument Aircraft Campaign, National Aeronautics and Space Administration, https://leonid.arc.nasa.gov/1966.html.

Powers, Harriet. "Bible Quilt, 1885–1886," Smithsonian National Museum of American History, Accession Number 283472, http://americanhistory.si.edu/collections/search/object/nmah_556462.

Powers, Harriet. "Pictorial Quilt," Museum of Fine Arts Boston, Accession Number 64.619, http://www.mfa.org/collections/object/pictorial-quilt-116166.

Secondary Sources

Cash, Floris Barnett. "Kinship and Quilting: An Examination of an African-American Tradition," *The Journal of Negro History*. Vol 80, No 1 (Winter 1995), 30–41.

Fry, Gladys-Marie. "'A Sermon in Patchwork': New Light on Harriet Powers," *Singular Women: Writing the Artist*, Kristen Frederickson and Sarah E. Webb, eds. Berkeley: University of California Press, 2003. http://ark.cdlib.org/ark:/13030/kt5b69q3pk/

https://publishing.cdlib.org/ucpressebooks/view?docId=kt5b69q3pk;chunk.id=ch06;doc.view=print.

Fry, Gladys-Marie. *Stitched from the Soul: Slave Quilts from the Antebellum South*. Chapel Hill: The University of North Carolina Press, 2002.

Georges, Robert A. and Michael Owen Jones. *Folkloristics: An Introduction*. Bloomington: Indiana University Press, 1995.

Glymph, Thavolia. *Out of the House of Bondage: The Transformation of the Plantation Household*. New York: Cambridge University Press, 2012.

Hicks, Kyra E. *This I Accomplish: Harriet Powers' Bible Quilt and Other Pieces*. Black Threads Press, 2010.

Hughes, D.W. "The World's Most Famous Meteor Shower Picture," *Earth, Moon, and Planets*, 68, issue 1–3 (January 1995): 311–322, Digital Library for Physics and Astronomy, High Energy Astrophysics Division, Harvard-Smithsonian Center for Astrophysics, http://adsabs.harvard.edu/full/1995EM%26P...68..311H.

Kennedy, Cynthia M. *Braided Relations, Entwined Lives: The Women of Charleston's Urban Slave Society*. Bloomington: Indiana University Press, 2005.

McCandless, Peter. *Slavery, Disease, and Suffering in the Southern Lowcountry*. Cambridge Studies on the American South. Cambridge: Cambridge University Press, 2011.

Milon, D. "Observing the 1966 Leonids," *Journal of the British Astronomical Association*, 77: 89–93, Digital Library for Physics and Astronomy, High Energy Astrophysics Division, Harvard-Smithsonian Center for Astrophysics, http://adsabs.harvard.edu/full/1967JBAA...77...89M.

Myers, Amrita Chakrabarti. *Forging Freedom: Black Women and the Pursuit of Liberty in Antebellum Charleston*. Chapel Hill: The University of North Carolina Press, 2011.

Perlerin, Vincent. "50th Anniversary of the famous 1966 Leonid storm," *American Meteor Society*, 17 November 2016. https://www.amsmeteors.org/2016/11/50th-anniversary-of-the-famous-1966-leonid-storm/.

Powers, Bernard E., Jr. *Black Charlestonians: A Social History, 1822–1885*. Fayetteville: The University of Arkansas Press, 1994.

Ulrich, Laurel Thatcher. "'A Quilt Unlike Any Other': Rediscovering the Work of Harriet Powers," *Writing Women's History: A Tribute to Anne Firor Scott*, Ed. Elizabeth Anne Payne. Jackson: University Press of Mississippi, 2011.

Vergano, Dan. "1833 Meteor Storm Started Citizen Science," Human Journey, *National Geographic*, August 30, 2014, https://blog.nationalgeographic.org/2014/08/30/1833-meteor-storm-started-citizen-science/.

Whitehouse, David. "The Night the Stars Fell," *BBC News*, November, 18, 1998. http://news.bbc.co.uk/2/hi/special_report/1998/11/98/the_leonids_98/213715.stm.

Winkler, Lisa K. "The Kentucky Derby's Forgotten Jockeys," *Smithsonian.com*, April 23, 2009.

Chapter 8: Even There

Notes

The title of this chapter is from: Wilson, Harriet. *Our Nig; or, Sketches from the Life of a Free Black, in a Two-Story White House, North, Showing that Slavery's Shadows Fall Even There*, first published by George C. Rand and Avery, 1859, this edition ed. P. Gabrielle Foreman and Reginald H. Pitts, New York: Penguin Books, 2005.

The South County History Center in Kingston, RI, holds the mural by Ernest Hamlin Baker, "The Economic Activities of the Narragansett Planters," 1939, which depicts overseers and enslaved people working on the South County plantations. Viewing this mural near Rhode Island's woods and farmlands is a stark reminder of the realities of enslavement in the north.

For more on the Great Swamp Fight, King Philip's War, and Massachuset, Narragansett, Wampanoag, and Nitmuk history and European colonialism, please see: Lisa Brooks, *The Recovery of Native Space in the Northeast*. Indigenous Americas. Minneapolis: University of Minnesota Press, 2008; Lisa Brooks, *Our Beloved Kin: A New History of King Philip's War*. The Henry Roe Cloud Series on American Indians and Modernity, Minneapolis: University of Minnesota Press, 2008; Jean M. O'Brien, *Firsting and Lasting: Writing Indians out of Existence in New England*. Indigenous Americas Minneapolis: University of Minnesota Press, 2010.

Recent texts on the intersection of Native American and African American history and enslavement include: Brett Rushforth, *Bonds of Alliance: Indigenous and Atlantic Slaveries in New France*. Omohundro Institute of Early American History and Culture and the University of North Carolina Press (Chapel Hill: University of North Carolina Press, 2014); Ellen Newell. *Brethren by Nature: Indians, Colonists, and the Origins of American Slavery*. Ithaca: Cornell University Press, 2016; Reséndez, Andrés. *The Other Slavery: The Uncovered Story of Indian Enslavement in America*. New York: Houghton Mifflin Harcourt, 2016; Warren, Wendy. *New England Bound: Slavery and Colonization in Early America*. New York: Liveright, 2017; Dunbar-Ortiz, Roxane, *An Indigenous Peoples' History of the United States*. Boston: Beacon Press, 2015; Gailay, Alan, ed. *Indian Slavery in Colonial America*. Lincoln: University of Nebraska Press, 2009.

p. 228, Zora Neale Hurston's *Their Eyes Were Watching God* opens: "Ships at a distance have every man's wish on board. For some they come in with the tide. For others they sail forever on the horizon, never out of sight, never landing until the Watcher turns his eyes away in resignation, his dreams mocked to death by Time. That is the life of men. Now, women forget all those things they don't want to remember, and remember everything they don't want to forget. The dream is the truth. Then they act and do things accordingly."

p. 238–239: The stones are now being cleaned to help preserve them. "Grave Concerns," *Newport Daily News*, April 10, 2016, http://www.newportri.com/newportdailynews/news/page_one/grave-concerns/article_da43936f-6f44-5ac3-ac96-21a006301963.html.

Primary Sources

Collection of The Historic Indian Agency House at Fort Winnebago.

Collection of the Old Slave Mart Museum, Charleston, SC.

Collection of the National Museum of African American History and Culture, Washington, DC.

Cooper, James Fenimore. *The Water Witch or, The Skimmer of the Seas*.

Equiano, Olaudah, *The Interesting Narrative of the Life of Olaudah Equiano, or, Gustavus Vassa, the African, Written by Himself*. New York: HarperTorch, 2014. E-book.

Goodnough, Abby. "Harvard Professor Jailed: Officer is Accused of Bias," July 20, 2009, http://www.nytimes.com/2009/07/21/us/21gates.html.

"Letter from Winthrop to Eliza Williams," July 29, 1839, Series F: Franklin Cushman's notebooks, Vol. 2: 139–140, (Elijah Williams Papers, Rhode Island Historical Society).

Stoney, Peter G. *List and Memorandum Book: Names of Negroes at Calibogue 1829*. South Carolina Historical Society manuscript, College of Charleston. 34/707.

White, Alonzo. *List book of negroes for sale*. 1853–1863. South Carolina Historical Society manuscript. 34/0350.

Young, Kevin. *Ardency: A Chronicle of the Amistad Rebels*. New York: Knopf, 2012.

Secondary Sources

Alford, Terry. *Prince Among Slaves: The True Story of an African Prince Sold into Slavery in the American South*. 30th Anniversary Edition. Oxford: Oxford University Press, 2007.

Braxton, Lisa and Alex Reid. "Boston: Origin of Slavery," Illustrated Talk, March 18, 2015, Royall House and Slave Quarters, Medford, MA, http://www.royallhouse.org/whats-happening/news-and-events/past-events/.

SOURCES

Bridenbaugh, Carl. "Charlestonians at Newport," *The South Carolina Historical and Genealogical Magazine*, 1767–1765. Vol. XLI, April, 1940, no 2.

Bridenbaugh, Carl. "Colonial Newport as a Summer Resort," *Rhode Island Historical Society Collections*. Vol. XXVL, January 1933, No. 1. (1–23).

Brown University Steering Committee on Slavery and Justice, *Slavery and Justice*. Providence, RI.

Camp, Stephanie M.H. *Closer to Freedom: Enslaved Women & Everyday Resistance in the Plantation South*. Chapel Hill: The University of North Carolina Press, 1994.

Cromwell, Adelaide. *Boston's Other Brahmin's: Boston's Black Upperclass, 1750–1950*. Fayetteville: University of Arkansas Press, 1994.

Davis, Paul. "Unrighteous Traffick: Rhode Island and the Slave Trade," *The Providence Journal*. Special Report, March 2006. Pettaquamscutt Historical Society, October 18, 2014.

Farrow, Anne, Joel Lang, and Jenifer Frank. *Complicity: How the North Promoted, Prolonged, and Profited from Slavery*. New York: Ballantine Books, 2006.

Fitts, Robert K. "The Landscapes of Northern Bondage," *Inventing New England's Slave Paradise: Master/Slave Relations in Eighteenth Century Narragansett, Rhode Island*. Studies in African American History and Culture. Routledge, 1998. Pettaquamscutt Historical Society, October 18, 2014.

Franklin, Susan B. "Early History of Negroes in Newport, An Address Before the Union Congregational Church," Newport, Rhode Island. Pettaquamscutt Historical Society, October 18, 2014.

Gaspar, David Barry and Darlene Clark Hine. *More than Chattel: Black Women and Slavery in the Americas*. Bloomington: Indiana University Press, 1996.

Gilkeson, John S., Jr. *Middle-Class Providence, 1820–1940*. Princeton: Princeton University Press, 1986.

Glymph, Thavolia. *Out of the House of Bondage: The Transformation of the Plantation Household*. New York: Cambridge University Press, 2008.

"God's Little Acre," *The Washington Times*, September 21, 2004, https://www.washingtontimes.com/news/2004/sep/21/20040921-110704-9800r/

Denease, Tammy. "Compelled to Servitude: The Story of Belinda," performance by storyteller Tammy Denease. 3 October 2015, Royall House and Slave Quarters, Medford, MA.

Jaffee, David. *A New Nation of Goods: The Material Culture of Early America*. Philadelphia: University of Pennsylvania Press, 2010.

Jones, Rhett S. "Plantation Slavery in Narragansett County, Rhode Island, 1690–1790: A Preliminary Study," *Plantation Society* II, no. 2, (December 1986): 157–170. South County History Center, Kingston, RI, October 18, 2014.

Kalin, Andrea and Bill Duke, directors. *Prince Among Slaves*. PBS Studios, 2008.

Kinzie, Juliette. *Wau-Bun: The "Early Day" in the Northwest*. Menasha, WI: The Collegiate Press, 1948.

Kirk, William. A Modern City: Providence, Rhode Island and Its Activities. Chicago: The University of Chicago Press, 1909.

Lemire, Elise. *Black Walden: Slavery and Its Aftermath in Concord, Massachusetts*. Philadelphia: University of Pennsylvania Press, 2009.

Lemons, J. Stanley. "Rhode Island and the Slave Trade," *Rhode Island History* 60, no. 1 (2002): 101.

Lewis, Catherine M. and Richard J. Lewis. *Women and Slavery in America: A Documentary History*. Fayetteville: University of Arkansas Press, 2011.

McBurney, Christian M. *A History of Kingston, R.I., 1700–1900: Heart of Rural South County*. Kingston, RI: Pettaquamscutt Historical Society, 2004.

Melish, Joanne Pope. *Disowning Slavery: Gradual Emancipation and "Race" in New England, 1780–1895*. Ithaca, NY: Cornell University Press, 2015.

Selig, Robert. "Washington-Rochambeau Revolutionary Route," Washington-Rochambeau Revolutionary Route Resource Study & Environmental Assessment, 2006. National Park Service. https://www.nps.gov/waro/learn/historyculture/washington-rochambeau-revolutionary-route.htm.

Smith, Andy. "Couple's burial ground research details black life in Colonial Newport," *Providence Journal,* 23 February 2014. http://www.providencejournal.com/features/lifestyle/content/20140223-couples-burial-ground-research-details-black-life-in-colonial-newport.ece.

Stokes, Keith and Theresa Guzmán Stokes. *God's Little Acre: America's Colonial African Cemetery.* http://www.colonialcemetery.com/.

Stokes, Keith and Theresa Guzmán Stokes. *1696 Heritage Group.* http://www.1696heritage.com/.

Chapter 9: Canuto Matanew

Notes

Bernardo (Nelson) Valmaseda Mendoza kindly provided information about the history and culture of Trinidad, Cuba, on a guided tour through the town and museums. I'm grateful for the time and knowledge he shared with me.

Email from Professor Manuel Barcia, University of Leeds, August 5, 2017 & August 7, 2017:

Dr. Barcia noted that we can't know for sure when the brick was made. He suggested that, though we have no way of knowing for sure, it might have been inscribed by a Creole slave or free man, perhaps an overseer, as the handwriting might indicate that the person was literate. He suggested searching the plantation archive, but I was told that there are no records to tell us more about the possible origins of the brick nor about Canuto Matanew.

For more on the transatlantic slave trade, please see: Marcus Rediker, *The Slave Ship: A Human History.* New York: Penguin Books, 2008; Thomas, Hugh, *The Slave Trade: The Story of the Atlantic Slave Trade.* New York: Simon & Schuster, 1999; Eltis, David and David Richardson, afterword David W. Blight, Foreword Brion Davis. *Atlas of the Transatlantic Slave Trade.* New Haven: Yale University Press, 2015; Lisa A. Lindsay, *Captives as Commodities: The Transatlantic Slave Trade.* New York: Pearson, 2007; Gregory E. O'Malley, *Final Passages: The Intercolonial Slave Trade of British American, 1619–1807.* Omohundro Institute of Early American History and Culture and the University of North Carolina Press. Chapel Hill: University of North Carolina Press, 2016; Sowande M. Mustakeem, *Slavery at Sea: Terror, Sex, and Sickness in the Middle Passage*, New Black Studies Series. Champaign: University of Illinois Press, 2016.

Katrina Browne, descendant of the DeWolf family, produced a film on her family's legacy, "Traces of the Trade: A Story from the Deep North," and speaks widely as part of her advocacy work. As part of the documentary journey, the family visited a DeWolf sugar plantation in Cuba. http://www.tracesofthetrade.org/family/ I viewed a screening at The University of Rhode Island during the 2014–2015 school year, followed by a Q&A with Katrina. Some family members maintain a website and have been active in helping to establish the Center for Reconciliation in Providence: http://cfrri.org/index.php/our-team/.

The Rhode Island Episcopal Diocese is planning a Center for Reconciliation in acknowledgement of both the state and the Diocese's long involvement with the trans-Atlantic slave trade in the 17th and 18th centuries.

Rhode Island merchants may have controlled as much as 90 percent of the American trade in African slaves in the years following the Revolution, and the state was once called "the Deep North" for its heavy involvement." https://www.episcopalri.org/rhode-island-episcopal-church-confronts-slave-trading-past-2/.

In addition to papers that include "Havana," there are many in the back of the quilt tops that mention Barbados and the West Indies. I chose to visit Cuba because of the existence of plantation ruins there.

For more on the history of Cuba and enslavement in Cuba, please see: Ada Ferrer, *Freedom's Mirror: Cuba and Haiti in the Age of Revolution*, Cambridge: Cambridge University Press, 2014; C.L.R. James, *The Black Jacobins: Toussaint L'Ouverture and the San Domingo Revolution*, New York: Vintage, 1989; David Wheat, *Atlantic Africa and the Spanish Caribbean, 1570–1640.* Omohundro Institute and the University of North Carolina Press, 2016.

p. 287, "Finding evidence of 'games' and leisure . . ." "Slave Life at the Royall House," Royall House and Slave Quarters, http://www.royallhouse.org/slavery/slave-life/.

SOURCES

Primary Sources

Belinda's Petition to the Massachusetts General Court, February 14, 1783, Massachusetts Archives, transcribed by the Royall House and Slave Quarters: http://www.royallhouse.org/belinda-suttons-1783-petition-full-text/.

Denease, Tammy. "Compelled to Servitude: The Story of Belinda," performance by storyteller Tammy Denease. October 3, 2015, Royall House and Slave Quarters, Medford, MA.

Digital Archive of Massachusetts Anti-Slavery and Anti-Segregation Petitions, Massachusetts Archives, Boston MA, 2015, "Council; Council Files March 13, 1788, GC3/series 378, Petition of Belinda Sutton", doi:10.7910/DVN/J8CWB, Harvard Dataverse, V3.

Digital Archive of Massachusetts Anti-Slavery and Anti-Segregation Petitions, Massachusetts Archives, Boston MA, 2015, "House Unpassed Legislation 1785, Docket 1707, SC1/series 230, Petition of Belinda Royall", doi:10.7910/DVN/1ZHSM, Harvard Dataverse, V2.

Digital Archive of Massachusetts Anti-Slavery and Anti-Segregation Petitions, Massachusetts Archives, Boston MA, 2015, "Senate Unpassed Legislation 1795, Docket 2007, SC1/series 231, Petition of Belinda Sutton", doi:10.7910/DVN/H5VLP, Harvard Dataverse, V5.

Franklin's note "fire-breathing southerner," Series F: Franklin Cushman's notebooks, vol. 2: 29–30, (Elijah Williams Papers, Rhode Island Historical Society).

Jason Williams Papers, Elijah Williams Papers, Rhode Island Historical Society.

"Letter from Winthrop to Eliza Williams," August 28, 1835, Series F: Franklin Cushman's notebooks, vol. 2: 26–29, (Elijah Williams Papers, Rhode Island Historical Society).

"Mary Ann: Plot maps of the grounds and gardens, ca. 1820," Double-oversized Box 1, *Sub-series 1. Mary Ann.* Series III: Plantation Accounts, 1818–1852 Records of supplies, maps, receipts and slave lists for the family's Cuban coffee and sugar plantations. MSS 382, DeWolf Papers, 1751–1864, Rhode Island Historical Society.

Passed Resolves; Resolves 1787, c. 142, SC1/series 228, Petition of Belinda, Digital Archive of Massachusetts Anti-Slavery and Anti-Segregation Petitions, Massachusetts Archives, Boston, MA, 2015 doi:10.7910/DVN/XFFLL, Harvard Dataverse, V3.

Survey of Federal Archives, *Ship Registers and Enrollments of Providence, Rhode Island, 1773–1939,* The National Archives Project, 1941, Hathi Trust Digital Library: https://catalog.hathitrust.org/Record/000968977.

Secondary Sources

Allahar, Anton L. "Slaves, Slave Merchants, and Slave Owners in 19th Century Cuba." *Caribbean Studies.* Vo. 21, No 1/2 (Jan.–June 1988), 158–191.

Barcia, Manuel. *The Great African Slave Revolt of 1825: Cuba and the Fight for Freedom in Matanzas.* Baton Rouge: Louisiana State University Press, 2012.

Clark-Pujara, Christy. *Dark Work: The Business of Slavery in Rhode Island.* New York: NYU Press, 2016.

Coughtry, Jay. *The Notorious Triangle: Rhode Island and the African Slave Trade, 1700–1807.* Philadelphia: Temple University Press, 1981.

hooks, bell. *Art on My Mind: Visual Politics.* New York: The New Press, 1995.

Marques, Leonardo. *The United States and the Transatlantic Slave Trade to the Americas, 1776–1867.* New Haven, CT: Yale University Press, 2016.

McBurney, Christian M. *A History of Kingston, R.I., 1700–1900: Heart of Rural South County.* Kingston, RI: Pettaquamscutt Historical Society, 2004.

Rediker, Marcus. *The Amistad Rebellion: An Atlantic Odyssey of Slavery and Freedom.* New York: Penguin Books, 2013.

Rodriguez, Garcia and Nancy L. Westrate. *Voices of the Enslaved in Nineteenth-Century Cuba: A Documentary History.* Chapel Hill: The University of North Carolina Press, 2011.

Smith, Roberta. "Sugar? Sure, but Salted with Meaning: 'A Subtlety, or the Marvelous Sugar Baby,' at the Domino Sugar Plant," *The New York Times.* May 11, 2014.

Trinidad, Cuba, Y El Valle De Lose Ingenios. Guia de Arquitectura. Trinidad: Assamblea Municipal del Poder Popular de Trinidad, 2003.

Chapter 10: An Abomination

Notes

Harriet Thorne (Hilton's wife) writes to Susan, 9 February 1837, the following account, explaining that Susan's enslaved people were sold. Until then, they had been rented out. Minerva was sick with scarlet fever in the summer of 1837, and Harriet wrote that they would sell her as soon as she was well in order to better "invest" the money from her sale. Eliza, Hilton wrote, paid her wages to the family from being rented out every month—six dollars and fifty cents. A man named Mr. Poole was renting the boy John, and since Mr. Poole had said he'd buy John's clothes (thus no expense to the Williamses), the Williamses decided to keep renting him out until they were ready to sell him. Harriet wrote, "Your negroes have been sold I suppose you have had an account of the sales from Winthrop so it would be useless for me to repeat them, we intend to let John stay with Poole a year longer, he is too small for us yet, and I do not think he could be in a better place you would scarcely know Jenny she has grown so fleshy and looks so happy she inquired after you and little Emily. My Negroes are all well. Hilton has Peter in the mill we get fourteen dollars a month. Lavinia behaves very well, she is so afraid of my selling her she would do anything I propose. I have no fault to find with her at all . . . they [Eliza] liked to have lost a negro the other night, Gilbert with the Quinsy, the same complaint that Osceola died with you must have seen an account of his death in the paper unfortunate Chief he would not let a Physician attend him. An old Indian doctor that had cured him before administered, he might of cured him again if they had been in the Woods when he could have had access to roots and herbs but it was folly to attempt it shut up as they were, he is no more, and his life could have been easily saved if they would have suffered a Physician to attend him however I think he would have died from grief, his countenance was the Picture of Melancholly—Tell Mother I have not had but one of the plates broken she gave me. Maybe she will think that is one too many but in our land of Slaves we think that is doing well in three months to have but one piece Broken." Series F, Vol. 8, 74–76 (Elijah Williams Papers, Rhode Island Historical Society).

Winthrop goes on to describe his encounter with Osceola in the letter that was also published in the *South Carolina Historical Magazine* in 1964.

Franklin makes note of the economic crisis. He writes that in "1836, The Second U.S. Bank was about to expire under Jackson's opposition, withdrawing the funds of the United States and distributing them in Pet Banks and Wild Cat Banks.12½ ¢ = York shilling (NY) 6¼ ¢ = sixpence (NY)." Winthrop's letter follows: "Enclosed I send $50.00 in Bills on the U.S. Bank, which I want Father to get into 10 cent and 5 cent pieces and ship them in an unsuspicious way to Hilton's care in Charleston who will forward them to me on their arrival there put them in such shape as they will come safe without being known what they are, say for instance in the middle of a Bbl. packed as Crockery or any way that you think the best and safest. 10 cent and 5 cent pieces pass here for 12½ cts and 6¼ cts and as I have an opportunity to get rid of a great many besides being very handy as change I will try to speculate for once in my life—say nothing to any one about it,—for if it succeeds well I may be induced to try it again, Whatever expense it may be to you, you can retain out of it I presume it will not be much trouble to get them if you do not let your object be known—You will write me immediately upon the receipt of this for I shall be anxious to know if it arrives safe." January 24, 1836, Series F, vol 1: 92 (Elijah Williams Papers, Rhode Island Historical Society).

p. 292–293, Information on Patty and Amelia was found by Sarah Nesnow.

p. 292, Winthrop shot himself in the hand: "Winthrop met with an accident on Thursday last which came very near being a serious one he started very early in the morning to shoot Marsh Hens, went over the River to James Island in a small canoe with only a negro man to paddle the Canoe in attempting to land on the Island, his gun went off he having the muzzle in his hand, the charge shot away the Fleshy part of his Thumb, Sixteen of the shot went into his arm + Brest two through his cheek into his mouth and one through his Ear, the Rim of his Hat is riddled." (Vol. 3: 31) I wonder if it was the man who paddled the canoe who saved Winthrop that day.

p. 294: For more on Nat Turner's rebellion and the subsequent history, see: David F. Allmendinger, Jr., *Nat Turner and the Rising in Southampton County*, Baltimore: Johns Hopkins University Press, 2014; Davis, Mary Kemp, *Nat Turner before the bar of judgment: Fictional treatments of the Southampton slave insurrection*, Baton Rouge: Louisiana State University Press, 1999; Foner, Eric, compiler, *Nat Turner*, Englewood Cliffs, NJ: Prentice Hall, 1971; Alfred L. Brophy, "The Nat Turner Trials," North Carolina Law Review, 91.5 (June 2013): 1817+; John Mac Kilgore, "Nat Turner and the Work of Enthusiasm," Publications of the Modern Language Association of America. Vol. 130, 5 (October 2015): 1347-1362; Shaun O'Connell, "Unhealed Cultural Memories: Styron's Nat Turner," *New England Journal of Public Policy*, Vol. 28, 2 (January 1, 2018): 1-...; Stephen B. Oates, *The Fires of Jubilee: Nat Turner's Fierce Rebellion*. New York: Harper Perennial, 2016; Patrick H. Breen, *The Land Shall be Deluged in Blood: A New History of the Nat Turner Revolt*, Oxford: Oxford University Press, 2016; Kenneth S. Greenberg, *Nat Turner" A Slave Rebellion in History and Memory*. Oxford: Oxford University Press, 2004.

Nat Turner's remains were recently returned to his family: Javonte Anderson, "Descendants of Nat Turner honored in Gary," *Chicago Tribune*, 7 October 2016. http://www.chicagotribune.com/suburbs/post-tribune/news/ct-ptb-nat-turner-skull-st-1008-20161007-story.html. Lon Wagner, "Nat Turner's skull turns up far from site of his revolt," *Baltimore Sun*, June 15, 2003, http://articles.baltimoresun.com/2003-06-15/news/0306150247_1_nat-turner-benjamin-turner-skull

For more on Denmark Vesey, please see notes to Chapter 4.

p. 301, The commemorative presidential fabric is printed in red with the date 1829. The URI Historic Textile and Costume Collection owns a length of the same fabric in blue. As for the black and white fabric with parrots, Colonial Williamsburg Foundation owns a similar piece of fabric donated by Franklin R. Cushman. The fabric in the Williamsburg collection is white and "china blue" (the pieces in the Cushman quilt are black and white), and it is dated 1774–1811. The piece at Williamsburg is said to have been a remnant from fabric used for chair and window seat covers, and window curtain tiebacks. Form No. 148, Curator's Worksheet, Accession No. 51-364, 1–2, The Colonial Williamsburg Foundation, Williamsburg, Virginia.

p. 304, In the 1960s, when the letter from Winthrop describing Osceola was published, the letter was held by the Gaud family in South Carolina; it's now in the Rhode Island Historical Society.

p. 308, There are several letters from Eliza Williams, Emily Williams, and Sarah Williams. In one, they mention that they've found a new doctor who knows about "breasts," and is able to help with issues around breastfeeding, and in another, they say they deterred a gossiping neighbor who asked whether or not Susan had a new beau.

p. 322, Sarah Nesnow found Jane Jones listed in these records. Jane Jones (previously listed in Zion Presbyterian's Records as Jane Thorn, "servant of Mrs. E. H. Williams," Hilton's wife) is not the same Jane as the woman who was owned by Hasell and Susan. There are no mentions of Jane Jones in the letters from Hilton. For now, we know only that she joined Zion Presbyterian on 6 March 1859, when she was "admitted on profession of faith," and that she was a member in 1866 and 1869, listed as Jane Jones, formerly Jane Thorn. In 1869, white church members "dismissed" black members and kept the name Zion Presbyterian Church along with the building on Calhoun Street. "Dismissed" is another term that disguises the ugliness of the truth—they were kicked out. The building that the white members kept is the one that Reverend Jonathan C. Gibbs, an African American preacher from Philadelphia, tried to have given to the Northern Presbyterian Church, a black congregation, because the building was constructed for African Americans. When his suit under the Civil Rights Act in 1866 failed, the church was given to the Southern Presbyterians, and many black members then left for other churches. Those who stayed, or left and then returned, were pushed out three years later. Jane Jones is one of the people listed as "dismissed" in 1869. White members had kept the records books just after the war, when they merged with Glebe Street Presbyterian.

Primary Sources

Admission to Zion: Zion (later Westminster) Presbyterian Church (Charleston, South Carolina, United States), Communicants' Roll Book, 1852-1861, p. 57-58, Jane Thorn, servant of

Mrs. E. H. Williams, admitted on profession of faith, 6 March 1859; Historical Foundation of the Presbyterian and Reformed Churches microfilm MFPOS 1552, item 2, Presbyterian Historical Society, Philadelphia.

Admission as member of Rev. Jonathan C. Gibbes Organization: Zion (later Westminster) Presbyterian Church (Charleston, South Carolina, United States), Sessional records 23 April 1858-1 April 1866, p. 59-60, Members of Rev. Jonathan C. Gibbes Organization received as members, list includes Jane Jones (formerly Thorn); Historical Foundation of the Presbyterian and Reformed Churches microfilm MFPOS 1552, item 1, Presbyterian Historical Society, Philadelphia.

Zion (later Westminster) Presbyterian Church (Charleston, South Carolina, United States), Session minutes, 1866-1885, p. 200-205, 5 August 1869, List of 345 members dismissed to organize a coloured [sic] church, list includes Jane Jones; Historical Foundation of the Presbyterian and Reformed Churches microfilm MFPOS 1552, item 3, Presbyterian Historical Society, Philadelphia.

Garrison, William Lloyd, ed. *The Liberator,* January 1, 1831–24 December 1831, v. 1, Digital Commonwealth, Massachusetts Online Collections, http://ark.digitalcommonwealth.org/ark:/50959/xw42p1401.

Higginson, Thomas Wentworth, "On this Day in 1831, a Bloody Uprising in the Virginia Countryside," *The Atlantic Monthly,* August 1861, reprinted online August 21, 2013, ed. Caroline Kitchener, https://www.theatlantic.com/national/archive/2013/08/on-this-day-in-1831-a-bloody-uprising-in-the-virginia-countryside/278905/.

Kinzie, Juliette. *Wau-Bun: The "Early Day" in the Northwest.* Menasha, WI: The Collegiate Press, 1948.

Letter from Arthur Tappan, New York, [New York], to William Lloyd Garrison, October 12, 1831, Digital Commonwealth, Massachusetts Collections Online, https://www.digitalcommonwealth.org/search/commonwealth:2z10zf85x.

"Letter from Hilton to Eliza Williams," September 13, 1840, Series F: Franklin Cushman's notebooks, vol. 3: 31–33, (Elijah Williams Papers, Rhode Island Historical Society).

"Letter from Hilton to his sister," (date) 1840, ibid, Vol. 3: 36.

"Letter from Winthrop to Eliza Williams," April 24, 1835, ibid., Vol. 2: 10–13.

"Letter from Winthrop to his sister," January 24, 1836, ibid., Vol. 1: 92.

"Letter from Winthrop to Eliza Williams," September 1, 1836, ibid, Vol. 2: 80–82.

"Letter from Winthrop to his sister," July 24, 1865, ibid, Vol. 2: 111–117.

"Letter from Winthrop to Eliza Williams," August 28, 1835, ibid, Vol. 2: 27–29.

"Letter from Hilton to Jason Williams," November 18, 1834, ibid., Vol. 2: 49.

"Letter from Winthrop to Eliza Williams," November 3, 1835, ibid, Vol. 2, 42–45.

"Letter from Winthrop to his Eliza Williams," October 4, 1835, ibid, Vol. 2, 36–38.

"Letter from Winthrop to his Eliza Williams," December 10, 1835, ibid, Vol. 2, 49–51.

"Letter from Winthrop to his Eliza Williams," July 10, 1836, ibid.,Vol. 2, 69–71.

"Letter from Winthrop to his Eliza Williams," July 27, 1836, ibid.,Vol. 2, 75–76.

"Letter from Hilton to his Eliza Williams," October 8, 1836, ibid.,Vol. 2, 91.

"Letter from Winthrop to Brother Harris," March 31, 1838, ibid., Vol. 2: 123–125.

"Invoice of six bales cotton shipped by Ewart Williams & Co. aboard Sch Pacific bound for Providence and consigned to WJ Harris," February 1, 1838, ibid., Vol. 2: 114.

"Letter from Winthrop to WJ Harris," October 9, 1839, ibid., Vol. 3: 3.

"Letter from Winthrop to his sister," December 6, 1865, ibid, Vol. 3: 142.

"Letter from Winthrop to Susan Crouch," marked "received January 3, 1866," ibid., Vol. 3: 147–148.

"Letter from Winthrop to his sister," February 12, 1869, ibid., Vol. 4: 97–98.

"Letter from Winthrop to his sister," September 22, 1873, ibid., Vol. 5: 3–4.

"Letter from Winthrop to his sister," April 25, 1876, ibid., Vol. 5: 34.

"Letter from Winthrop to Jason Williams," November 8, 1834, ibid., Vol. 7: 49–54.

"Letter from Susan to Eliza Williams," September 21, 1837, ibid., Vol. 2, 107–108.

"Letter from Winthrop to Eliza Williams," March 14 & 16, 1835, ibid., Vol. 2, 2–9.

"Letter from Winthrop to Brother Harris, October 31, 1837, ibid., Vol. 2, 111–113.

"Letter from Hilton to Eliza Williams," November 14, 1834, Vol. 1, 129–130.

"Letter from Abby and K.S. (Kelita) Elles to Eliza Williams," March 10 & 16, 1838, ibid., Vol. 2, 119–122.

"Letter from Winthrop to Brother Harris," February 3, 1838, ibid., Vol. 2, 114–115.

"Letter from Winthrop to Brother Harris," March 31, 1838, ibid., Vol. 2, 123–125.

"Letter from Winthrop to his sisters," August 22, 1838, ibid., Vol. 2, 126–128.

Map showing the lands assigned to emigrant Indians west of Arkansas and Missouri, 1836, United States, Topographical Bureau, Library of Congress, https://www.loc.gov/resource/g4051e.mf000044/.

Turner, Nat. *The Confessions of Nat Turner, The Leader of the Late Insurrection in Southampton, VA, as fully and voluntarily made to Thomas R. Gray.* Baltimore: Lucas and Deaver, 1831. Documenting the American South, University of North Carolina at Chapel Hill, http://docsouth.unc.edu/neh/turner/turner.html.

Yuan, Daojun and Zhonghui Tang, Maojun Wang, Wenhui Gao, Lili Tu, Xin Jin, Lingling Chen, Yonghui He, Lin Zhang, Longfu Zhu, Yang Li, Qiqi Liang, Zhongxu Lin, Xiyan Yang, Nian Liu, Shuangxia Jin, Yang Lei, Yuanhao Ding, Guoliang Li, Xiaoan Ruan, Yijun Ruan & Xianlong Zhang. "The Genome Sequence of Sea-Island Cotton (*Gossypium barbadense*) provides insights into the allopolyploidization and development of superior spinnable fibres," *Scientific Reports* 5, Article number: 17662 (2015), https://www.nature.com/articles/srep17662.

Williams, Winthrop. "A Description of Osceola: Winthrop Williams to Mrs. Susan M.S. Crouch, Charleston, January 6, 1838," *The South Carolina Historical Magazine*, Vol 65, No 2 (Apr. 1964), 85–86.

Secondary Sources

"A Note on the Language of the Narratives," *Born in Slavery: Slave Narratives from the Federal Writers' Project, 1936–1938*, Library of Congress, Digital Collections, https://www.loc.gov/collections/slave-narratives-from-the-federal-writers-project-1936-to-1938/articles-and-essays/note-on-the-language-of-the-narratives/.

Alexander, Michelle. *The New Jim Crow: Mass Incarceration in the Age of Colorblindness,* Revised Edition. New York: The New Press, 2011.

Bancroft, Frederic. *Slave Trading in the Old South,* intro. Michael Tadman. Columbia: University of South Carolina Press, 1996.

Dunbar-Ortiz. *An Indigenous Peoples' History of the United States.* Boston: Beacon Press, 2014. Kindle Ebook.

Freedgood, Elaine. "Souvenirs of Sadism: Mahogany Furniture, Deforestation, and Slavery in *Jane Eyre, The Ideas in Things: Fugitive Meaning in the Victorian Novel.* Chicago: University of Chicago Press, 2010.

Hoffer, Peter Charles. *Cry Liberty: The Great Stono River Slave Rebellion of 1729.* New Narratives in American History, Oxford: Oxford University Press, 2011.

Kennedy, Cynthia M. *Braided Relations, Entwined Lives: The Women of Charleston's Urban Slave Society.* Bloomington: Indiana University Press, 2005.

McInnis, Maurie D. *Slaves Waiting for Sale: Abolitionist Art and the American Slave Trade.* Chicago: The University of Chicago Press, 2011.

Pope, Nancy, "America's First Direct Mail Campaign," Smithsonian's National Postal Museum Blog, 29 July 2010, http://postalmuseumblog.si.edu/2010/07/americas-first-direct-mail-campaign.html.

Rankine, Claudia. "The Making of 'Citizen': Claudia Rankine," Woodberry Poetry Room, Harvard University, published 4 May 2015, https://www.youtube.com/watch?v=8RylFX9OG54&t=113s.

Sontag, Susan. *Regarding the Pain of Others.* New York: Farrar, Straus and Giroux, 2013. Kindle EBook.

Wagner, Lon. "Nat Turner's skull turns up far from site of his revolt," *The Baltimore Sun*. June 15, 2003, http://articles.baltimoresun.com/2003-06-15/news/0306150247_1_nat-turner-benjamin-turner-skull.

Wallace, Maurice O. and Shawn Michelle Smith. *Pictures and Progress: Early Photography and the Making of African American Identity*. Durham: Duke University Press, 2012.

Wiegman, Robyn. *American Anatomies: Theorizing Race and Gender.* Durham: Duke University Press, 1995.

Chapter 11: Living History

Notes

Juba Simons' life after 6 Cumberland Street: Winthrop writes that he sold Juba for $100 on January 12, 1838, but he doesn't say to whom he sold her. The proceeds from her sale are to go to Susan's daughter Emily, with arrangements made by Winthrop and instructions to Susan: "I also wish you to send me an acknowledgement to this effect 'that it was by your request that I sold Juba for One Hundred dollars and that you take all responsibility on yourself and hold me harmless for so doing. I have applied to a lawyer here respecting the transfer of this property (that is the Childs portion to her Guardian at Providence he says 1st Application must first be made in the proper court where the Minor resides) . . .'

He also notes that he "presented my account of the Estate today and the ordinary informs me I must have your receipt for all money paid you, the amt of Cash paid you, including your proportion of Housekeeping, passage, Board at Mrs. Dells + water is $48184/100 and for Blankets and Bed clothes, medicine, care +c taken by you 5825/100 this latter is to come from your proportion of the property so says the Ordinary. I wish you to send my by return of mail two receipts say 'Rec'd of E.H. Williams admin of Est. of Dr. H.W. Crouch 'Four Hundred + Eighty one 84/100 Dollars from 11 Jany 1837 to 1st October' 1837 inclusive for support of self and child." "Letter from Winthrop to Susan," Series F: Franklin Cushman Notebooks, Vol. 8: 76 (Elijah Williams Papers, Rhode Island Historical Society).

For more on the decision to remove Isaac Royall's shield from Harvard Law School, please see: Halley, Janet. "My Isaac Royall Legacy," *Harvard BlackLetter Law Journal,* Vol. 24 (2008): 117–131, posted online by *Harvard Journal on Racial and Ethnic Justice,* May 29, 2008, hjrej.com/wp-content/uploads/2012/11/vol24/Halley.pdf; Steve Annear, "Harvard Law School to Ditch Controversial Shield," *The Boston Globe,* March 14, 2016, https://www.bostonglobe.com/metro/2016/03/14/harvard-law-school-ditch-controversial-shield-with-elements-from-slave-owning-family/UIYgbyviFdwwGKjexZgWqN/story.html

p. 346, For more on Attucks, please see: Kachun, Mitch. *First Martyr of Liberty: Crispus Attucks in American Memory.* Oxford: Oxford University Press, 2017; Michael Lee Lanning, *The African-American Soldier: from the Crispus Attucks to Colin Powell,* Secaucus, NJ: Carol Publishing, 1997; Kachun, Mitch, "From Forgotten Founder to Indispensible Icon: Crispus Attucks, Black Citizenship, and Collective Memory, 1770–1865," *Journal of the Early Republic,* Vol. 29, 2 (Summer 2009); Stephen Kantrowitz, "A Place for 'Colored Patriots': Crispus Attucks among the Abolitionists, 1842–1863," *Massachusetts Historical Review,* 2016, Vol.18.

p. 348, For more on women in the Civil War, please see: Sharon Romeo, *Gender and Jubilee: Black freedom and reconstruction of citizenship in Civil War Missouri.* Studies in the Legal History of the South Ser., Athens: University of Georgia, 2016; Whites, LeeAnn and Alecia P. Long, *Gender, Military Occupation, and the American Civil War.* Baton Rouge: Louisiana State University Press, 2012; Nina Silber, *Daughters of the Union: Northern Women Fight the Civil War.* Cambridge: Harvard University Press, 2005; Libra R. Hilde, *Worth a Dozen Men: Women and Nursing in the Civil War South.* Charlottesville: University of Virginia Press, 2012; Hall, Richard, *Patriots in Disguise: women warriors of the Civil War.* New York: Paragon House, 1993; Elizabeth Leonard, *All the Daring of a Soldier: Women of the Civil War Armies.* New York: W.W. Norton and Co., 1999; Deanne Blanton and Lauren M. Cook, *They Fought Like Demons: Women Soldiers in the American Civil War.* Baton Rouge: Louisiana State University Press, 2002; Jami Ann Keegan, *Scandal of*

Patriotism: The forgotten contributions of Michigan's Native American, women, and African-Americans during the Civil War. Eastern Michigan University, ProQuest Publishing, 2000.

And on Cathay Williams: DeAnne Blanton, "Cathay Williams, Black Woman Soldier 1866–1868," *Minerva: Quarterly Report on Women in the Military,* Vol. X, Iss. 3 (Dec. 31, 1992): 1;

For more on the image, visual rhetoric, and representations of African Americans, please see: Raengo, Alessandra. *On the Sleeve of the Visual: Race as Face Value.* Lebanon: Dartmouth College Press, 2013. Weheliye, Alexander G. *Habeas Viscus: Racializing Assemblages, Biopolitics, and Black Feminist Theories of the Human.* Durham: Duke University Press, 2014. Hartman, Saidiya. *Scenes of Subjection: Terror, Slavery, and Self-Making in Nineteenth-Century America.* Oxford: Oxford University Press, 1997.

p. 356, please see Wells-Barnett, Ida B. *On Lynchings.* Mineola, NY: Dover Books, 2014.

Primary Sources

Aunt Sally: or, The Cross the Way of Freedom. A Narrative of the Slave-life and Purchase of the Mother of Rev. Isaac Williams, of Detroit, Michigan: Electronic Edition. Documenting the American South, University of North Carolina Chapel Hill, http://docsouth.unc.edu/neh/sally/sally.html.

Denease, Tammy. "Compelled to Servitude: The Story of Belinda," performance by storyteller Tammy Denease. October 3, 2015, Royall House and Slave Quarters, Medford, MA.

"Letter from Winthrop to Susan," November 15, 1864 ibid, Vol. 2, 105–106.

"Letter from Hilton to his sister," February 25, 1863, ibid., Vol. 2, 103–104.

"Letter from Hilton to Susan," June 25, 1865, ibid., Vol. 2, 106–108.

"Letter from Winthrop to his sister," 24 July 1865, ibid., Vol. 2, 111–117.

Truth, Sojourner. *Narrative of the Life of Sojourner Truth.* New York: Dover Publications, Inc., 1997.

Secondary Sources

Anderson, Carol. *White Rage: The Unspoken Truth of Our Racial Divide.* New York: Bloomsbury USA, 2016.

Barthes, Roland. *Camera Lucida: Reflections on Photography.* New York: Hill and Wang, 2010.

Barthes, Roland. *The Pleasure of the Text.* New York: Hill and Wang, 1975.

Blackmon, Douglas A. *Slavery by Another Name: The Re-Enslavement of Black Americans from the Civil War to World War I.* New York: Anchor Books, 2009.

Burns, Ken and Sarah Burns. *The Central Park Five,* November 23, 2012, Florentine Films, WETA.

"CDC Malaria Maps," Centers for Disease Control and Prevention, September 7, 2017, https://www.cdc.gov/malaria/travelers/about_maps.html.

Coates, Ta-Nehisi. *Between the World and Me.* New York: Spiegel and Grau, 2015.

Coddington, Ronald S. *African American Faces of the Civil War: An Album.* Baltimore: Johns Hopkins University Press, 2012.

Cromwell, Adelaide M. *The Other Brahmins: Boston's Black Upper Class, 1750–1950.* Fayetteville, IN: The University of Arkansas Press, 1994.

Davis, Miranda. "Monument to female Buffalo Soldier is dedicated in Leavenworth," July 22, 2016, *Kansas City Star,* http://www.kansascity.com/news/local/article91412232.html.

DuVernay, Ava. *13th : From Slave to Criminal with One Amendment.* October 7, 2016, Kandoo Films.

Freedgood, Elaine. "Souvenirs of Sadism: Mahogany Furniture, Deforestation, and Slavery in *Jane Eyre, The Ideas in Things: Fugitive Meaning in the Victorian Novel.* Chicago: University of Chicago Press, 2010.

Gabbatt, Adam, "What trans soldier Albert Cashier can teach Trump about patriotism," August 22, 2017, *The Guardian,*

Glymph, Thavolia. *Out of the House of Bondage: The Transformation of the Plantation Household.* New York: Cambridge University Press, 2012.

Hesseltine, William Best. *Civil War Prisons: A Study in War Psychology.* Columbus: Ohio State University Press, 1930.

Kelly, Annie. "Nestlé admits slavery in Thailand while fighintg child labour lawsuit in Ivory Coast," *The Guardian*. Monday, February 1, 2016. https://www.theguardian.com/sustainable-business/2016/feb/01/nestle-slavery-thailand-fighting-child-labour-lawsuit-ivory-coast.

McInnis, Maurie D. *Slaves Waiting for Sale: Abolitionist Art and the American Slave Trade*. Chicago: University of Chicago Press, 2011.

McMillen, Sally G. *Southern Women: Black and White in the Old South*, Second Edition. Malden, MA: Wiley Blackwell, 1992.

Powers, Bernard E., Jr. *Black Charlestonians: A Social History, 1822–1885*. Fayeteville, IN: The University of Arkansas Press, 1994.

Quigley, Shawn, Park Guide, "Peter Faneuil and Slavery," August 22, 2017, National Park Service, https://www.nps.gov/bost/learn/historyculture/peter-faneuil.htm.

Rankine, Claudia. *Citizen: An American Lyric*. Minneapolis, MN: Graywolf Press, 2015.

Reuters, "Supreme Court Rejects Nestle Bid to Throw Out Child Slavery Suit," January 11, 2016, *Fortune, MA* http://fortune.com/2016/01/11/nestle-supreme-court-child-slavery/.

Rudisel, Christine and Bob Blaisdell. *Slave Narratives of the Underground Railroad*. New York: Dover Publications, Inc., 2014.

Sharpless, Rebecca. *Cooking in Other Women's Kitchens: Domestic Workers in the South, 1865–1960*. Chapel Hill: The University of North Carolina Press, 2010.

Smith, Shawn Michelle. *American Archives: Gender, Race, and Class in Visual Culture*. Princeton: Princeton University Press, 1999.

Sontag, Susan. *On Photography*. New York: Picador, 2001.

Sontag, Susan. *Regarding the Pain of Others*. New York: Farrar, Straus and Giroux, 2013.

Ulrich, Laurel Thatcher. "Of Pens and Needles: Sources for the Study of Early American Women." *Journal of American History*. 77 (1990): 200–207.

Wallace, Maurice O. and Shawn Michelle Smith, eds. *Pictures and Progress: Early Photography and the Making of African American Identity*. Durham: Duke University Press, 2012.

Washington, Booker T. *Up from Slavery*. New York: Dover Publications, Inc., 1995.

Weigman, Robyn. *American Anatomies: Theorizing Race and Gender*. London: Duke University Press, 1995.

Winn, Patrick. "The slave labor behind your favorite clothing brands: Gap, H&M and more exposed," 22 March 2015, *Salon*. https://www.salon.com/2015/03/22/the_slave_labor_behind_your_favorite_clothing_brands_gap_hm_and_more_exposed_partner/.

Chapter 12: Portraits

Notes

p. 374–375 The opening, in which I imagine Juba Simons choosing her outfit for a portrait, and my subsequent imaginings in this chapter about her life post-war, are inspired by the work of Thavolia Glymph, *The Transformation of the Plantation Household*. New York: Cambridge University Press, 2008.

p. 375, Franklin mentions Moses Browns' involvement with the family Vol 2, 25; Vol. 4, 108; the story of Ava Harris Vol. 2, 95–99.

p. 376, Franklin's note, Vol. 2, 199: "For a year, Susan and her daughter Emily now Emily Hasell Crouch has been living in Providence in the household, free to come and go and enjoy her income but holding a tight rein over her father and mother. She lived there till 1902, reaching the age of ninety." When Emily was born, she was named Emily Harris Crouch, but after her father's death, Susan changed her middle name to Hasell.

p. 378, Franklin's note regarding Eliza Williams' marriage and inheritance, Vol. 2: 9: "Each Abby, Emily, Susan, Sarah received a $1,000 setting out at marriage. Eliza, whose marriage was prevented by the family, received nothing from her father—not even the $1,000 mentioned in his will, for everything had been transferred to Susan and every piece of furniture loaned to Eliza at Cedar Grove was recalled by Susan." Franklin notes, Vol. 2: 121, that Eliza Williams lived at Cedar Grove with her sister Emily Harris and her family, and continued living with the family after Emily died in 1895; she then moved with the Harris and Cushmans to a "600 acre farm" in Glocester, Rhode Island. Eliza's life at Cedar Grove is also mentioned in several letters, including: "Abby Elles to Susan," September 27, 1865, Series F: Franklin Cushman's notebooks, vol. 2: 123, (Elijah Williams Papers, Rhode Island Historical Society); "Letter from Hilton to Susan," July 4,1868, ibid, Vol. 4, 66; "Letter from Hilton to Susan," February 12, 1866, ibid, Vol. 4: 4. "Letter from Fred Elles to Susan," February 21, 1868, ibid, Vol. 4: 60.

p. 379, Susan kept a notebook of her knitting and sewing jobs and charity work. Jason Williams Papers, MSS 34, C (Eijah Williams Papers, Rhode Island Historical Society).

p. 380, Kay Siebler notes in "Far from the Truth: Teaching the Politics of Sojourner Truth's 'Ain't I a woman?' "When teaching Truth's speech, we need to articulate for our students that all its versions are only that: versions. Truth, unable to read or write, could not offer her own rhetoric in the written form. Her words (as we read them today) are never *her* words but a representation of her words by whoever transcribed them. These secondary rhetors were mindful of audience and purpose, *their* audience and purpose, which may have been a different audience and purpose from what Truth intended. We also need to help our student analyze why, for contemporary audiences, the Gage version is the one reprinted and performed while the Robinson version is ignored." For more on Sojourner Truth, see: Melissa Schramm Burnett, "The representation of truth: An interdisciplinary analysis of Sojourner Truth's Akron, Ohio speech," The University of Texas at Arlington, ProQuest Dissertations Publishing, 1998.

p. 384, for more on southern cooking, see: Witt, Doris. *Black Hunger, Soul food and America.* Minneapolis: University of Minnesota Press, 1999; Frederick Douglass Opie, *Hog and Hominy: Soul Food from Africa to America,* New York: Columbia University Press, 2008; Carrie Helms Tippin, "Defining authentic new southern identity in recipe origin narratives," Texas Christian University, ProQuest Dissertation Publishing, 2015; Elizabeth S.D. Engelhardt, *Mess of Greens: Southern Gender and Southern Food,* Athens: University of Georgia Press, 2011.

p. 389, After the war, Winthrop writes, "...We have one of the old servant women that used to belong to the Taylor Estate, who cooks and washes, and an old man of Dr. Trezevant's who is a capital waiting man and does all we have to do indoors and out so that Cassie is greatly relieved of the trouble of the house though she still has the chambers to look after but she makes the boys make up their own beds and in that way we get along better. . . . Cassie is in desire to leave here on account of the insubordination of the negro and I may be compelled to go from starvation, we are bound to have trouble in the South soon and it will be long years trial to get rid of the negroes. I consider the question settled as to their fate, it can be none other than that of the Indian in extermination and much more rapid than that of the Indian..."

Franklin notes that, "As Dr. Crouch's executor and administrator, Hilton Williams had never closed the estate and given an account to Susan tho thirty years would end in 1866. He invested the proceeds from time in southern property and sent enough money north to pay for clothing of Susan and the child Emmy and trips to Charleston or N.Y." Hilton noted that he and Harriet had noticed that Susan lived with few wants. When Susan sent a cloak down for Harriet and her daughter, Hilton encouraged her to also buy one for herself. He said if she needed anything, she could borrow money from her brother-in-law, Mr. Harris, and Hilton would reimburse him. Dec. 30, 1865, Vol. 3, 152–3.

The connections between family members in the north and south continued over many decades and were also evident in an anecdote from Hilton, in which notes that a woman of color came to his door in Charleston, saying that she knew Susan and Emmie (Emily) in Providence and was seeking a way home with her daughter; she explained she was destitute. She told Hilton she and Susan belonged to the same church in Providence. Hilton seems to have ignored her plea, blaming her plight on "our beautiful Radical government." December 27, 1876, Vol. 5, p. 56. Susan and Emily continued to spend time in Charleston with her relatives. Franklin notes: "From 1836 to the period just before the war, Susan and Emily Crouch lived at the old house unaided with the work, going South when they felt inclined." In the years after the war, Emily traveled south to visit with her relatives and maintained correspondence with her cousins until her death. Vol. 5,

p. 60 Franklin notes that "More than forty (40) years later after World War I Henry Williams still went annually to Flat Rock N.C. He was a widower for many years. His five daughters were brought up by their Grandmother. . . .Both sons are graduates of Yale University. [William's] wife was E. Middleton Henry and his wife 'Fan" live in Charleston restoring the Sword Gate House to which portraits, paintings and many articles of ancient days have been sent from this house relics of old George St. The marriage of Alice to a Northerner was not approved by the Charleston people. The girls lived for many years at one of the famous old houses on the Battery. Vol 5, p. 85. Whether the Sword Gate House contained—and still holds—items from the Williams family's George Street house is not yet known.

Primary Sources

"Abby Elles to Susan," September 27, 1865, ibid, vol. 2: 123.

Forten, Charlotte. "Life on the Sea Islands," May 1864, *The Atlantic Monthly,* https://www.theatlantic.com/magazine/archive/1864/05/life-on-the-sea-islands/308758/.

Godey's Lady's Book, The Online Books Page, University of Pennsylvania's Serial Archive Listings. http://onlinebooks.library.upenn.edu/webbin/serial?id=godeylady1830–1838, Hathi Trust via Princeton University. https://catalog.hathitrust.org/Record/008920204.

Hathi Trust, 1874, https://babel.hathitrust.org/cgi/pt?id=inu.30000111678110;view=1up;seq=11.

"Letter from AC & KC Elles to Susan," October 19, 1837, Series F: Franklin Cushman's notebooks, vol. 8: 146–148, (Elijah Williams Papers, Rhode Island Historical Society).

"Letter from Winthrop to Eliza Williams," July 29, 1839, ibid, Vol. 2: 139–140.

"Letter from Hilton to Susan," July 4, 1868, ibid, Vol. 4: 66.

"Letter from Hilton to Susan," February 12, 1866, ibid, Vol. 4: 4.

"Letter from Fred Elles to Susan," February 21, 1868, ibid, Vol. 4: 60.

"Letter from Winthrop to his sister," October 10, 1865, ibid., Vol. 2, 129–130.

"Letter from Winthrop to Susan," November 23, 1865, ibid., Vol. 2, 138–139.

"Letter from Hilton to Susan," August 27, 1868, ibid., Vol. 4, 72–74.

"Letter from Winthrop to Susan," November 13, 1865, ibid., Vol. 2, 135–136.

McGill, Denise, dir. "the Gullah Project, a documentary film" 2014, https://thegullahproject.org/team/.

Note by Franklin R. Cushman, ibid., Vol. 2, 136.

Outlaw, Penny and Elizabeth Ammons, introductions, and Tammy Denease, storyteller, "Giving Voice: 'Compelled to Servitude,' The Story of Belinda," Royall House and Slave Quarters, June 7, 2015.

"Paul Revere's Engraving of Crispus Attucks," The Gilder Lehrman Institute of American History. https://www.gilderlehrman.org/history-by-era/road-revolution/resources/paul-revere%E2%80%99s-engraving-boston-massacre-1770.

The Penn Center, 1862, St. Helena, SC, www.penncenter.com.

"Profile: Sojourner Truth's famous speech, 'Ain't I a Woman?'." News & Notes, National Public Radio, Feb. 9, 2005. Academic OneFile, http://link.galegroup.com/apps/doc/A161910171/AONE?u=lom_nmichu&sid=AONE&xid=8dfde641.

Vigil Reburial Celebration publication handout. *Stand in Honor of Those Forgotten.* May 20–23, 2015. The Portsmouth, New Hampshire African Burying Ground.

Secondary Sources

Ahmed, Sara "Happy Objects," *The Affect Theory Reader,* eds. Melissa Gregg and Gregory J. Seigworth (London: Duke University Press, 2010), 29–51.

Ahmed, Sara. *Willful Subjects*. Durham, NC: Duke University Press Books, 2014.

Anderson, Carol. *White Rage: The Unspoken Truth of Our Racial Divide.* New York: Bloomsbury, 2016.

Bailey, Anne C. *African Voices of the Atlantic Slave Trade: Beyond the Silence and the Shame*. Boston: Beacon, 2005.

Coddington, Ronald S. *African American Faces of the Civil War: An Album*. Baltimore: The Johns Hopkins University Press, 2012.

Eisler, Benita, Ed. *The Lowell Offering: Writings by New England Mill Women, 1840–1845*. New York: W.W. Norton, 1998.

Finefield, Kristi. "Profiling Portraits: Occupational Portraits of the 19th Century," Library of Congress, Oct. 5, 2017. https://blogs.loc.gov/picturethis/2017/10/profiling-portraits-occupational-portraits-of-the-19th-century/ Accessed Nov. 10, 2017.

Flint, Kate. *The Victorians and the Visual Imagination*. New York: Cambridge University Press, 2000.

Glymph, Thavolia. *The Transformation of the Plantation Household*. New York: Cambridge University Press, 2008.

hooks, bell. *Art on My Mind: Visual Politics*. New York: The New Press, 1995.

Kennedy, Cynthia M. *Braided Relations, Entwined Lives: The Women of Charleston's Urban Slave Society*. Bloomington: Indiana University Press, 2005.

Kinzie, Juliette. *Wau-Bun: The "Early Day" in the Northwest*. Menasha: The Collegiate Press, 1948.

Mitchell, W. J. T. *Picture Theory*. Chicago: The University of Chicago, 1994.

Mitchell, W. J. T. *What do pictures want? The Lives and Loves of Images*. Chicago: The University of Chicago, 2005.

Noble, Nigel, dir. "Memory," May 30, 2007, *Craft in America*, PBS, *http://www.craftinamerica.org/episodes/memory/*.

Powers, Bernard E. *Black Charlestonians: A Social History, 1822–1885*. Fayetteville: The University of Arkansas Press, 1994.

"Reburial Ceremony at African Burying Ground, Portsmouth, NH," video, Portsmouth African Burying Ground: In Honor of those Forgotten, http://www.africanburyinggroundnh.org/summary.html.

Sharpless, Rebecca. *Cooking in Other Women's Kitchens: Domestic Workers in the South, 1865–1960*. Chapel Hill: The University of North Carolina Press: Enhanced Ebook edition, 2013.

Twitty, Michael W. *The Cooking Gene: A Journey Through African American History in the Old South*. New York: Harper Collins, 2017.

University of Vermont, "Women's Clothing," Dating Historic Images. https://www.uvm.edu/landscape/dating/clothing_and_hair/1860s_clothing_women.php.

Waugh, Norah. *The Cut of Women's Clothes: 1600–1930*. London: Routledge, 1968.

White, Deborah Gray. *Ar'n't I a Woman? Female Slaves in the Plantation South*. New York: W.W. Norton & Co., 1999.

Additional Image Credits

Any unattributed photos are copyright of the author and cannot be reproduced without permission.

All images of the Crouch quilt top are courtesy of the Historic Textile and Costume Collection, University of Rhode Island. Photos taken by the author. All reproduction is prohibited without permission. Images found on pages: 1, 4, 5, 7, 8, 10, 13, 22, 27, 31, 33, 55, 89, 139, 244, 251, 301, 389, and 399.

Page 6: Images courtesy of Samarra Khaja.

Page 9: Courtesy of the Historic Textile and Costume Collection, University of Rhode Island.

Page 23: From *The Seaman's Friend* by Richard Henry Dana Jr.

Page 35: Courtesy of Wikimedia Commons.

Page 37: Courtesy of Pictorial Press Ltd/Alamy Stock Photo.

Page 45: Anna Williams (American, 1927–2010). Quilt, 1995. Cotton, synthetics, 76 ¼ × 61 ½ in. (193.7 × 156.2 cm). Brooklyn Museum, Gift in memory of Horace H. Solomon, 2011.18.

Page 49: Courtesy of the Division of Home and Community Life, National Museum of American History, Smithsonian Institution.

Page 53: Courtesy of Library of Congress, Geography and Map Division.

Page 56: Courtesy FCIT.

Page 67: Courtesy of the Library of Congress.

Page 80: Courtesy of The Metropolitan Museum of Art/Rogers Fund, 1942.

Page 108: Photo by C. C. Jones/U.S. Geological Survey.

Page 110: Courtesy of the Library of Congress.

Page 131: Anatomy full body. Courtesy of the Thomas Fisher Rare Book Library, University of Toronto.

Page 145: Illustration of Dr. J. Marion Sims with Anarcha by Robert Thom. Courtesy of Southern Illinois University School of Medicine, Pearson Museum.

Page 149: Portrait File, PR 052, "Sm"; image #74638. Photography © New-York Historical Society.

Page 150: Courtesy of Drexel University College of Medicine.

Page 153: Courtesy of Drexel University College of Medicine.

Page 156: Courtesy of the Library of Congress.

Page 160: Creative Commons license, Copyright © Michel Royon/Wikimedia Commons.

Page 162: Courtesy of the Wellcome Library.

Page 197: Courtesy of The Metropolitan Museum of Art, New York/Gift of Mrs. William R. Witherell, 1953.

Page 198: Brooklyn Museum Costume Collection at The Metropolitan Museum of Art, Gift of the Brooklyn Museum, 2009; Gift of Mrs. Alvah E. Reed.

Page 199: Courtesy of The Charleston Museum, Charleston, South Carolina.

Page 202: Courtesy of the Library of Congress.

Page 207: Harriet Powers, American, 1837–1910, Pictorial quilt, American (Athens, Georgia), 1895–98, Cotton plain weave, pieced, appliqued, embroidered, and quilted, 175 x 266.7 cm (68 7/8 x 105 in.). Credit: Bequest of Maxim Karolik, 64.619. Photograph © 2018 Museum of Fine Arts Boston.

Page 211: Courtesy of the Division of Home and Community Life, National Museum of American History, Smithsonian Institution.

Page 217: Detail of one of the squares of Harriet Powers' Pictorial quilt. Powers' description of this square is: "The falling of the stars on Nov. 13, 1833. The people were frightened and thought that the end had come. God's hand staid the stars. The varmints rushed out of their beds." Copyright © Bequest of Maxim Karolik. Photograph © 2018 Museum of Fine Arts Boston.

Page 236: Courtesy of the Collection of the Newport Historical Society.

Page 242: Courtesy of the British Library.

Page 243: Courtesy of the Museum of Art, Rhode Island School of Design, Providence.

Page 248: Courtesy of Redwood Library and Athenaeum, Newport, Rhode Island.

Page 254: Courtesy of University of Texas Libraries.

Page 298: Courtesy of the Library of Congress.

Page 314 Copyright © World History Archive/Alamy Stock Photo

Page 316: Copyright © World History Archive/Alamy Stock Photo.

Page 331: Courtesy, American Antiquarian Society.

Page 342 (top): Courtesy of The Art Institute of Chicago / Art Resource, NY.

Page 343: Collection of the Smithsonian National Museum of African American History and Culture, Gift of the Garrison Family in memory of George Thompson Garrison.

Page 344: Copyright © Wikimedia Commons/Daderot.

Page 345 (top): Photograph by Baldwin Coolidge, Courtesy of the Trustees of the Boston Public Library.

Page 345 (bottom): Copyright © Metropolitan Museum of Art/Gift of Mrs. Russell Sage.

Page 346: Courtesy of Underwood & Underwood Glass Stereograph Collection, Archives Center, National Museum of American History, Smithsonian Institution.

Page 347: Courtesy of the Library of Congress.

Page 352: From *The Kansas City Star*, July 22, 2016, © 2018 McClatchy. All rights reserved. Used by permission and protected by the Copyright Laws of the United States. The printing, copying, redistribution, or retransmission of this Content without express written permission is prohibited.

Page 367: Copyright © Wikimedia Commons.

Page 373: Woman in striped dress. Courtesy of the Yale Collection of American Literature, Beinecke Rare Book and Manuscript Library.

Page 384: Copyright © John D. and Catherine T. MacArthur Foundation.

Page 398: Image courtesy of the New York Public Library Digital Collections.

Acknowledgments

This book could not have been written without the help and wisdom of many scholars, writers, friends, and activists who took the time to educate me, read drafts, point me to resources, and talk about the project.

Heartfelt thanks to Don Fehr, Jessica Case, and Maria Fernandez, for ushering this project through its many phases. I'm especially grateful to Jessica, for your patience and feedback as I worked through this writing process. Thank you for continuing to rally for the book. And to the team at Pegasus for making it into a beautiful object of its own and for helping to send it into the world, thank you.

This book began thanks to Dr. Linda Welters "gifting" me these quilt tops to research and mentoring me in quilt studies. I could never have imagined, when I began, that I'd be here years later, finishing this book. Thank you for reading many drafts, and for trusting me with this story that has changed my life. Thank you also to Dr. Margaret Ordoñez, for crucial insights about the quilt's fabrics, and Susan Jerome, Collections Manager in the University of Rhode Island's Department of Textiles, Fashion Merchandising, and Design, where the quilt tops are held.

I'm indebted to the staff of the Rhode Island Historical Society, the South Carolina Historical Society, and the Carolinas Room at the Charleston Public Library, for your care in preserving these stories, and for your help accessing various collections and documents. I'm also indebted to the historians who educated me on nineteenth century Charleston and enslavement, especially Joseph McGill, who spent time with me in Charleston and in the Midwest and was incredibly patient with my many questions at Magnolia Plantation and Gardens. Thank you for teaching me to look for the back staircase and the fingerprints in the bricks. Thank you to Christine Mitchell, who works at Ryan's Slave Mart Museum in Charleston and showed me where slave agents did business in the neighborhood; I look forward to reading your book one day soon. Dr. Erin Dwyer offered invaluable feedback on several chapters of the book; thank you for your time, expertise, and many suggestions. Keith Stokes and Theresa Guzmán-Stokes, thank you for teaching me more about colonial Newport, the history of Africans and African Americans in Rhode Island, and the ways we can tell stories that offer empowerment. I'm also eternally grateful to Beverly Gordon-Welch; thank you for spending three incredible hours with me, on that difficult day, and for talking through ways to tell Eliza, Minerva, Jane, and Juba Simons' stories. I've been grateful to you every time I sat down to write.

Thank you also to Dr. Matt Haught, for corresponding and providing information on Mary Crouch, printer, and to Dr. Manuel Barcia, for generously offering your expertise on the brick from San Isidro in Trinidad, Cuba. I'm grateful, as well, to Gonzalo Alfredo López Turiño, for your time showing me the sugar plantations in Trinidad. Many heartfelt thanks to Franklin R. Cushman's descendants, Bob Cushman and D.D. Harrington, who sent me information about the family, including Franklin's memoir; it means a great deal to get to speak with the descendants of this story. Thank you for giving me your time and sharing your knowledge of your ancestors with me. Thank you also to Christine Lamar, whose genealogical work helped me find Bob and D.D. My gratitude, also, to Jennifer Rae Taylor, of the Equal Justice Initiative, who gave me her time to discuss the possibility of erecting markers in Newport, Bristol, and South County, Rhode Island. And to Nancy Wagner, Supervisor, of the Charleston Register of Deeds, for the assistance you gave me in tracing documents and seeking existing plots of land in Charleston.

Sarah Nesnow, my thanks to you for helping to trace in South Carolina archives the lives of the enslaved people. And to Sarah Schneider, tremendous thanks for critical help (and patience) transcribing and collating research, and encouraging me when I needed it most. And to Suzie Tibor, for your tireless help tracking down images and permissions.

Dr. Rae Ferguson and Dr. Kendall Moore, my gratitude for your wisdom and mentorship, from start to finish with this project. Thank you for reading drafts and letting me talk through this—among other things—even when you were in the midst of well-deserved down time. I'm eternally grateful to you. Thank you also to Dr. Anne Panning, Dr. Amy Hamilton, Judah Micah-Lamar, Dr. Will Arighi, and Matthew Lansburgh, for generously reading and critiquing drafts, offering your wisdom and keen eyes. And to Dr. Chawne Kimber, for talking with me about the sources of our quilting cotton, years ago.

Thank you to the Millay Colony, where I wrote sections of this project, and to Northern Michigan University, especially Dr. Michael Broadway, for facilitating funding that allowed me to travel for research to South Carolina. To my colleagues at Northern Michigan University who have offered support in a myriad of forms: Emily Lanctot, Matthew Gavin Frank, Dr. Russ Prather, Dr. Caroline Krzakowski, Dr. Norma Froelich, Dr. Sarah Middlefehldt. Dr. Lisa Eckert, Jon and Hilary Billman, and Dr. Lynn Domina, for conversations around the book, and for cultivating a supportive department.

My thanks to the University of Rhode Island's Center for Humanities, which allowed me my first visit to research in Charleston, and to those scholars at URI who supported me during my research on the quilt tops, especially Dr. Valerie Karno for your enthusiasm and support of this project and all other things textile, Dr. Peter Covino, for your wisdom, support, feedback, and time with many pages of my work as my advisor, and Dr. Annu Palakunnathu Matthew, Dr. Nedra Reynolds, and Dr. Jody Lisberger, for your critiques, mentorship, and guidance. Thank you also to Dr. Carolyn Betensky, for offering support throughout my time at URI (and for doting on 'the beastie').

To Shana Adams and Shani Gilchrist, my thanks for spending time with me in Charleston and Columbia, for welcoming me to your state and allowing me a glimpse of your friendship, and especially to Shana for allowing me to visit your family home.

I don't know how to properly thank all the people who supported me throughout the process. Danielle Krcmar, thank you for always being there and for helping me think about images, visual art, and the tactile allure of quilts. Dr. Wendy Farkas, for your friendship and support, and for joining me on the overnight with Joseph McGill's Slave Dwelling Project. Dr. Anna Brecke, thank you for conversations about domesticity, information about the Victorian era, and countless restorative breaks in our walks around Rhode Island; thank you for our endless dialogue and your many reminders, over the years, to keep my faith in this project. Megan Gannon, thank you for talking through the story and offering your wisdom and feedback on the final drafts, and for giving me deeper roots in the midwest. Nicole Walker, for your workshop, writing, and generosity. To Wendy S. Walters, my thanks for your time sharing your work with my students, and for your encouragement with this research. And to Jericho Brown, Carol Philips, Joy Cardillo, Alissa Kirchharr, Elizabeth Collins, Kristine Granger, and James Veil, for your friendship. And Thea Cawley, for an exceedingly patient ear and endless wisdom and support. To Rebecca Loren, and Alexis Deise, for friendship and lots of laughter as we quilt.

My gratitude to Jenn Scheck-Kahn, for taking time from your own writing to spend so much time with mine, and for countless conversations, which included a great deal of encouragement to keep going. I couldn't have started nor finished this book without your friendship and feedback. And to Brian, Naomi, and Eli, for the welcoming spirit of family you've always offered.

And to my family, especially my parents, and Josh, thank you for the various ways you helped me through this book. You know what they are. Mary May and Becky, thank you for visiting me in these hinterlands, and for always listening and for your encouragement. And to Melissa and Michele and your families, you have my gratitude, always and forever.